D0821084

PAUL RUTHERFORD is a member of the Department of History at the University of Toronto. He is author of *The Making of the Canadian Media* and editor of *Saving the Canadian City*.

During the last third of the nineteenth century a fierce rivalry among party 'organs,' sectarian dailies, upstart 'people's journals,' and revamped 'quality' papers fashioned a popular journalism for a large, chiefly urban audience in Canada. By the end of the 1890s, the number of daily and weekly editions of these newspapers exceeded the count of Canadian families. The country's first mass medium had arrived.

Professor Rutherford charts the growth of the daily press, describing personalities and events. He surveys the cultural prerequisites for mass communication – the growth of the city, of urban publics, and of mass literacy – and looks at the personnel, business routines, and worries of the new industry, showing how the news and views, ads and entertainment of the press changed as publishers competed for increased circulation. He also analyses the mythologies purveyed by the popular press across Canada, defines the press's connection with the 'establishment,' and shows how daily papers suited the libertarian model of a 'free press.'

This volume is a novel addition to our literature on nationbuilding, revealing the significant role played by the popular press in the making of Victorian society and the shaping of the twentieth century.

PAUL RUTHERFORD

A Victorian Authority: the daily press in late nineteenth-century Canada

UNIVERSITY OF TORONTO PRESS
Toronto Buffalo London

Toronto Buffalo London
Printed in Canada

ISBN 8020-5588-5 (cloth)
ISBN 8020-6459-0 (paper)

Canadian Cataloguing in Publication Data
Rutherford, Paul, 1944
A Victorian authority

Includes index.
ISBN 0-8020-5588-5 (bound). – ISBN 0-8020-6459-0 (pbk.)

1. Canadian newspapers – History – 19th century.
I. Title

PN4907.R87 071'.1 C82-094057-7

The plates in this book were obtained in the John Robarts Library at the University of Toronto. The plates on pp 55 and 90 are reproduced with the kind permission of the *Canadian Printer and Publisher*: Graham vol. 3–4 (Apr 1895), Berthiaume vol. 5 (Dec 1896), Sheppard vol. 5 (Jan 1896), Robertson vol. 3 (Nov 1894), *Mail* building vol. 4 (Nov 1895). The other plates appeared as follows: p 92 [Robert Hoe] *A Short History of the Printing Press* (New York 1902); p 120 Toronto *Mail and Empire* 2 Nov 1895; p 122 Toronto *News* 3 July 1899; p 124 Monsoon *Mail and Empire* 24 Oct 1895, Surprise ibid 31 Oct 1895, and *La Presse* 14 Apr 1899; p 150 Toronto *World* 28 and 31 Jan and 1 Feb 1899; p 152 Toronto *Globe* 24 July 1895; p 153 *La Presse* 3 Apr 1899.

FOR MY PARENTS

Contents

Illustrations

TABLES

FIGURES

PLATES

Acknowledgments

Scholarship is rarely unassisted.

I am especially grateful to the staff of the newspaper section of the National Library of Canada in Ottawa and of the microtext room of the John Robarts Library at the University of Toronto. Both groups gave me much assistance over the years in my efforts to find items in their newspaper collections. Dun and Bradstreet kindly permitted me to consult and quote from its holdings at Harvard Business School, Cambridge, Mass. Southam Press Ltd., likewise, permitted me to use material from its company archives, located in Toronto.

I am indebted, in various ways, to a number of people: Blanche Rutherford and Gail Rutherford, who did yeoman service typing out portions of editorials and the like; the late Donald Creighton, who guided my thesis work, out of which came much of the research for this book; Michael Bliss, Craig Brown, and Arthur Silver, all colleagues of mine at the University of Toronto, with whom I have talked over some of the questions raised in the book; and Tom Walkom, a doctoral candidate in political economy at the University of Toronto, whose excellent work on the rise of the popular daily in Toronto has provided me with many an insight.

I wish to thank Virgil Duff, my editor, who gave me useful advice and criticism through the various stages of turning a manuscript into a book, and John Parry, my copyeditor, whose reading of the manuscript corrected a number of egregious errors. Whatever errors remain are my own.

This book has been published with the assistance of grants from the Social Science Federation of Canada, using funds provided by the Social Sciences and Humanities Research Council of Canada, and from the Publications Fund of University of Toronto Press.

A VICTORIAN AUTHORITY

Introduction

The newspaper was commonplace around the Victorian home. Indeed, newspapers could be found almost everywhere Canadians gathered – in taverns and stores, in mechanics' institutes and public libraries, in clubs and associations, on street corners and in railway stations.[1] In 1853 Susannah Moodie, noted for her asides on the life of old Ontario, claimed that 'the Canadian cannot get on without his newspaper any more than an American without his tobacco.'[2] In 1872 George Rowell's *American Newspaper Directory*, one of the first such catalogues to attempt a comprehensive listing of Canadian publications, revealed that the Canadian press enjoyed a combined circulation of about 670,000 copies, or something over one journal per family.[3] That year the dominion post office faced difficulties handling the tidy bundles of newspapers and periodicals: roughly 24½ million issues were mailed in 1872, and this sum rose to more than 100 million by the end of the century.[4] In 1899 Toronto, the country's newspaper capital, boasted about 150 separate publications, some with multiple editions. In fact even a modest city like Woodstock, Ontario, sported three dailies, each with a weekly or semi-weekly in two.[5] 'Aujourd'hui, pas un famille pas un particulier ne peut plus se passer de son journal,' mused *Le Monde* (31 May 1893). 'Cest [*sic*] devenu un article de première nécessité, comme le pain et la viande. Malheur à celui qui prétend vivre sans cela.'

What impressed observers most was the rise of the big-city dailies, like Montreal's flamboyant *Star* or scandalous *La Presse*, each boasting tens of thousands of readers. New machinery, the marketplace, and public demand had enabled, even pushed, journalists to send their messages far down the social ladder and far beyond urban boundaries. The result?: 'la création du journal à bon marché, l'agent le plus actif, le plus prompt de l'éducation populaire dans nos sociétés democratiques.'[6] Newspapers now informed, sometimes inflamed, a huge reading public about the great issues of national policy as well as the mundane round of daily life. Politicians, at least the ones who survived, spent a good deal of time worrying about the notions which their so-called 'organs' dispensed to the voters. Clergymen, Protestant as well as Catholic, felt that they had a moral duty, if not a divine right, to watch over the news and views of a press that reached so many Christians. Businessmen had long been aware that newspaper advertising was a potent force in the marketplace, and newspaper advocacy a useful ally in the battle for government favours. The fans of the newspaper were legion: John King, a lawyer, was merely repeating a cliché when he called the press 'that great engine of intelligence' whose workings speeded the civilization of the country.[7] A smaller circle of critics feared the newspaper had become a source of evil: Joe Clark, himself an editor, blamed the 'indefensible' and 'baneful' influence of the press for the moral decline of that same country.[8] Whatever the truth, few observers denied the significance of the press. Rather, the Victorian was wont to invest the newspaper with an almost mystical omnipotence. 'As the matter stands to-day, for good or ill, the press is the most powerful factor in modern affairs,' declared J. Macdonald Oxley, a businessman and writer, in 1894. 'It reaches a wider audience than the pulpit; it uses more effective arguments than the platform; it smites harder and more enduring blows than the sword; and its work, when well done, lasts longer than that wrought by any other human agency.[9]

Such hyperbole was a common failing of Victorian prose. Even so, there was some justification for the excitement. Late nineteenth-century Canada was caught up in the throes of what has been called 'modernization.'[10] Oxley and company were witnesses to the birth of mass communications, a new phenomenon which in so many ways symbolized the promise and the perils of their 'age of miracles.'

I have set out to chart the growth of the daily press, Canada's first mass medium. Ideally, mass communication requires the regular and frequent transmission of a uniform message about life and affairs by a small group of experts to a large, anonymous, and heterogeneous public.[11] Few papers could claim such an exalted stature, especially not the plethora of little dailies that sprang up in Canadian towns toward the end of the century. That is why my study concentrates on the big-city dailies which did eventually offer a brand of journalism that approached the ideal of mass communication.[12] The story of this publicity machine spans almost 70 years. It began during the 1830s and 1840s when a few newcomers launched penny tri-weeklies boasting a modest fare of news and entertainment to cater to the tastes of a wider audience. It continued with the surging popularity of the party newspaper, notably among bourgeois readers, that filled cities after 1850 with competing dailies. I have chosen to lavish the most attention on the end of the story: the people and events of the last third of the century when the fierce rivalry among party 'organs,' sectarian dailies, upstart 'people's journals,' and revamped 'quality' papers fashioned a full-blown

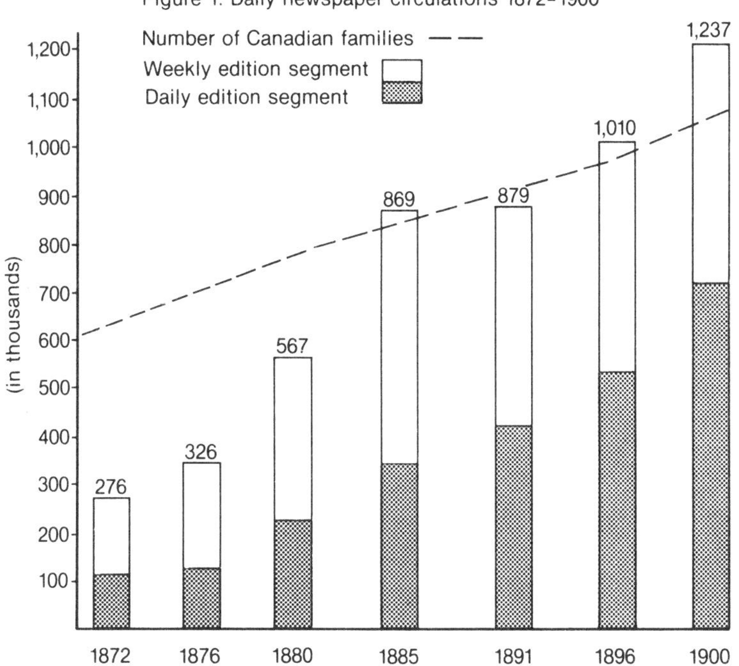

popular journalism for a huge public, mostly inside the cities but extending into the countryside as well. Indeed, by the end of the 1890s, the number of daily and weekly editions of daily newspapers exceeded the number of families in the country, a sure sign that Canada's first mass medium had arrived (Figure 1).[13] Always, my story-telling revolves around the theme of modernization, notably the part that the press played in the making of Victorian society. The result, I trust, is a novel addition to the already voluminous literature on Canadian nation-building.

Little study has been made of Canada's first mass medium. (Indeed, we know a good deal more about the role of the church or the public school.) The comment might appear ungenerous, since I have borrowed extensively from an assortment of scholarly pieces on nineteenth-century journalism.[14] However, almost all the existing material concerns only some aspect of newspaperdom (a journalist or a newspaper) and avoids a wider treatment of the press or the profession. That might appear surprising, given the pioneering efforts of Harold Innis and Marshall McLuhan – unless the reader realizes that their 'probes' served more to mystify than enlighten historians.[15] Here is the reason why the theoretical apparatus underlying my approach derives from the work of historians and sociologists outside Canada.

The approach requires some explanation. Every student of communications owes a debt of gratitude to Harold Lasswell. More than three decades ago he advanced what has since become the classic model of communications research, historical or otherwise.[16] Any act of communication, he asserted, might conveniently be described by answering one convoluted question:

Who?	control
says what?	content
to whom?	audience
in which channel	media
and with what effect?	impact

This formula neatly summarizes the many-sided character of the communications process. Put another way, only an account which tackles all of these characteristics can hope to sum up the experience of the daily press.

I do, of course, concentrate more on some aspects of the communications process than on others. That is normal. Harold Innis placed excessive emphasis on the importance of the 'media,' especially their technology.[17] Richard Altick, an analyst of popular culture, expended much effort discussing the evolution of the British reading public, the 'audience,' during the nineteenth century.[18] Recently, some of the most fruitful approaches have focused on the production side of the equation, notably the question of 'control.'[19] Lasswell's 'who?' refers not only to the actual publishers or journalists but also to advertisers and distributors, plus an assortment of powerful outsiders able to influence in some fashion or other the messages transmitted to a waiting public. Inevitably, the study of production necessitates a detailed analysis of the economics of communications – how the particular medium fitted into the business world. Thus the story of the press is linked to the complex games of power-seeking and money-making.

The cardinal advantage of this approach lies in its pursuit of concrete realities. It avoids the kind of methodological, and even worse epistemological, troubles that beset an Innis who hoped to prove that changing media were the key determinants in the rise and fall of all civilizations.[20] It eliminates the difficulties imposed upon an Altick who must eventually grapple with the unknown audience response. Instead, the scholar can assemble profiles of leading publishers, track down costs and revenues, often identify the motives of outside authorities, all of which lays the foundation for a believable explanation of the nature of journalism. Hence my study is replete with facts on the personnel, business, and the autonomy (or servility) of the press.

Unhappily, the approach also contains a dangerous bias. Inherent is an élitist assumption about the way things operated, which simplifies the communications process far too much. Sometimes we are left with the biography of an energetic press baron who manages to play god with his personal toy,[21] sometimes with the sinister conviction that the leading newspapers are, above all, instruments of the ruling establishment.[22] The press, then, appears primarily in the guise of an agency of domination. Too much attention to the 'Who?' can easily downgrade the importance of other aspects, notably the demand side of the equation, and mask the significance of other effects, outside the realm of power-seeking.

Worrying about the ordinary reader will offset the focus upon the masters of journalism. The 'audience' is too often a neglected factor in the standard histories of the press.[23] Sociologists tell us that modern consumers select from a range of channels and messages to please their convictions or suit their needs.[24] Even today's multimedia cater to a series of broad 'taste publics,' a fact which must give their messages a coherence and definition.[25] Why should we expect that things differed in grandfather's time? He too played favourites. Therein lay the power, albeit normally the sleeping power, of the ordinary reader: the press baron, whatever his idiosyncrasies, had to satisfy his clientele or else the popularity of his newspaper, and so his influence and revenue, would wane. This rule dictates an investigation of the reading public, notably the changes in the literacy, the class and occupation, and even the habits of the urban populace.

Sadly, the lack of public opinion polls means that any analysis of the public's wants must enter the realm of speculation. Much can be inferred, however, from a close scrutiny of exactly what was printed. Indeed, discovering the actual messages is necessary to any proper explanation of the cultural importance of communications. A new wave of scholars, trained in semiotics, has already begun to piece together the association between mass media and modern myth.[26] My study rests upon an extensive survey of the offerings, particularly the news and views, of the daily press. I have sampled the daily fare at various times to assemble statistics which illustrate the different happenings, and therefore worlds of experience, that the new dailies chose to report in their search for readers. I have paid attention to the language of journalism, the structure of argument, and the bias of editorial and advertising matter. And I have surveyed the ebb and flow of controversy, the sources of agreement as well as debate, to shed light on the predominant myths in that time of apparent strife.[27]

This brand of 'content' analysis supplies information for tackling the problem of 'impact.' The so-called power of the press remains at once the most confusing and intriguing aspect of the study of journalism. It is all too easy to assume the omnipotence of the press and speculate wildly. Cautious scholars avoid the problem, except perhaps for a few vague declarations about 'what it all means.' This is unfortunate. Again, sociology offers the historian some guides. First, the mass media cannot alter, either dramatically or quickly, an individual's decided views about well-known issues. Indeed, the media seem most effective when they endeavour to reinforce existing opinions. Second, over time, the media do have a wide variety of social, as distinct from personal, effects: agenda-setting (ordering the priority of issues or values in the public domain), mobilization (calling the people to arms), stereotyping (fixing images of particular ideas, events, or occupations), conferring of status (the creation of heroes and villains), manipulation of mood (emphasizing some collective emotion, such as optimism or resentment), and socialization (the education of people in the 'proper' ways of thinking and behaving). Much depends on the actual situation, since the media rarely act without the assistance of other institutions. The influence of print, in particular, is mediated by forces outside the communications process. Besides, cause and effect become fuzzy terms when applied to social phenomena: it almost always requires a long list of actors and events to explain why things happen when and how. Third, whatever the place or time, the mass media are a leading agency of 'legitimation.' They manufacture images of reality that justify certain sets of values and patterns of authority. The popular newspaper, in short, can exercise a good deal of ideological power.[28]

There are dangers in relying upon any theory of effects which explains the past in the light of the present. What is occasionally, perhaps facetiously, called the 'post-modern' society resembles a single, highly complex mechanism. Today's multimedia enjoy such prestige because life's routine depends on a continuous flow of public information.[29] Newspapers, magazines, radio, and television are normally the guardians of orthodoxy and consequently a source of stability. That was not so true in the nineteenth century. The emerging Victorian Canada was fragmented and plural, its institutions more autonomous and its consensus more troubled. Besides, the daily newspaper could not supply as much information and its printed messages could not carry as much weight. Its significance, ironically, can best be judged from the perspective of social change. The big-city daily empowered the forces of progress in the modernizing community.[30] It was in the nature of the beast: the very bias of popular journalism, its emphasis upon mass literacy, made newspapers leading antagonists of the force of custom which buttressed old ways. The logic of mass communication was then novel, akin to the process of industrialization or the idea of democracy in its ability to transform the social environment. No other major institution, excepting perhaps the public school, was so effectively the champion of what was called 'improvement.' The images merchandised might well be contradictory. Publicity did work to express as well as to counter class conflict. Either effort, though, spelled trouble for the traditions of popular deference and the presumption of the élite. The journalist was shaping a different sort of culture, first in the city and soon across the country.

This brings us back to Oxley and company. People upset by 'modernity' were bound to blame its messenger, even as the more numerous enthusiasts of progress would praise the assistance of the newpaper. Each did so, we shall see, with some justification.

1

The prerequisites of mass communication

Historians have cited quite an array of causes, from technological innovation to a triumphant egalitarianism, to explain the emergence of mass communication in the nineteenth century.[1] But, in truth, the actual story varies greatly from country to country. Popular journalism was pioneered in America by a new breed of cheap New York dailies during the 1830s, while in England the originators were a couple of London-based Sunday papers which became prominent in the 1840s and 1850s. Neither pattern was repeated in Canada. Even so, a common thread running through these stories is the way in which modernization generated new social needs that could best be satisfied by the birth of popular journalism.[2] So what follows is a discussion of the setting (the big city), the public (class and community), and the means (literacy and reading) – the prerequisites of mass communication.

THE BIG CITY

By 1901 one million people, roughly one in five Canadians, lived in or around the country's 12 largest centres of population. That was a bit surprising given the common impression then of a wilderness dominion. Admittedly, the primary engines of national growth had remained the expansion of the agricultural and resource frontiers. Their retarded development during the last decades of the nineteenth century explained in large part the exodus of native and immigrant Canadians to farms and factories in the United States. The very existence of this migration, though, highlighted the strides that cities had taken.

People in the 1890s seemed fascinated by the statistics of growth. Perhaps these were a necessary reassurance for the middle classes troubled by fears of national failure and a definite sense of social anxiety. Typical of the times was a paean of praise to Montreal published by Toronto's *Monetary Times* on 3 February

1893. Sparked by the discovery of a 50-year-old survey of Montreal's commerce, the anonymous writer waxed eloquent for three columns about the growth of just about everything. The choicest facts he saved for the conclusion. The Montreal harbour now handled '950,000 tons, and nine-tenths of it is steam,' earning a revenue of 'nearly $300,000.' The city's merchants imported in 1892 $7,627,000 worth of dry goods alone. 'Railways [the Intercolonial, the Grand Trunk, and the Canadian Pacific] connect her with either ocean.' And the city was the industrial capital of Canada: 'Rolling mills, sugar refineries, cotton mills, tobacco factories, foundaries, breweries, electrical works, flour mills push their modern smoke into the air within her bounds, her shoe manufacturers alone employing 5,000 men, and the great city uses 400,000 tons of coal a year.' Montreal was the embodiment of progress.

Big cities were massive concentrations of people, services, and wealth. True, the dominion had nothing to compare in size with London or New York. But what defined a metropolis was its function: the big cities acted as the brokers, the consumers, eventually the producers of goods. The cities existed in a wider 'urban system,' a hierarchy of places each competing for significance.[3] Here size was the key to success. The larger the city, the more its services and so its power were enhanced. The metropolitan rivalries of the victors and also-rans conditioned the emerging patterns of national life. In part, the success (and failure) of the cities served to knit the disparate territories of Canada into an integrated, albeit squabbling, whole – a nation-state beset by sectional ills.

Some measure of urbanization was understandable during the course of the nineteenth century. The particular ranking of the big cities, in contrast, seems a more chancy affair (Table 1). Why did so many people flood into only two bloated centres, Montreal and Toronto? The answer lies in the impact of Canada's 'industrial revolution' which, for historical convenience, is considered to have begun in the 1850s. Statistics told a story of advance everywhere. Between 1852 and 1857 official figures showed some 155,000 immigrants, mainly arriving to fill the still unsettled lands of Canada West.[4] Contemporaries recorded that the agricultural sector there experienced an unparalleled boom in wheat production and land values.[5] 'King Timber' flourished as never before because of an increasing demand at home and abroad for lumber, the value of exports rising from $5,200,000 in 1849 to $14,000,000 in 1865.[6] By 1860 about 2,000 miles of railway had been laid throughout British North America (66 miles had been in operation ten years earlier). Not surprisingly, most cities enjoyed a phenomenal rate of growth (Table 2). Of course, this giddy expansion was checked by another downturn at the close of the decade: Hamilton's population, for example, fell from 27,000 in 1858 to 17,000 in 1864.[7] But never again during the rest of the century would both the countryside and the cities – all cities – share so substantially in the fruits of progress.

TABLE 1

The ranking of big-city populations 1851–1901 (in thousands)

	1851		1871		1901	
1	Montreal	57.7	Greater Montreal*	144.0	Greater Montreal	360.8
2	Quebec	42.1	Greater Toronto†	115.0	Greater Toronto	238.1
3	Toronto	30.8	Quebec-Levis	66.4	Quebec-Levis	76.1
4	Saint John	22.7	Greater Saint John‡	41.3	Ottawa-Hull	73.9
5	Halifax	20.7	Greater Halifax§	31.8	Hamilton	52.6
6	Hamilton	14.1	Ottawa-Hull	27.9	Greater Halifax	45.6
7	Kingston	11.7	Hamilton	26.9	Winnipeg	42.3
8	Ottawa	7.7	London	18.0	Greater Saint John	40.7
9	London	7.0	Kingston	12.4	London	38.0
10					Vancouver	27.0
11					Victoria	20.9
12					Kingston	18.0
City total		214.5		483.7		1,034.5
Canada		2,436.3		3,689.3		5,371.3

SOURCES: *Census of Canada* 1871, 1901, 1911; George Nader, *Cities of Canada*, vol. 1 and 2 (Toronto 1975 and 1976); Richard P. Blaine and A. Lynn McMurray, *Toronto: An Urban Study* (Toronto 1970); M.C. Urquhart and K.A.H. Buckley, *Historical Statistics of Canada* (Cambridge 1965)

* Montreal Island

† Metropolitan Toronto

‡ Saint John and Portland (annexed 1889)

§ Halifax and Dartmouth

A change was already in the offing. How fitting that an engineer should be its prophet: in 1849 Thomas Keefer published a promotional piece entitled *Philosophy of Railroads* to sing the praises of that new machine which would liberate the country from the thrall of a harsh Nature.[8] City fathers needed little persuasion. Time and again, cities proved willing to mortgage the future (an over generous Hamilton faced bankruptcy in 1861)[9] to secure a rail connection. Montreal's Grand Trunk spanned the province of Canada, extending from the ice-free port of Portland, Maine (1853), to Sarnia (1859); Hamilton's Great Western (completed in 1855) criss-crossed south-western Canada West and terminated in Windsor and Toronto; Toronto's own Northern Railway reached north Collingwood (1855) to garner the lion's share of the north's agricultural and timber trade. By contrast, Quebec and Kingston, lacking railways, stagnated during the 1860s and never properly recovered in the later decades. Not until 1879 did Quebec City secure a direct connection with Quebec's railway network – and then too late: Montreal's commercial pre-eminence was too well established

TABLE 2

The growth rate of populations in big cities 1851–1901 (in percentages)

	1850s	1860s	1870s	1880s	1890s
Greater Montreal	50.7	22.1	34.1	43.7	30.0
Greater Toronto		16.6	49.0	83.4	14.8
Toronto	45.6				
Quebec-Levis		01.6	05.2	00.5	08.9
Quebec	42.7				
Ottawa-Hull			36.7	45.1	33.4
Ottawa	89.0	64.6			
Hamilton	41.1	40.8	36.4	33.6	07.5
Greater Halifax			25.5	12.0	02.0
Halifax	20.6	18.2			
Winnipeg				221.1	65.1
Greater Saint John			00.1	-05.3	03.9
Saint John	20.1	05.5			
London	64.2	55.8	45.9	21.7	18.8
Vancouver					97.0
Victoria			81.1	184.2	24.2
Kingston	17.5	-09.7	13.6	36.7	-06.8
Total	53.0	24.5	31.0	45.1	21.6

SOURCES: *Census* 1871, 1901, and 1911; Nader, *Cities of Canada*, vol. 2; Baine and McMurray, *Toronto: An Urban Study*

to brook a successful challenge from the leaders of the capital city. Similarly, on the seaboard, the slow expansion of railways hampered efforts to make Halifax or Saint John a regional metropolis. That crucial failure left the Maritimes a 'headless' region, ill prepared to meet the menace of central Canadian imperialism.

The construction of trunk-lines after Confederation, albeit much assisted by a protective tariff, did indeed turn the dominion into a commercial entity. The old cliché about iron bonds of nationhood has some validity. Ironically, Maritime promoters had often touted the virtues of an intercolonial railway to tap the wealth of the interior, a line finally guaranteed by the British North America Act and finished in 1876. It was ironic because neither Halifax nor Saint John became the booming ports of a Canadian hinterland; rather, the railway assisted the penetration of the Maritime market by central Canadian interests. In any case the most spectacular exploit was the building of the Canadian Pacific Railway across the prairies to the Pacific coast during the 1880s. That line ensured Winnipeg's destiny and created a series of towns, not the least of which was Vancouver (its original name, Granville, was altered at the request of William Van Horne, the railway's manager).[10] The railway's terminus enabled Vancouver's businessmen speedily to overcome Victoria's headstart and win commercial hegemony over the mainland of British Columbia.[11] So, what with trunk-lines and feeder-lines, Canada had more than 17,600 miles of track in operation by 1900, carrying that year about 36 million tons of freight. The enormous investment, valued at almost one billion dollars, was very sound – at least from the metropolitan standpoint.[12] The spread of railways had spurred the rise of the big city, especially in the new heartland of central Canada and its western tributary.

Hard on the heels of railways came manufacturing. Railway workshops and rolling mills were among the first factories on the urban landscape. Pre-industrial manufacturers (associated with the traditional crafts, the lumber and wheat staples, and shipbuilding) were common in the cities before mid-century. What characterized the next 50 years was the proliferation of small enterprises, a great boom in consumer manufacturing, and the arrival of heavy industry. The machine, of course, emerged as the key to industrial progress. But so too did mass labour, a novel source of urban growth. During the late 1840s and the early 1850s Montrealers again pioneered the new thrust of capitalism with Ira Gould's and the Ogilvies' flour mills, the Grand Trunk shops, or John Redpath's sugar refinery.[13] Quebeckers did not. Their city's continued dependence on the old economy spelled trouble after the mid-sixties when first the timber staple and soon the shipbuilding industry waned in economic importance. And other cities, Toronto perhaps excepted, lagged behind the trendsetter. So by 1880 Montreal was far and away the industrial capital of the dominion.

The next decade witnessed an extraordinary boom in manufacturing (productivity rose 72 per cent)[14] which benefitted almost all the major cities (Table 3). A languishing Quebec relied increasingly upon shoemaking, tanning, and textiles to employ a workforce no longer able to find jobs in the traditional port or shipbuilding industries.[15] Likewise, the merchants of Greater Saint John invested eagerly in the machine industry, rope and brass manufacturing, nail-making, and the like, doubling industrial output, to overcome the declining import (and profits) of their traditional pursuits.[16] None of the Atlantic ports regained its previous vigour. The boom was too little, too late. But elsewhere the boom fuelled a new jump in urban populations, notably Ottawa-Hull (pulp and paper) and Hamilton (iron and steel). Neither city matched the productivity of Toronto. That city's manufacturing output and productivity, already sizeable, more than doubled in ten years, making Toronto a serious rival to Montreal in the manufacture of goods for mass consumption.[17] Little wonder Greater Toronto's population rose by leaps and bounds to more than 200,000. In short, the manufacturing boom had fostered a new era of metropolitan expansion that approached the growth rate of the heady 1850s. This could not be sustained during the 1890s, though, because of the restricted home market.

TABLE 3

The manufacturing productivity* of big cities in 1881 and 1891
(in thousands of dollars)

		1881	1891	Percentage growth
1	Montreal and environs†	20,945	32,525	55.3
2	Toronto	9,585	22,546	135.2
3	Hamilton	3,906	6,903	76.7
4	Quebec-Levis	4,074	6,846	68.0
5	London	4,007	4,260	6.3
6	Ottawa-Hull	2,889	4,181	44.7
7	Greater Saint John	1,559	3,503	124.7
8	Halifax	1,891	2,786	47.3
9	Kingston	761	1,680	120.7

* Productivity = 'value of products' minus 'cost of materials' from table XX in *Census* of 1901, vol. 3.

† Montreal and environs includes Montreal proper, Lachine, Ste-Cunégonde, and St-Henri.

Industrialization had been lavishly aided by the state through railway subsidies, the National Policy tariff of 1879, and assorted tax exemptions. Not everyone gained. The changed environment worked to the distinct advantage of urban Canada, even more of the biggest cities; the countryside could hardly escape its effects. As early as the 1860s, older agricultural counties suffered for the first time a significant loss of population owing, at least in Canada West, to the inroads of the wheat midge and the fierce competition for land.[18] Some farmers escaped to the cities even then: Montreal once more became a predominantly francophone city because migration from the countryside of Canada East swamped immigration from overseas. Still, only after 1880 did rural depopulation in the older parts of Canada emerge as a troublesome and accelerating fact of life (Table 4). Local conditions played their part: the collapse of lumbering drove people out of Charlotte County and New Brunswick itself.[19] The attraction of the newly opened prairie lands also drew thousands in search of cheap farms and the simpler ways of wheat growing. Nonetheless, the phenomenon of rural depopulation was linked to the inordinate growth of the big cities, especially during the 1880s. That was obvious in Toronto, once an immigrant city, where by 1890 two-thirds of the residents were native Canadians.[20] The tragedy, claimed rural apologists, was that the cities drained towns and farms of the best blood, the youth of the countryside. The looming, sinister image of the swollen city was a great staple of agrarian rhetoric at the end of the century.

Industrialism's 'focusing effect'[21] had also disrupted the rough equality among the cities that had been apparent at mid-century. In 1884 Pelham Mulvany

TABLE 4

Rural depopulation in old Canada 1851–1901 (percentage of counties and number of people)

	1850s		1860s		1870s		1880s		1890s	
	%	N	%	N	%	N	%	N	%	N
Nova Scotia	–	–	–	–	–	–	44	7,848	61	14,204
New Brunswick	–	–	–	–	–	–	47	13,205	40	4,731
Quebec	5	678	32	30,362	15	7,282	38	22,233	30	25,066
Ontario	–	–	26	11,311	8	2,040	34	41,728	51	55,529

claimed that railways had made Toronto 'the metropolis, the mother-city, the mart of Ontario. With these arms she is enabled to pluck the choicest fruits that the fair Province of which she is the centre affords.'[22] Every railway that passed through enhanced the virtues of the city. Even Hamilton's Great Western had really placed the 'ambitious city' in the commercial orbit of the 'Queen City.' Toronto became the privileged location of the major business establishments in the province. Her businessmen created most; others she 'stole': the Board of Trade (1856), the Canadian Bank of Commerce (1867) which absorbed Hamilton's Gore Bank (1870), Eaton's nascent department store (1869), the Toronto Stock Exchange (incorporated 1878), the Massey Manufacturing Co. (from Newcastle, 1879), National Trust (1898), or Canada Life Assurance (from Hamilton, 1899). What, then, could be more natural than the arrival of Joseph Flavelle, a modestly successful Peterborough businessman, in Toronto in 1887? There he found other hopefuls, notably gathered around George Cox (also of Peterborough), intent on making a fortune and ready to challenge Montreal's suzerainty.[23]

In fact Montreal's suzerainty appeared unshakeable. Its businessmen had extended their influence across the dominion. Their city's diversified economy ensured success in the new industrial environment. The predominance of the ocean steamer finally gave Montreal the edge over Quebec as the province's premier port.[24] Soon after Confederation, Montreal's merchants had invaded the Maritime market,[25] and the completion of the Intercolonial Railway merely consolidated their hold. Later the Canadian Pacific Railway came to funnel a generous portion of the west's trade through the warehouses and harbour of Montreal. The city's shoe, cigar, textile, even wallpaper factories sent forth an array of cheap goods for the nation's selection, keeping Montreal ahead of Toronto in investment and output.[26] After 1890, Montreal's financial and industrial magnates steadily acquired a grip on the mass consumption and eventually the resource industries of the Maritimes.[27] That success had much to do with the city's banking supremacy. Montreal banks filled the land with branch offices – the arrival of

Hugh Allan's Merchant's Bank in Winnipeg (1873), for instance, signalled a desire to finance the exploitation of the new granary.[28] In 1880 the Bank of Montreal alone held assets amounting to $44.5 million, approaching the total of all Ontario banks.[29] Indeed Toronto's *Monetary Times* (3 February 1893) claimed that the city's Bank Clearing House handled the year previous $590 million, 'showing the chief city of Canada to be the tenth city on this continent in commercial importance.'

COMMUNITY AND CLASS

'Grand' is how Montreal and its rivals might seem to a sanguine, business-minded observer. Their's was hardly an unblemished success story, though. The rise of the big city – its extraordinary fetish of growth – had enormous social costs. The industrial city was a place filled with technological marvels, fine buildings and stately homes, a substantial middle class, piety, and pride; but, just as much a part of its life and landscape were slums, looming factories, polluted waters, human misery, vice, and crime.

Contemporaries were aware of this double legacy of growth. Witness the *fin-de-siècle* tract on Montreal by Herbert Brown Ames, a local manufacturer. He argued that the southwestern half of the city was in fact separated into two distinct enclaves, one fittingly high above the river and the other almost at river level. 'Looking down from the mountain top upon these two areas,' he wrote, 'the former is seen to contain many spires, but no tall chimneys, the latter is thickly sprinkled with such evidences of industry and the air hangs heavy with smoke.' The city above the hill was 'the home of the classes. Within its well-built residences will be found the captains of industry, the owners of real estate, and those who labor with brain rather than hand.' Here lived the masters of society. The city below the hill, by contrast, was 'the dwelling place of the masses' – the home of the 'craftsman, of the manual wage-earner, of the mechanic and the clerk,' of the 'submerged tenth' or poor. Here lived the workers, and the wastes, of society. It was a classic description of the social gulf that beset the big city.[30]

The ruthless ways of industrialism had made the big city a crucible of 'modernity.' Thrown together in these teeming places were all sorts of discordant people, the ritual warfare of the Orange and the Green (to cite one example) constantly enlivening urban life in central Canada.[31] A perennial source of instability was the transience of the city dweller: thousands of 'men in motion' moved through mid-century Hamilton, leaving little trace of their passage,[32] and 50 years later Ames discovered that half the poor he surveyed left their initial address within a year.[33] Such motion unsettled neighbourhoods and weakened social bonds. In 1882 an unofficial survey showed that less than half of Toronto's population attended Sunday services; the census of 1901 found a mere quarter of professed Protestants were church members.[34] And this was in a city renowned for its effusive devotion to Christianity. The traditions of an older world were twisted, sometimes destroyed, by the alien circumstances. Industrial discipline wreaked havoc with an inherited rhythm of a week's work broken by customary days of relief. So the Royal Commission on the Relations of Labor and Capital was distressed to learn employees would be dismissed by the Hochelaga Cotton Manufacturing Co. if they failed to arrive for work on a *fête d'obligation*.[35] The commission found as well that the demand for a plentiful supply of cheap labour had brought the 'evil' of child labour and the decay of apprenticeship, which was the traditional avenue of entry into the workforce for adolescents of an earlier generation. A second concequence of this demand was the influx of so many young women in search of factory jobs that the sex ratios were seriously unbalanced: the census of 1871 showed a surplus of adult women over men amounting to almost 5,000 in Montreal, 3,250 in Quebec, 1,600 in Halifax, about 1,000 in Saint John and Toronto. Before long, the results seemed all too visible: street arabs and wayward women, gangs and vice and crime.[36] Existing structures of control and service collapsed under the press of people and problems. The municipal governments appeared unable to keep up with the need for new sewers, better transportation, more police, and the like. During the 1870s a forward-looking council had constructed a series of pipes and pumps to bring Toronto drinking water; during the 1880s that service proved inadequate, if not dangerous, because of the decay of the wooden pipes and the raw sewage polluting the harbour.[37] No wonder people tried to reassert old values of order and harmony, to strengthen old authorities and forge new institutions, and so to ensure progress.[38]

The prime cause of social tension, though, was the abiding reality of inequality. Not that urban Canada had a simple or clear-cut class structure. What happened can best be introduced by an occupational profile of the industrial workforce (Table 5). Unfortunately, the conventions and vagaries of nineteenth-century census-taking make only the most outstanding shifts apparent.[39] The large group of tradesmen and skilled workmen, the artisans in 1851, suffered a steady attrition over the years. Their place was taken by white-collar employees, clerks, and officials, as well as by the semi-skilled and factory operatives. The fluctuating proportion of labourers and domestics reflected the eventual decline of female servants as a major component of the workforce. The changes in the highest occupational category were due to alterations in the numbers of businessmen. The percentage of professionals remained remarkably stable, 3.9 to 4.3 in Montreal and 4.3 to 4.7 in Toronto, over the six decades. The proportion of white-collar personnel (more store clerks than railway

TABLE 5

Occupational profile of the Montreal and Toronto workforces 1851–1911

	1851		1881		1911	
	Montreal	Toronto	Montreal	Toronto	Montreal	Toronto
Sample workforce (number)	8,260	8,375	49,578	30,001	184,212	169,433
Status (percentage)						
White-collar	26.1	20.3	28.2	31.5	31.9	34.8
Blue-collar	74.0	79.8	71.8	68.5	68.1	65.1
Occupations (percentage)						
Businessmen and professionals	18.8	14.0	15.5	18.9	13.1	12.4
Clerks and officials	7.3	6.3	12.7	12.6	18.8	22.4
Tradesmen and skilled workpeople	33.4	36.5	21.5	27.2	9.3	10.3
Semi-skilled and factory workpeople	10.3	6.4	20.7	19.2	32.1	31.7
Labourers and domestics	30.3	36.9	29.6	22.1	26.7	23.1

SOURCE: *Census of the Canadas* 1851–52; *Census* 1881 and 1911

magnates of course) grew substantially in the last decades of the century because of the rapid expansion of the service sector of the urban economy. Therein lay the origins of a lower middle class of salaried employees and small tradespeople. The apparent decline of the blue-collar workforce is really a fiction of the mode of analysis – artisans, especially in 1851, were not properly speaking blue-collar personnel. Indeed, the 'true' blue-collar workforce grew in significance over the years, reaching around two-thirds of the total by 1900. What happened, then, was the emergence of an increasingly visible separation of the workforce into 'brainworkers' and 'handworkers.'

Businessmen, professionals, even clerks all normally enjoyed a higher status, a degree of social esteem – and envy. That was reflected in their incomes (men only though!). Salaries were, by and large, more generous than wages. True, Montreal policemen, first class, earned a mere $450 a year between 1876 and 1891, which was raised by $100 in 1892, while the locomotive engineers had a standard wage of $700 a year during roughly the same period.[40] There were always stories about the unfortunate professional, such as P.S. Hamilton, who spent his waning years living in something called genteel poverty.[41] Neither case

TABLE 6

Comparative salary and wage levels in manufacturing 1901

	Salaried			Wage-earners		
Census districts	Number	Annual (dollars)	Weekly (dollars)	Number	Annual (dollars)	Weekly (dollars)
Montreal	3,930	958.16	18.43	36,846	333.20	6.41
Toronto	4,448	832.55	16.01	36.428	305.06	5.87
Hamilton	872	926.84	17.82	9,324	348.17	6.69
Quebec	772	843.83	16.23	8,612	284.73	5.48
Ottawa	591	746.49	14.36	6,532	291.83	5.61
London	629	796.17	15.31	4,973	344.83	6.63
Winnipeg	414	936.09	18.00	2,741	519.26	9.98
Saint John	508	863.35	16.00	5,122	300.45	5.78
Halifax	558	724.53	13.93	4,469	284.83	5.48
Vancouver	54	1,179.48	22.68	615	460.50	8.86
Victoria	269	921.68	17.73	1,300	519.92	10.00
Kingston	142	790.39	15.20	1,353	307.07	5.91

SOURCE: Data from *Census* 1901

was representative. In 1901 salaried employees in manufacturing earned on average two to two and one-half times more than wage-earners (Table 6). And the income of a successful, if modest, merchant, doctor, or lawyer could be quite substantial. The prospects for a decent living and a comfortable retirement were good in many a white-collar pursuit.

Even so, this middle class had its moments of definite unease. Very few people were insulated from the unpredictable whims of fate, be that the effects of illness or the workings of the marketplace. Failure was all too real a possibility – a grand entrepreneur such as Isaac Buchanan of Hamilton could suffer the collapse of his businesses after years of struggle and success.[42] Always, freedom was limited by the need to cultivate friends and to make connections that would ensure commercial safety or produce some promotion. White-collar employees were dependent upon the opinions of superiors, a special difficulty for the paid editor. And the self-employed, especially in business, faced the constant peril of competition. This unease, in part, led dentists to follow lawyers and doctors in creating a professional monopoly that limited entry to the pursuit, manufacturers to organize combines (notoriously unsuccessful) to end ruinous wars, small merchants to demand early closing by-laws to restrict shopping hours, and even homeowners to unite in ratepayers' groups against higher taxes. The middle-class conspiracy against the marketplace was a product of legitimate fears and a reasonable yearning for security.

The blue-collar existence was much more chancy, however. Not that all workers were poor or suffered in general misery, but many had difficulties, without the aid of wife or children, earning sufficient money to support a decent living for their families.[43] Real wages, on a grand scale, probably were increasing over the course of the late nineteenth century. The median salary paid each week by the manufacturing industry in the big cities rose $2 between 1881 and 1901, from $5.50 to $7.50.[44] This happened at a time when the prices of food and manufactured goods fell, even if rent did not.

Such figures, of course, did not always have much meaning to the workingman. Industrialism produced an economy which treated labour as a cheap, disposable commodity. The introduction of machines resulted in dismissal for a growing number of artisans, especially shoemakers and cigarmakers but also carpenters and some printers, reducing their wages and degrading their status. The artisan 'class,' consequently, dissolved over time into the wider mass of labour, even though the process was not complete before 1900.[45] The machine did create some new skilled workmen, notably mechanics, but many were specialized operatives whose skills were in fact minimal.[46] General labourers remained at the bottom of the social ladder, subject to abysmal wages and seasonal unemployment. Besides, the workers found themselves forced to submit to rules and conditions of work over which they had less and less control. The Royal Commission on the Relations of Labor and Capital uncovered much evidence of long hours, unsafe equipment, poorly ventilated factories, harsh industrial discipline, and the tyranny of the foreman. Even obedience could not ensure regular employment or a predictable wage because the worker had no tenure. One John Thomas, an old Saint John caulker, supplied the commission with a statement of 20 years of wages (an annual average of roughly $300) which showed an extraordinary variation from year to year.[47] Finally, the reality of inequality affected every aspect of the worker's life – not just unsatisfactory wages, but poor housing, a limited diet, much disease, few amusements, and only modest comfort.[48] By the 1870s the social landscape of the big cities was taking on a modern character – the well-to-do and the working classes more and more segregated in separate quarters of the city. And those families which slipped into poverty (a hardly uncommon fate) found that the more comfortable citizenry treated their condition as proof of some moral failing.

Early on, artisans and skilled workmen had organized against the power of industrial capitalism. This brand of self-reliance was the only way to win a degree of control over their fate. The new unions were not simply instruments of economic warfare. Typical were the Knights of St Crispin, a shoemakers' association born in the late 1860s, which preserved the traditions and rituals of artisans, organized recreational events, and assisted brothers in distress.[49] The shoemakers, the printers, the bakers, the railway engineers, and the like did endeavour to control their labour markets and to set the rate of wages as well as the conditions of work. Sometimes reluctantly, the unions went on strike to discipline a recalcitrant owner.[50] Before long, the crafts worked toward a wider union, evidence of a sense of fraternal solidarity. In 1867 Médéric Lanctot, a political adventurer and popular journalist, managed to organize La Grande Association in Montreal, hoping thereby to combine all the crafts behind a crusade for social amelioration. A few years later, Ontario's artisans joined in the Nine Hours Movement to bring Capital to heel.[51] And in the next decade arrived the national Trades and Labour Congress, a permanent body that would press for reform. Organized labour was a significant presence in the cities by the 1890s.

Organized labour did not pose a serious threat to the social order. The Royal Commission on the Relations of Labor and Capital recognized this in its two reports when it praised trade unions as instruments of worker betterment and even industrial stability. Fraternal solidarity was not class solidarity. The working classes never developed a mature consciousness that might translate into a revolutionary zeal. Industrialization did not convert all blue-collar workers into a classic proletariat. The work experience of the 'toilers' remained too diverse: how could a Halifax baker in a small shop fully comprehend the plight of a brother or sister in Moir's factory, a significant local establishment.[52] Likewise, the range of wages was sufficient to enable some skilled workers, eventually, to enjoy a style of life little different from the middle-class norm. No wonder the so-called labour aristocracy, the craft unions, pursued its own self-interest, accepted the virtues of respectability, and bowed to the demands of the bourgeois ethos.[53] Its less fortunate compatriots, the specialized operatives or unskilled labourers, lacked the traditions to launch an assault upon the factory system.

The tactic of accommodation, however, did not indicate a happy acceptance of industrial capitalism. During the 1880s a radical critique of society gained favour in working-class circles. That critique assumed a persistent conflict between the downtrodden 'masses,' be they even lowly brainworkers, and the privileged 'classes,' bankers as well as monopolists. Implicit was a commitment to the principle of equity that would inaugurate a social democracy. Occasional 'prophets of unrest' – some, such as Henry George, imported and others, like T. Phillips Thompson, homegrown – urged the 'masses' to strike down the evil of poverty.[54] So too did an assortment of noisy, but ephemeral labour journals.[55] The new Knights of Labor championed the alliance of skilled and unskilled labour to work a peaceful social revolution that would somehow replace competition with co-operation. None succeeded. But this radicalism did sap the legitimacy of the status quo. And the critique did justify that natural resentment growing out of the recognition of inequality.

This resentment could provoke violence. Time and again, frustrated workers damaged machines, threatened disorder, even assaulted enemies when employers refused to recognize the 'right' to collective bargaining. In 1878 at Lachine, for example, the men were so angered by a delay in their wages that they attempted to blow up one of the canal locks.[56] The surge of the Knights of Labor brought a crescendo of strikes which, briefly, suggested a species of class warfare: during 1886 and 1887 strikes by foundry workers, carpenters, bricklayers, and hod-carriers disturbed the industrial scene in London.[57] That kind of anger occasionally overflowed into the streets. So, in the fall of 1885, the francophone 'masses' in Montreal rioted against middle-class efforts (backed by Mayor Beaugrand) to impose vaccination to halt a smallpox epidemic. During the hard times of the early 1890s, the peace of Toronto, Quebec, and Ottawa-Hull was upset by mass demonstrations of strikers and the unemployed. In Toronto (1886) and again in London (1899), the 'masses,' including clerks as well as workers, eagerly took to the streets to humble that hated monopoly, the streetcar company.[58] These apparent outbreaks of anarchy seemed proof of the social gulf that worried men such as Ames.

Naturally enough, the idea of social harmony was sacrosant amongst the 'classes.' Across Canada the local establishments, long before the 1880s, had closed ranks behind the verities of the Victorian order. Montreal's assorted notables, for instance, were agreed on the priority of growth. Winnipeg's propertied electorate never doubted the wisdom of a city government run by businessmen. The royal commission received sufficient opinions from manufacturers to suggest an indifference to the plight of the 'masses' and a hostility toward workers' institutions. Certainly many a capitalist thought it only fair that he and his fellows combine in employers' associations to counter the union peril.[59] A consistent hard line, however, never won the general support of the élites or the middle class. Radicalism had its sympathizers amongst the comfortable public – Mayor Howland loudly championed labour's cause during Toronto's streetcar ruckus in 1886. Anyway, fear of social upheaval, alarm over urban degradation, a desire to improve life – a mix of motives – fostered a reform wave that promised to create a true urban community.

The umbrella of reform sheltered a host of different causes – different purposes as well, both social control and social service. Strengthening the police meant buttressing law and order, to defend property and to banish vice as well as to protect everyone from crime. Municipal reform in Toronto involved not only the streamlining of government but also checking neighbourhood power, which was a masked attack on the influence of the common man. Sabbatarians and prohibitionists clearly wished to discipline the leisure habits of the working classes, as well as to better their lot in life. Organized charities hoped to serve the deserving poor, to eliminate absolute deprivation and the cancer of pauperism. School reform planned to assist youth, through moral and commercial education, to better meet the challenge of bourgeois society. Public health schemes intended a high standard of personal cleanliness and an improved delivery of services which would save high and low from the scourge of disease. The Protestant churches set out to Christianize the city by bringing their message of hope and help to the unchurched masses. The Salvation Army, so successful in reaching the unwanted, tried to alter the habits of indulgence and laziness that it thought responsible for social decay. So it went. Bourgeois reform, like any reform, carried with it a heavy moral and class baggage.[60]

Ironically, the marketplace, the villain of this tale, had already begun to bridge the social gulf. Nothing could dampen the fires of social tension more than a greater share of the abundance created by the industrial machine. Some entrepreneurs came to realize the potential of the workingman as a consumer. Tavern proprietors and storekeepers, many having moved 'up' from blue-collar ranks, had long catered to labour. One Montreal proprietor, Charles McKiernan, alias Joe Beef, won celebrity status as a 'son of the people,' ever generous to his patrons irrespective of race or religion.[61] Like-minded entrepreneurs in that city, as early as 1870, had begun to organize sporting entertainments (horse racing and boxing and the like), especially on Sunday, to attract workingmen. That might have disgusted the puritan element, but it certainly pleased much of the so-called 'democracy.'[62] A sign of the times was the rapid expansion of cigar, clothes, shoe, and beer manufactures, selling to an expanding market. That too was sadly ironic. Minnie Phelps pointed out that ladies' underwear was cheap because of the success of the sweat-shop business.[63] And official figures showed that consumption of beer was up from two gallons per person in 1871 to three and one-half gallons in 1893, hardly a hopeful statistic for those people troubled by drunkenness amongst the working classes.[64] Another sign was the appearance of the department store, a novel retail institution which could boast low prices in a whole range of items. During the 1870s Timothy Eaton found favour with master and mechanic alike, because of his one-price, high-volume style of selling, complete with bargain sales. Two decades later, the central business districts of the big cities had a series of department or bargain stores competing for everyone's dollar. And a third example was the way the streetcar companies during the 1890s tried to cater to workingmen with special fares and Sunday service. The latter became a cause célèbre in Toronto: the city's 'Saints' mobilized the forces of Godliness to protect the sabbath (and incidentally the workingman's day of rest), though to no avail against the company's masterful propaganda and labour's interest in easy transportation.[65] Mass affluence was still a generation away. The share of abundance the workingman could claim for his family in 1900 did remain modest, whatever the improvements of the previous two decades.[66] Even so, that portion might give a family a sense of belonging.

Urban life, moreover, now provided a greater number of occasions for common celebration. Processions had always been a time of release, of festivity.[67] The St-Jean-Baptiste Day, Orange, or St Patrick's Day parades were grand rituals which drew together all sorts of people. The inauguration of Labour Day in the 1890s was designed to honour, in a similar fashion, the achievements of the workingman. Sometimes a city sponsored a special celebration: in 1883, for instance, Robert McGibbon arranged the first Montreal Winter Carnival.[68] The rise of sports, meanwhile, produced a new passion that cut across class lines and emphasized civic loyalties. The slow reduction of the work week, especially the beginning of the Saturday half-holiday, gave more families the leisure time to indulge this passion. Ned Hanlan's victory at Tyne, in 1879, winning him the world title in rowing, made the Torontonian a city hero. His successor, Jacob Gaudaur, was purportedly greeted by 'ten miles of procession' when he arrived in Toronto in 1896.[69] The appearance of lacrosse, hockey, and baseball teams, playing in intercity leagues, fixed spectator sports as a permanent feature on the urban scene. An early favourite in Montreal was the Shamrock Lacrosse Club, founded in 1868, which, although organized by leading Irish Catholics, was made up on the playing field of workmen and clerks.[70] About 5,000 people watched Montreal defeat Ottawa in the first Stanley Cup game (March 1894). Besides, the fact that these teams represented their cities added to the swelling tide of urban parochialism. By the 1890s organized sports, a middle-class invention, was already democratized.[71]

LITERACY AND READING

'Education is a public good, ignorance is a public evil.'[72] Egerton Ryerson's comment was an apt slogan for the new Canada. Sometime around 1850 society's leaders became devout believers in the efficacy of education. Their definition of education was decidedly utilitarian: James Wilson Robertson, a noted publicist of educational reform, claimed education was 'that which "helps to fit a man to bring things to pass."'[73] Their chosen method was mass schooling, a social innovation of enormous import to the course of Victorian culture. That innovation, of course, was shaped by the class presumptions of its bourgeois spokesmen. Ryerson and his ilk saw the public school as a panacea for all that ailed their land, especially the cities, as well as an instrument of intellectual progress. The school, they claimed, would educate the poor, defeat crime and poverty, save children, train a new workforce, ensure social cohesion, Canadianize forthcoming generations, speed industrial growth, and Christianize society.[74] The power of this idea led colonial and municipal governments during the 1840s and 1850s to invest extraordinary sums in creating what became a free and universal system of elementary education. That was a massive intrusion into the private lives of ordinary citizens by the state.

How successful was mass schooling? People, as usual, sought an answer in reams of statistics. At the end of the century, Léon Gérin, one of the new breed of social scientists, published in a Paris journal three lengthy essays on 'La loi naturelle du developpement de l'instruction populaire.'[75] Gérin focused upon an apparent indicator of intellectual progress, namely the spread of literacy. He used the census of 1891 to construct tables, and even maps, of the extent of adolescent illiteracy by city, county, and province. These figures, he argued, were a result of a dynamic social equation involving location, work, family, class, schooling, and race. What he found was a striking difference between the high literacy of English Canada and the persistent illiteracy of French Canada. He believed the Anglo-Protestant way of life engendered a generation of typically modern people – enterprising, instrumental, optimistic, individualistic, future-oriented.[76] Consequently, English Canadians had dominated the economic advance of the dominion. The French-Canadian way of life, by contrast, produced a 'traditional' people – dependent, communal, contented, parochial, present-minded, and past-oriented. No wonder they had fallen behind. An impassioned politics was their drug. Gérin called upon his fellows to emulate 'Anglo' ways or suffer the disaster of stagnation in an industrializing country. Ironically, he too espoused the fetish of schooling by ending his essays with a plea for 'écoles d'initiative,' which would shape a modern elite of French Canadians.

Gérin's focus on literacy, at least, was sound. Literacy skills were a crude but concrete measure of modernity. Admittedly, reading and writing were no more than 'basic' and 'minimal' abilities.[77] The illiterate is not necessarily stupid, ignorant, or even handicapped in an oral culture where custom reigns; his privileged colleague is not necessarily progressive or 'modern.' But an illiterate people do lack that essential 'technology of intellect'[78] which enables modernization. And a literate people enjoy the social capacity to absorb new ideas readily and to adjust to general change quickly in pursuit of some agreed goal. An industrializing society does not need, at first, a high level of literacy to sponsor growth. Literacy probably declined among ordinary people in the big cities of England and Wales during the early years of the nineteenth century.[79] Education becomes central when the economy demands more white-collar employees, the marketplace relies increasingly on advertising, and the society shifts toward a mass democracy. Then, perhaps within a generation, the personal significance of literacy mounts enormously. The illiterate, indeed, suffers not just the stigma of 'ignorance' but also the reality of an impotent dependency on others to win or enjoy a livelihood. Likewise, a society lagging behind in the educational race is crippled. So the social import of a high level and a high quality of literacy is enhanced as an oral culture is transformed into a print culture. That grand event occurred in Canada during the last half of the century.

Fortunately Canada possesses a nearly complete set of census statistics, from 1861, which allows a detailed analysis of the cultural transformation. The great advantage of this information lies in the fact that it is both comprehensive and uniform. Unfortunately the information requires careful handling to overcome, again, census vagaries. The 1861 census of the two Canadas noted only the inability to read among male and female adults, likely overestimating the number of people who had any competence.[80] The Nova Scotia census was far better, since it surveyed the ability to read and write among children and young teens as well as everyone over 15. New Brunswick did not bother to probe the illiteracy of its population, thus saving its masters the shock experienced by school teachers and politicians in the sister colony. The census of 1871 was a wider and apparently more accurate survey of all adults by place and sex.[81] In 1881 the census-takers did not publish information on literacy at all. In 1891 they provided an extensive breakdown of the statistics on the ability to read and write by age cohort, invaluable to demonstrate the advance of literacy over the decades. Most irritating, the census bureau in 1901 lumped all of its figures together in a silly attempt to discover the literacy of people aged five and over. Since people did not normally acquire competence in reading and writing until after a few years of schooling, around age ten, the findings contained an unknown number of children who had lacked the opportunity to become literate. That makes a comparison with earlier statistics difficult. Wherever possible, I have employed a definition of literacy which encompasses the ability to read and write. Reading alone amounted to semi-literacy, a rudimentary skill which could allow only a limited consumption of printed matter. Even so, other fragmentary data suggest that the census-takers exaggerated the actual competence of the public, especially in the first two surveys.

The apparent retreat of illiteracy was steady after 1871 (Table 7). Around 1850, about one-quarter to one-third of the adults in the mainland colonies could not read. That placed British North America behind such front-runners as 'white' America and Sweden (at 10 to 15 per cent illiteracy), or Scotland and Prussia (almost as accomplished), but on a par with England and Wales (25 to 30 per cent) and well ahead of Catholic Europe where illiteracy rates ranged from France's estimated 40 per cent to Italy's 75 to 80 per cent.[82] By the end of

TABLE 7

Illiteracy in Canada 1861–1901 (percentage of population)

	1861 (over 20)		1871 (over 20)		1891 (over 20)		1901 (5 and over)	
	Read	Write	Read	Write	Read	Write	Read	Write
Ontario	7.2	–	7.9	12.8	6.9	9.5	8.7	10.2
Quebec	35.9	–	35.9	45.8	29.6	36.1	17.7	22.1
Maritimes	22.6*	32.7*	15.8	23.3	8.1	13.9	14.6	18.8
West	–	–	–	–	11.9	12.8	22.2	23.2
Canada	–	–	18.9	26.1	15.3	19.5	14.4	17.1

SOURCE: Data from *Census of the Canadas* 1861; Appendix no. 25, *Journals and Proceedings of the House of Assembly of Nova Scotia* 1862; *Census of Canada* 1871, 1891, 1901. In each case the percentages are calculated on the basis of the particular population in question.

* Nova Scotia only, people 16 and over. For age 5 and over the respective percentages are 28.7 and 40.5.

the century the level of illiteracy (again the inability to read) among adult Canadians must have hovered around nine or ten per cent – a comforting reduction no doubt, but not altogether satisfactory: the dominion now ranked slightly behind France as well as England and Wales. Indeed, such overall statistics masked the range of both literacy and illiteracy in Canada, and elsewhere, at any point during the 50-year span. Actual competence always varied widely among the assorted groups of a population where the legacy of cultural isolation was slowly giving way before the onset of the mass society.

The young were naturally more accomplished than their elders (Table 8). True, the era of mass schooling did not mean that parents sent off their children happily each day. Especially at mid-century a mother and father did not always bother. One set of statistics indicates that the daily attendance of children in Nova Scotia's system at Confederation was just over one-half the supposed total enrolment. Ontario may not have reached this level until the late 1880s.[83] Still, long before Confederation, the majority of school-age children in Ontario were exposed to some teaching during their so-called 'formative years.' Indeed, the significant decade of educational advance in this province was likely the 1830s, prior to the famous Ryerson years. Thereafter each generation went to school more often and a bit longer.[84] That had something to do with the increasing numbers of free schools, first in the city and then in the countryside. By 1870, every province boasted at least three teachers per thousand people, more than sufficient to improve skills.[85] Then there was the social pressure to ensure each child a decent education, backed by the force of law in Nova Scotia (1865) and

TABLE 8

Literacy* in 1891 by age and date of schooling

Ages	Educational decade	Category	Maritimes (percentage)	Quebec (percentage)	Ontario (percentage)	West (percentage)	Canada (percentage)
10–19	1880s†	Male	85.0	73.2	93.5	86.3	85.2
		Female	88.0	82.5	94.9	86.0	89.3
		Total	86.5	77.8	94.2	86.2	87.2
20–29	1870s	Male	86.9	71.1	94.0	91.3	86.2
		Female	88.3	80.6	95.5	86.0	89.4
		Total	87.6	76.0	94.8	89.4	87.7
30–39	1860s	Male	85.1	63.9	92.1	90.6	82.5
		Female	83.0	72.5	93.1	84.1	84.4
		Total	84.0	68.2	92.6	88.4	83.5
40–59	1840s	Male	80.9	58.1	89.4		78.4
	and	Female	74.0	60.1	87.7		76.0
	1850s	Total	77.4	59.1	88.6		77.2
60 plus	Pre-	Male	73.4	39.1	83.4		67.9
	1840s	Female	59.3	36.5	75.2		59.5
		Total	66.6	37.9	79.6		63.9

SOURCE: Data from *Census* 1891

* Literacy means ability to read and write.

† The lower statistics for the adolescents in 1891 suggest that some pre-teens had not acquired the skills further normal schooling would give them in a few years.

Ontario (1871). Finally, most parents, whatever their station, had acquired the habit of sending their charges off for at least a modicum of schooling. All this seems to have produced an especially well-educated collection of pre-teens and adolescents during the 1890s, or so the findings of 1901 suggest.

Schooling – and death – were also narrowing the time-honoured gap between the skills of men and those of women. The accomplishments of the generation educated before 1840 pointed to a consistent pattern of discrimination against women. Thereafter, in Quebec, women not only caught up but also soon surpassed their partners. Was that an indication farmwives often took on the modest household duty of dealing with the world outside? Elsewhere, the duty remained a male job. In 1871 there was continuing proof of a social emphasis in the cities upon male literacy, especially the ability to read and write (Table 9). The census of 1901 did not provide a breakdown of skills by sex, but appearances suggest women and men were sharing more equally in the advantages of elementary and secondary (but not post-secondary) education by the end of the century.

The link between sex and literacy had varied in significance according to location. Usually, cities were more literate than the countryside.[86] Early nineteenth-century Quebec City, for instance, apparently had a much higher rate of male literacy than any of the surrounding rural countries.[87] That kind of distinction applied across the whole country, or so the census of 1871 and 1901 indicate (Table 10). The industrialization of Canada, then, did not result in any degradation of the overall skills of city dwellers – just the opposite. Big cities were more likely to contain concentrations of teachers and schools, even before the era of mass schooling, which ensured more children would receive a rudimentary education.[88] Besides, the utility of literacy was more obvious in an urban setting. The impersonal labour market, centred in the cities, produced a workforce that eventually had to operate in a sea of paper. The big cities boasted the department store, the trade union, the public library, the daily newspaper, and organized sports, all of which assumed literacy skills among their clients. In the countryside, especially on the frontier, the utility of the '3 Rs' was not so clearcut, which explains why Gérin found the highest levels of illiteracy in lumbering and mining areas. Still, the commercialization of agriculture made the successful farmer a reader of market reports, manuals of new techniques, perhaps agrarian tracts. By the 1890s, farming districts, especially in the vicinity of a big city, were obviously catching up.[89] Once again, the advance of 'modernity' was homogenizing the skills of disparate souls.

Even so, a substantial difference remained between the educational accomplishments of French and English Canadians. The census of 1871 allows a crude

TABLE 9

Sex and literacy 1871

	Read only		Read and write	
	Female (percentage)	Male (percentage)	Female (percentage)	Male (percentage)
Halifax	93.5	94.8	89.6	91.4
Nova Scotia*	(81.3)	(85.1)	(70.8)	(79.4)
Saint John	90.8	92.4	84.3	89.3
New Brunswick	(86.3)	(84.6)	(77.8)	(80.3)
Quebec City	80.3	77.7	69.4	72.4
Montreal	79.1	79.3	69.5	75.9
Quebec	(68.7)	(59.4)	(55.0)	(53.3)
Toronto	95.0	96.9	91.8	95.6
Ontario	(92.0)	(92.2)	(85.5)	(88.7)

SOURCE: Data from *Census* 1871
* Statistics for the province are given in parentheses.

TABLE 10

Big-city literacy 1871 and 1901 (in percentages)

	Able to write	
	1871 Over 20	1901 5 and over
Halifax	90.6	85.1
Nova Scotia 'remnant'*	(73.6)	(80.6)
Saint John	86.6	89.4
New Brunswick 'remnant'	(78.0)	(78.4)
Montreal and Quebec City	71.8	85.8
Quebec 'remnant'	(50.8)	(76.3)
Toronto	93.6	92.8
Ontario 'remnant'	(86.9)	(89.5)

SOURCE: Data from *Census* 1871 and 1901
* Statistics for the rest of the province are given in parentheses.

analysis of the link between 'nationality' and literacy (Table 11). Francophone districts in the countryside were invariably less literate than their anglophone counterparts. And the migration of French-Canadian country folk into Montreal and Quebec depressed the literacy levels of these cities. Here was a source of the charges of 'French backwardness' bandied about by nativists and bigots in the rest of Canada. The obvious reply was that French Quebec had

TABLE 11

Nationality and literacy* in Quebec 1871

	Population (number)	'French' (percentage)	'British' (percentage)	Adult literacy (percentage)
Montreal				
'East'	46,297	76.8	21.4	63.2
'Centre'	5,271	61.2	31.4	73.9
'West'	55,722	32.4	65.5	79.7
Quebec				
'East'	28,305	85.5	13.5	60.0
'Centre'	18,188	65.0	33.8	82.7
'West'	13,206	36.8	62.1	76.2
Kamouraska	21,254	98.9	00.7	35.6
Terrebonne	19,591	92.6	07.2	37.6
Trois-Rivières	8,414	91.4	07.9	59.8
Brome	13,687	25.4	68.9	85.4
Stanstead	13,138	24.4	71.4	87.6

SOURCE: Data from *Census* 1871
* Adult literacy refers to people over age 20 able to read and write.

inherited an unfortunate legacy of illiteracy which made any catching up difficult. In 1850 French Quebec likely ranked with the countries of Catholic Europe, the community's illiterates numbering somewhere around two-thirds of the total adult population. Thus by 1900 the statistical progress which the community had made along the road to full literacy was impressive.

But that reply begged an equally obvious question. Why was French Canada, not just in Quebec but elsewhere in the country, so 'backward' – especially when Ontario, as early as 1850, probably ranked with 'white' America among the most literate communities in the world? Ontario was peopled by immigrants, who perhaps were more literate than the stay-at-homes.[90] Early on, English Quebec received a high percentage of literate New Englanders. Far more important, though, was the effect of religion. The Protestant faith, and especially the intense piety of Dissent, placed an extraordinary emphasis upon reading 'the Word'.[91] Before 1840, Ontario was filled with all kinds of learning: not just state-supported common schools but many more local and private venture schools and Sunday and mission schools, as well as private tutors.[92] Much the same situation existed in English Quebec too: an enquiry into education in 1835–36 demonstrated that there were almost as many 'English' as 'French' common schools in the Quebec countryside.[93] The problem was that the traditional way of life in the Catholic countryside engendered what amounted to an Old World peasantry which saw little utility in education. As well, the Roman

Catholic church, never a great champion of widespread Bible-reading, was ambivalent towards popular education, its priests suspicious of the schoolmaster as a rival or an agent of anglicization.

Things did change after 1840. Then the colonial government and the church launched a major assault on the 'ignorance' of the countryside. The results of the assault showed how difficult it was to overcome the past. The mid-century effort to force local school taxation upon rural areas sparked a tax revolt, called 'la guerre des éteignoirs,' which even the church had difficulty suppressing. Gérin noted that the type of upbringing common among the French-Canadian masses fostered a dependent, unenterprising youth, hardly likely to see the virtues of much education.[94] The church was determined to extend its control over schooling to ensure that the liberal and his heresies secured no grip on the popular mind. In 1875, the church climaxed one campaign when the provincial government abolished the Ministry of Public Instruction and instituted a special council for Catholic education controlled by the bishops. Thereafter, the church easily disciplined the lay schoolmasters: the 'feminization' of teaching filled the profession with a vast majority of more submissive women (by 1900 95 per cent of all lay instructors were women) and the related 'clericalization' brought in a flood of religious personnel (by 1900 44 per cent of all instructors).[95] The consequent educational system was designed to impart a modicum of skills and a solid knowledge of Catholic dogma to the general populace. Indicative of the level of commitment to the quality of learning was the fact that in 1893 Ontario spent on education per person well over double the amount of Quebec.[96] Schooling, in short, was much more an instrument of preservation than progress, or at least the kind of progress the 'Anglos' touted. And the educational competence of the population suffered, producing, Gérin warned, new generations ill prepared for the challenges of the industrial world.

Similar doubts about competence afflicted the debate over class and education. Certainly, the rhetoric of the early school promoters and the later school reformers was filled with allusions to saving the children of the poor.[97] But, on balance, mass education better served the needs of the 'classes.' Schooling could not easily overcome the effects of inequality. Indeed, schooling often reinforced that reality.

Witness the famous public schools. Early attendance statistics demonstrated that boys and girls of the affluent went more often and more regularly to school than their poorer cousins.[98] During the 1850s, the Irish Catholics in Ontario's cities were only limited users of the new service until the proper organization of separate schools. Even compulsory education, which was not introduced in New Brunswick until 1908 and not until much later in Quebec, could not wholly defeat the bane of irregular attendance. Life's regimen meant that the children of the labourer might well have to move in the midst of the school year or even work to assist the family's finances, especially when the breadwinner lost his job.[99] At school, children found a kind of learning more congenial to someone brought up in a middle-class home. In 1889, Saint John's Albert School offered a curriculum full of reading, writing, arithmetic, grammar and composition, geography and history, some languages and sciences, plus singing and moral instruction.[100] That was not harmful obviously, but it was not especially practical either, beyond the '3 Rs,' and it was really geared to children destined for further education, or at least a white-collar occupation. Efforts to introduce more useful subjects resulted in little more than the addition of a few sewing and drawing classes, sometimes a study of agriculture.[101]

Then there was the bias of secondary and post-secondary education. Advanced schooling was very much a middle-class preserve, bolstered by special fees, entrance examinations, and the very style of teaching. Pelham Mulvany praised the 'social tone' of Toronto's Collegiate Institute, quite as appropriate for 'the gentlemanly lads and refined lady-like pupils' as any private school.[102] Quebec's classical colleges and universities were emphatically the vocational schools for the professions. Besides, adolescence was, for the 'masses,' the first entry into the work-force. Again, life's regimen deprived many youngsters of the leisure years necessary to acquire the secondary education important to a white-collar career. Educators did try to meet this problem by organizing evening classes at public schools in basic and technical subjects. There was a special 'école d'arts et métiers' in Montreal, schools of popular science and mining elsewhere. Ontario consistently funded a range of mechanics' institutes which did offer night courses in 'Book-keeping and Penmanship,' 'Arithmetic and Mathematics,' 'Architectural and Mechanical Drawing,' even 'Chemistry and Natural Philosophy.' Yet a government report indicated that between 1870 and 1880 only 15,261 pupils attended such courses, mostly in elementary subjects.[103] Supplementary education could not reach a sufficient clientele to upgrade the skills of the blue-collar work-force.

Did the middle-class bias mean the literacy of the 'masses' suffered? There was always some evidence that the schools had failed to educate the people at the very bottom of the social ladder. Jails and prisons throughout the half-century were filled with labourers and the like whose educational attainments were minimal. One account of mostly urban 'criminals' in Middlesex County, Ontario, in 1867–68 showed that only about one-fifth of the people arrested could read or write well.[104] The so-called factory schools, which were supposed to ensure some learning for labouring children, were never a great success. The Royal Commission on the Relations of Labor and Capital heard evidence from a manager of a Montreal cotton factory that many of his 'girls' were unable to read or write.[105] The records of the Hawkesbury Lumber Co. in the late 1880s and early 1890s showed only half of the work-force were literate.[106]

By the last third of the century, however, schooling and its partners were fast improving the overall quality of literacy skills among the wider populace. The popularity of the reading habit proved the competence of the masses was on the rise. Between 1868 and 1874 alone, the total annual value of imported books increased from $479,000 to $959,000.[107] The Typographical Society of Quebec City in 1864 had a reading room and a library of a thousand books.[108] That was an amenity trade unions commonly offered their members. In 1871 Montreal's Historical Society of Quebec opened its library on Monday and Saturday evenings for the convenience of working people.[109] During the 1880s middle-class reformers and the Knights of Labor urged with some success the establishment of public libraries for general use. By 1896 Toronto's public library claimed 'eighty-five thousand volumes, to which constant additions of the newest literature are being made; a large newspaper-room, displaying the latest journals from Great Britain and all the leading colonies; a separate reading-room for ladies, and a reference library of a most complete and up-to-date description.'[110]

Not that people were reading the kinds of things which enthusiasts of education had once hoped. Self-improvement was not high on everybody's list. Amusement was. Moralists, schoolteachers among them, lamented the craze for fiction. Pernicious literature, cheap fiction magazines, and dime novels, it seemed, had too wide a readership, especially among the youth of the land.[111] Forty-four per cent (1867) and 36 per cent (1874) of the books Samuel Dawson sold through his Montreal bookstore, presumably to an affluent clientele, were works of fiction.[112] John Ross Robertson, the proprietor of the Toronto *Telegram*, had a profitable sideline publishing pirated American or British 'trash' for sale at 10 to 50 cents a title.[113] A special irony was the conversion of the mechanics' institutes, emphatically a bourgeois institution run by the best people, into a series of reading rooms and circulating libraries. Over 80 per cent of the 33,000 volumes borrowed by members of Toronto's Mechanics' Institute in 1878–79 were works of fiction.[114] The gentlemen in charge admitted defeat. The clients had taken command.

Even more outstanding was the boom in periodical and newspaper circulation (Table 12). 'Newspaper literature,' mused one booklover in 1875, 'is ... the chief mental pabulum of our people.'[115] People of all ages, sexes, classes, and places were reading journals. Everyone, it seemed, could find a publication suited to his or her taste. Ontario claimed the most flourishing press: farm families, Thomas Conant noted, took 'a weekly paper, an agricultural paper, and generally some religious paper'[116] – and, he could have added, occasionally an urban

TABLE 12

Journals and readership* 1871 and 1891

	1871 (per family)	1891 (per family)
Nova Scotia	0.58	1.54
New Brunswick	1.05	1.73
Quebec	0.95	2.98
Ontario	1.29	3.57
Prairies	–	1.77

SOURCE: Data from the *Census* 1871 and 1891, Geo. Rowell's *American Newspaper Directory* of 1873; and A. McKim's *Canadian Newspaper Directory* of 1892

* Readership means the circulation of all journals divided by the number of census families. The figures for 1891 are very crude because journals with a national circulation are included in the provincial totals.

daily as well. The greatest readers, though, were in the big cities. There, the sheer number of publications and the soaring circulations suggested an insatiable hunger for newpapers. Popular culture had arrived in Canada, and with a vengeance.

2

The making of the daily press

The daily newspaper is a sophisticated result of man's ingenuity. It was never an easy task to produce, six days a week, so complete a medium of fact and fancy, editorials and advertisements. What enabled its making, of course, was a series of innovations in printing, paper manufacture, and communications. Yet if technology provided the opportunities, and established limits, technology did not create the daily press. Entrepreneurs did. They seized the main chance, sometimes aided by political overseers or inspired by foreign examples. Success required an assortment of skills, ranging from a good news-sense to business acumen. A talent for writing, especially in the beginning, was very useful. The knack of hunting down potential advertisers was always vital. But, above all, publishers had to be able to judge their markets, to decide how best to cater to the tastes of the reading public. At first, that public was grouped into special constituencies whose needs or interests were determined by religion, language, class, politics, locale. Over time, these constituencies lost definition as people became more obviously members of large or mass publics, if still separated by social boundaries. The upshot was that publishers developed, and scrapped, a series of formulas designed to give their papers a secure niche in the marketplace. The making of the daily press, then, is really a long drawn-out story of trial and error.

PIONEERS

Any birthdate for the daily press is bound to appear a trifle arbitrary. Up to the 1830s nearly all colonial newspapers were weeklies, run by a proprietor-editor (who was often a printer as well) with an assistant or two. Early efforts to launch part-time dailies, the Montreal *Advertiser* (1833) and the Toronto *Royal Standard* (1836), were dismal failures. More significant was the arrival of small-sized, penny tri-weeklies such as the Montreal *Transcript* (1836) and the Saint John *News* (1839) which sought to emulate America's cheap press by providing more family fare than their political brethren, the first time a group of Canadian proprietors consciously set out to win the favour of the lower orders. (The *News* announced that the penny paper was esteemed everywhere as 'the poor man's friend.'[1] Meanwhile, the larger sheets moved towards bi-weekly or tri-weekly editions, especially in the 1840s, to satisfy the thirst for news and the pressure of advertisments. The Montreal *Gazette* and *Herald* even started daily editions during the hectic commercial season in the summer. Only with the boom of the 1850s, though, did the year-round daily become a practical proposition.

There were newspapers galore in each city at mid-century. Only a few could trace their lineage back more than a decade. Changing fortunes and times had altered even the relatively 'old,' forcing conformity to the rituals of party warfare. The venerable Montreal *Gazette*, for a time little more than a commercial sheet, had become a zealot of the Anglo-Tory persuasion. Quebec's *Le Canadien* (1806), once Radical, was now a lukewarm supporter of the anti-radical Reform government. Most newcomers were launched with a definite purpose in mind: Hugh Scobie founded Toronto's *British Colonist* (1838) to aid conservative-minded Scots and the Church of Scotland[2]; Ludger Duvernay, back from an American exile, restarted *La Minerve* (1842) in the Reform interest; and William Annand saw in his Halifax *Chronicle* (1844) the new Liberal standard-bearer. These were only a handful of the chaos of organs: a contemporary anatomy of press opinion in the province of Canada, published by William Meikle in 1858, revealed that leading papers espoused an unholy array of ethnic, religious, and political 'principles'[3] – and the Maritimes was no better.

No paper could claim much more than a small circulation. Mass illiteracy severely limited the market for francophone papers to the well-educated, professional (less so business) element that dominated political life. Indeed, *La Minerve*'s circulation has been estimated at about 1,200 in 1845, the rival *L'Avenir* at about 1,500 near the end of the autumn of 1848.[4] Greater literacy in English Canada certainly enlarged the potential market for anglophone publishers. One observer thought that the effort to reach the half-educated 'lowers the tone of the press, and circumscribes both authors and speakers, as any allusions to history or general literature would be very imperfectly, if at all, understood.'[5] In any case, the plethora of organs meant that too many publishers were carving up the market. As late as 1858, Meikle claimed that the circulation of the 'few daily issues' in Montreal was 'nearly on a par, and that of the highest ... does not reach one thousand actual subscribers.'[6] Readership, of course, might be much greater than any subscription list suggested, since newspapers did travel from hand to hand. But a modest subscription list kept publishers closely in touch with the parochial concerns of their paying customers.

Susannah Moodie reported that the typical newspaper was 'a strange mélange of politics, religion, abuse, and general information. It contains, in a condensed form, all the news of the Old and the New World, and informs its readers of what is passing on the great globe, from the North Pole to the Gold Mines of Australia and California.'[7] An analysis of the contents of four leading newspapers in 1849 bears out her claim (Table 13). These four-page journals, at least bi-weekly and sometimes more frequent, furnished a little entertainment such as short stories or poetry, a lot of advertising for business or professional people and retail stores and patent medicines, plus a wealth of information that encompassed news briefs, parliamentary debates at home and in Britain, letters as well as editorials, features, and anecdotes. The second page was the grand domain of this information, and there the central attraction was the editorials or 'leaders,' long essays on the topics of the week, which had become a normal offering during the previous generation. Many happenings were not deemed especially worthy of much report or comment: civic affairs and life's routine, for instance, were usually slighted. The passion of all the papers was public affairs, notably the hot topic of a domestic politics upset by Reform Legislation, riots in Montreal, and the eventual clamour over union with the United States. Even the reports of things occurring in the outside world were sometimes selected because of their relevance to the fevered discussion in Canada of church and state, progress and trade. Publishers often mixed news and views in their columns to ensure a particular response from their readers. Political opponents, invariably, were a target of much abuse, as were rival journalists. This kind of bias was a natural extension of the newspaper's declared purpose, the advocacy of a dogma that thrilled the hearts and minds of the publisher's little public. The newspaper was a weapon of debate, not just a digest of facts.

There were differences between the anglophone and francophone varieties of journalism, of course. Take foreign affairs. Usually more of the happenings in the outside world would receive notice in anglophone columns. American news, in particular, was a constant item. If the foreign coverage of the *British Colonist* and the *Globe* emphasized the British scene, then *La Minerve* and *L'Avenir* worried more about European disturbances and especially an unsettled France. Likewise note the treatment of life. The Toronto journals carried a modicum of social trivia, especially about crime and disaster. The Montreal journals reported on the institutions and the beliefs that held together the community, notably the church and its views. In general, anglophone papers provided not only more information in each issue, but this information was more complete, more varied, and more factual. So the *Colonist* boasted a regular London

TABLE 13

Content analysis* 1849 (12 days, 1 from each month)

	Toronto *British Colonist*	Toronto *Globe*	Montreal *La Minerve*	Montreal *L'Avenir*
Line count of information	39,998	30,372	26,395	18,840
Contents				
Advertisements	49.8	50.6	54.3	39.4
Information	49.2	48.4	41.5	59.0
Entertainment	0.9	1.0	4.2	1.6
Information: locale				
Outside world	(46.0)	(39.0)	(26.1)	(15.4)
Great Britain	26.5	18.1	10.1	1.5
United States	8.2	6.7	2.6	4.9
Europe	7.4	12.9	11.6	9.0
Other lands	3.9	0.6	1.8	–
British North America	(36.3)	(38.2)	(47.7)	(39.1)
Province of Canada	31.2	32.6	46.6	39.0
Atlantic region	1.3	1.2	0.3	0.1
Other section	3.8	4.4	0.8	0.1
Local world	(14.2)	(20.2)	(20.9)	(32.9)
Home section	6.1	12.6	13.6	21.7
City	8.1	7.6	7.3	11.2
Information: subject				
Public affairs	(61.7)	(65.1)	(70.7)	(77.3)
External	20.0	16.3	9.3	11.0
Colonial	41.2	46.6	60.1	65.6
Civic	0.5	2.2	1.3	00.7
Economics	(16.0)	(11.5)	(11.5)	(4.4)
Life	(21.1)	(23.1)	(16.9)	(18.0)
The community and its ways	5.5	4.8	10.5	14.3
Culture and entertainment	2.3	1.8	0.4	0.6
People	1.5	2.1	0.2	–
Sports and recreation	0.1	–	–	–
Crime and violence	3.2	6.6	1.8	1.0
Death and disaster	3.8	2.5	1.2	0.3
Miscellany	4.7	5.3	2.8	1.8

* Some of the information could not be identified according to locale or subject; hence the percentages do not total 100. Percentages for major divisions of locale and subject are given in parentheses.

correpondent who supplied an opinionated survey of European and British imperial affairs. Both Toronto papers quickly realized the value of telegraphic news to keep readers abreast of the latest in foreign doings. The Montreal *Herald* and *Gazette* were renowned for the quality of their commercial information. By contrast, the francophone papers specialized in argument, be that copied, communicated, or editorial, suited to the sophisticated palate of the highbrow reader. Thus, in the late summer of 1848 *Le Canadien* was wont to fill its front page with such items as 'Sur le Communisme' and a 'Discours de M. Proudhon.' Abuse might routinely enliven the editorial columns of *La Minerve* and *L'Avenir*; so too did reasoned, philosophical disquisitions, often of first principles. The phenomenon of revolution, for example, led francophone journalists to ponder the very nature of European, and hence Canadian and American, institutions.

George Brown's *Globe* was the first newspaper to merit the term *popular*.[8] The paper had begun in the normal fashion: in 1844 a group of Reformers and Free Kirk Presbyterians contributed funds to enable Brown to set up a new Toronto organ. The novice publisher soon proved the outstanding newspaper entrepreneur of his era. His formula? – so improve the capacity and calibre of his newspaper that it created a demand in the city and countryside. He moved successively from weekly production, to semi-weekly (1846), tri-weekly (1849), and at last daily (1853). He expanded that four-page daily to enormous proportions, eventually using a 'blanket sheet' (folded once) measuring 31″ by 50″,[9] so that he could pack in 36 columns of reading and advertising matter. He launched in 1861 a new evening edition, slightly cheaper, to furnish late news and win more local readers.[10] He continued the weekly, thus making double use of news and views in the daily, for out-of-town subscribers. In 1864 he founded the fortnightly *Canada Farmer* to attract an even wider following in the countryside.

Improved capacity depended upon technology, and Brown was always aware of the newest inventions.

The printing press. The Hoe Co. of the United States manufactured steam-powered cylinder machines capable in time of producing thousands of sheets per hour, whereas the earlier hand presses were limited to about 200.[11] In 1844 Brown purchased the first such press in Ontario, capacity 1,250 copies an hour (he also became, for a time, Hoe's Canadian agent). By 1860 Brown's establishment boasted two double-cylinder A.B. Taylor presses, able to print 3,000 copies an hour each, plus a novel folding machine to prepare copies for delivery and sale.

Papermaking. Lavish amounts of cheap newsprint were necessary to feed these new machines. The traditional process of manufacturing paper from linen rags produced only limited quantities of expensive, if excellent, newsprint. Brown actually patented a new 'straw paper' process which he hoped would solve his difficulties – and make money.[12] Eventually, he gave his patronage to John Riordon whose St Catharines' mills were among the first in Canada to produce white paper from wood pulp.

The telegraph. The wiring of British North America took place in the late 1840s and early 1850s, thus giving to news an immediacy impossible before. In 1847 Brown and Scobie (*British Colonist*) shared the expenses of telegraphing Atlantic shipping information to please Toronto's merchants. Brown employed Thomas Sellars as his Montreal correspondent to send regular dispatches on the affairs of the commercial capital.[13] And Brown would fill his columns with telegraphed specials when interest warranted the expense – for instance, the *Globe* scooped the rest of the press by publishing the draft version of the British North America Act in February 1867.

No less impressive was the calibre of Brown's newspaper. Brown did not break with the prevailing conventions of journalism but rather perfected the normal range of offerings to attract a province-wide audience. He tried to supply something that would catch the fancy of the most wayward reader. Thus, over the years, he serialized some notable popular fiction, including Charles Dickens's works. Brown had an eye for the spectacular and the sensational: on 1 November 1856, the *Globe* provided four and one-half columns on the murder trial of George Brogdin, the jury verdict supplied by telegraph.[14] He made sure he furnished a lot of foreign news, sometimes filling up columns on the second page with round-ups of European affairs. What he specialized in was a fulsome coverage of colonial politics: parliamentary debates, political speeches, party business, and election campaigns. These would crowd other reading matter out of the columns.

All that Brown and his brother and their writers supplemented with ferocious editorials. These 'leaders,' of course, were often worthy analyses of events or statements of principle – indeed, the editor's purview extended over the whole of life and affairs: slavery, temperance and morality, education, trade policy, race and religion could furnish matter for thoughtful discussion. The famed and feared *Globe* editorial, however, struck without mercy against the foes of Reform. Brown and his cohorts seemed able to draw on an inexhaustible well-spring of moral indignation in their denunciations of Tory conspiracies. Repetition and slander were favoured tools. 'When a political opponent is torn to pieces some morning in the leading columns,' commented a British traveller, 'you will hear people say, "George Browne [*sic*] has finished him this time."'[15] The *Globe* in full frenzy was a marvellous engine of destruction.

The formula worked. Brown soon outdistanced his competition. He bought out his weak Reform rivals, the *North American* and the *Examiner*, in 1855. James Beaty of the Toronto *Leader*, the Conservative organ, seemed content with a modest circulation – much to the disgust of John A. Macdonald, the party leader, for Brown rapidly built up a huge readership, a lot of it outside the city. The variety of hard news made the *Globe* indispensable reading for the well-informed man, even should he be a Tory. Perhaps too, the fact that Brown was almost always in opposition freed the paper from charges of hypocrisy or bribery, enabling its forthright editorials to win readers by expressing popular grievances. Weekly and daily circulation stood at roughly 18,000 in 1856, 28,000 in 1861, and 45,000 in 1872. Much of the latest growth had come from the daily alone, when the subscription price was lowered from $6 to $5 in 1868 (and a new Hoe press added). Within three months, the daily's circulation more than doubled, from 7,700 to over 16,000, later reaching about 20,000, somewhat more than half the subscribers living outside Toronto. The *Globe* had become the political Bible of many a Reform household in western Ontario. No wonder people called the *Globe* Canada's 'Thunderer,' the equivalent of *The Times*, and worried about the onset of a newspaper despotism. An anonymous reporter for Dun's credit agency in 1876 called the *Globe* 'the most successful and profitable daily Journal in the Dominion,' boasting 'immense political influence and a large revenue.'[16]

No other publisher matched Brown's achievement. Some tried. Only one, John Dougall of the Montreal *Witness*, had much success. The fate of the others illustrated the difficulties inherent in this field of popular journalism. During the mid-1850s, Samuel Thompson endeavoured to make the assorted editions of the Toronto *Colonist* (morning and evening, bi-weekly and weekly) a mighty competitor, claiming in his *Reminiscences of a Canadian Pioneer* some 30,000 subscribers among 'all classes and creeds' inside and outside the city.[17] The commercial panic of 1857, plus a streak of bad luck, forced him to give up the newspaper, which in time was absorbed by Beaty's *Leader*. In 1862 John Livingston began his Saint John *Telegraph* as a tri-weekly for the city and a weekly for the country, tried daily publication briefly in 1864, and eventually amalgamated with the *Morning Journal* in 1869 to start a new daily. Livingston's *Telegraph* supplied a wide range of reading matter, including much hard news via the telegraph and a roving reporter, all of which brought the paper a daily circulation of 4,000 and a weekly circulation of 8,000 by 1872. Two years before, though, overexpansion and limited capital had led Livingston to declare bankruptcy.[18] Then there were John Ross Robertson and James Cook, who together launched the evening Toronto *Telegraph* in 1866, quickly branching out with a morning and a weekly edition. The *Telegraph* hoped to topple Brown's *Globe* by mixing Conservatism and sensation. Again, while the paper may have secured a sizeable circulation,[19] revenues never matched expenditures and the *Telegraph* disappeared when the Conservative party withdrew its backing in 1872. The effort to win a metropolitan audience required much capital and skill, all the more difficult if any competitor was in the business.

Far wiser to remain satisfied with a modicum of prestige and profit. Proprietors usually waited upon public demand before finally converting to daily publication. So for over ten years the business cycle seemed to dictate that the Montreal *Gazette* remain a winter tri-weekly and a summer daily. Only in 1854 did Robert Lowe and Brown Chamberlin make the permanent switch, and then because railways and telegraphs had fostered year-round commercial activity.[20] The Ontario boom furnished sufficient advertising revenue to ensure that the leading papers of Kingston, Hamilton, and London were all dailies by the late 1850s. Not so in the Maritimes: most similar journals remained tri-weeklies. Indeed, in June 1864, Halifax readers could enjoy eight different tri-weeklies, published morning or evening, or on different days, to avoid excessive competition! Lacking readers and advertisers, early French-Canadian ventures in the daily field came to naught. Then, late in 1864, *La Minerve* appeared as a daily, soon building a fair circulation (estimated at almost 5,000 in 1872). That event, as similar events elsewhere, forced its rivals to follow suit. Of course, the added expense might well mean disaster, suggested by the death of newspaper after newspaper during the 1850s and 1860s. But once a publisher took the plunge, and succeeded, then his competition had to do likewise. The public preferred dailies. By the end of 1872, there were eight dailies in Montreal (four English, three French, one bilingual); four apiece in Halifax, Saint John, Toronto – and Quebec (split evenly French and English); three each in Ottawa, Hamilton, and London; and two in Kingston.

Cluttered newspaper markets meant that publishers had to scramble to keep down costs and earn revenues. Montreal owners, for instance, agreed upon a single advertising tariff in April 1854 to regulate competition.[21] In 1864 Halifax publishers, led by J.T. Compton of the *Express*, arranged a sharing of the costs of the news service supplied by the Associated Press of New York.[22] In 1871 Montreal's *Le Pays*, a Liberal organ, commonly printed in translation and with citation telegraph dispatches initially sent to the friendly *Herald*. Less worthy, the editor of many an evening paper was often condemned for stealing the news of a morning rival. In Ontario especially the numbers of evening papers grew steadily. 'One reason is because in the evening the mass of workingmen and the bulk of families have most leisure to read,' noted a journalist in 1872; 'and another, the development of telegraphic enterprise, bringing news on the day it occurs with equal facility from the other side of the Continent and the other side of the Atlantic.'[23] Some dailies tried to cover all markets: the Ottawa *Citizen* in 1865 announced morning, noon, and evening editions of the daily.[24] Nearly every publisher maintained some kind of weekly, usually a reprint of selected daily matter, for country readers. Great success eluded all these hopefuls. Comfort many did enjoy.

THE SEARCH FOR POPULARITY

What disturbed that comfort, indeed the whole of the newspaper scene, was the discovery of the cultural and commercial significance of the social gulf in the big city.

During the 1870s and 1880s the count of daily newspapers doubled, from 47 in 1873 to 94 in 1892 (Table 14).[25] Additions came from the growing ranks of town dailies, which were often conversions of earlier weeklies, in the countryside, especially Ontario's countryside. Few of these papers enjoyed either a large circulation or a monopoly: the Belleville market, for example, was shared throughout most of the two decades by the Conservative *Intelligencer* and the Liberal *Chronicle*, each with a daily circulation of about 1,000 copies in 1891. As well, the daily press had moved out west, notably to British Columbia where Victoria and later Vancouver gave publishers a solid urban market. But, again, circulation figures remained small: Victoria's largest paper, the *Times*, could claim a daily circulation of only 1,750 and a weekly circulation of 2,250 in 1891. The most exciting scene remained the big cities of central Canada: there, publishers first experimented with new formulas to win ever larger segments of the rapidly expanding publics.

The changeover was already well advanced in Montreal at the time of Confederation. The presence of so many rival dailies created an extremely unstable market. An analysis of one week's contents of seven of the nine dailies[26] highlights the differing responses to common events (Table 15). The week of Monday through Saturday, 13 to 18 February, 1871 was full of news and contention: the war in Europe: Germany's victory assured and Paris on the verge of upheaval; the beginning of the Anglo-American negotiations in Washington that promised a normalization of relations between the Empire and the republic; in Montreal an upcoming civic election, debate over a railway subsidy, and a rape trial; in Ottawa the opening of Parliament. In short, it was an ordinary 'news week,' no single issue transcendent.

TABLE 14

Number of daily newspapers by region 1873–1901

	Maritimes	Quebec	Ontario	Prairies	British Columbia and Yukon	Total
1873 (R)	8	12	25	0	2	47
1877 (R)	8	12	22	1	2	45
1881 (A)	9	19	29	3	2	62
1886 (A)	10	22	38	3	4	77
1892 (M)	15	25	41	4	9	94
1897 (A)	18	16	52	5	7	98
1901 (A)	17	17	58	8	12	112

SOURCE: The newspaper directories are listed beside each date: A = Ayers, M = McKim's, R = Rowell's.

The city's prestige dailies were the four party organs. On the French side stood *La Minerve*, then at the peak of its influence, a profitable and important spokesman of 'old' conservatism, and *Le Pays*, near death (in December 1871), the rouge veteran of many a battle with churchmen and bleus. Both papers cost $6 a year, neither mentioning a single-copy or street price, appeared first in the morning (although *La Minerve*, at least, had an evening edition), and offered readers respectively 28 columns (*La Minerve*) and 32 columns (*Le Pays*). About 60 per cent of their space was the preserve of advertising, slightly over one-third went to information, the rest to entertainment, mostly the feuilleton. Ads collected under a variety of headings (such as 'Chemins de Fers,' 'Vapeurs Oceaniques,' 'Avis de Syndics,' 'Ventes par Encan' in *Le Pays*) dominated the front and back pages, leaving the inside pages, especially the second page, to information. Naturally, *Le Pays* and *La Minerve* lavished attention on politics and diplomacy, their editorials displaying a coherent perspective on the happenings of the world of affairs, though both papers also granted considerable space to the business scene and life in general. *Le Pays* was infatuated with events in Europe, especially the fall of France and the republican revival there, whereas *La Minerve* balanced a similar interest with excitement over the opening of Parliament. The two papers focused on the local world, a good deal of their interest in fact centred on Montreal, to the neglect of news in the other provinces. Little bits of trivia about people, high society, and the like in Quebec sprinkled the pages of *Le Pays*, perhaps as filler. By contrast, *La Minerve* offered considerably more telegraphic news (its cable news came largely via the Associated Press service), evidence the Conservative organ had greater resources to meet the expenses of buying and translating hard news. Even so, the two dailies were discernibly highbrow, their commentary and copied features above all learned.

TABLE 15

Content analysis* 1871 (Monday through Saturday, 13 to 18 February)

	Gazette	*Witness*	*Herald*	*Le Pays*	*La Minerve*	*Star*	*Le Nouveau Monde*
Line count of information	20,215	15,730	14,499	11,675	11,064	10,688	8,453
Contents							
Advertisements	(55.1)	(43.8)	(68.5)	(59.9)	(60.7)	(61.3)	(57.7)
Information	(44.6)	(53.7)	(30.8)	(34.0)	(36.9)	(35.9)	(37.1)
Telegraphic news	12.2	11.7	9.2	7.2	13.2	8.4	7.7
Entertainment	(0.3)	(2.6)	(0.7)	(6.1)	(2.4)	(2.8)	(5.2)
Information: locale							
Outside world	(40.9)	(35.4)	(36.7)	(48.4)	(34.4)	(33.7)	(44.0)
Great Britain	12.9	7.3	9.2	3.5	5.1	7.6	4.5
United States	18.7	15.6	14.1	9.6	8.2	17.1	5.4
Europe	8.8	11.3	12.8	34.8	20.4	7.8	33.4
Other lands	0.5	1.2	0.6	0.5	(0.7)	1.2	0.7
Canada	(29.1)	(25.4)	(19.8)	(17.4)	(26.7)	(20.6)	(10.0)
National scene	11.9	17.1	13.5	13.1	23.7	8.1	8.2
The other provinces	17.2	8.3	6.3	4.3	3.0	12.5	1.8
Local world	(29.1)	(32.5)	(42.0)	(34.2)	(37.2)	(40.0)	(46.1)
Quebec province	3.7	5.0	1.3	13.0	11.1	6.7	22.9
Montreal	25.4	27.5	40.7	21.2	26.1	33.3	23.2
Information: subject							
Public affairs	(48.1)	(44.9)	(42.8)	(56.4)	(65.1)	(38.9)	(56.6)
External	19.0	15.5	20.6	34.0	24.9	15.1	34.9
Canadian	22.4	19.5	16.1	13.6	25.7	12.6	9.3
Provincial	0.3	2.8	0.5	6.5	6.8	5.0	6.8
Civic	6.4	7.1	5.6	2.3	7.7	6.2	5.6
Economics	(22.9)	(14.5)	(32.7)	(17.8)	(16.2)	(7.3)	(9.4)
Life	(29.1)	(40.7)	(24.5)	(25.3)	(18.5)	(51.9)	(32.4)
The community and its ways	9.8	12.5	9.0	2.1	4.5	7.2	17.6
Culture and entertainment	1.9	4.3	2.5	5.3	2.0	2.5	1.5
People	2.9	1.0	2.4	3.1	0.8	4.6	0.7
Sports and recreation	4.0	1.3	1.8	0.4	0.2	4.8	0.3
Crime and violence	3.9	4.2	2.0	2.5	3.0	12.0	5.3
Death and disaster	2.3	6.1	3.8	3.3	1.0	11.9	3.0
Miscellany	4.3	11.3	3.0	8.6	7.0	8.9	4.0

* Some of the information could not be identified according to locale or subject; hence the percentages do not total 100. Percentages for major divisions of contents, locale, and subject are given in parentheses.

The typical party newspaper in French Quebec had remained a vehicle of argument.

On the English side stood the Conservative *Gazette*, then in the throes of reorganization under the new management of the Whites, and the Liberal *Herald*, its massive advertising patronage evidence of prosperity. Both papers cost $6 a year, appeared in the morning, and presented 36 columns of advertising and reading matter. The Whites, perhaps to boost local circulation, also offered a special rate for the paper delivered to the doorstep at $5 a year or ten cents a week, and $4 a year to bona fide clergymen. The format was roughly the same as the organization adopted by the francophone organs, indeed a format standard at the time. Still, on Friday and Saturday, editorials graced the *Herald*'s front page, advertising was cut back, all to accommodate coverage of the speeches in Parliament. The *Gazette* and the *Herald* did try to touch on a range of events, except in the province itself where the French fact made happenings of little interest to 'Anglo' readers. Foreign news remained a staple, but more attention was devoted to the United States and Britain (especially in the *Gazette*) than Europe or France, again proof that the outside world was an entity defined by the parochial concerns of the audience. The focus on public affairs was balanced by excellent coverage of the business scene and reams of market statistics from near and far, notably in the *Herald*. The *Gazette* showed a surprising interest in assorted happenings elsewhere in the dominion, whereas the *Herald* concentrated on the commercial routine of the city itself. Overall, the *Herald* was the peerless business journal: not just its swollen advertising columns or up-to-date commercial reports but also much of its general news were designed to please the 'Anglo' establishment in Montreal. The *Gazette* was the best medium of general knowledge in the city, heavily commercial but attempting a much more detailed coverage of affairs and life at home and abroad.

Le Nouveau Monde belonged to quite a different genre, the sectarian press. The doughty warrior for God and Race was born out of a reaction against the growing dominion of party over the press. Zealots found existing newspapers too often placed the goals of their church and nationality second to the partisan exigencies of the moment. So Orange and Green enthusiasts started up weeklies and tri-weeklies, mostly ephemeral, to air their righteous angers. By far the most elaborate network of such journals, however, belonged to the lay and clerical ultramontanes of Quebec, who were bent on making the province God's own Catholic utopia. Their inspiration was the famous Louis Veuillot, publisher of Paris's *L'Univers*, who for years combatted the liberal foes, inside and outside the church, of Catholic reaction. *Le Nouveau Monde* (1867) was Bishop Bourget's imitation, a tool that might win the hearts and minds of his flock away from the dangerous errors propagated by rouge heretics and too partisan bleus. By the close of 1872, its daily and weekly circulation had mounted to almost 4,000.

In February 1871 *Le Nouveau Monde* was a four-page, 28-column daily, costing $6 a year, and appearing in the evening for family reading. Its messianic purpose conditioned all but its advertising columns. Even the format differed: the paper adopted the so-called 'French front,' editorials and comment dominating the front page. Its editors were largely indifferent to the happenings in Ottawa and in the rest of Canada (really an alien domain), unless things Catholic or French were at issue. The business reports amounted to very brief collections of market statistics, although the editors' desire for northern settlement inspired interest in the railway question. What fascinated the ultramontane organ was France, the church's troubles in Europe (especially in wayward Italy), and the Quebec homeland. So the week's offerings included two long essays on Italy from *L'Unita Cattolica* and *La Correspondance de Genève*, an anti-republican critique of French events, articles on the Catholic nature of Quebec, and news about church matters. Trivia and filler there were, such as an item on a 103-year-old North Carolina mountain man and the inevitable police court news – but hardly sufficient to give the ensemble a common touch. The awful conspiracies of homegrown villains might for the moment be offstage, though not forgotten. *Le Nouveau Monde* had a moral, a divine mission to advance the Catholic way and the French race to some great North American destiny. It was very much the champion of what seemed a beleaguered faith and people on an Anglo-Protestant continent.

If *Le Nouveau Monde* spoke for an outpost of the worldwide Catholic empire, then the *Witness* did likewise for its Protestant foe. The *Witness* also belonged to the sectarian breed and so espoused a moral crusade. There the similarity ends. John Dougall, the *Witness* founder, was an entrepreneur of George Brown's ilk, though Dougall won much less profit or honour. He was a successful merchant but his devout evangelical beliefs led him in 1845 to start a weekly voice of the Protestant God, what he thought would be a witness to Truth. Fifteen years later he commenced the daily *Witness*, a half-penny soon to be one-cent evening paper designed to reach the Protestant masses and sold on the streets by newsboys, the first Canadian paper to adopt such a system. His special mission, again, it seemed, divinely ordained, was to free the province of its Catholic masters, to bring the boon of Anglo-Protestant liberty and progress to the benighted papists, and to impose a puritanical code of behaviour on public and private life. None of these causes mixed well with party journalism, at least not in Quebec: the *Witness*, if always political, was defiantly independent, usually in the Liberal camp by default but critical of both parties for their subservience to

TABLE 16

The circulations of leading newspapers (in thousands)

1872		1882		1891		1900	
Dailies							
Globe	20.2	*Globe*	24.0	*Star*	32.1	*La Presse*	67.8
Witness	10.5	*Mail*	22.0	*Mail*	27.0	*Star*	57.5
Mail	7.0	*Star*	17.8	*Globe*	27.0	*Globe*	47.1
Star	5.6	*Telegram*	15.2	*Telegram*	21.7	*Mail and Empire*	41.2
La Minerve	5.0	*News*	14.0	*La Presse*	20.4	*La Patrie*	27.5
Dailies and weeklies							
Globe	45.0	*Star*	89.8	*Star*	101.5	*Star*	175.4
Witness	23.1	*Mail*	89.0	*Mail*	89.3	*La Presse*	104.2
La Minerve	20.7	*Globe*	74.0	*Globe*	46.5	*Witness*	79.3
Mail	17.5	*Witness*	46.6	*Witness*	46.1	*Globe*	66.9
Star	15.6	*Le Monde*	31.7	*News*	31.5	*Mail and Empire*	59.1

the Catholic church and Big Business. In time, Dougall's mini-empire of publications included the daily, tri-weekly, and weekly editions of the *Witness*, the weekly *L'Aurore* (French Protestant!), the semi-monthly *Canadian Messenger* (temperance), and the *New Dominion Monthly* (a family magazine). The *Witness* was, at first, amazingly popular, reaching the peak of its influence by the early 1870s. In 1872 the paper had a daily circulation of 10,500, a combined daily and weekly circulation of 23,100, spread throughout Greater Montreal, into the Eastern Townships and eastern Ontario, up the Ottawa Valley, and even beyond into the Maritimes and western Ontario.[27] That ranked the *Witness* second among the leading dailies of the day (Table 16).

Dougall's intention infused every aspect of his paper in February 1871. Editorials normally took pride of place, appearing first on the front page and continued on page two; a mixture of ads, news, and opinion under different edition headings (noon, 2 and 4 pm, and 6 pm) cluttered page three; cable news, features, and entertainment were saved for the last page. The *Witness* carried only censored ads, never for patent medicines or liquors or questionable amusements. Prominent on page three were classified ads for jobs and places, say 'a Protestant cook wanted,' which were clearly aimed at the ordinary person. The entertainment was no less moral: 'At Last,' a temperance tale, or 'Herman the Hypocrite,' for children. The *Witness* did furnish a good variety of foreign, Canadian, and civic news, though its telegraph reports were often borrowed from the morning *Herald*. There was extensive coverage of public affairs, especially the speeches in Parliament, which evidenced the paper's determination to keep a Christian eye on politics. The commercial columns serviced the needs of shopkeepers and consumers by providing commodity statistics and reports on the local hardware or shoe markets. A very large amount of information (slightly over 40 per cent) pertained to life and society: news about churches, temperance societies, and other social authorities; both disaster and crime (a special item being 'The Spellman Indecent Assault Case,' itself a moral tale); and much miscellany, practical and curious. Among the features were didactic or useful articles on child-rearing and hymn music, assorted moral homilies or lessons, an article on agriculture and horticulture, plus items merely to feed curiosity: 'The Adulteration of Petroleum,' 'How a Spider Builds Its Web,' or 'Florida as a Winter Residence for Invalids.' Throughout, the language used was simple and direct, often colourful. Even the biting editorials were colloquial, respectable of course but never learned or difficult. This thorough determination to give the offerings a common touch explains the popularity of the newspaper.

The Dougall family could never build upon its early success. Part of the difficulty grew out of a lack of the funds necessary to finance further expansion. A magazine article rightly concluded that the various enterprises were more 'engines of usefulness'[28] than profit, though for a time the daily at least did make money. But subscriptions at $3 a year for the daily and $1 a year for the weekly could bring in only modest sums. Certainly the family finances suffered the travails of independence – no political patrons and little patronage to assist the meeting of costs. Dougall's high-mindedness deprived the *Witness* of the lucrative revenues which other publishers derived from patent medicines, liquors, theatres, and like advertising. In 1871 John himself set off for New York to launch an ill-fated daily *Witness* there, which placed a heavy burden on family resources. (The experiment proved an expensive flop, though John did salvage a weekly that lasted until at least the turn of the century.) Then, in 1875, the Catholic church placed a ban on the paper. 'Thence forward the Catholics might not read it, nor advertise in it, nor sell it,' noted a circular decades later. 'As many of the advertising men were Roman Catholics and as most of the newsvendors for a generation following the proscription, were the same, it was an incalculable blow to the *Witness* and benefit to its competitors.'[29] Most of all, however, the daily *Witness* stagnated because the stubbornness of the Dougall family prevented a significant shift to meet changing tastes and times. The paper's loyal readership remained, ensuring survival but not an advance.

Indeed the formula of sectarian journalism, for other papers as well as the *Witness*, would prove a dead end in the search for popularity. Two newcomers, the Montreal *Post* (1878) and the Toronto *Canadian* (1883?–84), tried unsuccessfully to win favour by offering an Irish Catholic slant on the world of affairs. In particular, the dailies were supposed to voice the Irish sense of grievance against what seemed the excessive power, and superior airs, of the French Canadian and the Anglo-Protestant in the new dominion. But there was insufficient money in serving so exclusively a disadvantaged minority, or in combating religious intolerance and racial bigotry, to meet the competition of rivals for the custom of the public and advertisers. The *Post*, apparently, survived only by becoming another organ of the Conservative party. Even *Le Nouveau Monde*, renamed *Le Monde*, ended up in the Conservative camp after 1880, as did Quebec's *Le Canadien* (briefly an ultramontane crusader). Sectarian journalism could not exploit or bridge the gap between the 'classes' and the 'masses'; its appeal was too specialized, too limited, to work as a technique of social outreach or to win many obliging patrons. No wonder most practitioners, the *Witness* excepted, sooner or later sought peace and profit (though ultimately with little result) in a party's warm embrace.

The Dougalls' most serious competition was undoubtedly the evening *Star*, a one-cent venture started early in 1869 by Hugh Graham and George Lanigan. The *Star* had little but contempt for its rivals: 'We neither aspire to be the "only religious daily" nor do we grovel so low as to bid for the support or countenance of the so-called aristocracy – in a word we try, however feebly, to be the organ of the people particularly the portion known as the working classes.'[30] Many a newspaper over the years had claimed no purpose but to serve the people, often with a bow to the penny press of New York as the parent of popular journalism. Some, such as the Montreal *Transcript*, had survived by becoming the purveyors of news and views, ads and entertainment for the bourgeois family, while others like the Saint John *News* had soon succumbed to the excitements of party warfare. Lanigan, an experienced journalist and Graham, a business manager, did not appear to have any special credentials that promised anything more novel. Indeed, the *Star* was at first a pitiful sheet, immediately threatened with extinction, in such a plight that Lanigan searched for American funding to turn it into an annexationist organ. What saved the paper was a coup by Graham who, with some unknown backers, took full control in 1870. He decided to make a blatant appeal for the support of the lowbrow public, the masses. In this way, he gave birth to 'people's journalism,' an ingenious formula that successfully flouted the conventions of newspaperdom.[31]

'What I want to see in the Montreal *Star*,' Graham told novices, 'is the sort of news, or item, or story, or article which if you saw it in some newspaper or book you would be tempted to read out loud to the next person to you.'[32] That translated meant a slangy style, sensation and crusades, much amusing or entertaining matter, and a surfeit of trivia. The *Star* in the second week of February 1871[33] supplied more tidbits of news than any other newspaper: so in the Monday edition alone the reader could find on the front page under 'Canada' some 30 items, mostly about Ontario; on page three more trivia under the headings 'Sparks from the Telegraph' and 'Round Town'; and on the last page almost a full column of names of people married or died outside and inside the country. America rather than Europe, the Canadian scene more than Parliament, above all Montreal fascinated Graham's editors this week. Much of the material the *Star* published, whether from near or far, was about life, such as 'Washington Society' reporting a splendid reception at great length. Disaster and crime (including the same Spellman case that intrigued the *Witness*) was there in abundance, the subject of nearly a quarter of the items offered. Much of this seems to have been clipped from foreign newspapers or stolen from rivals. Editorials could be long or short, often colloquial and crude. This week the *Star* editor criticized the Northern Colonization Railway, denounced the hypocrisy of the *Witness*, hounded a civic official, praised artisans, and published a long letter – 'How We Are Ruled' – which attacked George Cartier for the multifarious ills that had befallen Quebec.

However impoverished such offerings might seem compared with say the news and views of the lofty *Gazette*, they were definitely popular. What would later be called the 'down-market' strategy, in the jargon of the business, worked very well in an industrial city such as Montreal. As early as December 1876, the *Star* claimed a larger city circulation than all other English dailies combined. Certainly the paper had already surpassed the daily *Witness*. More readers meant more revenue, and that allowed improvements. In 1875 Graham purchased his first web press, a Prestonian, which delivered 8,500 perfected four-page papers an hour.[34] By 1880 the *Star* was a full 36 columns long, stuffed with a wealth of news and all manner of items: if the telegraph report was still published straight off the wires, now a group of local reporters and out-of-town correspondents gave depth to the news coverage. During the early 1880s the *Star* began the regular publication of illustrations; Graham realized people were not only 'interested in reading the day's happenings' but also 'like to see pictures of them as well.'[35] More famous were the *Star*'s crusades, an amalgam of news reports, sometimes interviews, and pounding editorials. The paper took up the cause of workers' rights at an early date, tariff protection and national independence, anti-partyism and manhood suffrage. It was always eager to find corruption or waste in high places, especially signs of civic mismanagement. The daily's circulation boomed during the 1880s (Table 17). So too did the subscription list of the *Family Herald and Weekly Star*, which became a national magazine for country folk, not just a compilation of used matter from the daily. Evidence of Graham's success was his acquisition in 1886 of two Scott perfecting presses, using the new stereotype process, which together gave his office a capacity of 44,000 copies an hour.[36] By 1891, according to McKim's *Canadian Newspaper*

TABLE 17

The listed circulation* of the Montreal *Star* 1880–90

1880	15,571	1884	23,048	1888	28,058
1881	16,946	1885	25,521	1889	30,175
1882	17,325	1886	26,096	1890	31,386
1883	20,391	1887	27,746		

* Each figure is for the first issue of the *Star* in November of the designated year.

Directory, the *Star*'s daily and weekly circulation stood at over 100,000, making it the country's premier newspaper.

What explains the phenomenal success? It had a lot to do with Graham himself. He loved to grandstand, to show off. Graham relished fighting the establishment: legend has it that he once faced 93 libel suits because of his 'righteous causes.'[37] He and his paper always worked loudly for the betterment of Montreal: during the smallpox epidemic of the fall of 1885, not only did the *Star* crusade for compulsory vaccination, in the wake of vociferous resistance from the French-Canadian masses, but Graham himself also ordered out the militia and liberated the Exhibition Building for use as an isolation hospital.[38] He was ever sympathetic to the plight of the underprivileged: the *Star* initiated in 1887 (following a New York precedent) a Fresh Air Fund which collected money 'for the purpose of giving working mothers and poor children a glimpse of country life and a bit of country health' in the summer.[39] He was ingenious: in April 1888, after the *Star*'s failure to move city hall, he personally organized 'The Star's Pick and Shovel Brigade' to clean Montreal's streets of winter filth.[40] Above all, he kept his paper fresh and flamboyant. 'It has earnestly advocated many reforms, and usually with some success, but when the immediate object in view is attained The Star passes on to some other popular matter and drops its old controversies into the waste basket of oblivion,' observed A.H.U. Colquhoun. 'Mr. Graham, I think, likes to be on the winning side.'[41] Indeed he did – not for him the consolation of moral victories; losing causes were for others. Graham succeeded by giving the masses their own paper, not only a digest of facts but also what seemed a fearless champion. He exploited, in short, the social tensions that afflicted the city of the 1880s.

Graham was not the only pioneer of people's journalism, of course. Its birth was well-nigh inevitable, given the stresses and strains that 'modernity' imposed on the life of the big city.[42] In Toronto the first successful practitioner was John Ross Robertson, who had failed so badly to make the grandoise *Telegraph* a paying proposition. He had learned his lesson well: in 1876 Robertson started the evening *Telegram*, soon a one-cent paper, to serve only Toronto households. That paper employed much the same formula of serial novels, tidbit news, sensation, life's trivia, maverick politics, and vigorous crusades. Robertson took special pride in replacing 'the long-winded and patience-wearing'[43] leaders with colourful, short editorial paragraphs, another American innovation. The key to his success, though, was that he kept the 'Tely' defiantly local. Consistently, the *Telegram* played down routine foreign or national news to emphasize items on city council, the water commission, the hospital, Toronto's amusements, local sports, and crime. His paper boosted civic ambitions and criticized civic leadership, always from the perspective of the ordinary citizen. Robertson was particularly keen on protecting the city treasury against raids by 'crackpot' schemers. So one of the first campaigns the 'Tely' waged was against a proposal that the city grant a bonus of $250,000 to the Credit Valley Railway, thereby enriching the promoters at the expense of the lowly homeowner.[44] The *Telegram*'s circulation leapt forward, over 5,000 in 1978, 15,000 by 1882, and almost 25,000 in 1889. That circulation was confined to Toronto – the *Telegram* was, claimed Pelham Mulvany in 1884, '*par excellence*, the family newspaper in the city.'[45] Consequently Robertson had a strangehold on local advertising. He had introduced in 1876 penny-a-word classified ads, about half the standard rate,[46] which soon filled his columns with want ads, and his blanket coverage of Toronto's homes brought him the patronage of the department stores, notably Simpson's and Eaton's, which purchased large display ads regularly to publicize their bargains. The 'Tely' was read so widely because of its ads as well as its news.

Robertson's achievement was all the more impressive because he soon faced energetic rivals. In February 1880 Billy Maclean and associates launched the one-cent evening *World*. Competition proved so stiff that the following year the *World* shifted into the morning field. Maclean's 'bright and breezy' four-page paper, beyond the offerings normal to a people's journal, became a forceful exponent of democracy, Canadian chauvinism, and the anti-monopoly cry, winning notoriety for its assaults on railway and utility corporations. That ensured the *World* a future as the country's first commuter paper, the darling of the morning streetcar hordes.

The career of the *News* was a good deal more colourful. It began in May 1881 as a new evening edition of the *Mail*, notable only because it was sometimes printed on pink paper.[47] Enter Edmund E. Sheppard, an American-trained journalist ready to import every 'Yankee' innovation conceivable, to whom the Riordon family transferred formal ownership in February 1883. Sheppard tried working in both the morning and evening fields, eventually to settle down in the evening arena only. His way involved not only the serial novel, much local news, and the like but also social slander (a 'Peek-a-Boo' column of local gossip), hoaxes (John A. Macdonald's retirement address), and a regular Knights of Labor column.[48] He dramatically altered the ordinary editorial style: pungent

Hugh Graham of the Montreal *Star*. The amazingly successful pioneer of 'people's journalism' in Canada

Trefflé Berthiaume of *La Presse*. The man who transformed French-Canadian journalism

E.E. Sheppard of the Toronto *News*. A fervent Americanizer

John Ross Robertson of the Toronto *Telegram*. A great champion of civic parochialism

language, many capital letters, imaginative punctuation, one- or two-sentence paragraphs, all to win the lowbrow reader who was frightened by an array of learned commentary.[49] And Sheppard made his *News* the organ of democratic republicanism, chanting the praises of a total Americanization of the country's political system. Such stunts produced a sensation all right but not a lot of money, and Sheppard lost control of the *News* in 1887. By 1889 the circulation of the *News* stood around 17,500 and the *World* over 10,000. Neither apparently secured much advertising revenue though, the *World* barely surviving and the *News* probably losing money.

The people's journals of Toronto and Montreal had perfected a sensational style and a Radical purpose suited to the tastes and interests of the common man. The *Star* or the *Telegram* might seem superficial if judged simply as agents of information, but they had succeeded by flouting convention, by writing for people with little sophistication and limited education. If not the pioneers, certainly Graham, Robertson, and Sheppard were the most skilful salesmen of news-as-entertainment, a kind of fact designed to divert as much as to inform the reader. (Why else would *News* editors be so interested in such oddities of nature as 'freak' births, bigamy, or comets?) Instead of catering to the 'classes,' their dailies voiced the resentments of the 'masses' toward social snobbery or economic privilege. Indeed they took great pleasure in poking fun at the assumptions and airs of the high and mighty (including their more staid competitors). And they proved adept at exploiting the ideas of nationality and democracy – against French Canadians or Irish Catholics, the British (and later the Americans), and party-rule – to justify popular prejudices. All this served to express class antagonisms (the poor against the rich) and yet emphasize a sense of community (the people or the nation against its enemies). The contradictory blend, perhaps best labelled populist, had proved a fine way to curry the public's favour.

Going 'down-market' might appear an excellent bet for a newcomer challenging established newspapers. 'Nothing goes to show the advancing power of the one cent papers so much as the manner in which the big, bad and bulkish sheets treat their breezy, brief and bright contemporaries,' enthused the Toronto *World* (22 November 1882): 'They pretend to ignore them, and yet they are constantly getting both news and ideas from them.' In truth, the ensemble could not always be exported to lesser cities because the lowbrow market was usually too small. What happened, therefore, was that newcomers modified the formula, often dispensing with its more outlandish techniques, to win a middlebrow clientele. James Carrel founded the Quebec *Telegraph* in 1875, so he claimed, to supply 'cheap and reliable news' and the working classes with a voice.[50] Crusading brought a modest success, but the small anglophone public kept circulation down, estimated at a mere 3,500 in 1883 and falling below 2,500 by the end of the decade. A variety of owners tried to make Winnipeg's *Sun* a people's organ, apparently not with that much result until they found Liberal backing and so changed their style. More successful in time were two independents, the Ottawa *Journal* (1885) and the Hamilton *Herald* (1889), both providing readers with a 'third option' to the existing party organs. On the Pacific coast, the Liberal Victoria *Times* (1885) and the Conservative *News-Advertiser* (1887) mixed party and people's journalism effectively. The same could be said of a number of evening dailies, such as Halifax's *Mail* (1878) and *Echo* (1888), satellites of morning organs (the Conservative *Herald* and the Liberal *Chronicle* respectively), or even established party newspapers such as the Liberal Hamilton *Times* or Ottawa *Free Press*. A modicum of lively news, more attention to the local scene, flirting with Radical causes had become standard ploys among evening dailies by the end of the 1880s.

There was an alternative route to popularity: 'quality journalism,' going 'up-market' to win a sophisticated readership by supplying a more extensive fare of up-to-date news, high-toned comment, and a wealth of special features. Unlike proponents of people's journalism who looked south of the border for guidance, their rivals looked overseas to Britain and the great dailies of London, especially the legendary *Times*. Here the lucky citizen found, wrote N.F. Davin, impartial 'political intelligence,' brilliant controversy, 'intellectual and moral force,' papers belonging to 'a cause, and not a party.'[51] Any similar formula in Canada required that a publisher create a metropolitan newspaper, reaching well into the provincial hinterland, since the cultured market was too limited even in the biggest cities. The 'up-market' strategy was best suited to the expensive morning newspapers, at two to three cents an issue, which could afford the cost of improvements – and realize savings by publishing cheaper evening editions for the masses as well as a weekly for the farm home.

It might appear that the newspaper in the best position to triumph as a quality journal was the mighty *Globe*. At least as early as 1868, the Browns had endeavoured to push their daily circulation throughout the province, and their efforts were continued by the new management even after George's death (1880) and Gordon's removal from the editor's chair (1882). In 1876 the Browns had commissioned early morning trains to Hamilton, and later London, absorbed the mailing costs of the daily *Globe*, and upgraded the weekly *Globe*.[52] In 1880 they installed new Bullock presses (using the stereotype process) which signalled an end to the old 'blanket sheet' and the arrival of the 'quarto page,' allowing more speed and flexibility in the process of production.[53] The daily *Globe* then became an 8-page issue, expanding to 12 or more on Saturdays, costing three cents in the morning and one cent in the evening. The daily maintained its emphasis on public affairs and the business scene, indeed becoming something of a journal of record noted for its detailed, accurate, comprehensive, and immediate news of the city as well as the province (the summaries of affairs in Ottawa or Hamilton, for instance), the nation, and the outside world, but supplemented all this with much soft news ('The Indians of British Columbia,' 'Bush-Rangers in Victoria,' or 'Profitable Poultry Farming') and life's trivia ('Lady Burdett Coutts and Her Fiance,' 'British Railway Accidents,' or 'Sports and Amusements').[54] The only significant change thereafter came in December 1885 when the front page was finally cleared of ads to make way for the leading news of the day, usually foreign or national. The Saturday edition was really a newspaper-cum-magazine, designed for family reading, with regular features on literature and art, the churches, fashions, entertainment and amusements, etc. Editors later added the first women's section in November 1882, initially called 'Bric-a-Brac' and eventually 'Woman's World,' plus increasing doses of American syndicated material (such as Marion Harland's 'Marrying for Money' or Ella Wheeler Wilcox's 'Women Who Gossip').[55] In May 1889 came a 4-page illustrated section, using drawings and two years later half-tone engravings from photographs. That began with a penchant for praising one small Ontario town after another, undoubtedly useful to circulation agents trying to drum up business in the hinterland. The Saturday paper of 1 February 1890 was a 20-page giant, consisting of 120 columns and three sections.

There was little reward for such noble enterprise. During the 1880s, circulation statistics told a sad tale of uneven or sagging growth (Table 18). On 2 February 1880, the daily *Globe* claimed an average sale in the previous week of 23,637 copies, 43 percent (or 10,064) in the city and 57 percent (or 13,573) in the countryside. The only bright spot in the picture over the next few years was the growth of the weekly, up from 25,000 (1879) to 50,000 (1882). Not only was daily circulation stagnant, but the Toronto *World* (29 March 1884) reported that the cheap evening edition had eaten into the circulation of the morning paper, now well below ten thousand copies, thus reducing subscription and even ad revenues. Things improved in 1886 and 1887, allowing a price reduction to two cents for the morning paper. The boom soon faltered, the price was raised once again, and by early 1890 daily circulation was not much ahead of the figure a decade earlier. Even the weekly circulation had sunk back to about 25,000. Everyone claimed the *Globe*'s influence was on the wane.[56] Brown himself had declared the last dividend in 1880. His old technique of spending ahead of demand had failed. Now the *Globe* faced strong competition, in the city and the countryside.

TABLE 18

The listed circulation* of the Toronto *Globe* 1880–90

	Average	Saturday		Average	Saturday
1880	23,637	28,400	1886	23,642	27,900
1881	23,888	26.012	1887	31,325	37,250
1882	24,075	27,500	1888	28,117	32,750
1883	23,858	27,000	1889	25,521	31,425
1884	24,158	27,000	1890	24,496	31,225
1885	22,636	26,050			

* Each figure is for the first issue of the *Globe* in February of the designated year.

A good portion of the *Globe*'s competition came from Toronto's second quality journal, the *Mail*. The *Mail* began as a political job, concocted by John A. Macdonald and John Sandfield Macdonald (the Ontario premier) to combat the *Globe*. T.C. Patteson, the managing editor, promised in his prospectus a raft of goodies: 'local items and city intelligence,' 'the impartiality of the leading English journals,' 'a summary of Sporting News,' 'a spirit of liberality[,] toleration and fairness,' 'the views of moderate Politicians.' Nothing low would ever disgrace the pages of this so very British paper: 'What is degrading and demoralizing is often best censured by silence.'[57] Such an ambitious paper soon boasted a morning and evening edition plus a weekly. Patteson even shared with Brown the considerable expense of running morning trains to Hamilton and London.[58] The paper's vigorous competition immediately killed off the faltering *Telegraph*, as John A. Macdonald had hoped, though the daily *Leader* lingered on for a few years as a conservative-minded independent. What the *Mail* did not do was unseat the *Globe*. By 1876 the daily and weekly circulations were only 9,000 each. Internal feuding among the shareholders, and even more importantly limited capital to support the grandiose ambitions, brought eventual disaster. In 1877 the paper was sold to its chief creditor, John Riordon.

John Riordon was a millionaire papermaker, known for his cheap newsprint. Rumour had it that he hoped to emulate the fame and fortune of the New York publishers of a generation previous, whose innovations had transformed American journalism.[59] Anyway, Riordon brought in new capital and new management, Christopher Bunting (who had a share in the enterprise) and W.J. Douglas, who proved to be two especially astute business managers. They presided over the paper's renaissance: more reporters and editorial writers were hired, arrangements made for special correspondence from the chief cities of the dominion, rights acquired to the New York *Herald*'s cable despatches, the

Associated Press copy supplemented by the National Press Association service.[60] By 1878 the circulation of the daily had purportedly jumped to over 15,000 and the weekly to over 25,000. In the summer of 1880 Bunting purchased new Scott presses, adopting the 'quarto page' format, and improved delivery services in the city and the countryside. The regular eight-page daily and the expanded Saturday paper carried much the same kinds of material as their *Globe* rivals. Three years later, daily circulation had risen to 22,000 and the management claimed a weekly circulation of a whopping 82,000. Not only was the *Mail* the loudest Conservative voice in the dominion, but it had overturned the *Globe*'s hegemony in western Ontario.

Then madness struck. Suddenly, in the mid-1880s, the *Mail* broke free from party 'fetters' to espouse its own views and hunt for a new party. The death of John Riordon in 1884 had placed in command brother Charles, a man more interested in making money than in advancing the Conservative cause.[61] The resignation of the loyal Martin Griffin (loyal, that is, to the Conservative party) in the fall of 1885 had brought to the editor's chair Edward Farrer, a brilliant writer but contemptuous of party, the Catholic church, and even Canada. The execution of Louis Riel in November 1885 provoked a storm of protest in Quebec that threatened the future of the government, sufficient to inspire the *Mail* to condemn 'French aggression' and thus solidify Conservative support in Ontario. Abusing the French Canadians proved so popular, though, that the paper's management decided to pursue an independent course whatever the desires of party chieftains. During 1886 the paper became a fanatical champion of Anglo-Protestant nativism, bent upon humbling the Catholic church and the French Canadians to ensure a British ascendancy in the dominion. A second variety of intransigence was manifested in the paper's conversion to that generation's new morality – fervent support of prohibition, municipal reform, and anti-partyism (the formal break with the Conservative party came early in 1887). Finally, just after the election of 1887, the *Mail* touted the panacea of Commercial Union, hoping some form of economic association with the American republic would energize the Canadian economy. All these policies the *Mail* forwarded with interviews, special reports, commissioned letters, and brilliant editorials.

'I cannot think that Canada has ever had a greater newspaper than was *The Mail* during this period of separation from the Conservative party,' J.S. Willison wrote many years later.[62] The *Mail*, in fact, had realized the ideal of quality journalism: full of news and features, boasting a superb editorial page devoted to 'a cause, and not a party.' The *Mail*'s crusades tapped the malaise, the anxiety of a bourgeois public upset by social change and national stagnation, to such an extent that it might fairly be called the leading organ of the 'classes' in Ontario.

Early in 1889, for example, Farrer set Ontario's heather on fire by urging the disallowance of Quebec's Jesuits' Estates Act as proof of Anglo-Protestant supremacy, a classic instance of the power of the editor in heat which resulted in the birth of the short-lived Equal Rights Association. By 1891 the daily's circulation had risen to around 27,000, the weekly's stood at 35,000, and the new cheap *Farm and Fireside* at 27,000. The apparent success of this splendid isolation likely did not translate into high profits, no matter how frightened were rivals or politicians. The old problem of competition re-emerged when Macdonald sponsored a new organ, the *Empire* (1888), which cut into the *Mail*'s market everywhere. Slowly, the *Mail*'s intransigence gave way, and in 1895 it returned to the party fold by acquiring the bankrupt *Empire*.

Some newspapers had virtually no choice but to pursue the formula of quality journalism because their professional and business constituency demanded the 'best' of news and views. By the mid-1880s, at least seven other dailies in English Canada had shifted to the eight-page format. Among these, naturally, were the two business papers of Montreal, the prosperous *Gazette* and the languishing *Herald* (a victim of the *Star*'s rise). In fact manager Peter Mitchell endeavoured during the late 1880s to capitalize on the anxiety of the 'classes' by championing a moral reformation of business and public life, a crusade no more profitable than the intransigence of the *Mail*. More surprising, perhaps, was the partial conversion of that other victim of the *Star*, the one-cent evening *Witness*, except that it too had to maintain a sizeable metropolitan readership against local competition. James and John Redpath Dougall diluted the intense bigotry of the early days but continued the founder's evangelical and puritanical thrust, ever in search of that elusive Kingdom of God promised good Christians. Enhanced offerings did not extend the paper's circulation, though the weekly performed very well during the 1880s, reaching over 37,000 homes by 1889. In London, where a degree of isolation limited the invasion of Toronto dailies, the Liberal *Advertiser* as well as the Conservative *Free Press* took the plunge, and both gained substantially at the expense of an old evening competitor.[63] Out in Winnipeg, again protected by distance, there were two eight-page dailies (evening papers though) in 1884, the Conservative *Times* and the Liberal *Sun*. Each eventually succumbed to the competition of the powerful *Manitoba Free Press*, a morning newspaper, which converted six years later, reaching a daily circulation of 7,000-odd and a weekly circulation of around 7,500 by the end of the decade. The only newcomer to adopt the quality format was, of course, the Toronto *Empire* which had to meet the competition of the *Globe* and *Mail*. Elsewhere the massive investment in machinery, if not newsgathering, necessary to support quality journalism frightened off publishers.

None of the trendsetters came from the ranks of the French-Canadian press. 'Il est de notoriété public que la plupart des journaux franco-canadiens ont jusqu'à présent marché clopin-clopant,' lamented Montreal's *La Patrie* (24 February 1879), 'n'evitant la banqueroute qu'au prix des sacrifices pécuniares des chefs des partis.' Why? Modernity had not yet reshaped popular culture, the evidence here coming from literacy statistics. The reading habit, though growing in popularity, simply was not as widespread in French Quebec as in English Canada. Sidney Bellingham, publisher of the Montreal *News*, claimed around 1870, 'as a rule the French-Canadian farmers ... never subscribe for or read a newspaper, save the curé or doctor, or the notary.'[64] In 1888 another journalist, Joseph Tarte, estimated only about a quarter of the francophone population read newspapers.[65] Contemporary wisdom had it that not only the well-educated French Canadians in the professions or business but also even their employees read and purchased anglophone newspapers. Indeed, the circulation of French-Canadian dailies based in Montreal (where the French-speaking majority was only about 56 per cent of the population in 1881) did not surpass that of their 'Anglo' rivals until the end of the century (Table 19). Other problems as well stemmed from the very presence and power of the English in Quebec and on the continent. So the 'difficultes particulières' of the francophone newspapers, claimed an obviously weary *Le Monde* (15 January 1881), arose because of their country's situation, 'où la population français n'est pas nombreux, où la plus grande partie du commerce est entre les mains des habitants de langue anglaise et ont à être traduites en français au prix des sacrifices additionels, etc.' Fewer readers, less advertising revenue, and more expenses all worked to hinder any general transformation of the French-Canadian press. Only slowly did francophone publishers try to imitate their more progressive brethren.

What persisted were the kept journals of opinion, happily engaged in the Good Fight for party or church. The argument might be stimulating, but Hector Fabre's stricture of 1867 remained true for too long: 'On fait généralement trois reproches aux journaux français en ce pays: ils publient trop d'articles politiques; ils ne donnent pas assez de nouvelles, et surtout ils ne les donnent pas assez tôt; enfin le choix des extraits s'y fait trop souvent au hasard des ciseaux.'[67] There was surprisingly little change in the nature of the old bleu press of Quebec City, *Le Journal de Québec*, *Le Courrier du Canada*, and *Le Canadien*. A new Liberal organ, the one-cent *L'Électeur* (1880), remained throughout the 1880s a specialist in public affairs and partisan rhetoric, a sign of its bias being the adoption of the 'French front.' In Montreal, where the pace of life was quicker, the once aggressive *La Minerve* made only a few feeble attempts to adjust to the times, apparently hamstrung by a lack of capital and will. Almost all of the short-lived newcomers – *Le National* (1872–79), *Le Bien Public* (1874–76), *Le*

TABLE 19

Approximate circulations of all editions of francophone and anglophone dailies in Montreal

	Dailies		Weeklies	
	Francophone	Anglophone	Francophone	Anglophone
1872	7,760	24,300	20,050	32,750
1876	9,317	29,787	15,134	61,031
1882	33,000	53,176	34,700	149,300
1883	32,709	49,810	45,487	133,984
1889	43,750	53,096	37,000	123,446
1891	50,181	57,064	48,612	110,207
1898	82,857	80,287	72,099	196,037
1900	104,060	98,742	61,370	193,583

SOURCE: See note 66 to this chapter.

Courrier de Montréal (1879–82), or *Le Temps* (1883) – were designed to forward a cause.

More impressive was *L'Étendard*, founded by F.-X.-A. Trudel and associates in 1883, as the castor or ultramontane flagship in Montreal and the province. Right at the beginning, *L'Étendard* gave evidence of its preferred public by sending its first issue free to clergymen, politicians, professionals, 'citoyens éminents,' and teaching and religious institutions.[68] The paper was decidedly a highbrow journal of opinion, weak on news but very strong in its commentary on the world of affairs and the clash of ideas. So on 26 March 1883, the front page was dominated by special features – 'Les prélats de France,' 'Le mouvement social au 19ème siècle,' and 'La franc-maçonnerie' (a special villain); the second page contained editorials, on freemasonry and temperance for instance, as well as news of doings in the provincial house; the third or news page provided religious and telegraphic information; the fourth page was given over to the feuilleton and 'Commerce et finance.' *L'Étendard* also stood out from the rest of the pack because of its strident and unusual views, especially its anti-modernism: symbolic was the fact that Trudel flew the flag of Bourbon France on top of his newspaper building.

L'Étendard did reach a knowledgeable constituency in the countryside as well as the city, its daily circulation being over 5,000 and weekly over 7,500 by 1889. That was eminently respectable by comparison with other journals of opinion. Joseph Tarte may have pushed his weekly *Le Cultivateur* into around 12,000 farm homes (1889) but his daily edition lagged well behind. The daily *La Minerve*, after declining badly in the mid-1870s, managed a modest gain to reach a highpoint of about 6,000 households by 1883. The many deaths, limited or falling circulations, especially in the late 1880s, suggest that the journal of opinion continued to depend on a small clientele and political handouts.

A more promising approach required some adoption of anglophone practices. As far back as 1863, Médéric Lanctôt managed a cheap Montreal *La Presse* whose Radicalism was intended to win a working-class audience.[69] Hector Fabre's *L'Événement* (1867) of Quebec City did enjoy a spurt of growth in the late 1870s, reaching a circulation of 6,000 by 1883, certainly because it dropped its price from $6 to $3 a year and possibly because of its determination to supply more news. The new L.-J. Demers management of the 1880s, though, ran a fairly unexciting 'journal populaire' thereafter. Honoré Beaugrand's *La Patrie* (1879) was a one-cent evening paper, soon with a weekly *Le Peuple*, which was intended to bring the Liberal gospel to the masses of Greater Montreal and its hinterland. The Radical Beaugrand carried a serial novel, much French and public affairs news, borrowed articles on the higher life of the mind, a modicum of sensation and city matter, and a surfeit of rouge opinion. Again, he used the classic 'French front.' The rouge bias distressed Liberal politicians seeking respectability and clerical approval, but the offerings and the low price pleased the public. By 1883 *La Patrie* had a sizeable audience, estimated at 8,000 daily and 12,000 weekly.

The most popular newspapers, however, were two cheap Montreal dailies, *Le Monde* (1881) and *La Presse* (1884), which embraced the techniques of people's journalism. Both had their origins in the murky factional politics of the city and the province. Behind the scene stood Adolphe Chapleau, a leading Conservative and sometime premier, plus his close ally Louis-Adélard Sénécal, very much the plutocrat. They worked through Arthur Dansereau, the foremost journalist in French Canada, and W.E. Blumhart, Sénécal's son-in-law.[70] The purpose of the clique was to establish an evening organ to counter the influence of Chapleau's enemies (especially the castors) in the Conservative party.

First *Le Nouveau Monde*, long lost to the church but until then still ultramontane, was transformed into *Le Monde*, signalled by the purchase of a new press and the adoption of a new style early in 1881. *Le Monde* promised (15 January 1881) to give to 'la population française catholique de ce pays un organe capable de rivaliser en progrès et un importance avec les journaux de langue anglaise.' A sign of the new spirit of enterprise, in April *Le Monde* and *La Minerve* (the Chapleauiste morning paper) arranged a special telegraphic service to transmit in French the debates of the provincial house.[71] *Le Monde* dropped the 'French front,' indicating a reduced emphasis upon opinion, offered a wider variety of abbreviated news, focused on Montreal, seemed to relish crime and fires, shortened as well as simplified editorials, and even experimented with illustrations. Late in 1884, however, Blumhart sold the newspaper to Hector Langevin

(Chapleau's rival!), likely because the very spirit of enterprise had encumbered the property with debt. The new management did not significantly alter the lowbrow fare, although by 1890 Saturday double numbers (that is, two four-page sections) had become common.

Meanwhile, within a week of unloading *La Monde*, Blumhart launched the new *La Presse*, even more Radical and populist. *La Presse* tried to specialize in news, and where possible sensation. Emulating the *Star*, it embarked upon crusades against what it claimed were corrupt dealings and wasteful management at city hall. Equally significant was the appearance of Saturday's 'Chronique ouvrière,' written by Jean-Baptiste Gagnepetit (Jules Helbronner), which took up such issues as a reformed debt law, early closing by-laws, night schools, and the local water tax. Indeed, the paper strove to present itself as a champion of social democracy, presumably to exploit the resentment the 'masses' felt toward the arrogance and influence of their 'betters.'

The presence of *Le Monde* and *La Presse* enormously complicated the press scene in Greater Montreal during the late 1880s. The competition did not slow the upward march of the *Star*'s circulation. *La Minerve* and *La Patrie* did suffer though, the former dropping by about 2,000 copies per day and the latter by 3,000. *Le Monde* initially had the edge, but *La Presse*'s ridiculously low price of $2 per year brought it more readers, if less revenue. Estimates suggest that in 1889 *Le Monde* reached over 12,500 homes, *La Presse* over 15,000. In truth, the vigorous competition seems to have impoverished both newspapers. *La Presse* underwent four formal changes of ownership during the five years, each presumably to bring in new capital to keep the enterprise afloat. Ironically, the search for a mass readership had produced two dailies which were still, in *La Patrie*'s phrase, marching 'clopin-clopant.'

Improved newspapers and circulation wars were signs of the arrival of the popular press in Canada. Overall circulation figures demonstrate a very substantial increase in the clientele regularly served by the daily newspapers. The cumulative circulation of the weekly editions of city journals jumped by 150 per cent between 1876 and 1883, assisted no doubt by a generally low yearly price of $1 or $1.50 and the lowering of postal rates (Table 20). Free postage was actually implemented in 1886, a clear indication of the political clout of newspaper publishers. They had indeed benefited from the spreading enthusiasm for reading (even in rural Quebec). During the late 1880s, however, the total weekly circulation began to slip (by 13.5 per cent between 1883 and 1891). The weekly editions faced competition from religious journals and imported magazines, even more from a host of small town dailies and country weeklies. New

TABLE 20

Circulation of the tri-weekly, semi-weekly, or weekly editions of city dailies 1872–91 (in thousands)

	1872	1876	1882	1883	1889	1891
Greater Halifax	7.8	15.9	12.6	12.7	[12.7]	12.8
Greater Saint John	15.5	11.2	10.8	13.9	[11.0]	14.8
Quebec-Lévis	8.6	6.6	23.9	29.6	[37.5]	19.5*
Greater Montreal	52.8	76.2	184.0	[179.5]†	[160.4]	158.8
Ottawa-Hull	7.9	4.5	9.1	12.4	[11.8]	12.0
Kingston	2.5	2.8	3.3	3.7	[8.3]	8.2
Greater Toronto	41.5	31.7	129.5	136.3	[107.5]	109.2
Hamilton	8.9	6.7	14.5	17.3	[13.8]	17.0
London	16.2	31.0	49.1	48.4	[39.5]	35.0
Winnipeg			8.4	14.1	5.0‡	13.2
Victoria						4.2
Total		186.6		467.9		404.7

SOURCE: See note 66 to this chapter.
* The 1891 statistic for Quebec-Lévis does not include *Le Cultivateur* which moved to Montreal in December.
† [ ] = estimated.
‡ The 1889 statistic for Winnipeg includes only the *Manitoba Free Press*.

distribution firms, such as Toronto News Co., born in the mid-1870s, had cut into the country market by organizing the mailing of thousands of foreign and Canadian publications throughout the land.[72] But a good deal more upsetting were the activities of the so-called 'boiler plate' manufacturers. 'Boiler plate' was simply ready-made press plates of news, features, perhaps ads, from which a subscriber could print a page or two of his daily or weekly. The pioneering Canadian firm was Auxiliary Publishing Co. of Toronto (initially Hamilton), by 1884 claiming a list of subscribers with a circulation of 120,000 copies a week.[73] The advantage of 'boiler plate' was that it freed the small-town publisher to concentrate on collecting local news and drumming up local advertising. And that enabled him to offer a better-quality product, suited to the locale, which could compete effectively against most weekly editions of city dailies.

The advance of the total daily circulation of the city press, by contrast, was permanent. Again, during the late 1870s and early 1880s, this circulation increased by almost 150 per cent, though afterwards that boom leveled off to a rate of growth under 30 per cent (Table 21). By far the greater portion of the growth occurred in and around the cities. Publishers used newsboys,[74] carriers, agents, and the mails to get their products into the hands of people downtown or

TABLE 21

Circulation of the daily editions of city dailies 1872–91 (in thousands)

	1872	1876	1882	1883	1889	1891
Greater Halifax	7.7*	8.1	15.6	15.7	[14.0]†	15.5
Greater Saint John	10.7	9.8	15.0	14.7	[13.3]	16.4
Quebec-Lévis	5.7	5.8	26.0	26.1	[23.0]	25.8
Greater Montreal	33.0	39.1	86.2	[82.5]	[96.8]	107.2
Ottawa-Hull	6.2	3.0	9.1	11.2	[13.5]	15.0
Kingston	1.5	1.5	3.0	3.5	[3.5]	3.9
Greater Toronto	31.5	[33.7]	84.7	85.9	[114.2]	102.2
Hamilton	3.5	6.3	19.7‡	15.3	[14.0]	26.0
London	4.1	5.7	16.2	14.8	[14.8]	17.3
Winnipeg			6.4	9.8	6.5§	8.2
Victoria						3.5
Total		113.0		279.5		359.0

SOURCE: See note 66 to this chapter.
* Figure adjusted
† [ ] = estimated.
‡ Figure doubtful
§ Figure is low (includes only the *Manitoba Free Press*).

in the suburbs. In 1875, for example, James Carrel arranged for the sale of his new Quebec *Telegraph* through newsdealers and their boys, not even bothering with advance subscriptions.[75] The Montreal *Star* organized a system of citywide delivery to newsdealers in 1877. Eventually these dealers sent orders in advance, and newsboys were required to purchase the paper at a wholesale price.[76] In 1876 the Toronto *Telegram* attempted city delivery via carriers, only to adopt the *Star* system some time later.[77] In 1880 the 'Tely' (31 August 1880) alone claimed 90 locations, many in the downtown core, where its editions could be purchased. The early mails probably still worked best for the quality or morning papers, especially after the post office established free city delivery. 'Nearly three millions and a half of papers were delivered under the free delivery system in the cities of Halifax, Hamilton, London, Montreal, Quebec, Ottawa, St. John, and Toronto,' asserted J.G. Bourinot, using statistics from 1879.[78] On balance, the galloping demand seems to have benefited local papers, in particular the people's journals and their followers. The market share of the quality and morning papers may actually have declined, as in the case of the *Herald* and *La Minerve*. By the mid-1880s, though, the city markets were clogged, at least outside French Montreal. Many urban families took morning and evening editions already. The popular press had conquered the city.

THE PRESS OF THE 1890s

An early fascination of the *Printer and Publisher* (1892) was the marvels of technology. That was a fitting subject for the house organ of the newspaper industry. During the 1890s machinery brought a significant lessening of the cost of production per newspaper, sufficient to complete the wholesale modernization of the daily press. In September 1892 the *Printer and Publisher* ran a special feature on the sophisticated papermaking process of the new, huge E.B. Eddy complex in Hull. The enormous capacity of such giant mills, in Canada and the United States, produced a surfeit of white paper and falling prices. Newsprint cost $3.70 per 100 lbs (delivered) in 1890, $2.90 in 1894, and $1.70 to $2.10 by 1899.[79]

Then there were the new typesetting and typecasting machines, the typograph, linotype, and monoline, which broke the last bottleneck slowing the speedy production of the newspaper. The linotype could cast and place a single line of adjusted type much quicker than any compositor, no matter how skilled. In February 1897 P.D. Ross, publisher of the Ottawa *Journal*, estimated the results of hand composition at 750 ems per hour at a cost of 30 cents per 1,000 ems, machine composition at 4,500 ems per hour at a cost of 14 to 15 cents per 1,000 ems.[80]

Finally there were the Goss, Cox, Scott, and Hoe printing systems which worked from rolls of paper to produced stacks of folded newspapers in seconds. The new Hoe system installed by the *Manitoba Free Press* in 1900, for instance, weighed 14 tons, included 'two complete presses and a folding machine,' and was capable of printing a 4- to 8-page paper 'at the rate of 20,000 per hour,' and a 10- to 16-page paper 'at the rate of 10,000 per hour.'[81] These machines made possible the general shift to the 8-page newspaper, larger on Saturday. By 1901, of course, the leading papers such as the Montreal *Star* or the Toronto *Globe* regularly printed more than 8 pages a day.[82]

Trefflé Berthiaume's *La Presse* was the first French-Canadian journal to make extensive use of the new technology. It acquired linotypes in May 1894, experimented with colour printing in June 1897, and employed photographs in 1900.[83] The paper's ad in McKim's *Canadian Newspaper Directory* of 1901 claimed 4 Goss duplex presses and 12 linotype machines, plus a 'complete photo-engraving plant.' The story goes that in 1889 Chapleau bestowed the paper and its debts on Berthiaume, a successful printer and publisher, while exacting a promise of Conservative allegiance.[84] It is hard to imagine a wiser choice. The paper's advance during the 1890s was astonishing (Table 22). Much of the boom occurred in the first half of the decade, notably in 1893 and 1895. In July 1895 a survey by the *Printer and Publisher* of the paper's circulation, which then stood at about

TABLE 22

The listed circulation* of *La Presse* 1889–99

1889	16,257	1893	33,249	1897	58,443
1890	19,076	1894	38,578	1898	65,738
1891	21,290	1895	52,836	1899	66,578
1982	24,950	1896	52,414		

* The figures are for the last week of each year. They are taken from the first January issue, in each case, of *La Presse*, and consequently pertain to the circulation for the week preceding.

50,000, revealed that its constituency extended throughout the province and into New England. 'In a place like Lowell, Mass., there are over 700 daily subscribers. The chief towns in Quebec are also good centres, like St. Hyacinthe, with 800 subscribers, Valleyfield, with 400, and the City of Quebec, with 1,000, sometimes on occasions running as high as 1,500. In the city of Montreal the circulation is between 28,000 and 30,000, and La Presse considers its growth there has been aided by rapid delivery in the afternoon.' In fact, as the reporter noted, the paper's 'phenomenal circulation' was a result of its discovery of 'a regular mine of readers, previously unworked and mostly unused to newspapers.'

How did Berthiaume succeed? Then and later, he was charged with importing 'Yankee' methods and yellow journalism into Quebec. The charge had substance. Immediately, Berthiaume had begun to fill his paper with illustrations, early in 1893 he launched a Saturday extravaganza stuffed with bright features, and in August 1894 he cleared the front page for news stories which by the end of the decade commonly sported a blaring headline. *La Presse* lavished space on crime and sensation, especially in the last years of the decade. The paper carried, for instance, a 'front-page sketch of the supposed mental visions of the murderess Cordelia Viau' on 3 February 1898, and two days later it scandalized again 'with a front-page illustration of Tom Nulty's scaffold decorated with scenes of his life and crime.'[85] Early in the new century came stunts, a classic form of self-puffery: Lorenzo Prince, a reporter who raced around the world in 66 days, or the steamer 'La Presse' whose March 1901 trip along the St Lawrence supposedly proved the river navigable year round.[86] Not only did Berthiaume imitate some New York innovations, as in 'père Ladébouche,' a comic strip, but he also actually used William Randolph Hearst's news and feature service.[87] All of this made *La Presse* Canada's closest approximation to a yellow journal.

And yet *La Presse* was also a very good *news*paper. An analysis of a week's contents of the four Montreal francophone papers (and the city's two 'quality' dailies) in 1896 shows its overall superiority (Table 23). Only the 'Anglo' journals supplied more reading matter. *La Presse* gave subscribers round-ups of

TABLE 23

Content analysis* of Montreal papers 1896 (Monday through Saturday, 9–14 March)

	Gazette	*Herald*	*La Presse*	*Le Monde*	*La Minerve*	*La Patrie*
Line count of information	41,956	36,706	27,771	16,664	14,893	14,729
Contents						
Advertisements	36.0	39.3	44.8	42.6	47.5	47.3
Information	61.6	56.1	50.6	47.8	47.1	43.7
Entertainment	2.4	4.6	4.6	9.6	5.4	9.0
Information: locale						
Outside world	(35.2)	(34.4)	(28.4)	(25.6)	(22.8)	(43.8)
Great Britain	8.0	9.5	2.1	3.1	2.7	1.4
United States	18.5	18.6	12.4	9.7	7.8	11.7
Europe	5.0	3.7	7.6	10.4	8.8	27.4†
Other lands	3.7	2.6	6.3	2.4	3.5	3.3
Canada	(24.9)	(24.8)	(19.7)	(33.4)	(32.6)	(19.0)
National scene	14.4	19.1	14.5	23.3	27.9	15.3
Other provinces	10.5	5.7	5.2	10.1	4.7	3.7
Local world	(33.5)	(29.9)	(43.6)	(37.6)	(37.6)	(32.3)
Quebec province	2.1	2.7	11.5	9.0	12.8	7.3
Montreal	31.4	27.2	32.1	28.6	24.8	25.0
Information: subject						
Public affairs	(31.6)	(27.7)	(30.8)	(46.3)	(45.9)	(45.3)
External	10.8	8.7	8.5	12.3	6.7	17.0
Canadian	14.9	16.4	14.1	24.0	26.1	20.7
Provincial	0.8	0.3	2.9	3.8	8.1	1.8
Civic	5.1	2.3	5.3	6.2	4.9	5.8
Economics	(25.4)	(22.6)	(17.5)	(9.2)	(24.1)	(9.5)
Business	24.8	21.8	12.2	8.5	20.8	5.1
Labour	0.5	0.7	3.1	0.3	1.0	4.3
Farm	0.1	0.1	2.2	0.4	2.3	0.1
Life	(42.9)	(49.7)	(51.2)	(43.8)	(28.9)	(44.0)
The community and its ways	8.6	8.4	8.4	15.3	12.5	7.4
Culture and entertainment	7.2	11.3	3.5	4.4	4.2	9.2
People and society	5.3	3.6	1.2	2.3	1.2	3.3
Sports and recreation	9.9	10.4	10.3	0.2	–	–
Crime and violence	4.7	5.5	11.9	11.6	3.6	11.8
Death and disaster	1.9	2.2	5.3	4.2	2.1	6.3
Miscellany	5.3	8.3	10.6	5.8	5.3	6.0

* Some of the information could not be identified according to locale or subject. Hence the percentages do not always total 100. Percentages for major divisions of locale and subject are given in parentheses.

† 82.1 per cent on France

provincial and national news and more surprisingly of Franco-American news as well. It displayed a definite preference for the local scene, sufficient to slake the thirst for news of city life. Its coverage of the economy was first rate, and included some attention to labour news as well as farming. Over 50 per cent of the information pertained to life's routine, the two outstanding specialties being the columns on sports and crime. Always, the newspaper cultivated its reputation as the people's tribune, ever the friend of labour. It is worth emphasizing that the major gains in circulation were made before the outlandish escapades of the late 1890s.

The success of *La Presse* had a dramatic impact upon the French-Canadian daily press. True, at first, the refurbished journals of opinion persisted, and their numbers were briefly increased by a couple of new arrivals in the early and mid-1890s. After 1892 the rival *Le Monde* tried to compete by espousing the gospel of independent journalism, which enabled the paper to pose as a social critic and a nationalist advocate for 'les classes intelligentes' (26 May 1893). The tactic failed, and before long the newspaper fell once more into Conservative hands. No alternative worked. The decade saw the death of old and new journals of opinion, no matter how brilliant their commentary: *Le Journal de Québec* (1889), *La Justice* and *Le Matin* (1892), *L'Étendard* and *Le Canadien* (1893), *La Bataille* (1896), *Le Monde* (1897), *La Minerve* (1899), and *Le Courrier du Canada* (1901). Papers which survived did so by conforming to the dictates of popular journalism. Joseph Tarte, for instance, converted *La Patrie* into a near replica of *La Presse* in the spring of 1897 – and the booming circulation figures showed the imitation had worked. When the Conservatives launched a new morning paper, Montreal's *Le Journal*, at the end of the decade, it too hunted popularity, whatever its claims about a more moral tone. When *Le Courrier du Canada* closed its doors, *La Presse* correctly remarked, 'Le dernier lien entre le vieux et le nouveau journalisme est disparu.'[88]

No similar decimation occurred elsewhere in the dominion. Publishers had by and large adjusted to the changing times. Faltering enterprises, such as the Montreal *Herald* or the Ottawa *Citizen*, were rejuvenated by new money and new management. Newcomers successfully broke into apparently closed or cluttered markets, often by taking up the standard of independent or people's journalism: the Toronto *Star*, London *News*, Winnipeg *Telegram*, Kingston *Times*, and Vancouver *Province*. Competition was alive and well in English Canada at the end of the decade. Every city had at least three competing dailies, Saint John had five, and Toronto once again six.

Newspapers everywhere were now engaged in the hunt for popularity. Contemporaries noted the declining importance of the editorial page in the typical newspaper. 'We say it, without fear of contradiction, that the standard of editorials in the daily papers of thirty years ago was higher than it is to-day,' a critic complained. 'The Gods of the Sanctum are now wordy weaklings, whereas they were once the Samsons of Thought. The brightest men in journalism to-day are writing news notes, head-lines and advertising puffs, while the prosy numbskulls grind out pages of emptiness, which are labelled "editorials."'[89] That was an exaggerated charge, of course. The lofty leader of the past still survived in the quality morning organs of Toronto and Montreal. The *Globe*'s editorial staff, and editor Willison himself, were renowned for the excellence of their comment on the routine of public affairs. Even Berthiaume kept the editorials of *La Presse* free from the taint of sensation which infected the rest of its columns. But the amount of space devoted to editorial opinion had not increased as papers ballooned in size. Many an evening paper was wont to abbreviate its editorials, unless there was some item of pressing interest. The Halifax *Echo*, on occasion, dispensed with editorials altogether to publish instead brief comments and homilies.[90] Besides, the role of the editorial writer was challenged by the arrival of the columnist who could specialize in anything from labour's affairs ('Chronique ouvrière' in *La Presse*) to social commentary ('The Flaneur' in Toronto *Mail*). He or she (in the case of the women's columnist) might cultivate a loyal following separate from the regular devotees of the editorial page. Indeed, on some dailies, the editorial writer was more and more restricted to debating the grave questions of immediate public import, leaving the wider sphere of life to the columnist and the newsman. And that writer might well find his copy supplemented by political cartoons, on the front page in the case of Toronto *Telegram*, to excite or divert the masses.

By far the greatest effort, even on the *Globe*, went into satisfying the news hunger of the populace. Symbolic of this shift was the change in the front page. The old 'French front,' featuring editorials, once a common format in French Canada, died with the journal of opinion. One of the last holdouts was *La Patrie* where the 'French front' was replaced only in February 1897, when the Tartes revamped the whole paper. Convention now dictated that the front page must be the showpiece of the daily, its pre-eminent news page (Table 24). The morning papers usually gave pride of place to diplomacy and politics, the trivia of public affairs, whether in Canada or abroad. The evening papers usually preferred local happenings, especially life's routine, and they were more likely to make use of headlines and illustrations. Each newspaper, however, arranged its own special blend of offerings: so *La Patrie* placed a virtual ban on foreign and national news, the morning *Globe* highlighted the outside world, the *Star* gave much attention to local politics, *La Presse* and the *News* had a weakness for crime, any crime. On rare occasions, a single theme might dominate: during the late fall of 1899, the Montreal *Star* turned its front page into a podium from whence to shout the

TABLE 24

Front-page content analysis* 1899 (a composite of four days–3 February, 10 May, 16 August, and 27 November)

	Toronto *Globe*	*Manitoba Free Press*	Montreal *La Presse*	Montreal *La Patrie*	Toronto *Star*	Toronto *News*
Edition	M†	M	E‡	E	E	E
Number of news items	54	98	43	61	101	158
Number of illustrations	1	0	7	4	2	2
Contents						
News	89.0	87.9	95.7	98.7	92.6	96.6
Advertisements	–	–	1.4	1.3	6.4	–
Miscellaneous	11.0	12.1	2.9	–	0.9	3.4
News: locale						
Outside World	57.3	41.2	24.4	3.9	26.4	37.0
Canada	20.2	35.4	2.2	–	25.1	10.7
Province	14.7	18.4	23.6	16.9	8.3	10.6
City	7.8	5.0	49.8	79.2	40.3	41.7
News: subjects						
Public Affairs	(76.1)	(51.3)	(39.0)	(26.2)	(64.3)	(41.5)
War and diplomacy	34.5	17.6	5.7	0.6	13.3	18.7
Outside world	17.0	8.0	13.4	1.0	13.4	3.9
Canada	21.0	15.5	1.6	0.5	14.7	2.6
Province	3.6	10.2	5.7	6.6	4.2	0.9
City	–	–	12.6	17.5	18.7	15.4
Economics	(12.3)	(15.7)	(3.6)	(5.6)	(16.4)	(5.3)
Business	10.0	9.2	3.6	3.3	15.2	4.0
Labour	1.5	4.4	–	2.3	0.9	0.9
Farm	0.7	2.1	–	–	0.3	0.4
Life	(11.9)	(33.1)	(57.4)	(68.3)	(19.4)	(53.3)
The community and its ways	0.8	9.3	15.9	20.3	10.8	15.0
Culture and entertainment	–	1.8	0.2	2.2	–	1.8
People and society	3.7	2.8	17.5	21.6	0.9	5.9
Sports and recreation	–	4.0	2.0	3.8	1.6	6.3
Crime and violence	0.5	3.0	17.8	5.8	2.7	13.5
Death and disaster	3.1	8.4	2.0	13.9	3.0	8.7
Miscellany	3.8	3.8	2.0	0.7	0.4	2.1

* Percentages for major divisions in news subjects are given in parentheses.

† Morning

‡ Evening

necessity of Canada's entering the Boer War. Then there was the idiosyncratic Toronto *Telegram* which covered its front page with want ads, not news, a striking display of Robertson's priority.

Changed altered the inside pages as well. 'The aim of the ordinary newspaper is to be all things to all men,' argued W.D. LeSueur in 1903.[91] What he meant was that the newspaper, especially on Saturdays, had become a conglomerate of fact and fancy organized into separate departments to please various sets of readers. The increased size of newspapers naturally fostered this kind of inflation. So there was a local news page, a women's page, columns of business news, often a column or so on labour's world, Saturday specials on churches or charities, popular science features, critiques of music and drama, children's matter, and fiction and humour. A regular item was the coverage of high society, proof of the importance of the 'feminine influence.' 'The newspaper to-day is the greatest of all feeders of social gossip,' lamented LeSueur. 'To-day, thousands who totally ignore the editorial columns greedily devour the social gossip.'[92] The other novelty was the marvellous array of sports news. 'Here the rising generation have come to their rights and perhaps a little more,' LeSueur reasoned. 'Sport is to the young man what the social columns are to the lady reader.'[93] Much of the reading matter might be light, with no obvious redeeming social value – indeed, the avid interest in sports depressed the appetite for politics. 'All this is not good for "the people"; but in a certain sense, it may be said, "the people" will have it so.'[94]

The search for popularity did produce significant, sometimes spectacular, results for the city papers. The overall circulation of weekly editions ceased its decline and the daily editions registered a gain of 60 per cent, mostly in the last years of the decade (Table 25). The primary market, of course, remained the city proper. The established dailies in Hamilton and London reduced their street prices to one cent to meet the competition of new, cheap challengers. The *Manitoba Free Press* offered the evening *Bulletin* free to morning subscribers to injure the rival evening *Tribune*.[95] The Montreal *Herald* tried to reverse its bad fortune by invading, late in 1894, the evening field and publishing sensation. Indeed, the paper 'invented' a 'newspaper slot machine' for streetcorners and, a year later, hired its own carriers to deliver newspapers to subscribers' homes.[96] A few years later, the renewed Ottawa *Citizen* also launched a one-cent evening edition which soon took great relish in publishing details of a local rape case on its front page.[97] This lusty competition, though, was really over respective shares of already cluttered markets. Even in French Montreal, the march of *La Presse*, and later of *La Patrie*, must have gathered in most of the households that hitherto did not subscribe to any newspaper. A number of evening or local dailies – the Halifax *Mail*, Quebec's

TABLE 25

Circulation 1891–1900 of daily and weekly editions of city dailies (in thousands)

	Dailies			Weeklies		
	1891	1898	1900	1891	1898	1900
Greater Halifax	15.5	21.1	24.5	12.8	7.6*	14.6
Greater Saint John	16.4	14.7	18.0	14.8	17.8	16.3
Quebec-Lévis	25.8	27.8	28.8	19.5	11.3	12.3
Greater Montreal	107.2	164.2	202.8†	158.8	238.1*	255.0*
Ottawa-Hull	15.0	17.9*	24.3	12.0	9.3*	10.0
Kingston	3.9	5.7	5.5	8.2	8.9	8.6
Greater Toronto	120.2	170.4	185.7	109.2	42.6	46.1
Hamilton	26.0	18.8	19.7	17.0	9.0	9.5
London	17.3	22.5	26.9	35.0	15.3	11.5
Winnipeg	8.2	21.4	25.9	13.2	24.0	23.6
Vancouver		4.3	6.2		3.8	2.5
Victoria	3.5	5.7	6.5	4.2	5.5	4.3
Total	359.0	494.5	574.8	404.7	393.2	414.3

SOURCE: See note 66 to this chapter.
* Figure adjusted
† Figure doubtful

L'Événement and *Telegraph*, all three Hamilton hopefuls – expanded their readership slowly, if at all. The mighty *Telegram*, disdainful of Toronto's suburban market, grew by only a mere 3,500.

A much more promising arena lay outside the city in the suburbs, the surrounding countryside, the province, and for a few enterprises the whole dominion. Success was difficult here. Witness the fate of the traditional intruder, the weekly edition. By far the most impressive performance was the sudden renaissance of Graham's *Family Herald and Weekly Star*, after a decade's rest: editor J.W. Dafoe, hired in 1895, carried out a thorough reorganization of the paper's offerings, using the now familiar technique of special departments to reach 'almost every class of readers' in a country setting, all of which boosted the nationwide circulation to 115,000 by the end of 1898.[98] The rival *Witness* maintained its national prominence by converting the old *Northern Messenger* into a weekly, costing 30 cents a year. The obstacle of language helped *Le Cultivateur* (Tarte's weekly) and the weekly *La Presse* withstand this kind of competition. Distance, and probably party assistance as well, enabled the Winnipeg and Halifax papers to win a sizeable rural readership. The real crisis centred in Ontario where publishers fought to regain ground lost in the previous decade. The Ottawa dailies published semi-weekly editions because, P.D. Ross claimed, 'they can hold their local field better against the Montreal and Toronto weeklies.'[99] The Hamilton *Times* and *Spectator* followed suit. The Toronto weeklies, the *Weekly Mail* and *Farm and Fireside* selling at 50 cents a year in early 1895, arranged special 'clubbing' deals with country publishers to charge $1.25 or $1.35 for both weeklies.[100] Efforts were made to use postal, customs, or police officers to curtail the circulation of American Sunday papers, supposedly flooding into southwestern Ontario.[101] These were to little avail. The circulation of urban weeklies in Ontario was cut in half during the 1890s. Hence this sermon from the *Printer and Publisher* (November 1898): 'All the signs go to prove that the country weekly – strong in local news, independent in tone, well turned-out mechanically – has an unassailable position if its proprietor knows how to use his advantages.'

Resourceful publishers in Ontario and elsewhere, however, realized that railways and better roads meant a growing provincial market for their wares. In 1892 the Winnipeg *Tribune* published a special 'Forenoon Edition,' sent out on the 'early trains,' for readers 'in all sections of the Northwest.'[102] The 1895 survey of *La Presse*'s constituency discovered that roughly 40 per cent of its circulation lay outside the city proper.[103] At the end of 1894, the Toronto *Star* and the *News* each clubbed with country publishers to sell the Toronto daily and the local weekly at a $1.50 a year.[104] The *News*, perhaps the first 'dollar daily,' offered a special morning edition (largely a reprint of the evening paper) at $1 a year to out-of-town subscribers.[105] That virtual giveaway boosted the newspaper's sworn circulation to 42,283 in 1898, though the total fell back to 30,000 and perhaps even lower two years later. More permanent was the amazing revival of both the Toronto *Mail and Empire* and the *Globe* which, after the mid-1890s, doubled their daily circulation in the next five or six years. Their competition made the future of morning editions elsewhere in the province very doubtful. First the Hamilton *Spectator*, early in the decade, and later the London *Advertiser*, at the close of the decade, withdrew from the morning field to concentrate on afternoon and evening competition.

Reflections on the state of the press at the end of the century were usually laudatory. A favourite boast was that the best of the British and American extremes had been adopted by the Canadian newspaper. 'They have as a rule infinitely greater dignity and love of fairness and accuracy than their American contemporaries,' stated W.C. Nichol of the Vancouver *Province*; 'they have, too, the spirit of enterprise in getting and presenting the news that the British press undoubtedly misses altogether.'[106] Perhaps there was some truth to this boast. The biggest papers could, as a rule, be grouped into one camp or the other, quality or people's journalism, indicating a different approach to the world of events. But each daily had its own personality, its specialties and causes and tone tailored to the immediate market and the urban community. So the *Telegram* was the stern maiden of Toronto's virtues, *La Presse* the workingman's friend but the *Gazette* the businessman's friend, Graham's exuberant *Star* an Imperialist organ while Willison's sophisticated *Globe* was a Liberal organ. And the search for popularity had made every kind of newspaper emulate the 'best' innovations, whatever their source. The variety of departments, the use of sensation, the fascination with life, the news emphasis, the Saturday specials, and the yearning for respectability were all common to the successful enterprise. A quality paper such as Toronto's *Mail and Empire*, its morning edition for the 'classes,' published an evening edition for the 'masses.' A people's daily such as the rival *Telegram* tried to push its way into every home in the city. Competition, in short, had forced newspapers to find readers among all classes of the community.[107] By the end of the century, the popular press was an authority that both reflected and bridged the social gulf in the big city.

3

The newspaper industry

There has always been some doubt about what newspaperdom really is. A wry J.S. Willison once remarked, 'Journalism is not exactly a profession, not exactly a trade, not always a means of livelihood.'[1] Then and later, this apparent ambiguity provoked a lasting tension between the professional and commercial aspects of journalism. During the late nineteenth century, new machinery and new labour 'industrialized' newspaperdom: those handsome buildings publishers put up to house their dailies were factories that produced cheap goods for a mass market of readers. The transformation of the place and routine of work took journalism far from its artisan roots. That transformation also inspired, but even more thwarted, a drive to professionalize the pursuit and its practices. Most important, the changes emphasized the links between the world of the newspaper and the world of commerce. Daily journalism became a business much like any other.

JOURNALISTS

All who laboured in the newspaper office were not journalists. Excluded, and by common consent, were the printing trades, office staff, sometimes even owners. A journalist was a reporter, correspondent, contributor, editor, or publisher – anyone engaged in the creation of news and views. Journalism might be only a 'bridging occupation' offering a young man a route to a more lucrative career, or a kind of 'out relief' enabling the civil servant and the academic to earn a bit of extra cash.[2] But it was also the primary means of livelihood, if not the passion, of most working journalists and that established the pursuit as a recognized occupation. Biographical compendia supply a surfeit of detail about the ranking journalists of the day, sufficient at least to allow a profile of the pursuit and its work.[3]

Why a person decided upon a career in journalism was sometimes a mystery. Women, of course, found it a congenial occupation at a time when other careers were closed. An obituary occasioned by the death of Joseph Tassé, longtime editor of *La Minerve*, talked about 'cette fascination puissanté que le journalisme exerce sur ceux qui aiment l'étude et la lutte.'[4] Perhaps too, journalism seemed an easy route to fame and significance, an excellent way for the idealist (thought Willison) to find the '"Balm of Gilead" for the humours and distresses of his time.'[5] Equally true was the offhand comment of Molyneux St John, then a young correspondent and eventually a peripatetic editor: 'If there is anything detestable it is being a Government Employee.'[6] There was always a home in some newspaper somewhere for a disenchanted soul in search of a modest but interesting living.

That fact did nothing for the status of the pursuit. The common euphemism 'the gentlemen of the press' did not really suit the public reputation of the journalists. Most were not granted the measure of respect normal to members of an established profession. 'When I first came to mingle among newspaper men as a working associate,' reminisced Hector Charlesworth, previously an accountant's clerk, 'it secretly amused me to discern that they held a much higher opinion of their importance in the world than the business and social community with which they were surrounded actually accorded them.'[7] Others were not so amused. An angry writer on *Le Monde*'s staff railed against a world which ranked lawyers, little better than paid opportunists, high above the committed journalist.[8] J.A. Cooper, a press apologist, flatly rejected 'the opinion that when a man fails at everything else he can become an insurance agent or an editor.'[9] Still, Walter Harte, an American critic, found the 'old Bohemianism' lingered on in Canada, fostered by 'a very decided prejudice against the profession.'[10] Journalism, so the sneer went, was too often the abode of the ne'er-do-well, the failed clerk, the dishonest scribbler, and the party hack.

The low reputation had something to do with the apparent lack of that special training, especially any course of studies, necessary to enter the liberal professions. The professionalizers at the end of the century looked to the university to remedy this lack: indeed, in 1903 the editors of the *Queen's Quarterly* sponsored a selection of essays by journalists entitled *Journalism and the University*, which explored the range of subjects desirable to train the prospective editor. In fact, on paper, the educational attainments of leading editors and publishers were quite respectable, in many cases impressive, by contemporary standards. Almost all but the oldest of hands had attended some sort of high school, then a near prerequisite for a middle-class career. A university education was not a requirement for success: witness the prominence of those self-educated editors J.W. Dafoe (editor, Montreal *Herald* and later the *Family Herald and Weekly Star*, 1890s), J.E. Atkinson (editor, Montreal *Herald*, late 1890s), even Willison himself (editor, Toronto *Globe*, 1890s).

But a sizeable minority of editors and publishers in English Canada were university men. Edward Farrer (editor, Toronto *Mail*, late 1880s) had attended the Jesuit College at Rome; William Maclean (publisher, Toronto *World*, 1880s and 1890s) earned a BA at the University of Toronto; Lewis Shannon (publisher, Kingston *News*, 1880s and 1890s) likewise received a BA, though from Queen's; P.D. Ross (publisher, Ottawa *Journal*, 1890s) graduated from McGill an engineer; Martin Griffin (editor, Toronto *Mail*, early 1890s) and John Garvin (editor, Montreal *Herald*, mid-1890s) studied law; H.F. Gardiner (editor, Hamilton *Times*, 1880s and 1890s) boasted an MA from Albert College in Belleville.

French Canadians were no less accomplished. Honoré Beaugrand (publisher, *La Patrie*, 1880s and 1890s) was enrolled in the Montreal Military School – before joining Maximilian's forces in Mexico during the mid-1860s! Narcisse Dionne, editor of various Quebec City papers in the 1870s and 1880s, studied first theology and later graduated in medicine from Laval University. Law, that most esteemed of professions among the French-Canadian middle class, contributed many, many 'scholars' to journalism: C.-A. Dansereau, the Conservative editor *par excellence*; Cléophas Beausoleil (editor, *Le Nouveau Monde*, early 1870s) and his successor Alphonse Desjardins; Joseph Tassé (editor, *La Minerve*, 1880s and early 1890s) as well as his successor, Joseph Royal; Thomas Chapais (editor, *Le Courrier du Canada*, late 1880s and 1890s); Godfrey Langlois, a new star (editor, *La Patrie*, late 1890s). Perhaps this accounts for the curse and charm of French-Canadian journalism, its passion for doctrinaire argument?

There was, as well, an unofficial system of apprenticeship: most editors and publishers served some time in the ranks before winning their place in the sun. Some had begun in the printing trades, once the standard route for the young man bent on a career in journalism. Their declining numbers included older publishers such as John Ellis (Saint John *Globe*, 1860s – post-1900), John Cameron (London *Advertiser*, 1860s – same), William Southam (Hamilton *Spectator*, late 1870s – same), and Trefflé Berthiaume (*La Presse*, 1890s – same), who started work around Confederation. Another group first tried its hand in small-town journalism – Joseph Tarte, who in 1871 started a newspaper at St Lin before moving on to greater things at *Le Canadien*, or Joseph Atkinson who put in long hours as a helper on the Port Hope *Times*. Becoming common, especially in English Canada, was an initial tour of duty as a reporter on a big-city newspaper. Gardiner (after some printing experience) was a reporter on Hamilton dailies; Graham's *Star* trained Ross and Dafoe; Garvin served on the Toronto *World*, *Telegram*, and *News*; H.-D. Tetu (though trained in law) began as a *La Presse* reporter in 1884, rising to the post of city editor a decade later.

Others jumped almost immediately into editorial work, especially the new flock of woman's journalists such as Kathleen Blake ('Woman's Kingdom' editor,

Mail and Empire, late 1890s) or Robertine Barry (Françoise,' *La Patrie*, mid-1890s). So too did the occasional university graduate: James Longley began writing for the press as a law student and became the chief editorial writer for the *Acadian Recorder* in the mid-1870s. That pattern was especially common in French Canada, where nearly all those 'ex-lawyers' moved into the editorial sphere without any other apparent experience. Clearly, the emphasis in big-city journalism was now on the acquisition of literary skills, no longer on printing expertise.

The reporter in French Canada, at least until the *fin de siècle* excesses of *La Presse*, was a virtual nonentity. This was not quite the case in English Canada: there a definite mystique had grown up about the reporter and his work because of the increasing 'fact-mindedness' of newspapers and their readers.[11] The ideal reporter was the public's eye, ubiquitous, impartial, and loyal to the facts. So: 'Unconsciously they are drawn to where some event is happening, or about to happen, and if the reporters are on the *qui vive*, but little need escape them.'[12] Also: 'his primary object, and, indeed, his only one, is to get the news he has sent for, and this does irrespective of his own likes or dislikes, whether they be of a personal, social, or political character.'[13] These notions informed the rules that city editors collected into reporters' guides. Thus, J.H. Maclean of the Toronto *World* warned reporters to avoid 'your own opinions,' 'don't get wordy,' 'be sparing in the use of adjectives.' Above all, 'be sure and get the news, all the news, in every case, and state it succinctly.'[14] Apparently, the reporter's was a life of mystery, sometimes high drama, full of variety; he was aware of secrets no others could share.

No doubt the reporter was a cultural innovation, a new breed of journalist necessitated by the complexities of the urban milieu and the new mood of social realism. Yet the reporter's existence hardly fitted the ideal. Never were reporters accepted into the journalistic fraternity as full-fledged members, whatever the rhetoric about the importance of news. Only a very few ever won a 'name' outside newspaper offices, men such as G.H. Pearl, the Montreal *Herald*'s celebrated municipal reporter in the late 1890s. More often reporting meant a life of dependence and anonymity, as much drudgery as excitement, long hours and low pay. Reporters might have special beats – the police docket, city hall, the local hotels, the sports world – but they were expected to fill in wherever and whenever necessary. An Ontario wage survey in 1884 found reporters made an average $550 a year for working about 62 hours a week.[15] In 1899 A.H.U. Colquhoun estimated that 'a good reporter' rarely received more than $1,200 a year, and the average was closer to $600.[16] And there remained an impression that the life of the reporter was disreputable, intemperate, or low: 'It has been considered a means of providing men of ability, but lax in morals and irregular in habits, a means of obtaining a precarious livelihood.'[17] The upshot was that good reporters almost invariably moved on, either out of journalism or into editorial work.

There was, however, one species of reporter, the Ottawa correspondent, who did enjoy much prestige, at least in 'Anglo' circles. These correspondents, really the first reporters, specialized in the higher politics of the dominion. Service in the Ottawa Press Gallery was usually a token of the editor's esteem, especially on a quality newspaper where public affairs was the banner offering. (Graham's editors on the *Star*, by contrast, seemed content to send out a green journalist such as J.W. Dafoe.) The Ottawa correspondent was neither anonymous nor impartial: John McCready, the *Globe*'s man in the early 1880s, was a Liberal who had to resort to skullduggery to squeeze news out of reluctant government departments.[18] Correspondents were expected not only to report gossip as well as fact, but also often to contribute columns or even lead editorials. During the mid-1870s the *Mail*'s Charles Belford was in constant communication with manager Patteson over matters large and small. Correspondents also had opportunities to free lance, since not all newspapers could or would afford a resident reporter in Ottawa. Witness Frederick Cook: appointed by the *Mail* in 1884, he served thereafter as the *Empire*'s and later the *World*'s correspondent, acted as well for a variety of other newspapers, and in 1894 took full charge of the Canadian news bureau established by *The Times* of London. Obviously, an excellent correspondent could win much fame, especially with the party faithful. Willison and Atkinson, for example, both made their 'names' while in Ottawa working for the *Globe*. Arthur Wallis moved directly from Ottawa into the chief editor's chair of the Toronto *Mail* in 1890. The Ottawa Press Gallery was a training ground for many a future editor or publisher in English Canada, and past membership and the memory of common work also served as a kind of professional bond which drew together journalists whatever their politics.[19]

Inside and outside the newspaper office worked an assortment of writers whose copy was more often in the realm of comment than simple news. Some were transients or part-timers, say a politician such as David Mills who (though called the editor) amounted to the chief editorial writer of the London *Advertiser* during much of the 1890s. French-Canadian politicians (such as F.-G. Marchand at *Le Temps*, 1883; L.-P. Pelletier at *La Justice*, 1886; G.-A. Nantel at *Le Monde*, 1896) were forever writing for, sometimes editing, their own organs to win some victory in the game of argument. Other contributors were noted intellectuals: Goldwin Smith, who had a long association with Robertson's *Telegram*; W.D. LeSueur, a civil servant and writer for the Montreal *Star*; Louis Fréchette, the poet and occasional rouge editor; or L.-O. David, a lawyer and inveterate journalist. The French-Canadian dailies, by and large, were much readier to turn over their columns to the intellectuals, especially for feature articles on history, literature, and philosophy. Much more novel were the woman's journalists who usually specialized in literary matters and, of course, high society. Only a few such as Eve Brodlique (London *Advertiser*) and Sara Jeanette Duncan (Montreal *Star*), served briefly in a wider field, both as Ottawa correspondents. Brodlique, by the way, went south in search of a better job: indeed, there was a definite tendency for the successful, and unmarried, woman's journalist to leave the restricted pastures of Canadian journalism. Then there were the specialists such as J.T. Lesperance (literary critic on the Montreal *Gazette*), John Bayne Maclean (briefly commercial editor on the Toronto *Empire*), John Boyd (longtime Montreal correspondent for the Toronto *Mail*), H.H. Wiltshire (the *Mail*'s famous columnist), and Edward Thompson (the *Globe*'s principal editorial writer in the 1880s). Finally, on the bigger papers, were a couple of sub-editors with a range of titles: the exchange editor, responsible for clipping news, views, and filler from other papers; the city man who handled reporters and watched out for libellous stories; perhaps a night or telegraph editor to collect wired copy; certainly a news editor (under whatever name) responsible for all the news. The apparent division of labour, of course, was not nearly as strict or as uniform as such a bare outline might suggest. But the very wealth of contributors, specialists, editorialists, and sub-editors showed how far the popular daily had moved from the simple days of the mid-century when the editor and a helper or two sufficed to bring out the newspaper.

Legend had it that the key man in the whole operation was the editor-in-chief, about whom again had gathered a special mystique. His work required, so N.F. Davin claimed, 'great and peculiar gifts, long and varied experience, and untiring energy.'[20] The editor was 'the guiding spirit of a newspaper. He writes the editorials outlining the paper's policy on every question, gives suggestions for future work, rejects matters that he considers valueless or untrue and has the whole supervision of the paper and is responsible for everything that appears in its columns.'[21] This godlike creature was expected to stamp the newspaper's 'persona' on the daily fare, so that its views and news were always consistent with its declared philosophy. Success won the mighty editor fame among his fellow journalists and accolades from a grateful public.

A small collection of reform-minded journalists, all in English Canada though, challenged this mystique during the 1890s. The burden of their complaints, and they did differ, was that even the editor-in-chief had become little more than a white-collar employee, writing for profit and publishers. Joe Clark, who worked on *Saturday Night* and the Toronto *Star*, denied his brethen any claim to professional status. 'They pass no examination as to knowledge; they possess no certificate of character; they foreswear no heresy; they subscribe to no creed; they are not under bonds to respect anything, to promote any good cause, or to overthrow any evil thing.'[22] A more common charge, however, was that the editor lacked both power and significance. 'It would be foolish for any reader to try to make himself believe that the policy of any great Canadian paper depends on what the editor thinks,' asserted the *Printer and Publisher* (October 1893). 'The editor is writing for a living, and the paper is run to make a profit. Policies are secondary considerations.' Another realist argued that popular journalism must produce 'a diminution of individual consequence. The editor must become more and more an anonymous inaccessible entity. He will simply be the engineer who has charge of the locomotive for one "run," or for one day.'[23] What did that leave of the editor's much-vaunted status, queried W.C. Nichol, a veteran journalist? The editor laboured to make profits for others, not even able to secure comfort in his old age, given the demand for 'young blood.' Editing was 'a sorry trade.'[24]

Who was right? Certainly, Clark's strictures were much too harsh. By the 1890s most leading editors, whether in French or English Canada, were seasoned journalists who had moved from one post to another in search of a better job.[25] The pay could be quite good. True, the Ontario Bureau of Industries estimated the average salary of editors in 1887 at $725 a year but that included small-town as well as big-city postings.[26] Ten years later, A.H.U. Colquhoun claimed the 'best positions' brought between $2,000 and $5,000, though only a few men earned more than $3,000. C.-A. Dansereau's annual salary as editor of *La Presse* in 1899 was around $6,000 or $7,000. As well, really famous editors could demand a fair amount of independence. Berthiaume apparently lured Dansereau back from the civil service with a promise of 'a free hand' in the editorial sphere.[27] Willison, albeit subject to much party advice – more, ultimately, than he could stand – was usually able to run the *Globe* during the 1890s in much his own fashion. Clifford Sifton, the owner of the *Manitoba Free Press*, eventually gave editor Dafoe considerable latitude in the day-to-day definition of policy. 'Great editors' were partners in the common task of managing the enterprise. But they too always worked within limits established by the proprietors. And a lesser editor such as Joseph Atkinson on the Montreal *Herald* had to accept 'frequent blue pencilling' of his editorials by the publisher, J.S. Brierley.[28] Not even the most famous, moreover, were assured they could survive a contretemps. So Edward Farrer's reputation as an annexationist brought dismissal from the Toronto *Globe* in 1892, and he never secured another position of comparable importance. When the *Empire* was sold off to the *Mail* in 1895, nearly all the organ's staffers were dumped out on the streets, only manager David Creighton receiving a slight reward for years of toil by appointment to the civil service.[29]

Little wonder many editors tried to escape from such an uncertain career. A traditional route out of journalism was into the comfortable arms of the civil service, so much so that the higher reaches seemed a retirement home for faithful editors. The longtime editor of the Conservative Toronto *Leader*, Charles Lindsay, was rewarded in 1867 with the post of registrar of deeds for the city of Toronto. Martin Griffin left the *Mail* in 1885 to become a parliamentary librarian in Ottawa, where he joined Alfred DeCelles, once editor of *La Minerve*. Louis Joncas, after six years running *L'Événement*, became in 1896 the provincial superintendent of fish and game. Younger men bridged out into law, politics, occasionally business. Cléophas Beausoleil, once of *Le Nouveau Monde*, found security in law and a greater excitement in Parliament. Alphonse Desjardins, his successor, chose to become a bank president as well as a leading politician. William Fielding gave up his post as chief editor of the Halifax *Chronicle* to take over as provincial premier in 1884. Still others moved into book or magazine publishing (Charles Belford or John Bayne Maclean) and weekly publishing in the countryside (T.H. Preston). This constant haemorrhage was a sign of the unprofessional nature of a pursuit which could not satisfy, and so keep, much of its experienced talent.

A more desirable fate for an editor, of course, was a final step forward to become a big-city publisher. Even J.B. Maclean, who had made his fortune building up trade journals, found the prospect of owning the *Mail and Empire* extremely attractive.[30] The mystique of the editor really suited the publisher. Very, very few publishers ever accepted the kind of self-denying ordinance that Joseph Flavelle took when he turned over the Toronto *News* to Willison in 1903. What has been called 'personal journalism' survived the industrialization of the press because the publishers continued to act as the grand controllers of their newspapers. Graham's *Star*, Robertson's *Telegram*, Beaugrand's *La Patrie*, Berthiaume's *La Presse* were all, in some measure, extensions of their publishers' views about life and politics.

The coin of the publisher's realm was not just money, sometimes in fact a scarce commodity, but also fame, excitement, at least the illusion of significance. Publishers were entrepreneurs, but entrepreneurs in the games of power and prestige as well as profit. Influence and respectability might matter more then making money. Publishers were men of stature, cultivated by businessmen, churchmen, and politicians. The aura of power and the sheer glamour of ownership inevitably appealed to many a veteran journalist.

Many publishers were or became politicos, inside and outside the parties, who relished the thrills of public life, even if they could be only kingmakers, never kings. Character and circumstance allowed that pioneer, George Brown, to exercise an extraordinary sway over the Reform hosts in Ontario after mid-century. C.-A. Dansereau, when a publisher of *La Minerve* (1871–80), was the *éminence grise* in the bleu hierarchy during the 1870s. The two White brothers of the Montreal *Gazette* achieved wide fame as political and business chieftains: Thomas worked his way up in the Conservative party to serve in Macdonald's cabinet while Richard took to collecting presidencies of assorted Montreal companies. Edmund Sheppard of the *News* made himself a force in Toronto's labour circles, even standing for election to the Commons in 1887 as a workingman's candidate. Honoré Beaugrand's significance was sufficient to win him the mayor's office in 1885, though he never could break into the upper ranks of the Liberal party. During the 1890s Francis Carter Cotton parlayed his importance as proprietor of the Vancouver *News-Advertiser* into a measure of influence as a local politician in British Columbia's legislature. John Ross Robertson and Hugh Graham, whose local influence soon became legendary, did move into a wider arena in the late 1890s: Robertson entered the Commons as an independent Conservative while Graham became a backroom Conservative power in Quebec.

Room at the top was in short supply. The lively competition in the cities of Old Canada made things difficult for ambitious veterans. Established properties were usually not for sale or too expensive. Indeed, the leading quality newspapers and party organs sometimes came under the control of wealthy outsiders such as John Riordon of the *Mail* or Robert Jaffray of the *Globe*, and by the 1890s company ownership was not an uncommon method of meeting the costs of popular journalism. Still, the example of the people's journals seemed to prove that nothing was impossible for the energetic newcomer. A journalist might win entry into the higher reaches through political preferment: witness the success of the Liberal Ernest Pacaud of *L'Électeur* (1880), the Conservative Berthiaume of *La Presse* (1889), or the Liberal Tarte of *La Patrie* (1897), all of whom received some form of party assistance. Sometimes, an editor could work out an arrangement with outsiders to allow him to acquire a share in the property, perhaps in time full ownership.[31] T.C. Patteson had been promised this opportunity should the *Mail* succeed. Walter Nichol, who had contemplated leaving journalism, bought first a half share (1898) and soon total control (1901) of the Vancouver *Province* he had managed from its recent beginnings (1897).[32] Joseph Atkinson's contract to edit the Toronto *Star* in the Liberal interest allowed him a salary of $3,000 plus 20 shares (valued at $100) per year.[33] Either course was safer than launching a new enterprise in a cluttered market without wealthy backers. That, mind you, was the plight of most newcomers, some of whom did succeed.

But publishing proved a very tricky business, more likely to end in frustration or disaster. Especially poignant was the case of John Livingston, whose grand effort to make the Saint John *Telegraph* a popular newspaper brought personal bankruptcy. Thereafter, Livingston served as a rootless editor on the Moncton *Times*, the Saint John *Sun*, the Montreal *Herald*, even the luckless *Empire*, before dying in harness as manager of the Calgary *Herald*. No less sad was the fate of

Gordon Brown who had worked so long to build up the *Globe* while George dallied elsewhere. George's extravagance left the paper in the hands of outsiders who removed Gordon as editor in 1882, because his views clashed with the prevailing wisdom of Edward Blake and the Liberal party. William Luxton might have turned the *Manitoba Free Press* into Winnipeg's dominant newspaper during the 1880s, but financial difficulties forced sale of control to the Canadian Pacific Railway, which fired him as managing editor in 1893.

Even the Dougalls, so devoted to spreading the Word, had moments of despair. 'We have to sell our papers for a cent to reach a multitude who hate it,' lamented John Redpath Dougall. 'I should like to sell out both businesses and go farming in the west.'[34] Some publishers actually did retire from the hurly-burly of daily journalism. Robert Lowe, a co-proprietor of the Montreal *Gazette* in the 1850s and 1860s, ended up in the civil service. C.-A. Dansereau disposed of his share in *La Minerve* in 1880 to join the civil service, in time becoming postmaster of Montreal, though he did return to journalism much later. Charles Mackintosh, after nearly two decades publishing the Ottawa *Citizen*, sold the paper in 1892 and the following year became lieutenant-governor of the Northwest Territories. Ill-health, perhaps too a lack of funds, led Beaugrand, bloodied by years of struggle with clerical and political foes (including Liberals), to retire altogether and dispose of *La Patrie* to Tarte's sons.

When Hector Charlesworth, bent on becoming a writer, entered Toronto journalism in 1891, he discovered a world regulated by a definite division of labour and a hierarchy of authority, wherein worked a host of white-collar specialists under the command of a few publishers. Looking back, he found that would full of picaresque types and much charm and excitement. Perhaps it was, but professionalizers at the time thought that the workers and the work needed a measure of improvement.

Rhetoric aside, since probably many working journalists sympathized, the cause of professionalism was at bottom impotent. There were a few signs of a new sense of brotherhood, one at least being the appearance in 1897 of a 'Toronto Newspaper Club' presided over by Willison and Wallis.[35] But the professionalizers lacked a practical formula to remake their pursuit. The sovereign remedy would have been, of course, a resort to unionism, except that required a change of outlook impossible in the 1890s. Ironically, professional aspirations made a unionist solution to the troubles of the editor anathema. Remember too that the working journalist might still reasonably dream of owning his own newspaper property somewhere. The root problem lay in the fact that journalism was effectively a headless profession. Its natural leaders, the publishers, were more and more entrepreneurs first; their worries differed, sometimes markedly, from the concerns of the rank and file. And it was the business side of journalism which dominated the pages of the *Printer and Publisher* as well as the sessions of the Canadian Press Association. So professionalism remained a strategy of criticism, never of action.

THE BALANCE SHEET

'A great newspaper now-a-days must be conducted on the same principles on which any other business is carried on,' John Bourinot claimed in 1881. 'The expenses of a daily journal are now so great that it requires the outlay of large capital to keep it up to the requirements of the time.'[36] That axiom signified the central importance of the business department to the health of the popular newspaper. Late in 1900, E.H. Macklin, the newly appointed business manager of the *Manitoba Free Press*, pleased proprietor Sifton and ensured the paper's profitability by aggressively securing new advertising; revenues were up about $1,500 in August and a huge $2,175 in October over the same months the year previous.[37]

Survival, not profit, was more often the priority of the hard-pressed manager. During the last three decades of the century, Montrealers witnessed the birth of 23 new dailies, and the death of 25 dailies. Only 4 of the 9 Montreal dailies around in 1870 survived in 1900, and none of these survivors was French-Canadian. Montreal, admittedly, was a special case, its very size exciting the ambitions of too many hopefules. But Winnipeg, a much smaller metropolis, was also a newspaper graveyard, mostly because of Conservative efforts to feed a loyal organ: all four of the dailies launched during the 1880s had closed down by the end of the decade. Indeed, the spectre of failure shadowed the career of many a publisher wherever he worked.

Starting up an enterprise did not necessarily require much capital. True enough, shareholders contributed $102,000 by 1876 to make the Toronto *Mail* a rival of the *Globe*, though that sum was far short of the declared nominal capital of $250,000[38]; but the story goes that Hugh Graham and George Lanigan founded the Montreal *Star* in 1869 with 'something under a hundred dollars in cash capital,' plus the goodwill of a local papermaker.[39] John Ross Robertson, it seems, was able to purchase the assets of the defunct Toronto *Liberal* for $6,000, paying $1,000 immediately, to allow publication of his *Telegram*.[40] In 1880 *L'Électeur*, the Liberal party's new organ in Quebec City, boasted capital of a mere $5,000.[41] Ten years later, Robert Richardson and Duncan McIntyre together amassed $7,000 to acquire equipment, again from a defunct newspaper, to start the Winnipeg *Tribune*.[42] Sometimes the publisher was able to depend upon the

TABLE 26

Yearly expenses of daily newspapers

	Total (dollars)	Wages/salaries (percentage)	Paper* (percentage)	Operations (percentage)
Toronto *Mail* (October 1875)†	120,000	47.7	35.3	16.9
Ottawa *Journal* (1892)	27,057	63.8	17.4	18.8
Ottawa *Citizen* (April 1900)	48,734	57.3	17.9	24.9
Toronto *Mail and Empire* (February 1903)	240,343	41.9	22.8	35.3
Montreal *Witness* (August 1905)	136,428	47.2	18.7	34.1
Hamilton *Spectator* (September 1905)	86,414	47.0	26.6	26.4
Toronto *News* (December 1907)	232,491	44.5	27.1	28.4

SOURCE: See note 45 to this chapter.

* Toronto *Mail* paper account includes ink, and expenses associated with the salary account; for the Ottawa *Citizen* the paper account is listed as 'supplies'; the Hamilton *Spectator* paper account includes ink.

† The dates indicate the year ending. Ottawa *Journal* figures are for the year 1892.

resources of shareholders – this was true of Patteson's *Mail*, Pacaud's *L'Électeur*. Trudel's *L'Étendard*, and Creighton's *Empire*, for example. Occasionally, the publisher had the backing of a wealthy patron: Robertson received a cheque for $10,000 from Goldwin Smith (never cashed though), P.D. Ross was able to reorganize the Ottawa *Journal* in 1891 because of the goodwill of a local banker, and E.E. Sheppard was funded in 1895 by the capitalist Frederic Nicholls who had purchased the Toronto *Star*.[43] What was called 'political money,' the generosity of well-off businessmen, ready credit, all made it comparatively easy, indeed a bit too easy, to launch a new daily.

The crunch came when the publisher tried to keep his new entry afloat. Essential was a line of credit with some bank or other to ensure solvency while the revenues dribbled in. Patteson, for example, wrote a desperate letter to G. Hague of the Merchants Bank in 1877 begging for $16,000 to tide him over the next few months.[44] The general problem was that yearly expenses were high, given the modest capital necessary to start up (Table 26). Whatever the type or size of the enterprise, the greatest expense was invariably the bill for wages and salaries. Paper costs fluctuated because of the newsprint market and the newspaper's style.

The Toronto *Mail* building ca 1895

The costs of operations grew slowly over the years because of increasing expenditures on plant, power, and delivery.

The first range of expenses was for housing, plant, and newsprint. Every newspaper needed a building, but the new publisher could get by with rented quarters and rents were not exorbitant. The *Mail* in 1875 listed on its profit-and-loss statement an expenditure of $4,666 (or 3.9 per cent of total costs) for rent, taxes, fuel, and light, the Ottawa *Journal* in 1892 a mere $800 (3.0 per cent) for rent alone, and the Ottawa *Citizen* in 1900 $1,200 (2.5 per cent), again for rent only. Almost every publisher, though, yearned to put up his own building, an event that symbolized permanence and success to the public at large. John Riordon and Christopher Bunting soon gave the *Mail* 'a local habitation and a name' by erecting an imposing domicile at an estimated cost of $100,000.[46] In 1896 the *Globe* proudly announced its new 'handsome structure' at the corner of Yonge and Melinda streets, 'the very heart of the business establishments of Ontario's metropolis.' Built of 'Don Valley pressed brick and red sandstone,' the three-storey home boasted a round tower on the Yonge Street front and an entrance decorated with 'Tennessee marble' – thus 'the whole building appears rich and solid,' a suggestive comment.[47] In 1899 *La Presse* emphasized its pre-eminence by building 'one of the finest newspaper offices in America.' supposedly for $250,000. 'Not to be outdone,' the *Printer and Publisher* (June 1892) added, 'the Star is also making preparations to build magnificent offices on St. James Street.' Publishers were a vain breed.

Expenditures for machinery increased because of the need for new technology to ensure speedy production. The *Mail*'s total bill for start-up equipment (1872) ran to only slightly over $8,000, which included the costs of a small Hoe press, a job press, a steam engine and boiler, and the estimated expense of a folding machine. But in 1878 an observer claimed the eight-cylinder Hoe press used by the Montreal *Witness* had a catalogue price of $30,000 and experience proved a new machine would be needed 'about every five years to keep up with the times.'[48] Prices fortunately held steady thereafter, or at least so the estimated expenditures for new presses in the 1890s suggest: $18,000 for a machine at the Toronto *News* (1892), $25,000 for the 'Scott rotary webb perfecting press' used by the Montreal *Star* and the *Mail and Empire* in 1896, $30,000 for 'a new fast press' sent to the Montreal *Gazette* (1898).[49] The much cheaper Goss and Cox duplex presses, retailing around $7,500, were considered suitable for smaller dailies such as *La Patrie*, the London *Free Press*, the Kingston *Whig*, or the Winnipeg *Tribune*.[50] In addition the publisher of the 1890s had to hand out more money for the new typecasting equipment, at first a bit tricky as P.D. Ross discovered when he bought the wrong brand. The machines Ross initially purchased were typographs at $1,500 each; the machines he later acquired were

SEXTUPLE PRESS

TEN CYLINDER ROTARY TYPE-REVOLVING PRESS

Giant presses

linotypes at $3,000 each, worth the extra cost because of their phenomenal speed.[51] The largest bill was paid by the Montreal *Star* in 1898, a total of $42,000 for 14 linotypes.[52] Once again, smaller dailies could get by with the cheaper monoline at $1,100 apiece: in 1900 *La Patrie* and *Le Journal* (also a Montreal paper) had 8 machines each, the Quebec *Telegraph* and the Quebec *Chronicle* 4 each.[53] That same year, the Ottawa *Citizen* calculated its depreciation expenses at 5 per cent on machinery, 10 per cent on shafting motors, and 20 per cent on the unspecified remnant of the plant.

Supply costs were a major and continuing expenditure and at times a very troublesome problem for the needy publisher. The cost of a new 'dress' of type, estimated at $3,000 a year in the late 1880s,[54] largely disappeared when newspapers switched over to the stereotype process and bought linotype machines. The yearly account for ink at one of the largest newspapers, the *Mail and Empire*, was $2,313 in 1902. The difficulty came with ensuring a generous and cheap supply of quality paper, and publishers constantly dickered with papermakers to find the best deal. Steadily falling prices, especially at the end of the century, were an extraordinary boon to the daily. True, out west scarcity made the publisher's lot seem a hard one: in 1898 W.C. Nichol of the Vancouver *Province* complained that he had on hand three carloads of newsprint at a cost of roughly $3,000, which works out to well over $3.50 per hundred pounds.[55] But in central Canada abundance had given the publisher a distinct edge in any negotiations. In 1899 that gigantic consumer, the Montreal *Star*, which used 12 tons (or one carload) of paper a day, signed a long-term contract with Canada Paper at $1.90 per hundred pounds, the low price because so huge an account was desired by every major papermaker. Even the Ottawa *Journal* was able to bring its costs down from $2.75 in 1896 to $2.03 two years later by playing off Canada Paper against the Eddy Co. Indeed, L.J. Tarte of *La Patrie* claimed he found occasional lots of paper as low as $1.75 or $1.85 (quality unspecified though) – but then Tarte was prepared to get quotes from far, far afield, once Vienna![56] Besides, the typical contract, even the small daily's, boasted a four-month period of credit, the right to return waste paper, and a guarantee of some advertising in the newspaper. It was all proof of how the free market sometimes did work on behalf of the consumer.

The link between consumer and supplier could be very intimate. George Brown and John Riordon enjoyed a profitable but mercurial liaison during the late 1860s and into the 1870s. Brown often placed large orders with Riordon, about $50,000 in 1869 and above $60,000 a year later, but never seemed satisfied with the delivery or the quality, one dispute over payment ending up in the courts in 1874. Ironically, Riordon had on occasion helped to carry the *Globe* with easy credit terms, in 1869–70 holding Brown's note for $25,000.[57] Such generosity was apparently very common, and sometimes abused. In 1876 James Dougall reported that Angus and Logan were supporting 'the Sun till it collapsed, the Star till it collapses and the Bien Public till it collapsed and practically owned everything connected with them.'[58] That could be a route to disaster, for the newspaper and the papermaker – in 1902 *L'Événement* may have owed as much as $130,000 to Canada Paper.[59] The point was that paper companies were a little too willing to bolster flagging enterprises to ensure a market for their newsprint.

A second range of expenses was chargeable to the news and editorial, production, and business departments of the newspaper office. Holding the line on news and editorial costs was always a worry. After all, 'a daily newspaper,' T.C. Patteson argued, 'is good or bad according to the money expended on the preparation of its news.'[60] That truism was supposed to justify Patteson's actions to dubious shareholders: the news and editorial department cost the *Mail* in 1875 $23,808 or almost one-fifth of the total expenditures, proof of Patteson's determination to build a quality newspaper. The *Mail* made very free use of the then expensive telegraph, at a cost of $9,028, which probably included the $20-a-week fee for the Associated Press service. Patteson's costs for editorial staff, correspondents and contributors, and subscriptions were even greater, $11,144, necessary because of the organ's responsibility to cover the public scene. Where he scrimped a bit was on 'Reporters and expenses,' spending a mere $3,636, which seemed to include the salary of the *Mail*'s parliamentary reporter. A breakdown of the actual staff showed the *Mail* employed only one city reporter and one junior reporter, hardly sufficient to supply much news about Toronto.

All but the most prosperous of publishers made some sort of trade-off in their choice of news coverage, although the exact nature of the compromise depended upon the state of finances, the style of the newspaper, or the actions of competitors. Quality newspapers tended to invest heavily in outside newsgathering services. In central Canada, at least, the telegraph's domestic press rates had fallen to 25 cents a hundred words in the early 1880s, cable rates to 5 or 10 cents a word from Great Britain by the mid-1980s, though the tariff was much higher out west.[61] Even so, an ad for the *Manitoba Free Press* in 1892 proudly proclaimed its exclusive rights to the services of the Western Associated Press, the United Press, and something called the Press News Association, which made the Winnipeg daily the premier source of foreign news west of Ontario.[62] A *Printer and Publisher* story in September 1896 showed the *Globe* and the *Mail and Empire* both maintained three representatives at Ottawa, the Montreal *Herald* and *Gazette* (but also the affluent *Star*) two apiece. In 1902 the *Mail and Empire* spent some $9,000 on 'Telegraphing' and $10,000 on 'Correspondence,' or about 8 per cent of its yearly expenditure, a reasonable sum given the stature of the grand tory organ.

Evening or people's dailies were at first more likely to make do with abbreviated dispatches, supplied cheap by the telegraph companies, and concentrate meagre resources on hiring inside staff. The Montreal *Witness* claimed 13 people in its editorial and reporting section in 1878. Ten years later, *La Presse*, hardly then a giant, boasted 4 editorial assistants and 7 contributors, whose subjects ranged as far apart as literature and the workingman. The Toronto *Telegram* steadily built up its staff of reporters from 5 in 1880 to 9 at the end of the decade and 21 in 1906. Smaller newspapers, of course, did things on a much more modest scale. The two leading Conservative organs in the Maritimes, the Halifax *Herald* and the Saint John *Sun*, shared an Ottawa correspondent in 1896. The prosperous but local Hamilton *Spectator* in 1903 spent a mere $548 on 'Correspondence,' $1,719 on 'Telegrams,' and employed 4 reporters. Clearly, the wise publisher was able to judge just how little the public would accept before it became disenchanted.

Ironically, the staff necessary to produce the newspaper usually cost more than the journalists who gathered the news. In 1875 the *Mail* spent $32,075 or over one-quarter of its budget on blue-collar employees. In 1878 the Montreal *Witness* employed 35 compositors, 15 pressmen, and 13 job-printers. Little wonder managers tried to cut wages or staff, which led, of course, to strikes because of the strength of printers' 'chapels.' In 1884 a combined effort of master printers in Toronto to lower wages by 10 per cent sparked a revolt at the *Mail* and *Globe* (apparently the *World* and the *News* agreed to pay the old rates) which hobbled production until both papers found non-union printers.[63] The arrival of typesetting machines seemed to be the means publishers could use to drive down labour costs, if not bust the unions. Indeed, the *Printer and Publisher* (April 1894) noted that the new machines had proved most popular in places such as Toronto, Vancouver, and Victoria where wages were high. The Toronto *News*, once famous as a labour advocate, claimed a saving of roughly $100 a week in its composing room bill in the spring of 1893.[64] A distinct advantage was that publishers could hire green hands – apprentices, and so much cheaper to use to run the machines. The Vancouver *News-Advertiser* and the Ottawa *Citizen*, purportedly, were both able to resist strikes because of the machines.[65]

In fact, the machine did not bring publishers the blessings of the open shop and cheap labour. The increasing size and circulation of newspapers necessitated the employment of many workers. The militancy of the printers meant the ever-present threat of a work stoppage that could harm any newspaper in the era of competition. Few enterprises were quite so vulnerable to disruption as the popular newspaper which had to produce its goods daily to make money. Early in 1892, R.W. Shannon of the Ottawa *Citizen* did use a lock-out to get rid of the typographical union; but some six months later a one-day strike forced him to come to terms with the union demand for workshop control.[66] Around the same time, John Ross Robertson, who had battled with compositors for several years, moved to ensure industrial peace by paying the union fees of his compositors.[67] The insecurity of management kept wages up. In 1898 W.C. Nichol of the Vancouver *Province* bitched about the crippling demands of labour that he had to accept. 'Printers get from $21 a week up. Pressmen and stereotypers the same. The foreman of a news-room thinks he is underpaid if he gets less than $25 a week.'[68] Even in central Canada, where labour costs were lower, savings were never sufficient. By 1902, for example, the *Mail and Empire*'s profit and loss statement showed an expenditure of $54,874 for 'wages (mechanical),' some $10,000 greater than the cost of salaried employees. The progressive mechanization of the printing process had brought, at most, only modest relief to the publisher.

That left only the business department, now very much the heart of the newspaper office. By 1903 the Hamilton *Spectator* employed ten business people, costing $118.50 a week: an advertising manager and two assistants, a city route man and two subscription assistants, two book-keepers, a stenographer, and an office boy. Just as expensive, if not more so, however, were the special salaries and operating costs of the business department. In 1902 the *Mail and Empire* spent $8,777 on its advertising canvass, and a few years later the Toronto *News* listed $2,346 for 'Special Representation.' Then there were the circulation charges: in 1902 the *Mail and Empire* spent a whopping $12,737, in 1903 the *Spectator* something over $2,000 for 33 carriers, and in 1905 the Montreal *Witness*'s 'stable a/c' stood at $2,060. E.J.B. Pense of the Kingston *Whig* estimated in 1900 that paid carrier delivery cost the publisher $1 a year per newspaper, at least in the smaller cities, a bit too rich for a man owning a daily sold at $3 or $4 per annum.[69] Delivery outside the city could be especially costly. In 1875 Patteson reluctantly agreed to pay half the $9,000 it cost for special trains to send the *Mail* and the *Globe* to points west. Few newspapers were so ambitious, the Toronto *News* in the 1890s, for instance, selling its paper wholesale to railway agents or news companies. Right at the end of the century, the elimination of free postage added another cost. Willison angrily charged early in 1901 that the new 'postal tax' cost the *Globe* $10,000 to $12,000 annually.[70] Even P.D. Ross thought that the change would add some $1,200 to $1,500 a year to his bills.[71] All of this showed that the daily had to spend a lot of money to collect its revenues.

Publishers could still earn ancillary revenues from property rentals, the sale of readymade prints, and the like.[72] A traditional sideline was the job contract business, indeed once an inevitable concomitant of newspaper publishing. What could be more natural given the expertise and the plant of the typical newspaper? General jobbing was a way of making good use of excess capacity, whether in skilled labour or machinery. There were quite a number of publishers who continued to operate a job department even at the end of the century: Tarte's sons (*La Patrie*), William Southam (Hamilton *Spectator*), the Dougall family (Montreal *Witness*), Frank Carrel (Quebec *Telegraph*). A couple of party stalwarts managed to get lucrative contracts out of the governments of the day: so, in Saint John, the Conservative *Sun* received contracts worth $50,844 (1891–96) and later the Liberal *Telegraph* $41,711 worth (1896–1901).[73] The bigger publishers, though, had turned away from the old sideline. None of the Toronto dailies, it seems, did job work, at least on any large scale, and neither did the Ottawa *Journal*, the Montreal *Star*, *La Minerve*, or *Le Monde*. It required special, smaller presses, since the giant newspaper presses were hardly suitable to job work. Besides, there was much competition in the field from specialized printers. Early on, the *Mail* had decided to rent its name and facilities to outsiders, eventually William Southam and William Carey. That was a wise move, since in time the Mail Job Printing Co. did very well. 'Few of the big dailies have ever made their job departments pay,' the *Printer and Publisher* (April 1895) claimed, 'but when they were taken over by independent concerns a profitable business was done.' The withdrawal, of course, left the publisher and his staff to concentrate on their primary business, mass communication.

By the 1890s subscriptions and sales generated only about one-third, advertising two-thirds of the general revenues produced by the newspaper itself (Table 27). That represented a change from the days of the first dailies when subscription revenues figured far more significantly in the balance sheet. As late as 1875 the *Mail* still earned more money from sales, though Patteson was aware things were changing. 'It costs, at least the first year's profit from any one subscriber [to the *Weekly Mail*] to get that subscriber,' he argued.[74] Anyway, sales revenues over the next couple of decades did not keep pace with the mounting costs of production. In 1903 the profit-and-loss statement of the Hamilton *Spectator* noted that the paper, ink, and wages necessary to put out the daily edition cost $45,333, with only $23,583 or just over one-half the expenses covered by earned subscriptions. A large circulation was a lot more important than a large subscription revenue.

Newspapers indulged in some strange shenanigans to drum up circulation. Typically, the office gave away all manner of premiums and prizes to people who submitted the names of new subscribers. In the winter of 1877–78, the Montreal *Witness* sent out '136 pairs of skates; 30 gold lockets; 125 gold rings; 40 photograph albums; 82 Pool's weather glass and thermometer combined; 6 magic lanterns; 4 McKinnon pens; 298 chromos of Lady Dufferin and 327 of the

TABLE 27

Yearly income* of daily newspapers

	Total (dollars)	Ads (percentage)	Sales (percentage)
Toronto *Mail* (October 1875)	112,643	48.8	51.2
Ottawa *Journal* (1892)	29,688	63.0	37.0
Ottawa *Citizen* (April 1900)	48,734	67.9	32.1
Hamilton *Spectator* (1902)	75,915	65.5	34.5
Toronto *Mail and Empire* (February 1903)	271,068	63.8	36.2
Montreal *Witness* (August 1905)	110,744	60.8	39.2
Toronto *News* (December 1906)	172,148	76.1	23.9

SOURCE: See note 45 to this chapter.
* Calculated at year ending, except the *Journal* and the *Spectator*

Earl of Dufferin.'[75] Other papers would sell cheap subscriptions to popular magazines or books (often American, sometimes British) or send out art work or even flags to new subscribers. In 1896 the Montreal *Herald* allowed readers to purchase with a book certificate and five cents any volume ('paper cover') listed in its printed catalogue of offerings. Around the same time, the Montreal *Star* pioneered in Canada the 'insurance idea,' paying $500 to the relatives of any *Star* reader or subscriber killed in a railway accident, a plan soon emulated by the Halifax *Chronicle* and the Saint John *Telegraph*.[76] The other classic technique was to whip up some artificial excitement via a special contest. Late in 1889, the Hamilton *Herald* offered readers a ballot they could clip and use to vote for the three best-known men in Hamilton, publishing early results to build enthusiasm. The ever ingenious *Mail* went a step further in 1891 with its province-wide popularity contest for clerics![77] In June 1890 *La Patrie* ran a contest for regular subscribers allowing any number of guesses of the exact number of Montrealers according to the new census, the winner collecting $100.

However silly, none of these giveaways or schemes cost much money. What did were 'bad debts,' price-cutting, and discounts. Every paper suffered the ills of 'bad debts' or unpaid subscriptions. The problem was so common that even Léger Brousseau, whose *Le Courrier du Canada* was popular with the clergy, had difficulties collecting his just revenues.[78] The Ottawa *Citizen* in 1900 allowed 25 per cent on unpaid subscriptions in its 'bad debts' account. The irony was that publishers often carried dead-beats on the books to keep up circulation. Price-cutting was usually a 'war measure' adopted to meet a rival's challenge. So, early in 1895, the Montreal *Gazette* reduced its street price from three to two cents, apparently because the morning *Herald* was at one cent.[79] An earlier estimate suggested that the *Herald*'s reduction had meant a loss of one and one-half cents per copy.[80] Discounting amounted to a hidden loss. The Montreal *Witness*, at least in 1878, sold its one-cent daily to newsboys at 12 papers for eight cents. The two-cent *Globe* in 1897 was offered at $4 a year to the public and $3.25 to dealers. Evening editions of morning papers were normally one cent, and thus cheaper. A common discount was the so-called parliamentary session, later the 'campaign year' subscription – in 1895 the Montreal *Gazette* offered its two-cent daily at the special campaign-year rate of $3. The Toronto *News* and *Star* had their 'dollar dailies' for the country subscriber. The upshot was that circulation was never a good guide to actual sales revenue. A May 1906 survey of the *Mail and Empire*'s circulation showed 38,296 sales which should have yielded, at two cents a copy, around $230,000 a year; in fact, the enterprise earned only $108,501 from sales and subscriptions.[81]

What the publisher did was sell his readers to the prospective advertiser. Indeed, during February 1899, *La Presse* ran on its front page almost a full column explaining the merits of newspaper advertising to the business community. Newpapers were forever touting their virtues as advertising media, whether because of their huge circulation or their special clientele, which suggests a casual recognition of the existence of different markets among the public. See, for instance, the assorted claims that publishers made in McKim's *Directory* of 1901: the London *Free Press* reached 'the classes with the morning, the farmers with the noon, and the masses with the evening edition,' the *Globe* went directly into the homes of Canada's leading people' and *La Patrie* was 'best liked by the better class' of 'French Consumers,' the Montreal *Gazette* influenced 'the minds and money of Montreal to a greater degree than any other newspaper,' and the Vancouver *World* boasted 'an aggregated circulation greater than that of any two newspapers in the west outside of Winnipeg.'

A survey of declared ad rates, published in Ayer's newspaper directories of 1881 and 1886, allows a crude appraisal of the rationale behind the charges that publishers exacted for the right to use their columns (Table 28). A large circulation was not necessarily any indication a publisher would ask the highest actual per-issue rate. The Montreal *Star* and *Le Monde*, both circulation leaders in their respective arenas, had very low charges by comparison with their rivals. True, the leaders in Toronto, the *Globe* and the *Mail*, did charge advertisers a comparatively hefty sum. The reason lay in the market strategy of the particular newspapers.

TABLE 28

Comparative advertising rates 1880 and 1885

	Circulation	Per month (dollars)	Per issue (cents)*	Comparison (percentage)
HALIFAX				
1880				
Acadian Recorder (E)†	2,250	5.00	0.0022222	40.2
Chronicle (M)‡	3,100	5.00	0.0016129	29.2
Citizen (E)	1,500	8.30	0.0055333	100.0
Herald (M)	3,000	6.00	0.002	36.1
Mail (E)	3,000	6.00	0.002	36.1
1885				
Acadian Recorder (E)	4,000	6.25	0.0015625	40.3
Chronicle (M)	3,432	5.00	0.0014568	37.6
Citizen (E)	2,142	8.30	0.0038748	100.0
Herald (M)	3,200	5.00	0.0015625	40.3
Mail (E)	3,600	5.00	0.0013888	35.8
SAINT JOHN				
1880				
Globe (E)	4,000	7.00	0.00175	72.9
News (M)	3,000	5.00	0.0016666	69.4
Sun (M)	2,500	6.00	0.0024	100.0
Telegraph (M and E)	4,500	5.00	0.0011111	46.3
1885				
Globe (E)	4,000	5.00	0.00125	62.5
Sun (M)	2,500	5.00	0.002	100.0
Telegraph (M)	4,800	5.00	0.0010416	52.1
ENGLISH MONTREAL				
1880				
Gazette (M)	5,000	10.00	0.002	60.0
Herald (M)	3,000	10.00	0.0033333	100.0
Star (E)	15,914	10.00	0.0006283	18.9
Witness (E)	13,377	8.00	0.000598	17.9
1885				
Gazette (M)	6,000	10.00	0.0016666	68.3
Herald (M)	4,100	10.00	0.002439	100.0
Star (E)	24,956	20.00	0.0008014	32.9
Witness (E)	14,265	10.00	0.000701	28.7
FRENCH MONTREAL				
1880				
Le Courrier (M and E)	3,500	6.00	0.0017142	60.0
La Minerve (M and E)	3,500	10.00	0.0028571	100.0
Le Monde (M and E)	8,350	4.00	0.000479	16.8
La Patrie (E)	5,000	13.50	0.0027	94.5

TABLE 28 continued

	Circulation	Per month (dollars)	Per issue (cents)*	Comparison (percentage)
1885				
L'Étendard (M and E)	6,000	10.00	0.0016666	91.7
La Minerve (M)	5,500	10.00	0.0018181	100.0
Le Monde (N§ and E)	15,113	5.00	0.0003308	18.2
La Patrie (E)	8,000	6.50	0.0008125	44.7
La Presse (M and E)	13,090	6.50	0.0004965	27.3
TORONTO				
1880				
Globe (M and E)	23,000	26.00	0.0011304	90.4
Mail (M and E)	22,558	26.00	0.0011525	92.2
Telegram (E)	14,000	10.00	0.0007142	57.1
World (E)	8,000	10.00	0.00125	100.0
1885				
Globe (M and E)	25,500	39.00	0.0015294	90.2
Mail (M and E)	23,000	39.00	0.0016956	100.0
News (M and E)	19,500	26.00	0.0013333	78.6
Telegram (E)	15,296	12.50	0.0008172	48.2
World (M)		10.00		

SOURCE: Ayer's newspaper directories, 1881 and 1886, which list for every paper their declared per-month rate for a ten-line block

* 'Per issue' cost refers to the rate for a ten-line block of advertising and is calculated by dividing the monthly rate by the circulation; the comparison is based on the largest per-issue cost.

† Evening

‡ Morning

§ Noon

An 'up-market' daily, a quality or party organ usually selling its main edition in the morning, reached a selected clientele of men (notably professionals, businessmen, and the 'leisured') with considerable purchasing power, so it could demand a high tariff. And since circulation totals were roughly similar between these rivals, their high monthly rates were often the same: the *Herald* and *Chronicle* in Halifax (1885), the *Gazette* and *Herald* in English Montreal, *La Minerve* and *L'Étendard* in French Montreal (1885), the *Globe* and *Mail* in Toronto.

A 'down-market' daily, a people's journal, might reach a much broader spectrum of the public, but that audience included lots of women and workingmen who would only excite advertisers interested in mass selling. Actual per-issue rates and declared monthly rates were likely to be lower. Competition in the evening market forced *La Patrie*, boasting the highest monthly rate (at $13.50) in 1880, to accept a dramatic reduction (to $6.50) to compare with the charges of *Le Monde* and *La Presse*, though Beaugrand's actual per-issue tariff was substantially higher. Success enabled the Montreal *Star* to jack up its monthly charge from $10 to $20, without disturbing the earlier ranking of comparative rates. The similar styles of the three Saint John dailies in 1885, plus the small size of the market, probably explains their common monthly rate of $5.

There were some anomalies, however, that defy explanation. Why in 1880 and again in 1885 did the lowly *Citizen*, the evening satellite of the *Chronicle*, charge the highest per-issue and monthly rates in Halifax? How could the *World* in 1880 and the *News* in 1885 demand so much more money by comparison with the *Telegram*, the dominant paper in city homes in Toronto? What accounts for the common monthly rate charged by those jointly owned papers, the morning *Herald* and the evening *Mail* in Halifax? Are we to question the business acumen of some publishers? In fact, not enough information has appeared to explain the reason for every action.

Still, we do know things were and remained pretty chaotic in the ad business. Publishers, it seemed, were forever discounting or selling off their space below the declared rate. Competition, especially in the 1890s, probably brought a slight decline in advertising charges. The *Printer and Publisher* (April 1895) gave the example of one national advertiser, the makers of 'Scott's Emulsion,' who, by dealing directly with newspapers, had been able to secure space for the lowest price less the 25 per cent commission hitherto paid an agency. Anson McKim, owner of an ad agency, claimed that Fortier's, a big cigarmaker, had persuaded 65 papers to insert six inches for one year for a box of cigars.[82] The pressures on the publisher or manager to reduce rates were, in fact, considerable. The very rhythm of the advertising year worked against the publisher: the post-Christmas and summer lulls could bring a serious cash-flow problem if he did not secure some business. The publisher, moreover, faced a particular difficulty that prevented any 'cast iron' adherence to rates. His 'commodity' was no more than 'blank space,' 'which has cost him a certain price and must be filled with something that will bring a return, else he makes a loss,' McKim argued. 'Unlike any other commodity, that which remains unsold immediately passes out of existence.'[83]

A lucrative source of revenue, indeed a circulation booster, could be the famous 'wants,' classified ads for jobs or workers, houses and rentals, articles for sale, and so on which made the paper popular with the masses. That was why the people's journals took special pains to win this custom. In April 1870 the Montreal *Star* introduced cheap rates for wants, 'solely with the hope of receiving them in sufficient numbers to make them a feature of news.[84]' *The Globe*'s early dominance in the field – 'the wants of masters and servants being an especial source of revenue'[85] – was eventually overthrown by the Toronto *Telegram*, dubbed the 'penny-a-word emporium' because of Robertson's low rate.[86] By 1886 the Toronto *News* advertised a rate of ten words for 5 cents. Even the *Globe* broke down, by 1895 offering ten words for six days at 40 cents to employees only. In short, the charges for classified ads fell dramatically, again to meet competition and please readers. In 1901 the *Manitoba Free Press* boasted more 'wants' than any other morning paper in Canada, apparently to attract big-name advertisers.[87] Most papers probably garnered only a modest sum from their classifieds: in 1905, for example, less than 10 per cent or $6,426 of the total $70,139 the Hamilton *Spectator* earned in ad revenue came from classifieds. Only a very few, notably the *Telegram*, got fat off the 'wants' of the masses.

Far more important, then, was display advertising, particularly for retail outlets and, by the 1890s, brand-name goods. The birth of mass-consumption industries could well mean a golden stream of money for the shrewd publisher, since the manufacturer and the department store needed considerable advertising space to sell their wares to the greater public. Again rates varied. In 1895 Ross remarked that he charged a regular advertiser $45, or two cents a line, for a one-time, full-page ad in the smallish Ottawa *Journal*.[88] An agent in 1899 claimed he could buy a thousand lines in the Montreal *Star* or *La Presse* for $50 each, or five cents a line.[89]

What all publishers wanted, though, was a large volume of contract ads which would ensure a regular income as well as filler throughout the year. Competition here could be brutal. Early in 1886, the Toronto *Telegram* bragged that it offered city merchants an exceptional rate, a mere $300 a year to run daily a 40-line ad which would reach well over 15,000 homes in Toronto. By contrast, the 'Tely' continued, the overblown *Globe* charged $900 for an equivalent ad that reached only 7,000 odd homes in the city, however many the subscribers in the countryside.[90] Perhaps in response, the *Globe* a short-time later offered a new scale of $748.80 for a 40-liner.[91]

Publishers strove to regularize this kind of custom – the Montreal *Herald*, for instance, eventually insisted clients demanding a page or half-page now and then insert at least 20 lines a day to keep their option alive.[92] Newspapers also usually charged more for large type or illustrations, so the Montreal *Witness* told clients such ads must pay a double rate.[93] Similarly, the Ottawa *Citizen* in 1902 had a standard rate of $6 a line per year for an insertion in 'first position,' at the top of the column and alongside reading matter where it was more likely to catch the consumer's eye. When the Hamilton *Spectator* took front-page ads, the most favoured location, apparently the rate was around $8 a line.[94] Success, however, could be a trifle embarrassing: late in 1900, swollen advertising columns threatened to overwhelm the reading matter necessary to the reputation of the *Manitoba Free Press*.[95] The whole task of adjusting space, setting rates, and dickering with clients or agents had obviously become a very complicated business.

This discussion raises the crucial question of the worth of a newspaper. Unfortunately, that is difficult to answer since the determination of 'worth' depends on the eye of the beholder, and therefore the result is different to the credit agency, a prospective buyer, or the proprietor himself. The newspaper usually had such tangible assets as cash or savings, real estate and perhaps a building, the actual plant and inventory, but these might be encumbered by debts. Especially important was the amount of business done, that is the actual expenditures and revenues, as well as the result – either a profit or a loss. The final component was something called goodwill, a term that nowadays represents 'the potential of a business to earn above "normal" profits.'[96] In the nineteenth century, however, even the name of a losing property might enjoy some value. Indeed, on occasion, political exigencies set a value on a newspaper far higher than any commercial considerations could warrant.

The credit ledgers of Dun's mercantile agency, assembled by anonymous reporters, make clear that most of the first dailies were pretty modest enterprises. In 1858 Donald McDonald, a publisher of the Montreal *Transcript*, had a printing office valued at about $8,000, debts of $3,000, and a personal worth estimated at $9,000 or $10,000, no doubt buoyed up by his good reputation. A few years later, S.B. Foote, a tea merchant and owner of the London *Prototype*, purchased the Quebec *Chronicle* for around $16,000, a high price for the day but reasonable given the paper's significance to the local business community plus the favour of the government. Charles Annand in 1871 supposedly had 'means' of $10,000 to $15,000 and his Halifax *Chronicle* was called 'a very good ppty in itself.' In 1877 Ellis and Armstrong, owners of the Saint John *Globe*, were thought to be worth $8,000 to $12,000 and their paper prosperous because it was a 'Government organ.' Then there was the praiseworthy Dougall family who by dint of hard work had brought their *Witness* up to a value of $50,000 by 1875, purportedly paying them $10,000 to $15,000 a year.[97] A hidden asset was John's marriage into the Redpath family, the sugar barons, which may well have helped him overcome the effects of an insolvency action in 1864.

New competition and bad judgment could easily undo past gains. Rollo Campbell, publisher of the Montreal *Pilot*, was one such victim of changing fortunes: in 1857 the Dun reporter estimated his personal worth at $25,000 to $30,000, in part because of generous printing contracts from the government; but in 1862 his paper folded, hurt by the competition of the *Witness* and the fall of a friendly government, perhaps too by 'his love of strong drink.'[98] Another victim was James Beaty, a leather merchant and landowner, whose Toronto *Leader* (managed by nephew Robert) was purportedly making a profit of $10,000 a year in the mid-1860s. The competition first of the *Telegraph* and then the *Mail* ate away at Beaty's profits, and soon the Dun reporter began to note a decline, a final entry in 1873 suggesting his means (including more than the newspaper, though) had fallen from $250,000 to $150,000.[99]

Much the most interesting tale, however, arose from the troubles of George Brown who, great entrepreneur though he might be, proved a rotten business manager. Even in the beginning, Dun reporters had commented critically on his penchant for getting into debt and his failure to pay debts promptly. The business depression of the late 1850s and land speculation in Lambton County put him in desperate straits and he was saved only by the prosperous *Globe* which was supposedly bringing in $800 to $900 a day in receipts in 1861. Although Brown worked his way out of the mess, helped by good times and the sale of his Lambton properties, he soon invested in another loser, the Bow Park farm, which by 1873 was draining off *Globe* revenues. A reporter in 1874, totalling up mortgages and debts, decided the Globe Printing Co.'s 'needy condition seems to have become chronic.'[100] The strain of competition with the *Mail* and the expense of new machinery left the company in debt to the tune of $61,308 in 1880, just before Brown's death.[101] Worse yet, Brown's extravagance had forced sale of control of the paper to outsiders, thus defeating his determination to ensure the future security of his family.

Penury was a constant problem in press circles during the new era of competition. Too many publishers seemed never to have sufficient capital, and they quickly fell into debt to support not just improvements but routine operations as well. Robertson's *Telegraph*, after years of fruitless activity and heavy losses, was valued in 1872 by Hunter & Rose at $24,000, 'plant & establishment' worth $21,000 and 'subscription list & goodwill' at $3,000.[102] Patteson's *Mail* seemed to begin well, with at one point $102,000 paid-up capital, but $70,000 of this was sunk into 'establishing a business and a goodwill.' At the beginning the enterprise was actually losing $100 a day, though Patteson claimed that figure had been brought down to $15 in 1875. In fact, the *Mail* lost $7,000 in 1875 and $9,000 in 1876, its efforts hamstrung by the *Globe*'s hegemony and the commercial depression. Patteson admitted the plant was 'not worth more than $15,000 at a forced sale,' an argument used to justify issuing a chattel mortgage to the papermaker Riordon. In the autumn of 1877, Riordon took over the paper in payment of a debt of more than $26,000, other creditors (including a second paper company) accepting 25 cents on the dollar.[103] Then there was that classic hardship case, the Toronto *World*, begun in 1880 with a hope and a prayer. It was forced to suspend publication briefly in April 1884.[104] Rejuvenation did not much change its fortunes: during the early

1890s, Hector Charlesworth remarked, 'it had seldom supplies of paper for more than a few issues and sometimes hardly enough for one.'[105]

Similar difficulties dogged efforts of francophone publishers; these kept the value of their newspapers low. The highest price paid for any French-Canadian newspaper was the $38,000 which Dansereau and associates collected for *La Minerve* in 1880, and that was overpriced given the paper's weak performance thereafter.[106] Maurice Laframboise reportedly lost $30,000 trying to make the Liberal *Le National* of Montreal a viable journal during the 1870s.[107] W.E. Blumhart had unloaded *Le Monde*, debts and goodwill, on Hector Langevin in 1884 for $28,000; a company formed four years later went into liquidation in the summer of 1892, with the property soon purchased by a syndicate (including of all people Berthiaume) for $22,000 and then quickly sold to the Sénécals and associates in October for $1,000 more.[108] Joseph-Israel Tarte of *Le Canadien* declared bankruptcy in late 1892, leaving assets of $17,500 and liabilities of $32,700.[109] *L'Étendard*, a shareholder's concern, failed in April 1893, leaving assets of $32,700 and liabilities of $69,132.[110] Publishing was definitely not a route to financial security in Quebec, however much it might pay off in terms of prestige or influence.

The unsteady career of the Montreal *Herald* showed that even a lot of money could not ensure success against severe competition. Once, back in 1857, a Dun reporter had called the *Herald* 'the best paying paper published 'in the city, and it remained in fine shape during the next decade and a half.[111] During the mid-1870s the property was purchased by a new company for $60,000 cash and $20,000 in stock, Lucius Seth Huntington (a Liberal chieftain) being the largest shareholder with an investment of $40,000. The fierce rivalry engendered by the challenge of the *Gazette* and the *Star* so hurt the paper that the new company never payed a dividend.

Perhaps in 1881, one William Glendenning bought Huntington's *Herald* shares for $30,000, only to discover the paper was losing $10,000 to $12,000 a year. That brought on a financial crisis three years later, when such creditors as Buntin and Boyd ($15,000) and Canada Paper ($7,000) demanded payment. A syndicate headed by Peter Mitchell offered $20,000 cash, plus the $15,000 realizable on existing accounts, for the property.[112] Mitchell did get the paper, though for what price is unclear, and proceeded to run it into the ground. Indeed, in 1891 the *Herald* went to the New England Paper Co. for a mere $9,000.[113] The next year, Liberal money bought the paper back to serve again as the party's mouthpiece. Fire, which twice cursed the *Herald* in the 1880s, struck once more in 1893, consuming the whole building. Fortunately, in June 1894 Alexander McLean and J.C. Rogers, two former queen's printers, came with $30,000 to rejuvenate the luckless enterprise.[114]

The last shuffle occurred in January 1897 when J.S. Brierley arrived from Ontario, where he had owned two small papers, to turn the *Herald*'s fortunes around. An early move, unsuccessful, was an offer to merge with the *Witness*, also on the rocks, and thereby leave one strong Liberal daily in the morning and evening markets.[115] What helped Brierley was the return to office of friends, in Ottawa and Quebec city: the Liberal government in Ottawa, between 1896 and 1901, lavished advertising and printing contracts worth almost $100,000 on the *Herald*. Meanwhile, the circulation figures in McKim's *Directory* of 1901 at last indicated that the paper's total switch into the evening arena had begun to produce more readers. The *Herald*, clearly, was an indispensable daily to Liberals, which gave it a worth far greater than the market might assign.

In contrast, the Riordon story demonstrated the distinct advantages that a generous capital could bring to a newspaper. Charles Riordon was the millionaire papermaker fortunate enough to control the Toronto *Mail* and the Toronto *News* – two prime consumers of newsprint. He had, as well, some excellent business talent on hand, Christopher Bunting, longtime manager of the *Mail*, and his successor, W.J. Douglas (related to Riordon by marriage), plus Thomas Dyas, one of the best of the new breed of advertising managers. The *News* mattered little, except as a newsprint buyer. Riordon called in his $75,000 mortgage on the property in 1887, turning the management over to Douglas. During the 1890s the paper embarked on a wild career as a dollar daily, which, whatever its results, must have pleased Riordon's paper mills. In 1903 he sold off the newspaper for an estimated $150,000, an inflated figure given the huge losses the *News* suffered thereafter (perhaps as much as $255,000 in five years).

The *Mail* was treated with much greater care. Rumour had it that by 1893 the paper actually cleared $7,000 the year previous, something of a feat considering the crowded Toronto market.[116] The great coup, engineered by Bunting, was the acquisition early in 1895 of the *Empire*, an organ whose seven-year losses were estimated at around $150,000.[117] The deal gave the *Empire*'s shareholders $125,000 of paid-up *Mail* stock and a guarantee of the paper's loyalty to the Conservative cause. Better yet, the *Mail*'s proprietors had the right to purchase back the stock for $30,000 after 18 months, an option exercised in November 1896.[118] The merger may not have brought any immediate circulation gains but it clearly did bolster ad revenues. And the circulation boomed during the halcyon days at the end of the century. In 1902 the *Mail and Empire* made a profit of $30,725, or over 10 per cent, on revenues of $271,068. That made the paper a worthy property indeed.[119]

The success of the Southam family was of a different sort, a rags-to-riches tale which proved devotion to the work ethic sometimes did bring an earthly reward after all. The story began with William Southam, once a newsboy for the

London *Free Press*, and later an apprentice printer and member of the local mechanics' institute, who eventually acquired a part interest in the *Free Press*. In 1877 Southam and William Carey, a friend, purchased the flagging Hamilton *Spectator*, perhaps for as little as $6,000, aided by a consortium of local capitalists (including John Riordon) whose shares were soon bought up by the partners. The Hamilton *Spectator* proved a great little moneymaker, even when the one-cent *Herald* entered the lists in 1889, and by the end of the 1890s the *Spectator*'s profits had risen above $10,000 a year.

Meanwhile, the Southam-Carey partnership had expanded into the printing business, taking over the *Mail*'s job work in 1881 and sending Southam's son Fred off to start up another printing shop in Montreal in 1889. Both experiments were successful: the Montreal operation earned a net profit of $30,000 in 1900 and the *Mail* company almost $20,000 in 1902. Then in 1897 William Southam financed two more sons by purchasing the troubled Ottawa *Citizen* for $9,000 plus book debts. Wilson and Harry Southam moved the paper to new quarters, bought a Goss press, and soon invaded the evening market. Success came again – the *Citizen* started showing a profit in 1900.

Already, the wise Southams were spending their surplus profits on a range of investments. The financial statement of Southam Ltd. in December 1904 indicated holdings of $15,000 in Cataract Power, $35,000 in 'Hamilton and Fort William Nav. Co.,' and a whopping $67,500 in Hamilton Steel and Iron. Indeed, the total assets approached $900,000, including half interest in the Spectator Printing Co. ($130,000) and full control of the Ottawa Citizen Co. ($247,000). Of course, these values were inflated, a common practice in those days of casual accounting, but the achievement remained impressive, especially given the firm's humble beginnings.[120]

The Southam's success story, and even less the *Mail and Empire*'s triumph, were hardly outstanding in the annals of Canadian capitalism. A phenomenon of the age was the arrival of superprofits and large pools of capital, in finance, transport, and resource development especially, sufficient to create a 'Big Business.' No newspaper ranked with the true giants such as the Canadian Pacific Railway, Dunsmuir and Son, to say nothing of the assorted banks. Indeed, Dun's mercantile agency displayed a certain disdain for the run-of-the-mill daily (Table 29). Its listing, for example, placed the three Hamilton newspapers far behind the 18 local firms that could boast an 'estimated pecuniary strength' greater than $125,000. True enough, a proprietor might well disagree with such a view, his balance sheet showing a good range of assets. But these valuations were wildly optimistic: the statement of the Ottawa *Citizen* in 1900, for example, claimed assets of $107,340, including $22,333 in goodwill and $46,000 of treasury

TABLE 29

The worth and credit of selected newspapers 1899

	'Estimated pecuniary strength'	'General credit'
Saint John		
Globe Publishing Co	10,000–20,000	Good
Sun Printing Co	5,000–10,000	Fair
Quebec		
Frank Carrel (*Telegraph*)	3,000–5,000	Fair
Thomas Chapais (*Le Courier du Canada*)	3,000–5,000	Good
Montreal		
Graham and Co (*Star*)	300,000–500,000	High
T. Berthiaume (*La Presse*)	35,000–50,000	Good
Ottawa		
C.W. Mitchell (*Free Press*)	50,000–75,000	High
Ottawa Citizen Co	20,000–35,000	High
Journal Printing Co	10,000–20,000	High
Toronto		
J. Ross Robertson (*Telegram*)	125,000–200,000	High
Hamilton		
Spectator Printing Co	10,000–20,000	High
Times Printing Co	20,000–35,000	High
Herald Printing Co	10,000–20,000	
London		
Free Press Printing Co	35,000–50,000	Good
News Printing Co	10,000–20,000	Good
Victoria		
Times Publishing Co	10,000–20,000	Good

SOURCE: R.G. Dun & Co., *The Mercantile Agency Reference Book* (1899)

stock, which meant in fact only a one-third of the total value was made up of tangible assets. And the profit margins of the popular newspaper did not inspire any great excitement, even among publishers. 'Only a baker's dozen of the Canadian press are making over a few thousand dollars a year,'' W.C. Nichol complained, 'and the majority of them barely manage to keep their heads above water.'[121] A bit extreme perhaps, but not far off the truth: among a sprinkling of profit figures from the 1890s that have come to light, the highest were Robertson's supposed $20,000 a year in 1891 and Graham's reported $45,000 in 1898.[122] Finally, the assorted sales figures at the end of the century show most properties could still be purchased cheap: Tarte's sons acquired *La Patrie* in

1897 for around $27,000, Clifford Sifton valued his new share in the *Manitoba Free Press* at a little over $60,000, Frederic Nicholls sold the Toronto *Star* in 1899 for $32,000, and the same year B.F. Pearson bought the Halifax *Chronicle*, its evening *Echo*, and its weekly *Nova Scotian*, for a paltry $16,500.[123]

Perhaps had an ambitious soul prepared a 'Top 200' of the leading manufacturing or retail firms, then a property such as the Montreal *Star* or the Toronto *Globe* would have ranked well. The transformation of the newspaper business was akin to changes in merchandising and manufacturing. This A.H.U. Colquhoun, editor of the *Printer and Publisher*, recognized in a short, reflective essay on the business in December 1898. He pointed first to 'a marked cheapening in the principal processes of publishing a newspaper.' Twenty-five years earlier, 'the price of paper was much higher, matter had to be set by hand, and the expense of telegraphing and correspondence was considerably heavier.' The fall in the unit cost of newspaper production had sparked an expansion of the daily press. Yet the savings 'appear not to have gone into the pockets of the publisher, but into the pockets of the public.' Indeed, the vigorous competition had made the publisher's life more precarious. 'Advertising rates have fallen and subscriptions have declined, until it is becoming a question in the newspaper business, just as it is becoming a question in mercantile life, where [sic] the present condition, being abnormal, can last.' The true beneficiaries of a transformed journalism, then, were the readers. The popular newspaper, like the department store or the shirt factory, had adjusted to the regimen of the mass market.

THE BUSINESS IMPERATIVE

'The chief aim of this paper will be to more thoroughly unite the Printers and Publishers of Canada,' declared the *Printer and Publisher* in its first number (May 1892), 'and through such united effort to increase the diminishing revenues of the printing office.' J.B. Maclean's brainchild was supposed to be the authentic voice of a nascent industry. Maclean, never a slouch, wished his publication to speak not just for big city dailies but also for country weeklies, town dailies, magazine and book publishers, job printing shops (even adding later a special section on the pulp and paper business). Still, during the 1890s at least, the special favourite was the newspaper industry – an industry, Maclean thought, that the big city publishers should lead toward some golden future. His way of binding together the new constituency was to preach a gospel of profit. 'Is it not a fact that we are all too busy looking after the interests of everyone but the printer to think of ourselves?' asked the *Printer and Publisher*? 'Co-operation is the great watchword of the latter half of the nineteenth century,' this preacher said a few months later, 'and the lack of it has caused the printing and publishing trades to suffer more and bear heavier burdens than other classes of the business community.'[124] So the gospel of profit combined that obligatory sense of grievance, a devotion to the idea of mutual protection, and a determination to make newspapering a proper business.

In fact, Maclean was preaching to the converted. Little wonder the periodical became the official organ of the Canadian Press Association, an Ontario body with a Montreal tail that was the model for press organizations across the country. Indeed, the CPA was the first ever press organization, its birth dating from a Kingston meeting of assorted journalists back in 1859.[125] Then, and for many years afterwards, the life of the CPA had been determined by a kind of fraternal imperative. True enough, CPA leaders did do some lobbying on the issue of postage rates and libel laws and even extracted from the railways a reduced fare for members that was valuable to the working journalist. But CPA meetings were usually occasions for good times and high-falutin rhetoric about the glories of the press, CPA energies devoted mostly to organizing a summer excursion bigger and better than the year before. The most memorable was a trip west in 1882 when the Canadian Pacific Railway supplied a special train for these special tourists. Ironically, the organization was hobbled by the indifference of big-city publishers, and especially the distrust of George Brown who looked upon the CPA as a platform for his enemies. (The founding father of the CPA was a deep-died tory, William Gillespie of the Hamilton *Spectator*.) The CPA represented little more than an idea, since neither a profession nor an industry was really in existence.

Things changed suddenly in the late 1880s as a result of the lean times linked to the industrialization of journalism. What admirers liked to call 'live publishers,' particularly in the big cities, began to take an interest in the proceedings of the CPA. In 1888 the decision was made to hold a winter business meeting. The first was organized for the following February. Its proceedings were published in an annual report, which thereafter became standard practice. The summer parties and the normal excursions died out because of a lack of interest. The revamped CPA was emphatically a business association first, a professional gathering second. 'We are a band of business men gathered together for the advancement of our business interests,' claimed J.S. Brierley, a future president, 'and incidently for the promotion of good-fellowship.'[126] The meetings collected publishers and managers, or at least their representatives: suggestive of the new mood was the role of one Arthur Samalice of *La Presse*, who noted that he was 'speaking for Mr. Berthiaume' in a debate on the postage issue at the meeting of 1897.[127] The topics dominating the decade's agenda were the virtues of typecasting machinery, proper delivery systems, what to do about national advertising, subscription rates, the postage tax, libel laws, and so on. Papers on the ethics of journalism or the way to make a better newspaper there were, but never in great numbers. Even the presidential addresses focused on the problems of the industry.

The hot gospellers of profit wanted an end to the Bad Old Days of 'senseless competition' when partisan and business rivalries had made publishers bitter enemies. The protective impulse was no less a force among publishers than among lawyers, merchants, farmers, or workers. 'Much more can be done by associated action than by individual effort,' declared CPA president A.F. Pirie in 1894.[128] In Toronto and Montreal, for instance, there was a good deal of chatter about strengthening ties to meet the menace of organized labour. Indeed, during 1892 the *Printer and Publisher* took up the cause of the United Typothetae of America, a body then headed by a Canadian (W.A. Sheppard), who called for a union of master printers to defend managerial prerogatives against 'the arrogated rights of trade unions.'[129] In a smaller arena, P.D. Ross was one publisher who listened well to the siren song of restriction – he and his fellows in Ottawa in 1895 agreed to keep up advertising rates and drop 'dead-beat' subscribers, so defeating citizens who tried to exploit press rivalry.[130] That agreement did not prevent a fight a few years later when the Southams upset the market with an evening *Citizen*, though.[131] The wages of competition, it seemed, were too high for even a great nag such as the *Printer and Publisher* to persuade proprietors of the wisdom of some kind of newspaper combine.

Besides, both the *Printer and Publisher* and the CPA displayed far more interest in press dealings with partner enterprises. The boom in consumer advertising during the 1890s sponsored a series of advertising agencies, the recognized leader being A. McKim's, which had the skills necessary to manage nationwide campaigns. At first, many horror stories gathered around the activities of this classic middleman. 'In one case it was discovered that Mr. McKim was offering advertising to one paper at about one-third the rate he was proposing to his principal,' asserted Ross. 'In addition, out of the newspaper's third he would have got his usual 25 per cent commission.'[132] In fact, much of the blame lay with the publishers themselves, something A. McKim and the *Printer and Publisher* soon made clear. Big newspapers managed to get on well with agencies: the Montreal *Star* and the Toronto *Telegram* allowed only 15 per cent on all contracts, and the Toronto dailies generally never paid commissions on local advertising.[133] The *Printer and Publisher* urged publishers to deal honestly with the agency, even open their circulation books to prove good faith. The CPA championed the idea of a uniform advertising contract to ensure a fair price for newspaper space. The agencies were 'useful,' as C.N. Taylor, the *Globe*'s manager, put it, because they encouraged new business.[134] The *Printer and Publisher* noted in 1898 that McKim's was placing ads with dailies everywhere for 'Whitlam's "never-slip" rubber sole shoe' and 'Sir John Power's Irish Whiskey,' the next year spending almost $15,000 on Toronto, Montreal, Ottawa, and Winnipeg dailies for advertising Kennedy's '"Semi-Ready" clothing.'[135] When McKim died many years later, grateful publishers arranged a special memorial fund, proof of the happier times that his efforts had brought the press.[136]

Dealings with news agencies caused another set of problems. The complaint here was not over charges so much as quality. The demand for news had made dailies heavily dependent on the world reports supplied by American agencies via the telegraph companies: according to a survey in 1895, 33 papers subscribed to the 'United Press' service, 14 to its 'Associated Press' rival.[137] The difficulty was that the agencies furnished a biased version of happenings. 'Le plus petit incident survenu dans un village inconnu des Etats-Unis pour est télégraphée avec force details,' argued *Le Monde* (28 September 1892), 'et c'est à peine si nous recevons un maigre feuillet des nouvelles d'Europe.' 'To extol all that savors of America; to deprecate all that is truly British,' wrote another critic, 'seems to be the inspiration of the news cabled from Great Britain.'[138] A swelling patriotism, and even more the profit motive, led publishers to demand a less Americanized news, more British and European coverage better suited to the tastes of the reading public.[139] Agitation was pointless, since the Canadian custom was too small to persuade American agencies to change their ways; and an alternate world service, funded independently, was far too expensive to attract publishers.[140] Not surprisingly, the two Imperialist dailies, the Montreal *Star* and the Toronto *Telegram*, took the initiative by each financing a special cable service from London. In 1903 the 'Tely's' service was transformed into the Canadian Associated Press, assisted by a grant of $15,000 from the Canadian taxpayer and a like sum from a few daily publishers, to supplement American copy.

In 1900 that last partner enterprise, the newsprint industry, provoked a crisis. After years of falling prices, very pleasing to publishers, a new Papermakers' Association moved swiftly to increase the cost of newsprint via a price-fixing agreement among Canadian firms and a no-trading compact with American rivals. Publishers raised an immediate outcry at the May meeting of the CPA, and the next year the association called upon Ottawa to act under the authority of the anti-combines clause of the Tariff Act, the first time such a demand had been made. A compliant government soon arranged a royal commission inquiry which established and condemned the existence of the price-fixing agreement. Even before the commission hearings got under way, the Papermakers' Association had voluntarily rolled back prices, though not to what it considered the ruinous levels of 1899. And, early in 1902, Finance Minister W.S. Fielding (himself an ex-editor) lowered slightly the duties on imported newsprint.[141] It was a modest victory for the free market, a grand victory for the CPA which had won wide support among publishers. Indeed, the newspaper industry had proved it had some clout in the higher reaches of government.

That seemed a welcome change after years of neglect. A persistent cry during the 1890s was for the Canadian government to extend its protectionist embrace over journalism. Much effort was expended trying to get provincial authorities in Ontario and Quebec to alter the libel laws so that publishers would not be threatened by every disgruntled reader and needy lawyer. There were hopes that the customs officers and the police would act to block the arrival or sale of American Sunday papers which cut into the market for the publishers' Saturday specials. The CPA as well as the *Printer and Publisher* wanted Ottawa to reduce import duties on a range of supplies and machinery necessary to the manufacture of newspapers. Then there was the demand the post office do something to hinder the circulation of advertising 'fakes,' masquerading as newspapers and thus mailed free of charge. That issue died when in 1897 Ottawa moved toward the reimposition of mail rates for newspapers. Ironically, here, the CPA could take little action because its members were split between local and metropolitan publishers. But the point is that the press, like so much of the business world, had become a supplicant at the government's door. What could be better proof of the industry's coming of age?

4

The daily fare

'It is absolutely necessary to make a good paper in order to do a good business,' declared a smug E.E. Sheppard in 1895.[1] Perhaps this was the case. But what made a 'good paper'? Sheppard's two tries, the Toronto *News* in the 1880s and the Toronto *Star* in the mid-1890s, did not show that he had any magic answer. Newspapers always sold a package of advertising, entertainment and education, news and views. Convention certainly, sometimes technology as well, ruled what would appear and how it would be presented. That might suggest the newspaper was a settled product. However, the search for popularity ensured that the newspaper's offerings would alter or shift each decade to suit a wider and wider audience.

FORMS: THE MID-CENTURY NEWSPAPER

Journalism, like any significant cultural activity, employs definite forms through which it brings its particular kinds of messages to the public.[2] Newspapers have a distinct 'look' and 'feel' that sets them apart from, say, magazines or books. That way any reader knows roughly what he may expect to find. The analysis of forms can tell us something about the purpose of journalism as well as the place of the press in the wider network of social institutions.

The following investigation of forms employs a close description of the issue of the Toronto *Globe* which appeared on Thursday, 11 April 1850. The *Globe* was then a solidly established tri-weekly, as representative of the genre as any other leading paper. But the investigation also compares the *Globe*'s 'look' and 'feel' to the forms used by other papers of the late 1840s and early 1850s, to ensure that the distinction between convention and eccentricity stands out.

The *Globe* offered the reader 28 columns of matter on four pages. The four-page format was well-nigh universal at mid-century because the printing press was designed to imprint one large or blanket sheet. The need for the occasional extra space to publish some accumulated surplus (usually brought on by an excess of ads) could be met with a supplement, such as the two-page addition which Toronto's *British Colonist* offered on 15 July 1845. Competition or prosperity might induce a permanent increase, but this was met by adding more columns and using an even larger sheet. By 1855, for instance, the daily *Globe* and *Gazette* (of Montreal) were mammoth sheets boasting 36 columns an issue. The limits of technology dictated that papers, whatever their size, remain four pages long.

The result was a newspaper densely packed with all the material that the publisher could stuff into his four pages. Nearly always, the news or ads, whatever, were placed in rigid columns running unbroken down the page. In the sample *Globe* the column straitjacket was relieved only on the last page – by three ads on the left-hand side which cut across two columns. Display ads were occasional, and really quite similar in style to their lesser rivals. The straitjacket was a matter of convenience and custom, since the markers separating columns came only in full-length size and breaking them required special effort. Each column was filled with print: neither George Brown nor his comrades believed in the virtues of white space. Only the occasional woodcut of a crest or a steamer and the like in the advertising columns plus the use of large capitals and varying type sizes, again mostly in ads, broke the monotonous array of print. The masters of these compact journals were engaged in the business of publishing a continuing book of affairs useful to readers, not a display of pyrotechnics pleasing to the eye.

Slightly less rigid were the conventions which governed the arrangement of material throughout the newspaper. Immediately below its name, the *Globe* printed its special motto, taken from Junius: 'The subject who is truly loyal to the chief magistrate will neither advise nor submit to arbitrary measures.' That identified the paper's devotion to the Reform cause in politics. But the front page was filled with small ads, pride of place on the left-hand side given to a business directory. Advertising consumed all the space on the last page as well as four and one-half columns on page three. This huge section suggested that the *Globe*'s primary function was to speed the course of commerce, whatever the rhetoric of the day. Indeed, the pride taken by the *Globe* and its fellows in their list of 'new advertisements' each issue proved that the publisher looked upon his commercial messages as a feature of the news.

The other offerings were clustered on the second page and overflowed onto the first two and one-half columns of page three. The important European news opened this section on page two; the lesser news as well as a brief market rundown and a 'By Telegraph' quarter-column closed the section on page three. In between were six editorials, printed in a bit larger type for emphasis, on almost seven columns. The prominence bestowed on editorial views demonstrated that the tri-weekly was very much a journal of opinion committed to battle in the arena of public debate. The limited space given to news left this offering only a third priority, although on other days the news columns could expand greatly to encompass important British information or the debates of the legislature. The sample paper did not carry any features, entertaining or educational, presumably because the rush of other matter left no room for filler. (The *Globe*, nonetheless, was noted for its occasional offering of quality serial novels, such as Charles Dickens's *Dombey and Son*, begun on 11 November 1846.) This layout, with some variations of course, was standard across English Canada and even employed by occasional francophone papers as well, notably *La Minerve*.

A different layout, however, normally found favour among journalists in French Canada. *L'Avenir* (6 September 1850), for example, banished ads from its front pages to carry a long item on literature, an editorial on 'Politique Honnete [sic],' plus rundowns of European news and the provincial acts of 1850. The second page was no less exclusive, offering mostly opinion and a long news story on the execution of an American criminal, a story which extended to page three, where the editor also located additional foreign news and a market report. Ads finished off the third page and filled page four. The different arrangement highlighted the difficulty that some francophone publishers had attracting advertising. French-Canadian newspapers, usually, were not so important to local commerce as their anglophone rivals, an observation strengthened by the fact that a lot of *L'Avenir*'s fourth page carried patent medicine ads rather than the retail or real estate notices that the sample *Globe* offered in its advertising section. No wonder these French-Canadian weeklies and bi-weeklies compensated by emphasizing the priorities of education and opinion (*L'Avenir* proudly identified itself as a 'Journal républicain, publié dans les intérêts populaires').

What was striking was that the forms used by ads, news, and editorials in both kinds of journals were so various, though a detailed analysis would probably conclude that convention reigned here too. The *Globe*'s business cards gave only the barest information. Each real estate notice briefly elaborated a property's virtues. An ad for a new Reform weekly, 'The Post,' amounted to an extended essay on political philosophy. The lead editorial was part of a continuing academic treatise on the history of the clergy reserves, replete with a mass of heavy quotes from government documents. A second editorial, entitled 'The Customs Regulations,' amounted to a sneering critique of a letter which had appeared in the columns of a Conservative rival. The 'By Telegraph' news was little more than a collection of market statistics. By contrast, *L'Avenir*'s 'Execution de John White' was a lengthy news story which dwelt on the little details of the man's final day. And its large ad for 'Pilules Moffatt' seemed a kind of editorial on the incredible benefits of this vegetable compound to everyone's health. The language and style employed in the longer items in both papers, however, could suit the knowledge and taste of only the well and truly literate. That extraordinarily detailed *Globe* discussion of the clergy reserves was not meant for anyone hesitant about his ability to read. It is hard to imagine that the ad for 'Pilules Moffatt' would be understood by the ordinary workingman. Indeed, a goodly portion of the contents of the *Globe* and *L'Avenir* would have been beyond his comprehension without the assistance of an educated friend.

The mid-century was a time in the history of journalism when the publisher or editor could indulge his idiosyncrasies. What news to feature, which causes should be served, whether or not to entertain readers were the prerogatives of the journalist. Little wonder the offerings (advertisements aside) deemed important differed from paper to paper and from week to week. But the ways to locate, arrange, and write the messages were largely fixed by a few conventions. This conformity was a necessary balance to the freedom allowed the journalist to select his messages. Indeed, the conventions ensured that the newspaper would be primarily a compendium of information for the literate bourgeoisie, whether the particular reader be an Orange Conservative or an Irish Liberal. Rare were devices such as colourful headlines, illustrations, white space, an easy or casual prose style that might make the paper appeal to a wider and consequently less literate public. Even the titles or headlines used to identify an item or a group of items were bland statements of fact ('News by the Europa,' 'Sale of Real Estate,' or 'Commercial') which avoided any hint of sensation. Newspapers were meant for the better people.

ADVERTISING

Ads might consume as little as one-third or as much as three-quarters of a daily's space. Much depended on the vigour of the business manager. Late in 1900, A.J. Magurn of the *Manitoba Free Press* expressed his exasperation to young E.H. Macklin, the new business manager, whose admirable energy made the ten-page paper 'too small to contain our advertisements and news as well.[3] Magurn feared the flood of ads had shrunk the 'news hole' to a size that must hurt the paper's credibility. Perhaps too, like many editors, he had a certain disdain for advertising. After all, an ad was a sponsored message designed to 'sell' either a product or a service, and so not readily subject to the editor's stamp. Ads were, however, a crucial service to the business community, especially local merchants. 'Advertising is to business what steam is to commerce – the great propelling power,' a Macaulay aphorism, was reiterated here by the *Monetary Times* (16 December

1881). Throughout the nineteenth century, newspapers were the primary medium of advertising, not without competition, of course, but far and away the best vehicle to reach the most consumers. What changed was the nature and style of this advertising.

Advertising at mid-century was already a highly stylized form of communication. Let me select one example, the ads published by the Montreal *Transcript* on Tuesday morning, 23 January 1855. Just over two-thirds of the newspaper, or 23 out of 32 columns, were given over to advertising. Almost 300 separate items promoted a limited collection of goods, services, and firms: many business cards for lawyers, doctors, and merchants (the 'yellow pages' of the day); retail outlets, especially drygoods and grocery stores; patent medicines, the first brand-name items, but sponsored by local druggists; coal and wood supplies; real estate; forthcoming auctions; a few 'wants,' mostly about jobs and lodgings; amusements, books, a lecture series; club announcements, hotel accommodation (no restaurants though) and government and insurance notices. Missing, probably because of the season, were shipping firms (but there was a card for a telegraph company).

The ads were arranged under special headings such as 'For Sale,' 'Clothing Stores,' 'Sales by Auction,' 'Wanted,' or 'Business Directory.' Most were fairly straightforward announcements of goods and services, often placed months before. D. MacGregor offered an itemized series of woolen goods, the ad dated 20 September. Slightly more recent (13 October) was the special pleading of Cheapside, or the London Clothing Store, which promised cash sales only and a fixed price, so 'the most inexperienced may buy with perfect confidence.'[4] The language used was usually restrained, even respectful: Glenfield Patent Starch thought 'Gentlemen should see that their Linens are dressed with this starch; they will be delighted with its elasticity and beautiful finish.' The space allowed each item was usually small, bare of illustrations, cluttered with type (admittedly different sizes of type). Only J.&M. Nichols, whose clothing store ad was highlighted by a woodcut of their establishment, broke the normal column straightjacket – they had a small square in prominent display on the front page. And even this ad, placed on 4 December, merely stated the merchants 'would respectfully invite the public' to view a variety of unspecified wares 'at greatly reduced prices.'

That kind of propriety did not rule the patent medicine ads. They were anything but timid. Even the names of these marvels struck a different note: Dr M'Lane's Celebrated Liver Pills, Bryan's Pulmonic Wafers, Davis' Pain Killer, Balm of a Thousand Flowers. Patent medicine ads usually took up more space than other kinds of advertising, 'THE RENOWNED REMEDY!!!' Holoway's Ointment, running to two-thirds of a column. Some sort of woodcut, or fancy layout,

"I AM AS WELL AS I WISH TO BE."

Miss Blake, of Hamilton, Ont., After Using Paine's Celery Compound, is a Picture of Womanly Vigour and Beauty.

A Story For All Who Stand in Need of Perfect Health.

Miss Isabella Blake, of 303 Hughson street, Hamilton, Ont., is one of the fairest and best known young women in the ambitious city. To-day she is a picture of womanly health, vigour and beauty, and joyfully declares, "I am now a new woman, can enjoy life, and am as well as I wish to be."

When Miss Blake makes the declaration that she is a "new woman," she does not wish it to be understood that she has entered the ranks, and adopted the fads of those light-brained women who would usurp the legitimate positions of men, and go through life clad in half masculine attire, with the fixed idea of altering the plans of an all-wise Providence, and turning the world upside down. Ah ! no ; this is far from what Miss Blake wishes to imply when she makes the statement that she is a "new woman."

The "new woman" that the world values is not the modern creature that dons the open vest, exposed shirt front, four-in-hand tie, straight and high collar, stiff Derby hat, who walks out on our streets with cane in hand, giving evidence of empty brain and unsatisfied vanity. The true "new woman" is perfectly represented by Miss Blake, made healthy, vigorous, strong and active by the use of Paine's Celery Compound. This is the "woman" that sensible and rational beings honour and appreciate—the type of "woman" that blesses home, friends and the world at large.

Miss Blake, though a young woman, can relate a tale of sad experiences. In the past, lions have stood in her way threatening destruction ; she knows what sore afflictions are, owing to the rough grasp of disease ; and at times, the cold touch of the destroyer, death, has made her shiver, and caused her to think of the dark gloom of the silent tomb.

When Miss Blake's heart was faint, sick and void of hope ; when all the doctors and medicines failed to do good, and when threatened with that relentless foe, consumption, an angel of mercy suggested the use of a remedy that has brought new life to thousands of poor sufferers in the past. Yes, it is Paine's Celery Compound that is recommended ; it is used, and in a short time makes a "new woman" from the material that the grave had battled for.

These facts, dear reader, are not overdrawn or coloured in the least. Miss Blake and her friends will gladly vouch for the truth of the statement that Paine's Celery Compound, and it alone, under God's blessing, was the agent that saved life at a critical juncture The following letter from Miss Blake is surely of sufficient weight to convince the most hardened unbeliever :—

"For years I suffered greatly, and was under the care of doctors who finally told me I was going into consumption. I was becoming worse through the use of medicines, and I gave up my doctors. While in a very critical condition, not able to sleep or rest, always faint and weak, appetite and digestion bad, and my system run down and little life left in me, I commenced to use Paine's Celery Compound. After taking one bottle I felt much relieved. I have used in all seven or eight bottles, and am now a new woman, can enjoy life, and am as well as I wish to be. Many thanks for your great medicine."

A patent medicine ad of the 1890s

graced the bigger ads. Their extravagant claims promised cures to an incredible range of ailments. Not only would Dr Hoofland's Celebrated Bitters work wonders with jaundice and constipation, but it would also relieve 'Constant Imaginings of Evil, and great Depression of Spirits.' Balm of a Thousand Flowers would bring 'a beautiful complexion' (by eradicating 'tan, pimples, and freckles'!) as well as serve as a tooth cleaner and a shaving lotion. Often, the claims were backed up by stilted testimonials from American newspapers, assorted notables, or 'just plain folks' who cited some miraculous cure of a disease that had defeated the best efforts of doctors.[5] Nineteenth-century Canadians, it seemed, were sorely troubled by the state of their health, perhaps too by the inadequacies of the medical profession.

Gentlemen could not but disdain all this outlandish promotion of cure-alls and beauty aids. S.P. Day, a British visitor in the 1860s, found the 'system of puffing and charlatanry' both amusing and saddening, proof of 'the infinite credulity that obtains among the uneducated classes.'[6] (Bourgeois presumption, no doubt, made him fail to see that his own kind of people could be equally credulous.) Dougall refused to carry patent medicine ads (indeed, ads for any questionable product, and that included liquor and tobacco) in his Montreal *Witness*. Most publishers, especially French Canadians whose papers publicized a lot of cures, were much less discriminating about this kind of trade, since the monies quack nostrums brought in were all too necessary. But the prejudice against what was called 'puffery' (exaggerated language or lavish praise) was sufficiently common to ensure other spiels remained dull, suited to the sensibilities of the oh-so-proper Victorian. Dougall opposed using even 'large and varied type,' an unseemly display, which made for 'a very ugly and vulgar looking paper.'[7] All this meant that the normal commercial advertising was bland, less opinionated than many a news report, hardly geared to the needs of mass consumption. Similarly, the fact that a lot of ads were weeks, if not months, old suggested a more leisurely marketplace which did not require the constant seduction of a horde of buyers. Mid-century advertising catered, on the whole, to a small clientele of respectable, comfortable consumers.

The social outreach of the daily newspaper evolved a new style of popular advertising. The first striking change was the emergence of the special classified columns after 1870. Almost 2 full pages of Saturday's 12-page Toronto *Mail*, 16 November 1889, was given over to classifieds. Normally, each item was very short, rarely fancy, mostly abbreviated, since the client was charged according to the number of words used. Here could be found something for everyone, whether of high or low station – business cards, real estate listings, articles for sale (including machinery), personals, board and lodging, above all jobs available and

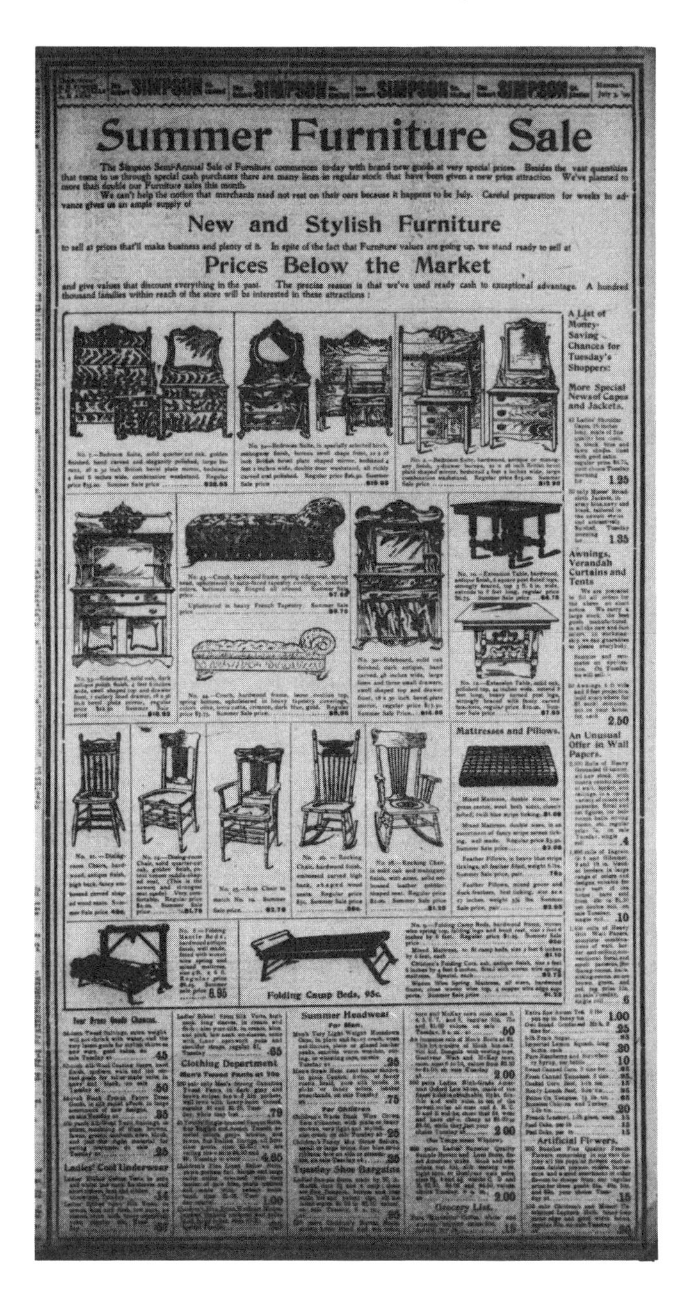

Summer Furniture Sale

The Simpson Semi-Annual Sale of Furniture commences to-day with brand new goods at very special prices. Besides the vast quantities that came to us through special cash purchases there are many lines in regular stock that have been given a new price attraction. We've planned to more than double our Furniture sales this month.

We can't help the notion that merchants need not rest on their oars because it happens to be July. Careful preparation for weeks in advance gives us an ample supply of

New and Stylish Furniture

to sell at prices that'll make business and plenty of it. In spite of the fact that Furniture values are going up, we stand ready to sell at

Prices Below the Market

and give values that discount everything in the past. The precise reason is that we've used ready cash to exceptional advantage. A hundred thousand families within reach of the store will be interested in these attractions:

A List of Money-Saving Chances for Tuesday's Shoppers:

More Special News of Capes and Jackets.

Awnings, Verandah Curtains and Tents

Mattresses and Pillows.

An Unusual Offer in Wall Papers.

Folding Camp Beds, 95c.

Summer Headwear For Men

Clothing Department

Ladies' Cool Underwear

Tuesday Shoe Bargains

Grocery List.

Artificial Flowers.

The department store ad: the 'better way' in merchandising

jobs wanted. The Toronto *Telegram* (17 January 1898), the classified specialist, even had small sections devoted to 'Education,' 'Patents,' and 'Marriage Licenses' on its front page. The modern type of community billboard had made its appearance.

No less striking was the transformation of retail advertising. Some stores had always employed one gimmick or another to win the reader's eye: a large ad for 'la maison Plamondon' in *L'Avenir* (17 February 1849) began by repeating three times 'Attention!' and announced 'Progrès des reformes radicales!' which celebrated the transient liberal mood of the time, and concluded by proclaiming a radical reform in the prices, quality, and quantity of the store's clothing goods. But it was the new department stores after 1870 which overturned the old prejudice against puffery by taking up an American style of advertising that was suited to the needs of mass buying.[8] Not for Eaton's, Simpson's, or the Mammoth House (all Toronto firms) the small, stale ad that stayed for weeks or months in a newspaper – these clients regularly placed new ads, often a couple of times a week, which consumed lots of space, on occasion a full page. The typical ad began with the company's name or some grand promise in bold print. Then the ad chatted with the consumer, sometimes touting the company's democratic spirit and business success,[9] sometimes trying to create a special mood linked to the season. The real meat of the ad, of course, was the itemized list of goods on special, always with price, usually some description, and occasionally illustrations. A full-page ad for Blumenthal's in *La Presse* (2 July 1897) promised 'Des valeurs extraordinaires' because the store was overstocked and needed ready cash and then specified a series of garments for men and boys, cheap hats, 'costumes de bicyclistes,' etc, etc, all neatly and clearly printed, well arranged on the page by special sections, and complete with assorted illustrations. This technique had proved so successful that even speciality stores sometimes emulated the lead taken by department stores, though naturally on a much more modest scale. The result? – an enormous variety of sales and bargains, changing from day to day, was offered the city public.

The third innovation, and the last to mature, was a flood of brand-name advertising, at first mostly for foreign goods though soon for many Canadian-made items as well. A reader could find brand-name ads for patent medicines, liquors and cigars, sewing machines, and the like in the dailies of the early 1870s. But the great surge in this type of advertising really dated from the late 1880s when a series of cleaning agents and foodstuffs, soon clothing and household items as well, tried to sidestep the middleman by building consumer loyalty to a particular brand which would force retailers to stock the product. That required almost constant advertising, not necessarily much space though – Salada Tea, for example, had a little square on the front page of the Toronto *Star* thoughout much of

Harmonie dans les Vêtements

o o o

Quand vous achetez des meubles de haute qualite vous ne les achetez pas " tout faits."

Vous choisissez le genre "d'ameublements" que vous voulez avoir et vous consultez un rembourreur dont le gout, l'experience et le jugement vous aident a decider quelle sera la couleur et la sorte de marchandise que vous choisirez pour la " couverture "—qui le finira pour etre en harmonie avec son entourage futur.

Il en est de meme quand vous achetez des vetements " Semi-ready " la seule difference est que c'est plus avantageux pour vous.

—Plus avantageux parce que vous choisissez la couleur et le genre de marchandise en essayant les vetements et en voyant l'effet qu'ils ont sur votre mine.

Vous choisissez l'habillement ou le vetement fait jusqu'au point ou " la confection generale " finit et le " fini " commence.

Ils sont ensuite completes par des tailleurs habiles suivant leur individualite conservant vos petits gouts et eliminant vos degouts.

Les changements ne laissent pas de traces qui gatent l'apparence des vetements et il n'est pas necessaire de les "refaire" comme pour les " hardes faites"

Vous n'etes pas oblige d'attendre le bon loisir du tailleur qui est occupe, comme cela arrive pour les vetements faits sur commande.

Ils ne coutent pas plus que les " hardes faites " et de la moitie a un tiers de moins que les vetements faits sur commande.

Finis et livres deux heures apres avoir ete commandes.

Nous vous remboursons votre argent si vous n'etes pas satisfait.

$20, $18, $15, $12, $10 l'habillement ou le pardessus.

La Garde-Robe Semi-Ready

THE KENNEDY COMPANY, (Limited).

2364 rue Sainte-Catherine,
231 rue Saint-Jacques, MONTREAL.

TORONTO, WINNIPEG ET OTTAWA.

Brand-name advertising in the 1890s: the effort to organize new markets

1899. Normally, these ads emphasized the product's name, sometimes added a picture, usually complete with a slogan or a small spiel. Castoria broke with the still common extravagance of most patent medicine puffs by running small notices with the slogan 'Children Cry For Castoria.' Drewry's 'All Canada Malt' Lager (note the patriotic label) in the *Manitoba Free Press* (2 October 1896) began a small statement with the boast 'A light refreshing beer.' More impressive, a half-page ad for Hires Root Beer in *La Presse* (5 July 1897), graced by a picture of a poor soul suffering the heat, argued that nothing was so pleasant or healthy as its marvellous stimulant. The Kennedy Co. employed what was called the 'reason-why' approach to push sales of 'the Respira shoe' via the Toronto *News* (19 November 1898): the ad explained how important, how comforting was an 'insole conforming, when borne upon, to shape of footsole, and responding to the movements of each bone and muscle.[10] All this brand-name advertising was the siren-song of an emerging affluent life-style, mostly confined to the white-collar classes of the cities. The ads promised ready gratification of such new consumer 'wants' as convenience, comfort, cleanliness, refreshment, good looks, and on and on. Put another way, brand-name advertising was by the late 1890s the first spokesman of the gospel of mass consumption, the great ally of North American abundance.

At the end of the century, the reader might well discover substantial differences among the ads of his newspapers. People's journals regularly carried short ads masked as news items, on the front page in the case of the Toronto *World*, a 'disgraceful' practice that the quality daily normally avoided. The Montreal *Gazette* (14–19 November 1898), a morning daily, published nary a department store ad, very few classifieds, but instead many patent medicine and brand-name ads, a lot of transportation and financial notices, even a full-page spiel for 'Church's Auto-Voice Institute' which guaranteed relief from 'various forms of speech impediment' (over 2,000 stammerers cured!). That aside, nearly every newspaper had become a showplace for the new style of popular advertising. The old column straitjacket had not altogether disappeared, but it no longer ruled when an advertiser demanded a big display. These ads, small ones too, often made an imaginative, pleasing use of white space, pictures, and type. The ads looked good. And they were interesting – if some ads remained staid, many others employed slogans, wit, specific information, testimonials, 'reason-why' explanations, or little chats to capture the reader's attention. The pedantic tone of an earlier time had given way to the 'plain talk,' even the 'Tall Talk,' of a democratic age.[11] In sum, a new art of huckersterism had matured to appeal to the variety of different tastes and means among the consuming public.

FEATURES

No doubt features were less important than the editorial page or the news columns, to say nothing of the ads, to the success and even more the fame of the daily newspaper. Yet features could fill up a lot of that paper's space, and these features might well entrench upon the preserve of news or editorials. Normally, what defined the feature was its freedom from the pressure of time (if not always the dictum of timeliness), the fact that its message was distanced from the world of significant happenings. Listed among features, then, might be a philosophical disquisition on man's condition or a piece of romantic fiction, a sermon on poverty or an anecdote about Napoleon, a personal column on labour's troubles or a traveller's account of life in Cuba. Features served to broaden a newspaper's appeal, not just to inform or persuade but also to educate, beguile, amuse, or entertain the reader.

Features were nothing new to the offerings of the press. Even the first publishers, and certainly their colonial successors, ran assorted features, often in some place of prominence, especially when the dearth of news or ads threatened to leave their columns blank. By mid-century newspapers might carry a column or two, on the first or fourth page, entitled 'Miscellany,' 'Extraits Divers,' 'Odds and Ends,' or the like. The change that the search for popularity brought was to expand this miscellany into regular, more specialized fare. First the increase in the column size of newspapers, then the birth of the expanded six- or eight-page Saturday newspaper in the 1880s, and finally the inflation of the ordinary daily edition during the next decade ensured the editor would nearly always find features a necessary filler. Besides, his features (listed on the front page in some cases) were a great selling point of his Saturday paper to a family audience. Whereas he once would have scalped his features from another journal, now he not only made arrangements with outside agencies but also hired special writers whose task was to prepare regular columns. And these features were designed to fit or express the newspaper's special personality.

There were three distinct genres among this plethora of features. First to mature was entertainment. Whatever the eccentric practices of an earlier day, it was those pioneers of popular journalism, the publishers of the penny tri-weeklies, who tried to feature entertainment in every issue. So the 'principal object' of the Montreal *Transcript*, asserted its prospectus (28 September 1836), was 'to amuse,' even promising readers contributions from 'several gentlemen of high literary attainments' and 'the first Literary Works published in England and the States.' Perhaps more surprising was the fact that within a decade or two nearly all kinds of papers, including the high-toned journals of opinion in French Canada, even if they might disdain such a low purpose as merely to amuse, did meet the new competition with their own brand of entertainment.

The particular routes that each newspaper took to realize popularity, of course, affected the amount of entertainment it supplied readers. The quality dailies with their 'up-market' strategy came more and more to confine this feature to the Saturday edition when women and teenagers, not just the head of the household, would read the paper. The majority of city papers had to be less discriminating since their limited market required a daily dose of fantasy to satisfy everyman and everywoman. That was especially true of francophone papers during the late nineteenth century when the daily feuilleton was a continuing staple. The 'down-market' strategy of the people's journals ensured that they would place a high priority on lavish quantities of entertainment to please their lowbrow readers. Right from the beginning, *La Presse* gave a big play to its serial novels, even trying to drum up interest with editorial columns and sometimes running two feuilletons at once. At times, the feuilleton seemed the main item: on 6 October 1892, a Thursday, the paper gave over to '*Jacques L'Honneur*' some four pages!

Entertainment came in various forms. Poetry, once very common at mid-century, was usually shunted off onto the woman's page, or the boys and girls' section, by the end of the century. Do-it-yourself features such as the Toronto *Telegram*'s song sheets or the chess and checker problems of the Toronto *Mail* appeared in Saturday editions. Ponderous witticisms abounded, especially in 'Anglo' newspapers where they might serve to finish off a column of print. (Witness this sample from the Toronto *Telegram*, 10 June 1895: 'Parliamentary oratory is a flattering name for the sound of ignorance effervescing when a bottle of silence is broken by speech.') More amusing were the occasional samples of American humour, tall tales, and anecdotes, such as Bill Nye's column carried by the Toronto *News* in 1887 or 'M. Quad' syndicated in a number of anglophone papers during the next decade. Then there were short stories, such as 'Benedict' by one 'Roy Compton' about that old tragedy, lost love, which appeared in the Ottawa *Free Press* (3 July 1894). But the most important of these features was the serial novel, an item supposed to keep the reader interested and so loyal to the newspaper. In fact, even after cheap books, periodicals, and public libraries became commonplace, the newspaper serial remained a leading medium of popular fiction for the classes and masses, especially the masses.

Newspapers had to exercise some care selecting their novels. Editors were well aware of bourgeois sensibilities, especially the disdain for low and immoral works. An editorial announcing the appearance of Henry Gréville's *Sonia* in *L'Électeur* (22 December 1880) promised 'pas un mot qui puisse blesser l'oreille la plus chaste, la plus délicate.' The effect its reading must produce 'est une émotion saine, c'est celle que produit la contemplation de la vertu la plus élevée.'

(By contrast, the paper set this novel against the works of a nature 'de plus repoussant et de plus immoral' written by Emile Zola!) Clearly, *L'Électeur* did not wish to alienate any moralist, which might well lead to a ban on family reading. However, neither *L'Électeur* nor any newspaper wished to bore a reader and so defeat the purpose of the feature. Thus, with considerable fanfare, *Le Monde* (19 May 1893) announced its coming attraction, *Le Fantôme*, supposedly 'un des grands romanciers de l'époque.' Its capsule description claimed, 'l'amour y coudie le crime et toutes les angoisses de l'un et les palpitantes émotions de l'autre y sont analysées de main de maître.' The editor felt he somehow had to find a novel that would satisfy, in the words of *L'Électeur* (2 August 1892), 'les goûts de tous.'

In fact the result was that the serial novel reflected not the tastes of all but the newspaper's market. In the spring of 1881, the Montreal *Gazette* carried a piece of didactic fiction entitled 'Ploughed Under! The Story of an Indian Chief Told by Himself' which showed the trials and tribulations of North America's native peoples. The Toronto *Globe* featured the quality novels of the age, such as Jules Verne's *Mathias Sandorf* (1885) or Robert Louis Stevenson's *David Balfour* (1893). The Toronto *Telegram*, in contrast, furnished over the years a lot of social melodrama, normally situated in England or America among the well-off – a special favourite were the novels of May Agnes Fleming, a Canadian-born author who had won fame in the United States.[12] Francophone papers displayed a penchant for adventure and gore as well as romance, or so titles such as *La Noce sanglante* (*La Minerve* 1871), *Les Sabotiers de la forêt noire* (*La Patrie* 1883), or *Un Drame du nord de la mer* (*L'Electeur* 1892) suggest.

Much of this fiction was trashy, the nineteenth-century version of hack writing – witness *The Fate of Fenella* written by 'Twenty-four Authors' which appeared in the Ottawa *Free Press* in 1894. Almost all the novels were foreign imports, from Britain, America, or France (though *L'Étendard* did run *Le Chien d'or*, a 'légende canadienne,' late in 1884). Francophone dailies even published translations of English works, such as Wilkie Collins *La Femme en blanc* in *L'Électeur* (1887). By the 1890s publishers often made arrangements with publishing houses, foreign newspapers, or various agencies to secure the rights to a constant supply of fiction: on 6 and 7 June 1895, for instance, the Toronto *Star* carried 'Told by a Brass Button' under the copyright of the American Press Association.

A newspaper that could entertain might also educate. But what to teach? The rampant dogmatism of the century ensured that all too many features would amount to blatant propaganda for the publisher's causes. So readers were cajoled by articles that ranged over the meaning of liberty, the virtues or sins of monarchy, the splendour of free trade but the necessity of protection, and on and on. In truth, borrowed or communicated essays were much more common in French Canada where journalists took very seriously the task of educating readers. An important distinction emerged, moreover, between the Catholic and Protestant approaches to matters moral and spiritual.

French-Canadian journals early evinced a determination to educate their readers in the details of the Catholic church's history, philosophy, and practice. Why else would *Le Canadien* (22 August 1832) publish on its front page 'Influence de Christianisme sur la legislation,' dealing with the laws of the later Roman Empire? Or *Le Journal de Québec* carry a historical series, written by one abbé Dasange, entitled 'Pourvoir du Pape au moyen age' (concluded on 8 July 1845)? Bleu newspapers after 1850 made that great Catholic champion Louis Veuillot a household name amongst the upper crust, so often were his polemics reproduced. The ultramontane newspapers were always selecting features that fitted the world view of an embattled church: right away, *L'Étendard* published the series 'Le mouvement social au XIXe siècle' to buttress its doctrine of defiance. Even *La Presse* was prepared to carry the arguments of local churchmen on whatever subject, such as R.P. Slevin's Lenten sermon, 'Rome et raison' (9 March 1896).

In contrast, English-Canadian papers were more likely to specialize in moral guidance or homespun philosophy. The Montreal *Witness* was replete with rules and uplift in the form of reports of Christian lectures, temperance tracts, moral tales, and Sunday School lessons. The sermons of the American preacher T. DeWitt Talmage on right thinking and right doing were widely syndicated in the press of the late 1880s. Book review columns often analysed literature from the standpoint of propriety, concerned with good taste and the triumph of virtue as well as the evils of 'sensational writing.' French or English, Catholic or Protestant, these approaches, of course, embodied the assumed relevance of Christian teachings to the daily routine in Victorian Canada.

Equally, the utilitarian thrust of this age of improvement dictated that newspapers would provide some practical instruction to guide a person's living and working. Even *L'Avenir*, so zealously rouge and highbrow, published in 1849 an occasional column entitled 'Connaissances utiles' that might delve into cures for ordinary ills. Throughout, the weekly articles on agriculture focused on what to do, when and how, influenced at least in the closing decades of the century by notions of scientific farming. Around about the 1860s, newspapers searching for a family audience began to carry regularly notes on fashions, child care, household management, and so on for the wife and mother; these teachings later found a permanent home on the woman's page. In the mid-1890s, for instance, the Montreal *Herald* routinely offered the 'Herald's Table Hints,' a complete day's menu. Children too received some assistance in their play – Saturday's Saint John

Sun (3 January 1880) told how to build 'scientific snow-forts'! In a more parochial vein, the francophone dailies were wont to give language lessons to protect the purity of French, whether against anglicisms or slang. So, for at least three years (1893–95), *La Patrie* published a Saturday special entitled 'A travers le dictionnaire et la grammaire.' A hint of things to come, Saturday's *Mail and Empire* in January 1897 helped all readers with 'Questions and Answers' and 'Legal Answers,' which responded to queries on all manner of subjects.

More and more of the teaching, however, tended to avoid outright advocacy to satisfy instead the reader's curiosity, and much of this interesting matter was taken from foreign sources. History was ransacked for bizarre anecdotes or exciting episodes, *La Presse* in the summer of 1897 running on Saturdays a serial history of the Franco-Prussian War. Celebrities of all kinds received their due: illustrated biographies of local public men (Toronto *Telegram* 1878), world-class personalities ('Célébrités contemporaines' in *Le Monde* 1890), or unusual souls (*La Presse*'s front-page extravaganza on 'Les hommes forts,' 1 April 1893). Thomas Edison became a household name in the 1880s, in French and English Canada, so often were he and his inventions featured in the press. Another fascination was the 'Scientific Miscellany' (in the Saint John *Sun* 1893) or 'Chronique scientifique' (in *La Minerve* 1896) replete with trivia about the newest discoveries and technological marvels of the day. Amongst the Montreal *Gazette*'s Saturday specials of 14 March 1896 were 'Extracts from Dr. Hunter's Famous Lectures' which dealt this time with 'Why Consumptives Lose Flesh.' *La Presse*, in particular, was an enthusiast for any and all progress, one of its earliest features on 'Torpilles et torpilleurs' discussing advances in weapons technology.

But the great favourites were accounts of life in places beyond the immediate bounds of the community. So the Toronto *News* (30 April 1887) proudly announced 'the Porter letters, describing life in old London,' especially 'the slums and social problems of the metropolis of the world.' Often the locale was exotic: such pieces as the Toronto *Globe*'s series on British India (spring 1895), *La Patrie*'s 'Chez les Japonais' (2 January 1895) and 'À travers les colonies françaises' (14 March 1896), or *La Presse*'s 'L'Abyssinie' (10 March 1896), dispensed interesting facts about the outside world. Sometimes the feature focused on a land nearby: in August 1896 *La Presse*'s special correspondent for the 'Chronique vagabonde' was tramping through the nether regions of Quebec. All of this had nothing to do with tourism, not then a mass passion. The point was that a constant supply of travelogues strove to exploit that sense of wonder believed common among the classes and masses.

Last to mature was the genre of personal comment, a unique blend of news and views, sometimes angered, sometimes whimsical, but above all original to the newspaper itself. This offering, as well, could trace its roots back to the early days of publishing when letters to the editor, invariably bearing a pseudonym, were a valued filler. Indeed, reader's letters commonly furnished the only bit of spice and controversy in the otherwise bland gazettes. And the tradition continued: letters remained ever useful to probe a sin, buttress an editorial opinion, even provoke a laugh. In 1878 Robertson's *Telegram*, then so innovative, launched 'Our Complaint Book' to allow irate citizens to air grievances about 'public wrong-doing.'[13] The *Mail*'s feature 'What the People Say' (28 August 1880) enabled the editor to tout the virtues of protection with a choice missive from a Hamilton reader on the benefits of the National Policy. Five columns of 'Communications' in a Tuesday issue of the *Globe* (24 August 1880) provided space for a mostly anonymous crew of readers to deal with 'Temperance on Steamboats, 'Workingmen and Their Grievances,' 'The New Tariffs,' 'Condition of New Zealand,' and so on. Convention dictated that the assorted pseudonyms, such as 'Citizen,' 'A Labourer,' 'Philopatris,' 'Pro Bono Publico,' would suggest a representative of a group or a cause, something greater than one person's opinions.

Enter the columnist. During the 1880s the Saturday columnist came to challenge the letter to the editor as the most interesting source of personal comment in the newspaper. This new kind of journalist was granted the freedom to select whatever subject might catch his or her fancy. The columnist was expected to sport a unique style of writing, the copy stamped by the author's personality, to win readers' affections. That could well make the column another tool of advocacy. So in 1883 *L'Étendard*, emphatically a social conservative, offered every Saturday an uplifting, reflective essay by 'Lisette' under the forbidding title 'La politique d'une mere de famille.' The 'Ladies Column' of the Saint John *Sun* (spring 1889) carried a mix of news and views which depicted women as social helpmates, perhaps mothers to a nation's morality, certainly deserving a just measure of sexual equality.

Labour columnists were even more forthright. During the late 1880s and early 1890s, *La Presse*'s Jules Helbronner, who wrote the weekly 'Chronique ouvrière' under the pseudonym 'Jean-Baptiste Gagnepetit,' caused excitement by stridently championing labour's rights and causes. When *Le Monde* finally decided to imitate its rival's fame, the editor apparently promised Urbain Lafontaine, a local labour leader, a free hand. No purchased pen this man – 'je serai seul responsible des idées émises dans ces causeries ouvrières' (15 October 1892), an obvious effort to ensure credibility. Perhaps these men did enjoy a lot of independence. The Ottawa *Journal*'s labour columnist in 1900, G.W. Patterson, chose each Saturday a range of news items, from near and far, that allowed him to condemn trusts and combines, praise unions, or favour a redistribution of wealth with a vigour unknown to the editorial page.

This kind of impassioned commentary, though, was comparatively rare. More often the columnist eschewed any grand desire to spread the true word. 'I shall express opinions and sometimes speak plainly,' promised 'The Flaneur' in his initial remarks (Toronto *Mail*, 17 December 1887), 'but with no intention either to proselytize or preach.' What flavoured the normal column was a special attitude or pose which can only be called a sort of opinionated inquiry. Thus H.H. Wiltshire ('The Flaneur') might roam over the woeful condition of France or Ireland, the arts world, Toronto civic politics, displaying a conservative bias but not in any strident fashion. No less eclectic, 'Jean Badreux,' *Le Monde*'s daily columnist in the mid-1890s, wrote on such diverse topics as 'La langue simiesque' (7 May 1895) and 'Le monopole des avocats' (26 March 1896). 'M.J.G.,' author of 'At Dodsley's' in the Montreal *Gazette* (11 March 1899), mused over the career of the two Napoleons. Woman's columns, likewise, seemed designed in the 1890s to satisfy curiosity, to serve and entertain but little more. Wiltshire's equally famous partner, Kathleen Blake or 'Kit' furnished a good deal more gossip than argument about women's affairs – and fashions. So too did 'Mary Dean' and 'Gaétene de Montreuil,' respectively of the Montreal *Gazette* and *La Presse* in 1899. The casual, chatty style ruled as well in those intermittent specials such as Lynn C. Doyle's 'At the Art Gallery' and 'L.B.D.'s' 'The Library Table' in the Toronto *Globe* or 'Ignotus' and his (?) 'Notes et souvenirs' on literature and history in *La Presse* during the spring of 1899. The columnist, at least these columnists, tried to please, not excite, the public.

Nonetheless, the personal column had not made the kind of splash in Canadian journalism one might expect. As late as 1899 many a newspaper, including the Toronto *Telegram*, the Saint John *Sun*, or the *Manitoba Free Press*, did not bother with any columnists. The Toronto *Globe*, a pioneer of the woman's page in the early 1880s, had neither a woman's columnist not a proper woman's page in its huge Saturday editions of 1899. Even *La Presse* had done away with the 'Chronique ouvrière.' What had hindered the spread of the column, indeed limited the amount of features, was the surging fascination with news.

NEWS

'It is a fact, now pretty well understood, that the first duty of a newspaper, whether metropolitan or local, is to give news,' declared one observer. 'This being the case, it is in the interest of every paper to have within its pages the news most suited to, and most desired by, its particular constituency.'[14] The public's hunger for news was nothing new. What had changed was the publisher's ability to satisfy demand. In the first couple of decades of the century, newsgathering facilities were sadly inadequate. Early publishers had to depend on local gossip and rumour, the occasional correspondent, what the mails or the ships brought in, and clippings from far-distant journals to furnish a modest survey of the recent past. Technology, the steamship, the railway, even more the telegraph supplied the means to publish a record of the immediate reality. During the week of 13–18 February 1871, around one-quarter of the news and views (including editorials and commentary) in the Montreal press arrived via telegraph. A reporter in 1882 estimated that the central office of Great North Western Telegraphs sent about 20,000 words of copy, roughly half of it political, on election evening to dailies across the country.[15] By the last decades of the century, the new hordes of reporters were able to prepare a surfeit of articles especially about happenings near at hand. That was why news could fill the expanding pages of the daily.

The hunger for news was rooted in human nature, or at least that nature wrought when custom began to fall victim to the sweep of fashion. 'News,' Bernard Roshco tells us, 'is a consequence of the human desire – and need – to know the state of the surrounding social and political environment.'[16] The function of news, Robert Park once remarked, is 'to orient man and society in an actual world.'[17] News amounts to 'the exercise of power over the interpretation of reality'[18] – something Clifford Sifton instinctively recognized when he told E.H. Macklin of the *Manitoba Free Press* that the news columns had a greater effect on 'the simple-minded farmer' than any number of editorials.[19] Fact had taken place of the miraculous, the traditional.

This sociological truth seems a trifle abstract to explain everything. Publishers realized news might satisfy a clutch of needs – to be informed, of course, but also to be excited, even amused. The belief that readers liked to be jolted lay behind the most controversial innovation on the news scene, namely sensationalism: the selection and presentation of stories to provoke an emotional response. 'What is a newspaper published for if not to produce sensations – to make an impression upon its readers and the public?' asked the Hamilton *Herald* (6 May 1890). 'The sleepy, old style of journalism which contents itself with printing the stereotyped "news" never created a sensation, but it never accomplished anything worthy of mention.' Yet even the *Herald* supplied a lot of news that could hardly be called sensational. Indeed, publishers knew they had to furnish much dull, routine copy about Parliament, the stock exchange, and, later, sporting events or high society that served the particular concerns of readers. Hence the instruction Ross of the Ottawa *Journal* delivered to his city editor in 1906: 'Police Court must be inserted daily without fail as it is too important to be lightly left out.'[20] The commonplace as well as the unusual, the predictable and the unexpected shared news columns where servicing readers was as important as sensation-seeking.

What made news? News, so a contemporary celebration of journalism argued, was 'an unpublished event of present interest,' served up 'hot,' any item which touched 'either the heart or the pocket-book of human affairs.'[21] The key was timeliness. Nothing was more sinful, it seemed, than stale news. 'To habitual news readers news forty-eight hours behind date is almost as ancient history, and only interesting as a memorial of how people lived so long ago.'[22] News was above all a perishable commodity, 'transient' and 'ephemeral' in Park's words because linked to 'the specious present.'[23] Now the timeliness of an event, Roshco asserts, depends upon 'the conjunction of: (1) *recency* (recent disclosure); (2) *immediacy* (publication with minimal delay); (3) *currency* (relevance to present concerns).' And the actual definition of timeliness, he adds, implies 'the existence and interaction of a news source, a news medium, and a news audience.'[24] Put another way, the editor played a crucial role as a gatekeeper who selected from the detail available the items which he thought would satisfy the tastes of readers. Not to downplay the importance of fate: the ebb and flow of happenings, the course of a war, or the end of an election campaign might determine the news on any given day. But the news was, like almost everything else in the popular press, a product of convention. Formula reigned even in the description of reality.

Each newspaper had its own 'map' of the world of happenings which focused attention upon a limited number of places and lands. Only in moments of extraordinary crisis, such as the Boer War in 1899, were events outside Canada likely to dominate news columns. Still, foreign news remained a regular staple in people's and even more in quality dailies. Life and affairs in the United States, of course, were an inexhaustible source of copy, the American scene becoming, so it seemed, a grand stage whereon the follies and fancies of mankind were acted out to please Canadian readers. Less attention was given to the two mother countries, France and Britain, and that attention preferred affairs over life. Naturally, 'Anglo' dailies, even more quality newspapers, did keep a close eye on British politics and imperial diplomacy, whereas the French-Canadian press was more intrigued by France's career (*La Patrie*, during the mid-1890s, actually had a daily 'Courrier de France' running along the bottom of the front page). Crisis journalism, a focus on strife or accident or upheaval, characterized the coverage of happenings elsewhere – readers did get bits of information about Russian terrorism, Italy's fractious politics, the Brazilian 'revolution,' Japan's new militarism, the European acquisition of Africa, and the like. Parochial or idiosyncratic concerns also influenced the notice editors took of certain kinds of events. Canada's colonial status dictated a keen interest in the course of international diplomacy, both the troubles of Europe and Anglo-American relations, as well as the trivia of British and French imperialisms. The Montreal *Witness* watched for signs of advance anywhere in the grand moral war to perfect human life. The Toronto *Mail* during the 1870s worried a lot about the collapse of conservatism in post-Napoleonic France. During the next decade, in contrast, *La Patrie* cheered on the spirit of democracy which it thought imbued France's republican rulers.

Ironically, the coverage of the outside world might well be more varied than the survey of Canadian happenings. Of course, a spectacular event, the Northwest Rebellion in 1885 for instance, would win the editor's eye. Also, Central Canadian dailies, even in French Quebec, displayed a continuing interest in the progress of the prairies. But the idea of Canada seemingly fixed in the editor's mind – at least when it came to news – was less a single community, more a political nationality. Newspapers concentrated upon Ottawa, especially when Parliament met, to keep readers abreast of partisan doings. They worried about the affairs of other regions when these might impinge on the great game of party or affect sectional interests. Thus Ontario dailies during the late 1880s were upset, some horrified, by the apparent popularity in Quebec of French-Canadian nationalism and its mentor, Honoré Mercier. French-Canadian dailies a half-decade later concentrated on Manitoba's campaign against the privileges of the Catholics and the Métis.

The province or region, then, was the more substantial community, at least so the news columns suggest. Here, too, much coverage looked at happenings in the domain of public affairs, again seasonal to suit the meetings of the local assembly. But editors did assume that readers were interested in all kinds of doings. The 'Maritime Miscellany' of the Saint John *Sun* on 19 March 1889 offered abbreviated mention of a new brigantine nearing completion at Bear River, Scott Act (temperance) cases in Cumberland County in Nova Scotia, a thumb amputation in Moncton, and the fortunes of finnan haddie shipping. *Le Nouveau Monde*, and later *L'Étendard*, were infatuated with the workings of the community in Fortress Quebec. Worth noting, 'Anglo' papers in Montreal were much less interested in the daily routine of the province, except its politics, because the community was Catholic and French. Toronto's quality dailies specialized in columns of news about Hamilton, Ottawa, even smaller places, just as the *Manitoba Free Press* took pride in its prairie surveys – the papers did, after all, embody the metropolitan ambitions of their cities. And, across the Rockies, the press of Victoria, New Westminster, and later Vancouver seemed in a constant state of agitation about the feuds, troubles, and progress of their isolated province. All of this news fuelled the fires of sectionalism, perpetuating the image of distinct regional communities each boasting separate ways.

By the 1890s, however, the centre of nearly every newspaper's 'map' was the home city itself. Till mid-century the city scene had never struck editors as a source of news equivalent to the political arena or the outside world. The growth of the city, an increasing democracy and social tension, and the rise of organized labour as well as organized sports contributed to an urban parochialism among both classes and masses. Their chaotic society required definition, and celebration. The people's dailies first capitalized on the mood by filling columns with items on civic institutions and amusements, maybe exposing the greed of the streetcar company or the quality of workingmen's houses, not to mention the mundane routine of city life. The *Telegram*'s amazing success, or so its chroniclers thought, had a lot to do with the paper's determination 'to go heavily for local matters' which quickly established it's reputation as the ratepayer's watchdog.[25] Rivals could only hire their own teams of reporters to meet the challenge. But the upshot was a constant stream of news about everything and anything. The popular newspaper, consequently, was far and away the most effective agent of a sense of community, a civic consciousness in the big city. It told people about their civic leaders and government, how the local sports heroes had fared, what the market was like, and where to go to find amusement.

Formula likewise dictated what subjects, what events would merit publicity and emphasis. Take public affairs, that passion of nineteenth-century life. 'The attention paid by nearly every male adult in Canada to the science of government,' protested one business editor in 1882, 'has earned us the reputation of having more politics to the square mile than any country in the world.'[26] The press served, indeed perpetuated this enthusiasm. A good portion of the routine news in any newspaper was bound to look at international diplomacy or homegrown politics. A domestic or foreign crisis, most especially a Canadian election, lent itself to sensational treatment. So the *Printer and Publisher* complained in May 1896 (in the midst of an election campaign) that 'the daily press continues to groan with the load of political news poured into them,' temporarily abandoning 'all standards of condensation.' Especially important, the political news focused on personality, not just on leaders but also on the lesser chiefs as well, what the mayor or the premier did and said, giving a human dimension to the issues of the day. News, then, made public affairs a grand spectacle, full of excitement and significance, heroes and villains.

Even so, the search for popularity had brought a substantial change in the amount and quality of this brand of news. Invariably, the quality dailies strove to supply a routine, detailed survey of public affairs everywhere, suited to highbrow tastes, whereas the people's dailies rigorously abbreviated their coverage, afraid of boring the lowbrow reader. Morning newspapers made a specialty of foreign news: the front page of the *Mail and Empire* on Monday, 10 June 1895, contained four columns that noted 'Nasrulla Khan's Visit to London,' the 'Eastern Troubles,' and 'Imperial Politics.' Party organs continued to feature parliamentary proceedings and speeches (though often abbreviated), assorted Ottawa and party gossip, summaries of government reports or political tours, all designed to please the Conservative or Liberal reader. The evening, people's dailies scrutinized the affairs of the civic government, the police commission as well as the municipal council, since its decisions touched directly the lives and pocketbooks of ordinary citizens. Right away, *La Presse* had probed into the management of Montreal's business, soon finding the requisite scandal (over paving contracts) to justify a crusade. None of the dailies, neither a highbrow *Gazette* nor a lowbrow *La Presse*, however, devoted as much space to public affairs as their predecessors a generation earlier. The single-minded infatuation with politics at home and abroad had died with the disappearance or transformation of the francophone journal of opinion in the early 1890s. The popular newspaper, as a rule, offered a much more balanced account of the day's happenings.

The watch on the economy took an increasingly generous share of the news space. Here the first priority was servicing the business public. The publishers of colonial weeklies had usually supplied a short market round-up to assist local merchants. The arrival of the telegraph allowed the new tri-weeklies and dailies to add a more up-to-date summary of events on American and even European markets. And, in time, the quality newspapers, notably in Montreal, combined these kinds of information to create a distinct financial and commercial page. That page was bare of personality but replete with statistics on the commodity and money markets, the stock exchange, trade patterns (at home and elsewhere – sometimes western Europe, but always the United States), occasionally supplemented by predictions or warnings. Rarely was there much on a particular company or industry – indeed manufacturing received little attention.

The style of this news varied little. The amount and focus did vary. Not every publisher followed the lead of the great servants of capitalism. That peculiar hybrid, the Montreal *Witness*, carried by 1871 a regular survey of the local market for hardware or shoe merchants, grocers or importers, in short for the small businessman. If *La Minerve* normally furnished a competent review of financial and commercial dealings, the more popular *La Patrie* remained content with a column of statistics plus a weekly 'Revue commerciale' (borrowed from *Le Moniteur du Commerce*). In 1886 the Toronto *News*, hardly a businessman's paper, merely published a brief 'Business and Prices,' coyly described as 'Information Collected for Practical People.' A comparison of the news on Wednesday 14 July 1897 showed the *Mail and Empire* (ten pages) and Montreal *Gazette* (eight pages) giving their readers a full-blown financial page, the morning *World* of Toronto (eight pages) five columns of ads and statistics, the evening *La Presse* (eight pages) and Toronto *Star* (four pages) a very modest rundown of business affairs.

The broader workings of the economy did generate events that deserved some treatment on the ordinary news pages. A tycoon such as William Van Horne of the Canadian Pacific Railway had little difficulty getting his views on business into the press.[27] Bank statements, board of trade meetings, and company announcements usually won attention, though once again the most complete reports appeared in the quality newspapers. Occasionally, newspapers offered reports on the wheat harvest or the British market and the like – on 14 July 1897, for example, the Toronto *World* allowed a column and one half for a special discussion of 'The Atik-okan Iron Range.' Perhaps the most interesting novelty was the focus on labour. During the mid-1880s a variety of newspapers, quality as well as people's, began to supply regular columns on trade union affairs. So the London *Advertiser* had its 'Work and Wages' as well as 'Knights of Labor Corner' to recount the trivia of the workingman's world.[28] By the mid-1890s *La Presse* published daily a 'Nouvelles ouvrières,' admittedly not always very extensive, on its front page. The labour scene, of course, sometimes produced a piece of spectacular news, such as Toronto's streetcar troubles in 1886, which required detailed, even sensational treatment. This watch on the economy suggested first a preference for news about growth and second a deepening concern over the signs of industrial warfare, both of significance to the progress of the city.

A striking attribute of popular journalism, however, was the almost obligatory concentration on life, which furnished the most digestible news for any soul. Once again, the style of a newspaper determined what aspects of this 'life' deserved prominence. The oldest focus was on the doings of the assorted social authorities or their leaders. By the 1870s the sectarian journals, in particular, had made a specialty of the close scrutiny of the church, churchmen, and moral agencies. After all, an ultramontane organ such as *Le Nouveau Monde* was bound to feature Catholic news, just as the crusading *Witness* highlighted the affairs of the evangelical world. French-Canadian papers, whatever their stripe, usually proved willing to give space to religious news or the St Jean-Baptiste society. Once, on its front page, *Le Monde* (9 March 1896) actually carried a one-and-a-half column summary of a lecture on miracles! In English Canada, though, the quality dailies were better known for a routine coverage (notably on Saturdays) of schools and universities, the courts, temperance bodies, charities, or churches. The rest of the dailies were more lax, their coverage dependent on the editor's prejudices or the flow of events.

Vying for attention was news from the expanding realm of leisure. Here too the high-toned, eventually quality, newspapers were its most careful chroniclers, not surprising given the fact that the prosperity of the 'classes' meant they could better sample the new delights. In dailies such as *Le Pays* and *La Minerve* in the early 1870s or the Toronto *Mail* and *Globe* in the early 1880s a reader might find reports of lectures, plays, balls, and other highbrow amusements. And at first it was the quality press of English Canada which recognized the sports world: Saturday's *Mail* (16 November 1889) had a respectable two-column 'Sports and

Pastimes' which roamed over baseball, bowling, the ring and the turf, even a bit on athletics. Space limitations held back other papers, but even so the people's journals always kept an eye on popular recreations like skating or concerts plus local sports heroes. In fact, the rise of spectator sports dictated that these dailies offer a sports round-up, far more interesting for their readers than the financial columns. In the 1890s, for instance, *La Presse* pioneered the regular coverage of sports in French Canada, hitherto neglected by the francophone press.

The last preference was for incidents in what Park has called 'the game of life'[29]: births and deaths, marriages, the rituals of high society, the comings and goings of celebrities, accidents and disasters, above all crime and violence, but also the unusual and the exotic. Publishers had always found brief items about everything from a local suicide to Indians on the rampage a useful filler to close off a column. What set Hugh Graham and John Ross Robertson off from the pack was their decision to supply a surfeit of such trivia, and that remained a hallmark of people's journalism. The lowbrow fascination with the game of life never seemed to flag: E.E. Sheppard's editors at the *News* had an especially keen eye for news about bigamy, lynchings and graft, freaks of nature, any and every American vice. Nearly all publishers, though, soon realized readers loved to learn about celebrities: the Queen and other royalty or aristocracy in the Old World,[30] sports heroes such as Ned Hanlan, the grand inventor Thomas Edison, actors or generals, and on and on. Incidents in the social swirl of local and international snobs came to curse the woman's columns of the 'best' newspapers in the 1890s.

Likewise, publishers found the game of life a constant source of sensational copy. Not even the quality dailies were able to resist the urge to exploit some horrors: in November 1890 the Toronto *Mail* published an autobiography of Reginald Birchall, a famous murderer. People's dailies, of course, had no compunctions about booming such news. Berthiaume's *La Presse* sensationalized a host of fires, disasters, and murders throughout the 1890s. One Wednesday, for instance, the whole front page of *La Presse* (31 July 1895) reconstructed in all its gory detail 'la sanglante tragedie de la rue Bonsecours,' a lover's quarrel that ended in death. This type of coverage was trivial, morbid, inane, but invariably exciting, a classic instance of news as a form of entertainment.

The news came in many sizes and shapes. That variety was as important as the choice of locale or subject. Indeed, the form could, sometimes, determine the substance: popular journalism was committed to accuracy, getting all the facts right,[31] but not to the ideal of objectivity. Editors had few scruples about slanting the news to favour some particular point of view or provoke some kind of response. J.S. Willison admitted as much in his reminiscences: 'Even if no editorial opinions were expressed, the news columns would advocate a cause or a party, reveal the convictions or betray the prejudices of the responsible editors.'[32] Put another way, 'Fact' was often seconded to 'Truth.'

The round-up, a very common form, conveyed reasonably pure fact. At least until the general inflation of the dailies in the 1890s, the round-up prevailed in the telegraphic columns (whether about the outside world or the domestic scene), the financial and commercial section, and the local and sports surveys. In 1886 the Toronto *Globe* carried atop its first column on the front page 'News of the Day' in which an editor might stuff any kind of fact.[33] More imaginative, the Hamilton *Herald* three years later styled its telegraphic summary 'Echoes from the Hours' and 'Ticks that Tell the Tale of Human History.' The paper was following the lead of the Toronto *Telegram* which used the round-up to convey the news from all arenas of life and affairs. Much of this news amounted to little more than tidbits of information to alert the reader to change. Why was the round-up popular? It so effectively suited the necessary task of servicing the public. Businessmen and sports fans, for example, were interested in discovering simply and briefly exactly what routine events had occurred. The publishers of people's dailies reasoned that their readers were interested in a boiled-down version of ordinary news, which assumed the masses had a short attention span. Even into the 1890s many newspapers still cluttered their front pages with a large number of abbreviated items. Superficiality survived because it sold papers – and it cost little.

It was easier to bias the information in supposedly verbatim copy, another old form of news. Newspapers had always acted as a vehicle for the views and arguments of significant people. In 1849, for instance, the Toronto *British Colonist* and the rival *Globe* carried large chunks of the debates in the British houses of Parliament pertinent to the Canadian crisis. In French Canada, nearly every daily opened its news columns to the letters and *mandements* of Quebec bishops on topics of the day. In season the party organs, at least till the 1890s, would fill columns with the speeches of MPs, often granting their favourites extra space to elaborate the right views. On 1 June 1876 the Toronto *Globe* gave slightly over six full columns to a speech Alexander Galt delivered on the financial condition of the dominion, a speech which expressed opinions generally sympathetic to Liberal aims. More novel was the straightforward interview with some sort of celebrity. *L'Électeur* (29 July 1892) tried to capitalize on a short-lived political excitement by publishing a lengthy, front-page interview with Elgin Meyers, called 'un des chefs du parti annexationiste.' What the reporter did here, of course, was structure the interview, asking the correct questions to elicit the desired responses.

The so-called 'news-letter' was expected to mix opinion and fact to furnish readers with an explanation of the news. News-letters usually came after the fact, perhaps an elaboration of an event announced in an earlier dispatch. They were written by a regular correspondent, who in French Canada might have a byline. The most celebrated news-letters analysed the affairs, occasionally the life, of some place in the outside world. As early as 1849, the Toronto *British Colonist* boasted a London letter which regularly appeared on its editorial page. This kind of news-letter was soon a standard offering in the leading dailies of English Canada. The correspondents were typically masters of arrogant commentary, if not invective, on people and events. Witness this unrestrained judgment which appeared in the 'European Correspondence' of the Montreal *Herald* (14 February 1871): 'The monstrous bubble of lying which M. Gambetta has been believing so long, and with which he has dazzled and misled his unhappy country, ha[s] collapsed at last.' The ultramontane journals were especially careful to select correspondents who would provide a fitting interpretation of the European scene. *Le Nouveau Monde*'s 'Correspondance romaine' (14 February 1880), after surveying the problems of poverty and the charity of Italian authorities, noted the 'contraste entre le cynicisme cruel et rapace des gens officiels et la charité douce et tendre de l'Eglise.' An equivalent bias ran through the various Ottawa letters that party organs used to supplement their political coverage. *La Minerve*'s 'Courrier politique' in the 1890s was expected to reflect the party's view as well as recount interesting gossip. By this time, though, the news-letter was definitely on the wane (especially in English Canada), a victim of the emphasis on up-to-date news.

In fact two related forms, the 'report' and the 'story,' had triumphed, at least on the general news pages.[34] That was proof of how central the reporter (including the men hired by news agencies, which now supplied expanded dispatches to their clients) had become to the process of newsgathering. The report or story was an especially versatile way of conveying the news. Editors could easily slant copy via the imaginative use of headlines, illustrations, and loaded words. Neither the report nor the story carried a byline, so the reporter was the anonymous voice of the newspaper. Typically, the report took the shape of a lawyer's brief, logical but hardly impartial, suited to the task of instruction and persuasion, whereas the story smacked more of melodrama and thus was the preferred technique of sensationalism. Naturally, the quality daily favoured the rational style of the report, the people's daily the emotional style of the story. Even so, many a news item shared attributes of both forms. And every newspaper employed the report as well as the story to communicate information or sensation.

The structure and the language of the report suggested its cerebral purpose. It began with a headline, often supplemented by a few subheads, and offered a summary lead sentence or paragraph. Note the opening of this report in *La Presse* (9 March 1896):

DAVIS CONTRE LA VILLE

Condamnation de $3,487

On ne renvoie pas les employés
publics sans raisons

L'honourable juge Doherty a rendu jugement cette aprês-midi, dans la cause d'Adolphe David dit Davis, ex-surintendant du département de l'aqueduc, contre la cité. On se rappelle que le demandeur réclamait la somme de $50,487 dont $50,000 de dommages-intérêts et $487 de salaire.

Thereafter, the report, if lengthy, summarized exactly what happened and why, where fitting carrying the opinions of the principal actors, usually in a bold and sparse style. The editor might easily slant the news by employing a biased headline: so the Liberal Montreal *Herald* (10 March 1896) asked 'TRICKERY OR BACKDOWN?' in its account of a speech by Charles Tupper, while the Conservative *Gazette* (14 March 1896) labelled a speech by George Foster 'GREAT' and referred to 'LIBERAL INJUSTICE.' Or the writer could include a casual comment which bespoke the paper's view: thus a *Gazette* report (11 March 1896) on a proposed by-law closed with the opinion 'the characteristic apathy' of the aldermen was bound to delay passage. These techniques made the report valuable when the daily embarked on a crusade since moral indignation and bias could be cloaked in the garb of fact and logic. The reader was left with the impression of an ordered, rational investigation of the issue or event.

The story, by contrast, strove to reach the reader's 'heart,' as well as 'mind,' indeed to involve the reader in whatever joyful or tragic item the newspaper was serving up. Murders, suicides, heroism, virtue, or villainy all readily lent themselves to a story treatment. Headlines were striking: the Hamilton *Herald* (26 December 1889) announced 'An Attempted Robbery/Atrocious Attack upon a Defenceless Woman/Beaten into Insensibility and then Robbed.' The opening sentence or paragraph tried to evoke a mood, not merely summarize the happening. Thus the first lines in this human interest story about a child's death taken from the Toronto *World* ('A Little Tot's Pitiful Fate,' 23 March 1893): 'Only a sash of white crape suspended from a doorknob, between two streamers of white satin ribbon, swaying back and forth in the gentle spring breeze! Many people passed 39 Bulwer street yesterday evening, but perhaps not a dozen gave a second thought to this badge of mourning, the index to a most pathetic story.' The storyteller became an eyewitness, using a lush, dramatic language to keep the mood alive. A suicide story, set in Niagara Falls, in the Saint John *Sun* (2 January 1880), for instance, told how the poor soul 'gazed intently into the rivers,' 'suddenly threw up his hands,' 'jumped into the awful abyss,' entering that 'maelstrom of the whirlpool.' *La Presse*, in particular, went to great pains to reconstruct a murder: not just a description but quotes, illustrations, even maps, following up with an account of the hunt and arrest of the villain, his trial and conviction, all of which produced a 'true life' feuilleton.[35] The story turned news into revelation, enjoyable but not always decent.

The difference in style and tone was obvious in the ways the *Globe* and the *News* covered one local crisis, the Toronto streetcar troubles of 1886. On the morning of 10 March company officials, acting on orders from the owner, Frank Smith, had locked out employees who, he suspected, had broken or intended to break their contracts by joining the Knights of Labor. That action sparked a general walkout, and when the company tried to run cars downtown crowds of clerks, workingmen, and youngsters gathered to block passage, a striking display of the public hatred for the streetcar monopoly. For three days a near riot disgraced Toronto's streets until the civic authorities arranged a compromise solution. Both the *Globe* and the *News* furnished lengthy descriptions of exactly what happened. The *Globe*, however, published 'reports,' the *News* 'stories.'

The *Globe*'s reports ('Street Car Lock Out' 11 March, page eight; same title 12 March, page eight; 'Street-Car Troubles' 13 March, page sixteen) mixed description and interviews to attempt a balanced survey of the dispute. The various attacks on the cars, on the scabs and police, the recklessness of the mob, and the efforts to maintain order all were noted. At times, the reporters suggested that people were merely having fun, indulging in a bit of 'horse play.' Much was made of the 'stalwart police' who on the whole kept things in hand. Both sides were allowed to speak their minds, since reporters interviewed Smith and his officials as well as the labour leaders. (On 13 March the *Globe* even published a brief letter from Smith correcting an error made in an earlier report.) And the public interest was not forgotten, the *Globe* men keeping a close watch on the mayor and the aldermen whose purpose became to get the dispute settled fast. These reports took no definite stand, though implicit was the priority of maintaining order. The *Globe*'s account left the impression of troubles, but always under control and anyway rooted in a breakdown of communications. The orderly world of Toronto the Good was only briefly disrupted.

The *New*'s account was much more excited. The two stories on 10 March, 'Warring against Labour' (page one) and 'Locked Out' (page four), were chatty, eyewitness descriptions of the troubles, and these descriptions clearly favoured the employees' cause. Reporters gave a blow-by-blow account of the crowd's successful efforts to stop traffic. At fault was Smith, typecast as a reactionary who, because of his anti-union views, who had infringed upon that 'principle of freedom and liberty of action' enjoyed by all people. And the *News* emphasized that the men had behaved 'in a most orderly manner' and 'wisely refrained' from taking part in crowd actions. The arrest of one of the drivers even sparked a reporter's complaint that this was 'extraordinary,' given the fact no charge had been laid. The next day's stories, 'Still the Same' (page one) and 'The Mayor Speaks' (page four), merely picked up the tale from the previous afternoon, supplying more lengthy descriptions of the street scenes, this time complete with illustrations. A new concern over the threat of anarchy offset the earlier question of justice, though. Indeed, the *News* admonished readers against acts of violence, especially property damage, which endangered the peace and order of the city. Friday's story, simply entitled 'The Mob' (page four), recounted in great detail the battle for control of the streets, twice commenting on instances of police excess. The Saturday finale, aside from a brief item on the settlement, was just a repeat of the previous day's story – with some new illustrations. What stood out was the *News*'s desire to convey the drama of the troubles. This unique event, the crowd's furious anger, deserved a sensational treatment. The community was in upheaval, the dread spectre of anarchy and mob rule just below the surface. At the same time, the paper's account boosted labour's cause and later defended law and order, views natural to so bourgeois a champion of democracy. The villain of the whole affair was undeniably Frank Smith. The victors were rightfully the carmen. The truth had been revealed, justice had triumphed, peace restored, and readers entertained.

THE EDITORIAL PAGE

'La carrière du journalisme est une vie de contentions et de luttes.' That was the opening line in *L'Étendard*'s extraordinary statement of purpose, 'le journalisme militant,' featured in its prospectus (23 January 1883). Apparently the duty of every newspaper was to 'combattre pour le triomphe des principes qu'il croit bons, et dans nos divisions, défendre ce qu'il croit être la vérité.' True, the zeal for controversy should be gentled by a commitment to that grand Christian rule, love thy neighbour. So *L'Étendard* promised to take the high road, to avoid abusing people and their views, indeed to respect adversaries. But the force of this promise was immediately nullified by the joyous 'cri de guerre.' The paper had been born with 'une constitution plus robuste,' necessary because of its devotion to 'la cause du bien.' And this 'cause' was in peril, threatened on all sides by 'ennemis acharnés.' No one could doubt the paper would do everything in its power to combat error.

In fact, *L'Étendard* had merely repeated a maxim of the age, albeit with a good deal more energy than was normal. Journalists stubbornly insisted that a newspaper had not fulfilled its mission unless it swore allegiance to some cause, and worked hard to ensure the victory of that cause. After all, it was 'the business of the journalist to develop public opinion, to liberalize and energize the social and industrial forces, to utter the voice of the people, and go on his way stoutly,' Willison told a university audience.[36] Even Ross, so the story goes, was wont to proclaim 'the outstanding glory of any journal is to create, to correct, to guide and mould public opinion.'[36] That was why newspapers were forever publishing manifestoes – that and the need for self-promotion, of course, to give the newspaper an identity in people's minds. Every newcomer proclaimed its views to the waiting public: *L'Étendard*'s prospectus made abundantly clear that its news and features, not only its editorials, would sustain the ultramontane cause. A change of ownership or control usually produced another declaration: late in 1883 E.E. Sheppard signalled his new authority over the Toronto *News* with a marvellous rundown of the measures he saw necessary to realize an American-style democracy. So too a change of course: during the winter of 1886–87 the Toronto *Mail* not only publicized its break with John A. Macdonald but also espoused a series of Radical views that would thereafter condition its news and comment.

All of this exalted the editorial page, whatever the necessity of increased advertising or more news. There, the newspaper brought its principles to bear on the issues of the day. 'If it be true that the editorial page is to disappear then it must be that we are to become more and more a race of mere triflers and gossipers, stuffed with the raw, crude odds and ends of the world's happenings, and seeking always for the new sensation in the earth, and never for the new sign in the heavens,' warned a critic. 'There is no other agency so calculated to promote keen independent thinking and acute public controversy.[38] Editorials were never just the property of the actual writer – hence the rule of anonymity: 'The candid impersonal opinions of a newspaper are usually of great weight and value, and enhanced by the impersonality of the writer.'[39] The editor could select from a regular arsenal of weapons to elaborate the paper's opinions. True, the old-fashioned leader, sometimes full of grace, sometimes just turgid, was on the wane. Brevity found special favour with the people's journals. Especially after 1880, editorials came in all sizes, though the substantial editorial pages of the quality dailies still offered at least one lengthy essay as a matter of course. The editorial could simply report a choice piece of information (the *Globe*'s 'The Grasshopper Plague in Manitoba'), inquire into some phenomenon (the *Manitoba Free Press*'s 'Diabolism Rampant'), survey a series of events (the *Mail*'s 'Statesmen and Ecclesiastics'), or spoof a pompous official (the *Telegram*'s 'Hooray for Shippy Spurr').[40] The turn of the seasons brought year-end reviews and New Year predictions or resolutions, laudatory articles occasioned by the queen's birthday or Dominion Day, celebrations of autumn in Canada. Yet the classic form remained polemic, long or short, which marshalled logic, irony, wit, insult, statistics, and principle to rip apart an enemy or demonstrate a truth. Although the usual tone might be a trifle more dignified, less bitter than in times past,[41] the traditional pose of editorial infallibility survived little changed. The editor's world remained a place of crisis. Conspiracies abounded. Paranoia was not uncommon. The quality daily, the ordinary party organ, and the people's journal could not resist the urge to argue and attack.

Inspiration came from everywhere. Sometimes, a prominent outsider, politician or businessman, might furnish a useful thought, maybe an actual article. Then there were the eccentricities of the editor or publisher: so Martin Griffin used the Toronto *Mail* in the early 1880s to worry about the decline of Christianity at home and abroad, John Cameron a little later employed the rival *Globe* to boost his temperance views, Honoré Beaugrand around 1892 and 1893 allowed his annexationist leanings to infect the editorials of *La Patrie.* A special source of inspiration, though, were the opinions of friends and enemies in the press. Unknown is the extent of simple plagiarism, a natural recourse when an editor might be exhausted and newspapers exchanged copies. On 19 April 1889, for instance, the Vancouver *World* carried 'Peace and Honour,' an editorial on the Jesuits' Estates Act copied from the Saint John *Sun* of 14 days earlier. A bit more selective, the Liberal *Chronicle* of Halifax (28 June 1892) printed with slight changes a nice attack on the National Policy as the primary cause of rural depopulation, an attack first published four years previously in the Montreal *Herald.* Lusty arguments, like good ideas, never lost their merit. More obvious, of course, were the admitted borrowings from other newspapers: in one month (26 December 1881 to 26 January 1882), *La Patrie* copied three editorials from *L'Électeur*, two from *La Concorde*, even one translated from the *Globe*, all papers in the Liberal camp. The very fact of publicity might bring a novel topic to the attention of a whole gaggle of editors. Exactly that happened when, early in 1887, the *Mail* raised the issue of Commercial Union, soon a matter of consuming interest to dailies of all stripes in Ontario. Then there were the opinions of a rival. If repeated enough they were bound to set off a cycle of abuse that might well degenerate into sheer name-calling. The smaller dailies and country weeklies, in particular, were all too ready to surrender their editorial freedom to parrot the arguments of the big-city papers on the major questions of the day. A party organ might then cite these parrotings to prove how popular its views were in the country at large! This form of incest was the nineteenth-century version of what would later be stigmatized as 'pack journalism.'

Inspiration, however, was subservient to the newspaper's loyalties. The first, sometimes the foremost, loyalty was to a party. Any reader, whether in 1870 or 1900, could easily predict the response of most newspapers to the inevitable government scandal. But, on occasion, the surrounding region might exercise an even greater influence on the editorial page. During the early 1880s the emphatically city-rendered *Telegram* blasted away at the grumpy,greedy farmers of Ontario who exercised too much sway over the policies of the provincial government and opposition. The big metropolitan dailies crafted the new regional credos that upset and enriched the dominion's life by the 1880s. The *Manitoba Free Press*, for example, pioneered the notions of an energetic west and an effete east and all the related stereotypes that were repeated ad nauseam by prairie newspapers thereafter.[42] Race and religion added another layer of conditioning. Montreal's anglophone press watched closely the legislation of the Quebec government to ensure the preservation of the English presence and power in the province. Finally, there was the novel force of class. Sheppard's *News*, intent on winning over the workingman, was a loud champion of the Knights of Labor; Farrer's *Mail*, pursuing the 'classes,' favoured the 'free workingman' and the open shop. The editorial page, in short, catered to the presumed tastes of a newspaper's constituency.

That might suggest press debate was always an unholy chaos, rabid but formless. Just the opposite was the case. Recall the editorial was a type of popular literature and consequently constructed around fairly well established structures of thought.[43] The editors, excepting a few doctrinaires, were slaves of chance, men of strong opinions perhaps but rarely of deep convictions, forced to explain the ephemeral or the transient to a mass of readers. This situation did not so much liberate the imagination as necessitate conformity to structures that had worked in times past. New thoughts succeeded by fitting into an existing philosophical framework, which intensified rather than altered the message of their philosophy. Newspapers became the champions, in whole or part, of distinct perspectives on life and affairs which repetition made familiar, indeed welcome to their audiences. The term 'perspective' is used here to indicate a unique collection of stereotypes, a cluster of priorities (often boasting a style or ritual of argument), grounded in the immediate past and the present. The perspective, not surprisingly, lacks rigour, consistency, and depth, attributes normally associated with a doctrine; rather the perspective is superficial, simpleminded, and cluttered with contradictions, no matter how dogmatic the expression. Yet it does serve to guide the response to things as they are, or appear to be, making easier the task of the editor. Then, at least, it proved a powerful tool of explanation, highly saleable to publics that wished to understand the meaning of events.

Readers could choose from among that quarrelsome trinity of Conservatism, Liberalism, and Radicalism. The Conservative banner was carried by a wide assortment of organs, many reborn or first launched in the 1870s, as well as a couple of ultramontane mavericks. This label meant a fulsome commitment to the community, supposedly bound together by tradition and self-interest, which translated into a strategy of preservation emphasizing resistance to social and political change – anything from 'Godless Schools' to 'Senate Reform' – as well as a strategy of nation-building emphasizing growth and bigness, railways and factories. Conservatives happily dressed up in the garb of nationalism – hence their frequent use of the notorious 'Loyalty Cry' to doom their foes. The perceptive reader might wonder to which nation the loyalty lay: the nation *L'Étendard* defended was usually a Catholic Quebec, whereas the Toronto *Empire* boosted a British Canada.

The Liberal alternative, also voiced by a party press, revolved around the concept of liberty, freeing the individual from the rule of privilege and the dead hand of the past to deliver up a better world, a credo that could justify free trade, provincial rights, even prohibition. Sometimes Liberals seemed the quintessential Victorians, so pure were their motives, so zealous their morality. Ironically, leading Liberal papers such as the Toronto *Globe* or the London *Advertiser* were the great proponents of a moral regulation that would hobble personal freedom to ensure social regeneration.

The Radical challenge suffered by far the most confused credo, perhaps because there was no major party to effect its priorities. It was born, of course, in the people's journals, but it appealed as well to a number of mavericks and independents who found the status quo oppressive. Generally speaking, this perspective stressed the idea of democracy, the liberation of the 'masses' (or, in the case of the *Mail*, the 'classes'!) that would work a grand transformation of society and politics. That goal led its champions to boost a grab-bag of schemes: protection, anti-monopoly, national independence, later imperial unity, an Anglo-Protestant ascendancy, or Fortress Quebec. A Radical paper fell easily into the pose of a populist tribune striking out against the powers of the day, be they plutocrats (the Victoria *Times*), Catholic bishops (the Winnipeg *Tribune*), or sabbatarians (the Toronto *World*).

Each of these camps cut across the boundaries of language, religion, locale, even party. The rise and fall of these perspectives gave coherence, indeed a unity, to the press debate over nation-building. The general question of Confederation had temporarily exhausted the wellsprings of innovation, leaving editors little but party or parochial issues to satisfy their zeal for controversy. It was after the early 1870s that the three perspectives took a rough shape around competing visions of the ideal Canada: hence the extraordinary excitement over the National Policy, Provincial Rights, Manhood Suffrage, Canada's Destiny, and the like. Quite abruptly, in the mid-1880s, the mood of debate changed. A sense of malaise, a dissatisfaction with things as they were, fostered a growing volume of dissent, Liberal as well as Radical. Pessimism was in vogue. Old and new disputes – over race and religion, regional ambitions, Capital and Labour, moral reform – threatened the social as well as the political order. After 1890, however, a new theme of celebration, especially evident in Conservative rhetoric, overcame the Radical frenzy. In fact, by the late 1890s, the quarrelsome trinity had lost, for the nonce, some of its force, leaving behind a consensus of sorts.

Convention had decreed the editorial page was the brain as well as the heart of the newspaper. 'A paper is much more than a collection of news items,' assumed N.F. Davin, later editor of the Regina *Leader*. 'It is a political "persona," which must preserve its individuality at the peril of complete failure. Nor is it enough to do this. It must have intellectual and moral force; in its voice their must be no uncertain sound – not to speak of contradictory notes – and though many minds contribute, the unity must remain intact.'[44] The emotions and thoughts bared on the editorial page must resonate throughout the whole newspaper. The aim was not always realized in practice. Even so the daily fare (including, at times, the ads) could usually claim a certain coherence, with at least the chief items reflecting the paper's views. The good newspaper remained an instrument of propaganda.

FORMS: THE POPULAR DAILY

A mid-nineteenth-century reader would have easily recognized the daily of 1900. The long search for popularity had not worked any spectacular change in the basic design of the newspaper. But this reader would likely have been unsettled by the new ensemble. The conventions governing form had undergone substantial modification to suit the successful market strategies of popular journalism.

Once again my investigation views form through the medium of the Toronto *Globe*. The sample selected was the morning edition of Tuesday, 15 May 1900, 12 pages in length, seven columns on each page. Advances in technology now allowed the publisher to inflate the number of pages to suit the rush of daily material, although costs usually kept the ordinary weekday edition modest. But the column straitjacket remained the essential skeleton about which editors placed their material. The most striking innovation was the wealth of headlines and subheads, the latter often a summary of the report. On occasion, a headline, in large black type, might cut across column boundaries: 'Gen. Buller Fighting,' for instance, covered two columns to introduce the *Globe*'s lead front-page report on the Boer War.

Also common were display ads in self-contained blocks, coming in different sizes of course, which broke up the straitjacket on the inside pages: so in the top

The front-page cartoon: a new editorial form increasingly popular in the 1890s as a way of grabbing the reader's attention

middle of page five a three-column block advertised the virtues of 'Dr. McLaughlin's Electric Belt' (electric belts were apparently a popular item, promising cures for such male troubles as a weak back or persistent impotency). These ads were notable for the number of illustrations used to capture the eye of the casual reader: the Eaton's display ad, for example, contained small drawings of the 'Tempting Buying Chances for Wednesday.' Aside from the front-page cartoon, depicting the onward march of the British forces to victory in South Africa, illustrations were largely absent from the news columns, the *Globe* supplying only two drawings of leading figures in a mildly sensational trial. Popularity, then, had only slightly altered the stern appearance of Brown's earlier *Globe*.

But now the arrangement and the style of material emphasized that the *Globe* was, first and foremost, a *news*paper. Symbolic of this enthusiasm was the inclusion on the front page of an index to that edition's 'Special Features' in the news columns on the inside pages. The front page, cleared of ads, was dominated by two lengthy reports on British fortunes in the war. Happenings in the sports and business worlds received attention on two special pages. The other news filled the non-advertising columns on all but one page. The exception to news, of course, was the editorial page, at the centre of the newspaper still (page six), where the *Globe*'s old motto could be found – albeit in small print. Ironically, the editorials, even the lengthy essays, whether argumentative or reflective, took on the guise of the report, marshalling facts to persuade or inform.

Ads occupied space on all the inside pages, including two columns on the editorial page. Classifieds were assigned six columns on page three. A variety of small commercial and financial ads, in blocks, dotted the business page. The department stores boasted the largest ads: Eaton's took a half-page (plus a small block elsewhere), Simpson's three-quarters of page four. These ads, as well, borrowed from the style of the news report (especially by their emphasis upon concrete facts) to sway the buying public.

Much the same could be said of the rest of the daily press. But the forms, employed by the *Globe*'s weekday edition were not common – at least in detail. Both the Montreal *Gazette* and the Saint John *Sun* still carried ads on their front pages in 1899 (a practice which likely allowed them to charge a higher tariff). The *Manitoba Free Press* turned over the first column on its front page to tidbit news about happenings from near and far. Half the centre column of *La Patrie*'s front page (3 May 1899) went to promote a forthcoming 'feuilleton' (two serials were already being carried by the paper). The so-called editorial page of the Toronto *News* (23 May 1900) was in fact dominated by a huge top-to-bottom block, covering the middle columns, for Eaton's; the shortened editorials were squashed into the first two of the paper's eight columns. That

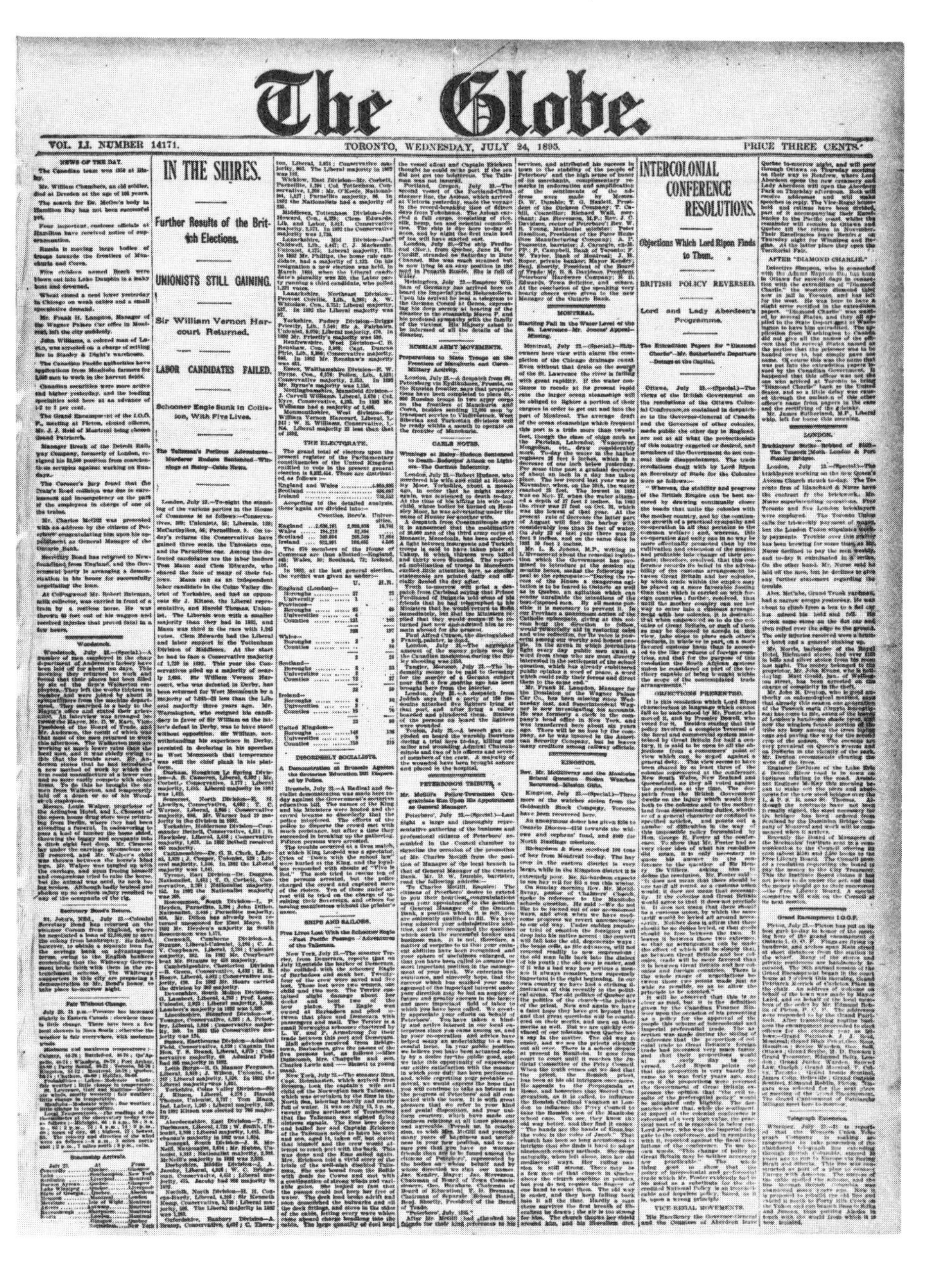

The Globe.

VOL. LI. NUMBER 14171. TORONTO, WEDNESDAY, JULY 24, 1895. PRICE THREE CENTS.

NEWS OF THE DAY.

IN THE SHIRES.

Further Results of the British Elections.

UNIONISTS STILL GAINING.

Sir William Vernon Harcourt Returned.

LABOR CANDIDATES FAILED.

Schooner Eagle Sunk in Collision, With Five Lives.

THE ELECTORATE.

RUSSIAN ARMY MOVEMENTS.

CABLE NOTES.

MONTREAL.

INTERCOLONIAL CONFERENCE RESOLUTIONS.

Objections Which Lord Ripon Finds to Them.

BRITISH POLICY REVERSED.

Lord and Lady Aberdeen's Programme.

AFTER "DIAMOND CHARLIE."

LONDON.

LE PLUS FORT TIRAGE QUOTIDIEN AU CANADA

LA PRESSE

66.246

QUINZIEME ANNEE – N° 128 MONTREAL, LUNDI 2 AVRIL 1900 HUIT PAGES – UN CENTIN

CATASTROPHE MIRACULEUSEMENT EVITEE

La journée d'hier pleine d'emotions pour nos braves pompiers. — Une conflagration de plus de $100,000 au magasin Paquette, rue St Laurent. —Incidents tragiques. —Une collision avec un tramway. —Plusieurs pompiers blessés. — M. Dufort, marchand, se fracture le bras. —Le pompier Magnan raconte les impressions d'une chute d'un troisième étage et d'un ensevelissement sous une dizaines de pieds de débris.

MAGNAN du Nº 11 — GUTHRIE du Nº 5 — LECOMPTE du Nº 4

LE POMPIER CASAVANT LUI-MEME

The front page of the 1890s: two different styles

nicely symbolized the importance of department store advertising to the evening people's daily. *La Presse* and *La Patrie* both made more liberal use of illustrations to please their lowbrow readers. On 10 May 1899, for example, *La Presse*'s front-page account headed 'Encore 1030 Doukhobors' contained a sizeable block illustration of the crowded deck of a boat. The third page of *La Patrie* (3 May 1899) included two columns of illustrations devoted mostly to people involved in a recent fracas at an Indian reserve, without any supporting story. Indeed, all the major newspapers adopted a different form to house the variety of features contained in their Saturday editions, some of which were more than double the size of the weekday paper. The *Globe* itself added a front section of four pages featuring a story with photographs (on 29 September 1900 the North West Mounted Police were celebrated) as well as other light fare. The Saturday special was designed to 'look' like a magazine as well as a newspaper, because it was meant for leisurely family reading.

A similar variety characterized the language of the daily press. 'The flippancy of the American headliner and the partiality of American newspaper writers in general for colloquialism, irreverence and slang are continental in their scope,' argued Samuel Moffett in 1907, 'and sharply distinguish both American and Canadian journalism from that of England.'[45] That was only true in general. Ads, in particular, employed an easy language and simple sentence structure to reach a mass audience. The Simpson's ad in the sample *Globe*, for instance, spoke of 'A Score of Stores,' 'dependable quality' and 'great economy,' the need to 'push' a lot of goods in 'ever-so-short a time' which, naturally, resulted in 'money-saving chances' for the consumer. Slang infected the sports news as well: a story on a baseball game in the Toronto *News* (23 May 1900) praised the local team for fighting 'gamely,' noted 'wild throws' and 'bad throws,' and decided Toronto had been forced 'to take the small end of the purse.' Headlines, in some papers, strove to excite rather than just inform: so *La Presse* (27 November 1899) offered stories under headlines such as 'Le gibet ou le bagne' and 'Combats sur combats,' both cutting across three columns. But headlines in a quality paper such as the *Globe* were more staid, if occasionally expressing bias (witness the headline 'Boers Misuse White Flag,' supplemented by the subhead 'British Cavalry Were Treacherously Entrapped'). And the editorials remained long and complicated, requiring a person to bring to his reading a sophisticated knowledge of English as well as affairs, whereas a reader of the *Telegram* would not need to worry that its simple editorials might test his competence in either field. What had lost force somewhere during the years, obviously, was the conviction that all readers shared the same kind of literary skills and tastes.

Clearly, the arrival of popularity had not fostered any rigid standardization of form across newspaperdom. In some ways the publisher of the popular newspaper actually enjoyed more choice than his colonial predecessor. Technology now made this choice possible. Besides, uniformity of design, appearance, and language were no longer so important now that the idiosyncrasies of individual journalists had been tamed by the discipline of mass communications. Convention was tailored to suit the particular market strategy of any given newspaper. That allowed the *Globe* to appear so serious and staid, as befitted a quality daily, while *La Presse* could adopt a flashy packaging to suggest the sensations inside. The popular daily was, in short, specialized. Sheppard's 'good newspaper' remained very much a creature of convention but the conventions were more numerous and their sway less strict. Publishers had to fashion out of the formulas available a form and a substance that would assure a profitable share of the market in their particular arenas.

5

Mythmaking

Graeme Patterson has called myth 'a complex of symbols and images imbedded in narrative' which works 'as a sort of lens or screen, whereby certain features of a subject are ignored or suppressed, while others are emphasized or distinctively organized.' Shared myths can serve to promote 'group identities, cultural stability, and social harmony,' to legitimate 'status systems and power structures,' and even to justify 'social and political revolution.'[1]

Every leading authority, from the school to the church and party, sponsored myths. But the daily press was the prime mythmaker. Here the editorial excelled: although the teacher's lessons or the preacher's sermons dealt in symbols and images, neither form could reach so many people so often on all manner of topics. During the last decades of the nineteenth century, editorials elaborated a series of mythologies of nationhood which sometimes challenged but usually justified the existing or emerging patterns of dominance in the country at large. These mythologies, of course, were rough-hewn, incorporating unresolved tensions and outright contradictions. And they might well suffer a somewhat different fate in the hands of a Radical than a Conservative, a French-Canadian instead of an English-Canadian editor. Still, their very presence in a welter of rhetoric suggests that the ways of a modernizing dominion rested on a firm foundation of shared myth. Their prominence in francophone and anglophone rhetoric indicates that an important ideological bridge joined the 'two solitudes,' of French and English Canada. Their nature points to the emphatic class bias of Canadian life, the fact that the new dominion was very much a bourgeois domain.

THE DOGMA OF MODERNITY

The daily press popularized, above all, a particular dogma of modernity cobbled together out of the clichés of the editors' world. The dogma was built upon three apparent certitudes, the ideas of progress, nationality, and democracy, accepted (if sometimes reluctantly) by journalists of nearly every stripe. And it incorporated what would remain a lasting tension in Canadian thought over the proper role of the state in the making of a modern society.

The idea of progress was the most hallowed maxim of the age. It rested on the presumption that change ruled man's life. 'Aucune période de l'humanité n'a vu autant de transformation que celle de 1840 à 1890,' exclaimed an excited Benjamin Sulte in *Le Monde* (24 June 1893) in one typical outburst. People had experienced 'dix existences dans à court laps de temps.' The result was the successive breakdown of the way things were. 'Old systems are tottering and new ideas are being pushed rapidly to the front,' mused the Montreal *Herald* (27 March 1886). 'New social forces have been created and are at work,' causing 'problems before the statesmen and philanthropists of today which cannot be solved by rules and precedents of former ages.'[2] Such a view was likely to please any journalist. Newspapers had an institutional bias that ensured their editors would believe everything was in flux. The news pages chronicled change, be that scientific or medical discoveries, upheavals in the realm of affairs, novel doctrines or movements, even the ordinary swirl of events. Was it any wonder that the journalist would assume the change his paper detailed had some grand significance for his readers? There is something ironic about the possibility that an occupational hazard of journalism assisted the growth of a structure of myth.

Not everyone was charmed by incessant change. Editors recognized that change had not always brought sweetness and light in its wake. Pessimism was a mood that could strike any writer upset by some sin or other. In French Canada, where Catholic beliefs perpetuated a ritual anti-modernism, newspapers looked askance at 'l'esprit de progrès à rebours' (*Le Nouveau Monde*, 18 February 1880), the cause only of error, revolution, and destruction. In English Canada, where Protestant beliefs fostered an equally impotent anti-materialism, newspapers might well explode into anger over the 'extravagance, waste, ostentation, barbaric display, pride of wealth' (Hamilton *Spectator*, 29 April 1887) – attitudes and habits that marred modern life. In fact, editors sometimes suffered from a nineteenth-century version of 'future shock,' afraid society was being swept off its moorings. So *La Minerve* (10 September 1880) felt called upon to warn youth especially to remember always the value of tradition and the lessons of history. Likewise, the Toronto *Mail* (28 January 1876) lamented the speed of change which had brought much dissatisfaction to people and vitiated that old-time spirit of contentment. Nostalgia was a not uncommon failing of the moody Conservative.

Such doubts, however, were only the intellectual equivalent of indigestion. Far more common, even among the doubters, was an extraordinary faith in 'le mouvement de progrès,' 'the eternal law of progress.'[3] A survey of cynics and cynicism left the Toronto *Globe* (13 July 1889) with the conviction that 'the tendency of the world and the race is still upward.' The approach of Dominion Day elicited from the Vancouver *World* (30 June 1890) the cheery declaration that 'the civilization of these later years is tending gradually to the loftiest point to which it is possible to attain.' Editors found the signs of progress everywhere, citing, for instance, the spread of Christianity, the advance of literacy, the rise of workingmen, even the headway the English language (or the French) had made in the world and at home. But these editors recognized their's was above all a century of material progress, when the marvels of science had granted man an ever-increasing command of nature. *La Patrie* (10 September 1891) devoted a front-page editorial to celebrating the story of electricity, startling evidence of man's new-found powers. *L'Électeur* (30 October 1894), excited by the technology of petroleum, praised 'le mouvement industriel de plus en plus étonnant, de notre epoque.' Editors romanticized the smoking factory as proof of progress or the railway as civilization on wheels – 'Ce progrès matériel est bon lui-même,' thought an optimistic *La Presse* (5 September 1903), 'et il peut devenir une cause de progrès moral.'[4] A classic example of this innocence was an editorial simply entitled 'Notre progrés' in *La Minerve* (25 May 1892), which listed all the signs of growth, from canals built to charities multiplied, in one grand litany of progress. Besides, whatever the social troubles or the moral ills of the present, editors were convinced 'the march of progress will not be stayed with the close of the nineteenth century' (Saint John *Telegraph*, 31 December 1895), sure that future generations would clean up the debris left behind by change. The editorial pages, in short, were imbued with the smug conviction that things must turn out right eventually.

The idea of nationality, a partner of progress, had won its entry into the pantheon of Canadian myth only around the time of Confederation. True, long before then, francophone journalists had been enthusiasts of nationality because of its utility in the battle for 'la survivance.' Also, dreams of a British nationality had pleased generations of anglophone journalists. But the key event was the success during the 1860s of the unionist movement, which employed the idea of nationality to justify what otherwise seemed a prosaic bargain among petty colonies. The London *Free Press*, in particular, popularized the phrase 'a new nationality' to describe the result of a British North American federation, a phrase which briefly enjoyed much currency in anglophone circles and found its way into the first throne speech of the dominion's Parliament. The erstwhile anti-unionists, such as the Halifax *Chronicle* or Montreal *Herald*, only came to admit the idea's force as they came to accept the reality of Confederation.

Ironically, the rhetoric of nationality quickly proved a source as much of contention as of agreement. The francophone press, from the beginning, sanctified Confederation as the guardian of a Québécois nationality, whereas the anglophone press soon portrayed the same union as the foundation of a pan-Canadian nationality.[5] The later recognition of this fundamental disagreement led a few dailies, notably the Toronto *Mail* in the late 1880s and *La Patrie* in the early 1890s, to use the idea of nationality to reject Confederation and justify the search for a better home. This indicates that the so-called 'Canadian Question' has rested not so much on the absence of nationalism as on the presence of competing nationalisms.

Even so, francophone and anglophone alike shared a liking for the stereotypes which the idea of nationality advanced to explain past and present. Humanity, it seemed, was naturally divided into rival nationalities, which thus must constitute the primary communities everywhere, whatever the claims of party, class, or creed. What made a nationality? History supplied one answer. Editors sponsored a view of the past which highlighted the theme of survival. Throughout the Canadian experience, reflected the Toronto *Empire* (27 July 1889), there ran 'a vein of intense interest, of romantic action and of heoric deeds' as Canadians strove to overcome the wilderness and block the ambitions of the American giant. 'Not only have they preserved through all the difficulties and dangers of the early years the continuity of the British traditions, but they have in addition built up the foundations of a great nation out of unsettled wastes and an untilled wilderness, and have proved their right to the possession by genuine patriotism and undoubted loyalty.' No less clichéd was the francophone counterpart. Abandoned by an errant France to the tender mercies of 'une puissance étrangère,' recounted *L'Électeur* (19 August 1892), a pitiful handful of French Canadians had by heroic effort and great devotion become 'plus de 2,000,000' strong, 'maîtres d'une province représentant dans l'Amérique du Nord toute une civilisation, tenant incontestablement dans la Confédération canadienne la balance du pouvoir, commençant à exercer même dans la République voisine une légitime influence.' Canadians and Canadiens were facts of history. That belief explains why the press gave fulsome support to proposals to teach patriotic history in the schools and to bigger and better celebrations of national holidays, notably St-Jean-Baptiste Day, Queen Victoria's birthday, and Dominion Day (outside of the Maritimes that is), when people could recall their glorious pasts.

A second answer was supplied by the attributes of culture and race. 'Chaque nation a son caractère et ses intérêts distinctifs,' according to *Le Nouveau Monde* (20 June 1868). 'La différence des lois et ces institutions contribue tout autant que celle du langage à créer la nationalité.'[6] A lengthy series of feature editorials on 'Our Destiny' in the early days of the Montreal *Star* concluded the Canadians were 'the last of the Germanic series' of races, 'the nation nearest the climax' because 'our national ideas embody the nineteenth century' (11 March 1869).

Central to the nationalist credo in French Canada was the Catholic fact ('Pour les Canadiens, la catholicisme c'est nationalité!' declared T.J.J. Loranger in *La Minerve*, 3 July 1880) which made the Québécois bearers of a splendid tradition in an Anglo-Protestant continent. The Catholic fact served as well to separate Quebec, a purged New France, from its European mother country, a republican France, where the church was under attack.

Central to the nationalist credo in English Canada was the country's un-American heritage, more presumed than proved of course: the boundary, stated the Toronto *News* (13 January 1888), divided 'two peoples different in their form of government, in thought, in mode of life, in aims, in idiom[;] almost the only point of similarity is that the English tongue is generally spoken in both.' One must not discount the effect of the environment though, since the New World had worked to create what the Saint John *Telegraph* (2 April 1887) called 'The Un-British Provinces': 'The prevalent ideas, habits, sympathies and predelictions of the people are democratic and American, not European, or aristocratic.' Anglophone nationalists would have it both ways, declaring a British or American ethos, the style of argument depending upon whether the momentary target was an arrogant Republic or a paternalistic England. But the force of these arguments justified the care with which editors watched the racial composition of the newcomers arriving on Canadian shores. Keeping out the blacks, Asians, perhaps Jews and Slavs as well, certainly the Mormons, seemed a sound policy to preserve the nation's purity.

The final answer, not surprisingly, lay in that most powerful of emotions, self-interest. Everyone's fancy was captured by a naïve vision of a spacious Canadian future. Supposedly, every nationality was caught up in the logic of competition, something francophone editors loved to call 'la lutte pour l'existence,'[7] which meant a 'rivalité dans de domain du progrès' (*La Patrie*, 8 September 1880). And a generous Providence had blessed Canada with well-nigh limitless vistas. 'Here are boundless stretches of virgin soil crying for the plough and the hoe,' went one typical rhapsody which appeared in the Halifax *Herald* (1 January 1885). 'Here are interminable forests waiting for him who is mighty to lift 'up axes against trees.' Here are inexhaustible mineral treasures beneath our feet. Here is wealth unknown, swarming in our bays and teeming in our seas.' The great want was people. The francophone editor devoted his best efforts to speeding the colonization of Quebec's north, 'notre chateau-fort,' 'le foyer des vieilles traditions et des vieilles moeurs; le centre de la sécurité, la garantie de notre autonomie' (*La Minerve*, 14 November 1870). Whereas the anglophone editor urged settlement everywhere, especially in the west (one estimate held that Canada boasted sufficient 'arable land' to sustain a population '300,000,000' strong)[8] to ensure Canada's glory in North America. But all could expect marvellous things from the grand Canadian barbecue: loads of wheat for world markets, more commerce and new industries, booming cities and contented farms. Not surprising, then, was the concern which gripped editors whenever the government released a census report, even more the paranoia over the so-called 'Exodus' of Canada's youth in search of opportunity in the factories or on the farms of the United States. The statistics of growth, it seemed, were the acid test of Canadian fortunes.

By the 1890s the idea of democracy was accorded about equal honour by editors. That amounted to a substantial change in the accepted wisdom, not unrelated to the social outreach of the daily press. At and after Confederation, a common editorial reflex was to shower praise on the old constitution of Great Britain, because British institutions required voters prove that they had 'a stake in the country' and balanced the powers of plebeian and aristocrat, crown and crowd. The trouble with manhood suffrage, always the symbol of democracy, was that it ruptured this balance, allowing the mob to run rampant. 'The besetting sin of Democracy is its inevitable tendency to level down,' cried the Ottawa *Times* (12 May 1869). 'It is characteristic of democracy to debase everything to its own level, to pull down, never to elevate,' concluded the Quebec *Chronicle* (2 February 1864). 'Democracy is a ruthless deity that must be worshipped by sacrifices of nobility, and it is as insatiable as it is ignoble, as pretentious as unworthy, and has a precocity and growth that is only bounded by its self-destruction.' Such horrors had been amply demonstrated, or so the Conservative argued, by the debauched régimes of a democratic United States and a republican France. Typical of this view of history was the charge aired by *Le Monde* (2 July 1886): 'Le suffrage universel a perdu la France, a déshonoré à jamais le drapeau tricolere et a mis notre antique Mère-Patrie, la fille aimée de l'Eglise, au rang des barbares persécuteurs de l'Eglise et des institutions catholiques.' Fears that manhood suffrage and its ilk would work a similar havoc in Canada justified, throughout the 1880s, the Conservative's stout defence of the Senate as a necessary counterpoise to the unruly Commons. Indeed, even on its deathbed, the ultramontane *L'Étendard* (4 February 1893) warned one more time the reformers intent on abolishing the legislative council that their 'marche à la perfection' was really 'vers la démogogie,' ever the fruitful source of revolution and anarchy.

In fact, *L'Étendard*'s warning was out-of-date among its peers. Democracy was on the march in Canada as elsewhere. That triumphant cry was first echoed by the people's journals which seemed hell-bent on transforming Canada into a democratic utopia. Democracy, in the words of the Toronto *News* (26 November 1883), was 'nothing but a government of the people, by the people, for the people.' Manhood suffrage was more than a measure of simple justice, one of the 'full rights of citizenship' (Toronto *World*, 19 November 1881) owed to every Canadian. Radicals imagined that manhood suffrage was a magic formula which would speed the purification of a corrupt politics and eliminate the remnants of 'caste supremacy' (Toronto *News*, 17 July 1884). The principle of popular sovereignty, indeed, justified a Radical frenzy against the old constitution, especially the Senate, 'the most useless political lumber room that a perverse ingenuity ever invented' (Montreal *Star*, 18 March 1882), which appeared a special affront to the dream of a democratic simplicity. Only two leading dailies, Sheppard's *News* and Beaugrand's *La Patrie*, were sufficiently impressed by the American constitution to favour outright republicanism. But, during the late 1880s, first Liberal and more slowly Conservative organs joined the people's journals, and admitted the merits of manhood suffrage, especially since Gladstone's Reform Act had set Britain firmly on a democratic course.[9] And the daily press soon raised a grand, if useless, clamour against the expense as well as the complexity of a system of over-government, where 'every twentieth man is a tax-eater more or less voracious' (Toronto *Mail*, 24 January 1887).[10] Retrenchment, Economy, Reform – recurring slogans – bespoke the new-found enthusiasm to recast that vast establishment once thought vital to good government.

'Democracy is upon us,' reported the Victoria *Times* (19 June 1890). 'We cannot get rid of it if we would. We must, therefore, make the best of it.' That seemed a simple statement of fact; was not Canada, in *La Patrie*'s words, 'ce pays démocratique' (10 February 1882) in 'ce siècle démocratique' (18 June 1885) where even 'toutes les inventions modernes contribuent à la diffusion des séntiments démocratiques' (18 June 1890). Gone from the press were phrases such as 'the conservative influences of rank and property,' 'l'équilibre entre les trois pouvoirs monarchique, aristocratique, et démocratique,' or 'the tyranny of the mob' and in their place were clichés such as 'the right to vote,' 'le voeu du peuple,' or 'equal rights.'[11]

These clichés had a significance beyond the realm of politics. The era of the common man was 'dawning' in society as well, requiring that publicists (and especially editors in search of popularity) pay lip-service to dreams of equality. What excited the Radical sometimes frightened the Conservative, namely the impact of democracy on the Women's Question, the power of the churches, the separate school or language issues, the relations of Capital and Labour. Democracy could become a universal solvent. It did not, of course. Rather, editors of all stripes, when not in heat over some blight on the social landscape, tried to persuade readers that Canada was a blessed land unmarred by the entrenched class privileges or systems of oppression apparent in the Old World, if not in the American Republic. *Le Monde* (26 July 1886) claimed that it was not the poor but the rich 'qui paie le taxe et qui gorge le trésor public.' For farmers: 'The truth is that the farmers have been making steady progress during the last number of years,' reported the Toronto *World* (26 May 1887), 'not only in the improvement of land itself and the building thereon, but [in] stock, implements and everything that tends to lessen toil and given him a fair and equitable remuneration for his labour and capital.' For workers: 'What burdens ... do the workingmen labour under in British Columbia?' asked the Vancouver *World* (19 May 1890). 'They are as free as the air; are paid good wages and allowed reasonable hours of work; and are permitted – as they should be – to have a full share in the government of the country.' Canada offered a fair field for anyone, and honoured honest toil above good birth or inherited wealth: 'Whether on the farm, in the shop or behind the counter, success is largely a matter of brains' (Montreal *Star*, 17 April 1886). Such arguments made believable the extravagant boast of the London *Free Press* (4 September 1894) that there was 'perhaps no country in the world more homogeneous and purely democratic in all its ramifications and interests.' Thus was born a myth, of an egalitarian Canada, necessary in an age of modernity.

Not surprisingly, champions of modernity would look to the state to realize their special brand of progress. The trouble was that this idealization of the powers of the state clashed with other myths about the dynamics of progress. The upshot was a fierce debate over the relative merits of 'aller faire' and 'laisser faire' (in the words of the London *Advertiser*, 21 May 1889). Controversy broke out first over the validity of economic protectionism. That strategy of nation-building had enjoyed some popularity with unionist editors during the debate over Confederation. A little later, newspapers as different as the Conservative *Chronicle* of Quebec City or the Radical *Star* of Montreal in English Canada, and the Conservative *La Minerve* or the Radical *Le Pays* in French Canada, flirted with economic protectionism. But the cardinal event was the conversion holus-bolus of the Conservative press in the mid-1870s, necessitated by its great propaganda campaign in praise of the National Policy. The Conservative effort, too, was seconded by the people's journals, whose nationalistic juices were excited by visions of a Big Canada. And, by the early 1880s, the new protectionist zeal embraced not just the technique of the tariff but of assisted enterprise (notably the Canadian Pacific Railway) as well. The Liberal response, excepting only a few papers, mingled horror and incredulity at the astonishing Conservative infatuation with discredited economic heresies. The Liberal counter-attack defended the tenets of political economy, emphasized the sins of protectionism, and threw off assorted alternative strategies of nation-building (including that wild scheme of Unrestricted Reciprocity in the late 1880s). No single question so polarized the press for so long as this issue of economic protectionism.

The protectionist case rested upon a couple of maxims endlessly repeated. Central was the conviction, here expressed by the Halifax *Herald* (6 February 1877), 'that the end of Government is not merely to collect and spend taxes, but rather to develop and protect industries, to increase the value of land, to encourage immigration, to diversify, and to be a chief factor in the national prosperity.' Protectionists referred, time and again, to the fact Canada was an infant nation, its capitalists lacking the means to engender unaided the necessary growth. These zealots saw one answer to the Canadian plight in the panacea of industrialization, à la England and the United States, which promised to generate new wealth, diversify employment, and attract foreign capital as well as new immigrants. They employed, and with gusto, the language of war (the Montreal *Gazette*, 9 August 1875, headed one editorial 'War of Extermination') to highlight how the laws of national rivalry overrode the laws of political economy: the international marketplace seemed the plaything of a few giants, in particular the United States, whose industrial prowess enabled her to turn Canada into a 'slaughter market' for surplus manufactures. So tariff protection, the Halifax *Reporter* (10 September 1875) argued, was 'a fence placed around an enclosure to prevent waste or subtraction by outsiders.' The other answer lay in the rapid development of railways which promised to open up Canada to settlement, join frontier and heartland as well as city and countryside. The Canadian Pacific Railway, admittedly very expensive, became 'a great arterial highway' (Toronto *Mail*, 12 January 1874) along which would pass the wealth of a continent. All of this rhetoric was topped off with an appeal to the public's patriotism. The National Policy, broadly defined, added that material dimension necessary to bind together the political nationality built by Confederation. Indeed, it gave Canada, proclaimed an enchanted *Le Monde* (5 November 1890), 'les avantages et la gloire de former sur cette partie du continent, un empire indépendant, pouvant vivre par lui-même et assez fort et puisssant, pour revendiquer et prendre sa place dans le débat des affaires, sur ce continent d'Amerique.'

The rival case was no more sophisticated. Central was the conviction, repeated here by *La Patrie* (16 April 1879), that 'la prospérité ne se crée pas par des actes de législation.' In fact, according to the Montreal *Herald* (10 February 1880), 'Governments do best when they confine themselves as much as possible to governing, leaving all other business to their citizens in their individual capacities.' Liberals put their faith in the laws of political economy, better yet the workings of the free market, to realize growth. Always singing the praises of the 'cheap society' (a favoured phrase), they expected that farmers able to sell in the dearest market, and buy on the cheapest, would produce that wealth and activity necessary to ensure the birth of 'natural industries.' Commercial Union or Unrestricted Reciprocity promised to tie Canadian fortunes to the dynamic

American giant, thereby making the dominion a frontier of American capital and ensuring entry to a gigantic market. The National Policy, by contrast, restricted the course of trade and burdened people with high prices, higher taxes, and a growing debt. The Liberal blamed protectionism for any and every evil, from sectional animosities and class tensions to the exodus of young people to the United States and the corruption of national politics. Just as the Conservative employed the rhetoric of nationality, so the Liberal turned to the rhetoric of democracy. He saw in the National Policy nothing more than a scheme to rob the many (especially farmers and workingmen) for the few (especially manufacturers and railway promoters) that could only foster a new aristocracy of wealth in the dominion. 'The ownership of Canada and control of her political affairs,' proclaimed an angry Halifax *Chronicle* (15 September 1894), had been 'wrested from the hands of the people by a conspiracy between greedy and selfish capitalists and a gang of venal politicians.' Privilege, that enemy of yore, had emerged in a new form.

Meanwhile, controversy had erupted over another brand of protectionism, this celebrating the state as an agent of moral progress. During the early and mid-1880s, a collection of editors rushed to defend sabbatarianism, demand the censorship of pernicious literature, crush out the vices of gambling and prostitution, and eliminate the liquor evil. This time, the champions were not confined to either partisan camp, though such Liberal stalwarts as the Toronto *Globe* and the London *Advertiser* as well as their Radical sympathizer the Montreal *Witness* were in the forefront. There was, however, an ethnic split of sorts, since nary a one of the francophone papers espoused the whole range of moral protectionism. That said, almost all editors found some cause which captured their fancy. Even *L'Étendard* (23 February 1893), anti-statist to the core, could speak out in favour of prohibiting the sale of tobacco to children. All of this made for a confused debate, although the opposing lines of argument were clear enough.

The warriors against vice made much of what the Toronto *Mail* (9 November 1881) called 'the ethics of restriction,' the social right to limit individual liberty to ensure the general weal. 'In society duly organized,' argued the London *Advertiser* (13 August 1890), here defending sabbatarian laws, 'no one can possibly enjoy the unlimited rights and untrammeled freedom of nature.' Put another way, this time by *Le Monde* (28 January 1895) in support of compulsory education, 'il est necessaire, pour le bien général, que chaque individu cèdu une portion de sa liberté.' What justified the aggressive extension of the state's moral authority, though, was the dark vision of a Canadian society somehow menaced by Satan and his works. Censors pointed to the widespread circulation of irreligious and immoral books among the public, especially the young, which could not but foster vice and crime. 'Like seeds' this 'mental poison' sinks 'into the mind,' warned the worried Montreal *Star* (18 February 1875), 'and spring up yielding a sorrowful harvest, if not of wrong actions, at least of impure and unholy thoughts, which taint the whole character with weakness and instability.' Sabbatarians argued that Sunday must be 'an oasis in the desert of daily toil' (Toronto *Mail*, 23 July 1883), else materialism would consume all life, and a day of spiritual renewal, else vice would spread and 'Christianity itself will be undermined' (Winnipeg *Sun*, 3 February 1883). They liked to point to the 'continental' or 'American' Sunday, all too secular, as a source of evil in those foreign lands. Temperance champions, even more prohibitionists, found in the demon booze the grand cause of insanity, ill-health, crime, and vice. Even *La Presse* (31 May 1980), no friend of over-zealous reformers, admitted that 'au Canada, l'histoire du *roi alcool* est une histoire de honte et de corruption, des cruantes et des crimes.' Was it any wonder women were so prominent in the prohibition movement, queried a sympathetic Toronto *Globe* (1 April 1889), when drink destroyed so many happy homes? The promise of redemption was great: 'All social virtues and all public reforms would thrive in our country if it were relieved of the accused and demoralizing liquor traffic,' cried the Montreal *Witness* (5 August 1876), the most dedicated advocate of temperance anywhere in the daily press. Indeed, the *Witness* and its occasional allies made the prohibition the key to increasing productivity, strengthening the family, eliminating most vice and crime, saving vast sums of public money. The war on vice ultimately had as its goal the creation of a puritan version of God's Kingdom in the dominion of Canada.

The difficulty was that the heroic measures necessary to attain this goal smacked too much of moral tyranny, even if practical. This seemed all too obvious to francophone dailies such as *La Presse* (27 August 1894) which charged that the assault on gambling was 'au nom de la moralité anglaise combattant l'immoralité française.' Indeed, *La Patrie*, a harsh critic of Protestant schemers, consistently employed the rhetoric of democracy to foil 'les cliques qui, sous prétexte de vertu supérieure entendent imposer aux gouvernements l'exercise au pouvoirs à leur gré et à leur caprice' (27 July 1894). The same approach was followed by some critics of sabbatarian laws or prohibition in English Canada who denounced the 'ethical dogmatism,' the 'extremism' and 'fanaticism' of puritans and reformers. In fact, a Radical paper such as the Toronto *World* (17 February 1885) made clear that 'blue laws press more heavily upon the poor than upon the wealthier classes,' because wealth could 'command the comforts of life by evasion.' But far more common was an appeal to the principle of individual liberty. 'A cardinal point to be kept in view of this – that we are not responsible for one another's morality,' intoned the

Toronto *Telegram* (26 February 1877), 'not to any extent which justifies us in putting restraints on our neighbours with a view to making or keeping them moral.' Any excessive reliance on legislation could not but sap that 'sense of responsibility' among individuals (Montreal *Star*, 7 June 1884) upon which public morals ultimately depended. Besides, the state lacked the right 'to say just what the nature and the extent of the moral obligation is, and just how and where the moral obligation is binding' (Halifax *Chronicle*, 4 April 1889). There were, most dailies agreed, certain individual liberties upon which the state could never trench, no matter how noble the cause.

There were certain collective rights that enjoyed an equal sanctity as well. That, at least, was the conclusion of the last controversy, over the use of the state as an instrument of cultural protectionism. Anglo-Protestant nativism had been born back in the 1870s when newspapers such as the Montreal *Witness*, the Toronto *Leader*, and the Toronto *Telegram* (with the modest assistance of the Canada Firsters)[12] wedded the legacy of Protestant bigotry to the novel idea of nationality. Not until the 1880s, and especially after the Riel crisis of 1885, did this nativism become a staple of Radical advocacy in English Canada. Then, and for almost a decade thereafter, the *Mail* (especially when Ned Farrer was editor) led a clamour for a kind of cultural revolution that attracted the sympathies of the people's journals in Toronto, eventually the Ottawa *Journal* and the Winnipeg *Tribune*, usually the Dougalls' *Witness*, plus occasional intransigents here and there in the dominion.

The vitriol, the sheer hatred of things Catholic and French, evident in nativist outbursts was sufficient proof of the new sense of crisis. Central to the nativist case was an assumed conspiracy to extend special religious and ethnic privileges, perhaps to build a dual nationality across the length and breadth of Canada (so the *Witness* early warned of a 'flowing tide of French population' overcoming 'the English settlements' in Quebec and Ontario).[13] The conspiracy was an affront to an Anglo-Protestant majority whose efforts had made Canada, and posed a threat to their dream of a pan-Canadian nationality in which race and creed differences would be forgotten. This was why the *Mail* (2 January 1890) could claim the roots of nativism lay in 'the instinct of self-preservation.' Considerable effort was devoted to detailing the picture of the enemy: a machiavellian Catholic clergy, 'reactionists of the most pronounced type' (Toronto *World*, 17 April 1888) and grasping French politicians, especially that ogre Honoré Mercier 'the Moses of his race' (Toronto *World*, 28 July 1891).[14] Their strength depended first on the insulated Quebec bastion, a backward province filled with ignorant French habitants, 'the cowardly and irreconcilable foes to nineteenth century progress, liberty, order and good government' (Toronto

News, 30 September 1885), and second on the docile Catholic masses everywhere, 'taught to obey the command, nay, even to respect the wishes of the priest' (Charlottetown *Guardian*, 20 March 1891). Singled out for abuse were bilingualism ('Unity of language tends to unity of purpose,' according to the Winnipeg *Tribune*, 5 October 1893, 'and disunity of language just as inevitably to diversity of purpose') and the assorted Catholic or French schools ('the nurseries not merely of an alien tongue, but of alien customs, of alien sentiments, and of a wholly alien people,' in the words of the *Mail*, 24 November 1886). No wonder nativists urged not merely the elimination of Catholic schools in Ontario and Manitoba and an end to bilingualism on the prairies, but the creation of a national school system, where 'the children of this country would not be educated as Nova Scotians, Lower Canadians, or as Manitobans, but as Canadians' (Toronto *News*, 23 August 1892), and even an assault on the Quebec church itself, 'stripped of those powers which enable her to retard the welfare and curtail the liberty of the Queen's subjects' (Toronto *Mail*, 25 August 1886). Nativist rhetoric billed the cultural revolution as, at bottom, a struggle between 'progress and reaction' (Toronto *Mail*, 6 December 1886). The reality, of course, was a demand to employ the state to realize an Anglo-Protestant ascendancy.

The nativist crusade almost immediately brought denunciations of cultural protectionism. 'It is not the business of Government either to create society or to create nationalities,' argued the London *Advertiser* (6 November 1885) at the time of the Riel crisis. This maxim won favour for very different reasons. Francophone editors, aghast at what seemed a revival of Protestant bigotry, insisted time and again that Confederation rested upon a guarantee of the rights of French and Catholic minorities, indeed a guarantee of the Québécois nationality. Thus was fixed in Canadian rhetoric a new myth of Confederation, defined as 'un pacte entre les races parlent l'anglais et le français dans le pays' (*La Minerve*, 4 December 1885), and a new vision of a Canadian mosaic, 'fondée sur l'égalité des races, et non sur l'absorption d'un élément par l'autre' (*L'Électeur*, 24 April 1889). These myths were occasionally echoed in anglophone circles. So the Toronto *Globe* (21 August 1886) claimed 'the Canadian Idea is the establishment of a nation united in the aim to make Canada great and good and rich, though long to be bi-lingual and of diverse creeds.' Indeed, the *Manitoba Free Press*, back in the 1870s always a critic of Métis rights, by the 1890s declared that the term 'Canadian,' like the term 'British,' should comprehend 'many nationalities and many languages.' A Canadian unity was possible without people 'giving up the language and the customs of their forefathers, without forgetting their history and without sacrificing their pride of nationality' (6

August 1892). But the dream of a polygot Canada never became very popular, at least not in the daily press of English Canada. After all, the aim of Confederation, according to the Saint John *Sun* (29 August 1883), was 'to mould all the better qualities of every blood into one grand strong nationality, and employ the peculiar genius of each in the development of its common resources and the achievements of its aggregate civilization.' Time alone would realize the goal of a pan-Canadian nationality, time and the superior ways of the Anglo-Saxons would slowly undo the Québécois nationality. 'The time will come when English only will be spoken throughout Canada,' thought the Hamilton *Spectator* (24 February 1890), 'and a peaceful conquest will have been made of the French tongue as a peaceful conquest has been made of the French heart.' That kind of simple confidence eventually convinced even nativists that the advance of progress was on their side.[15]

All of this highlights the contradictory impulses which moved journalists and their newspapers to take one stand or another. True, editors of all stripes displayed an abiding suspicion of Big Government. Events transpiring outside Canada, especially in such authoritarian lands as Germany, suggested that the old, supposedly discredited paternalism of times past was on the march again. Even in Canada too many people, Labour and Capital, every species of reformer, worried the Victoria *Colonist* (23 October 1888), had 'lost faith in themselves' and placed 'unbounded trust in the wisdom and energy and patriotism of governments.' In part, anti-statist views flourished because of the enemy on the left, whether called 'Georgeism,' 'collectivisme,' or 'socialism,' which planned the use of the state to realize some bizarre notion of the proper social or economic order. Partly, too, these views reflected the sound assumption that the state was 'neither honest god nor angelic demiurge, but simply the Tory machine or the Reform machine, as the case may be, with all its malefic influences' (Toronto *Mail*, 12 April 1887). Then there was the impact of democracy which had entrenched a fear of 'la bureaucratie, la pire des tyrannies anonymes' (*La Minerve*, 9 January 1895). But above all editors were obsessed by the notion that Big Government must restrict that liberty of the individual necessary to the progress, especially the growth of the country. The trouble was that paternaliam on any grand scale could only produce 'la ruine de l'initiative privée' (*La Patrie*, 29 March 1893), 'the weakening of individual enterprise, which is the cornerstone of a nation's commerce' (*Manitoba Free Press*, 19 July 1890). Even a convinced believer in the wisdom of the National Policy, such as the Halifax *Herald* (2 January 1890), warned that 'the great danger' inherent in any recourse to government control or assistance was 'the repression of individual enterprise and the weakening of individual confidence and self-reliance.' So well-established was the belief in the magic properties of liberty that editors rarely felt the need to elaborate or explain.

And yet the so-called ethic of individualism could never rule unchallenged the thoughts of such determined modernizers. 'If all men were honest, scrupulous in all their dealings with each other, individualism would be practicable,' observed the Radical Victoria *Times* (5 March 1890), often a critic of Big Business. 'Withdraw the protecting arm of government to give place to individualism, the moral law disregarded as it now is, and the masses, unless they resorted to force, would become the victims of the scheming few.' Pragmatism alone dictated a rejection of 'laisser faire.' How else to clean up the city, improve factory conditions, benefit farmers, save children form vice, if not by using the power of the state? Even the liberal fervour of the Liberal organs waned dramatically, some joining in the partisan game of demanding assistance for necessary enterprises. So *L'Électeur* (17 October 1888) called for 'action immédiate,' by the federal government of course, to organize a rapid steamship service connecting Europe and Asia via Canada, more properly Quebec City. The justification for any state intervention rested on common sense:

> The tree is known by its fruits, whether it be native or transplanted, or by whatever course of experimentation it has come to be what it is. It is the same with a policy. It is to be judged by its results. If it quickens and stimulates invention and enterprise, promotes social progress, increases the people's prosperity and multiplies opportunities for the extended use of all these gifts and advantages, it is to be commended; if through short-sightedness, obstinacy or apathy, it turns the key on opporunity, bars the course of human endeavour and leaves unattempted what might have been beneficially accomplished, then it merits only condemnation, on whatever philosophic plea it may excuse its neglect of duty. (Montreal *Gazette*, 8 July 1891)

By the closing decade of the century, then, the daily press had accepted that protectionist myth which depicted the state as a crucial instrument of modernity.

THE GOSPEL OF ORDER

The ethic of individualism fell victim as well as to a second mythology of nationhood. The famous catch-phrase 'peace, order and good government,' enshrined in the British North America Act, suggested a social emphasis on order, not on liberty. Indeed, 'the prosperity and the civilization of the nation,' declared the Conservative Charlottetown *Examiner* (10 June 1891), 'are dependent upon the enforcement of discipline and the preservation of order.' That maxim presumed the restriction of individual liberty throughout the whole realm of ordinary life. The Toronto *Mail* (13 May 1893) preached the virtues of propriety, in itself a form of social tyranny: 'Avoid even the appearance of evil ... for the semblance of evil is prima facie evidence of the wrong itself, and one impropriety is often the parent of a long procession of crimes.' That labour sympathizer *La Patrie* (3 May 1887) nonetheless warned 'les serviteurs qui acceptent un contrat avec un maître être obligé de respecter leur contrat, absolument comme le maître a l'obligation de respecter ses engagements.' The message was similar in a piece which the Toronto *Telegram* (5 February 1887) carried on the ideal of 'Social Purity': 'It would revolutionize society if the same inexorable rules were followed in regard to impure men as in regard to impure women.' Sometimes, an editor would anguish over the merits of a law because it threatened to relax normal restraints – *La Presse* (17 January 1890), for instance, argued that any bankruptcy legislation, always a contentious issue, must establish 'une différence entre le commerçant honnête que des circonstances malheureuses et imprévues ont mis dans la nécessité de suspendre ses paiements, et celui qui, par malhonnêteté, indélicatesse ou insouciance avérée, a manqué à ses engagements.' Not even this Radical saw the irony inherent in the fervent emphasis upon conformity. Obedience, it seemed, was a social duty.

The daily press popularized the belief that the community was shaped by a thicket of moral and social disciplines.[16] The overarching discipline, of course, was Christianity itself, an assertion constantly repeated by editors Protestant and Catholic. 'La region est la principe de notre force,' declared *Le Monde* (20 December 1887); 'respectons-là, protégeons-là.' Christianity, the London *Advertiser* (9 October 1893) agreed, was 'the chief cornerstone' of civilization, 'a religion of progress, enlightenment and happiness.' Surely it was obvious that 'Christian influences ... cannot be eliminated without razing to its foundations the entire fabric of society' (Toronto *Mail*, 21 January 1882)? This line of argument assumed that the Christian faith was the fundamental social cement, uniting all classes, creeds, and races in one fellowship. No aspect of the community's life, from the home to the Parliament, was unaffected by its presence. Such a conviction made the Toronto *Mail* during the early 1880s, when its chief editor was the Roman Catholic Martin Griffin, a great worrier, ever troubled by the apparent spread of irreligion in the Christian world.[17] Likewise, that conviction buttressed the paranoia of ultramontane dailies, notably *Le Nouveau Monde* or later *L'Étendard*, whose editors feared an advancing liberalism abroad threatened Catholic truth and at home endangered a Québécois nationality. Protestant editors, given less to apocalyptic visions of a religious collapse, nonetheless agreed that 'the religious element' (Montreal *Gazette*, 22 October 1874) was the key ingredient in the drive for moral progress. 'Our improved circumstances – the higher civilization of the present age – the comforts of the present and the prospects of the future,' stated the London *Advertiser* (3 November 1883), 'are the results of the religious influence, enlarging and developing our better nature, and lifting humanity higher and higher day by day.' Whatever the angle, every editor shared the belief in the utility of Christianity.

No less were they sure of the utility of the family, 'la force et la modèle de la société' (*Le Monde*, 10 July 1897). The family was a necessary fortress against the hurly-burly of a busy world, an abode of those civilized values that must guide a person's life.

> The true unit of society is not the individual but the family. No individual in fact is fit to take his place or discharge his duties to society unless his better nature has been developed by family life; unless he has family affections and sympathies; unless he has been enabled to realize with some degree of fullness what are the normal feelings of father, mother, brother, sister, child. The family has thus a most important preparatory work to do, and if that work is not done, or if circumstances render it abortive, society has thrown into it elements that it cannot properly assimilate, and whose presence in the body politic must be a source of irritation and injury. Upon the right ordering, therefore, of family life in all social well being depends; and just in so far as home influence breaks down or loses its efficacy, will society be filled with adventurers, whose one object and law will be the gratification of their own appetites. (Montreal *Star*, 17 March 1883)

This romance of the family explains the jaundiced view which editors took of any moves to weaken the ties of marriage. On that a fervent Catholic paper such as *L'Étendard* ('La sainteté de l'état du marriage est la plus forte digue qui se puisse opposer aux torrents de crimes qui debordent dans ces pays, où l'on méconnait ces vérités') agreed with a Protestant stalwart such as the Toronto *News* ('Anything which has a tendency to interfere with the sacredness of the marriage relation or render it less binding, is fraught with danger, and is certain to result in ruined lives, unhappy homes and a low standard of morals').[18] Marriage and the home fostered self-control, restraining not just the sexual urge but rampant selfishness (in short man's bestial nature), so making for a moral populace.

What supplemented the influence of the home was the training of the school. At times, a newspaper would raise education to the status of a panacea. Typical of such an extravagant view was the description of education, in *La Patrie* (21 March 1887), as 'l'un des agents le plus actifs de progrès, dans l'ordre matériel, intellectuel et moral, l'un des plus puissants leviers de la civilisation.' That kind of claim rested on the assumption that education was a boon to the individual

('C'est l'éducation qui fait l'homme libre').[19] Even more though, the press was fascinated by the social utility of education. 'Whatever else they do,' a pragmatic editor in the *Mail and Empire* (10 June 1895) remarked about schools, 'they certainly inculcate in the child a habit of obedience to rule and regularity of life. They begin the work of making a good citizen of him.' Indeed, education or some kind of reformed education, was touted by the Radical *Pays* (20 August 1868 and 24 April 1871) as a catalyst for a free and progressive (read anti-clerical) Quebec, by the Montreal *Witness* (21 March 1878) as the source of an intelligent democracy, by the Halifax *Herald* (14 October 1880) and the *Manitoba Free Press* (27 February 1896) as a way of building a pan-Canadian patriotism. In particular, the press looked to education, be that 'l'enseignement religieux' in Catholic Canada or 'ethical education' in Protestant Canada, to shore up people's moral fibre, if not work a moral miracle.[20] And the press, French as well as English, boosted commercial training, evening or industrial schools, even courses in home economics, to equip a work-force with the skills necessary to assist the economy. *Le Monde* hoped 'les écoles commerciales, agricoles et industrielles' would end 'l'insuffisance d'initiative' that seemed a part of the French character.[21] In short, the press had identified education as another key agent of progress (one among many) in that 'struggle for existence' in which individuals, classes, and nationalities were caught up.[22]

But 'if a justification can be found for making education compulsory,' thought the Montreal *Star* (7 February 1883), 'still more could one be found for making occupation compulsory.' The work ethic, usually associated with Protestantism, had its champions in Catholic Canada too. But one of the more extraordinary statements of faith did come from an anglophone daily, the Montreal *Star* (3 January 1887):

> Man is as much a working animal as he is a 'land animal.' As soon as he emerges from infancy man delights in the exercise of brain and muscle. How restless children are and how proud they are to be of use. How long and perseveringly some of them will work to accomplish some object on which they have set their hearts. The purest, the keenest as well as the most lasting enjoyment that men are capable of consists in the exercise of mind and body for some useful purpose. Who has not felt that the very act of working irrespective of the object to be gained by it is a positive pleasure. Take any man who is worth anything and ask him if he has not enjoyed life more when he has been at work, than when he has been idle and the answer will be in ninety-nine cases out of a hundred an emphatic affirmative. And this is only according to Nature's great plan. Nature never works aimlessly. When she gives powers and capabilities, she also gives the will to exercise them and a delight in their exercise ... We are inclined to believe that the man doomed to ceaseless, resultless work is less to be pitied than one compelled to pass an

existence without employment of any kind. Such an existence for a rational being would be simply unendurable.

Work, hard work was the surest means to personal success in a land such as Canada, reasoned the Toronto *Mail* (24 January 1879), 'where victory rests with the most industrious, most skilfull and most daring.' But again the greater value of work lay in the fact that it produced habits of self-reliance in the populace which could only benefit the community at large. A copied article in *Le Nouveau Monde* (23 January 1880) argued 'le travail est l'un des plus précieux éléments de moralisation.' Editors quickly got excited when they spotted some threat to the discipline of work. Anglophone journals, for instance, were ever ready to denounce gambling (based on 'the hope ... of getting suddenly rich without any labour, exertion or the giving of any value')[23] in whatever form, though especially Quebec's lotteries. The Montreal *Witness* recommended a regimen of work to defeat the 'criminal laziness' of paupers who would otherwise live off the fat of the land.[24] *La Minerve* voiced a common opinion when it claimed that the arrival of a host of poor, uncouth immigrants from England, Bernardo's children, would create 'une véritable plaie nationale,' sapping the morality and the wealth of the country.[25] A willingness to swear allegiance to the ferocious faith in work was a sine qua non for any Canadian welcome.

Another reason to fear any flood of 'mauvaise immigration' was the danger it posed to law and order ('almost every murderer in Canada ... the thieves, burglars and "fancy men" whose exploits we are chronicling daily,' lamented the Ottawa *Free Press*, 25 January 1883, 'are in every instance late importations or the children of such'). Editors bothered little with descriptions of the law; rather they emphasized the necessity of obedience. 'The basis of society is obedience to law,' reported the Toronto *Mail* (31 July 1893), 'and if the law is not strong enough to carry out its edicts society falls to pieces.' Such a presumption made crime a sin, the criminal someone beyond the pale, whose actions were proof of wickedness, deserving only punishment. 'La société a droit, et un droit naturel, d'être vengée des attentats commis contre elle,' noted *La Minerve* (2 December 1896), 'outrement elle se trouverait à la merci des brigands et des assassins.' No wonder the press was never a fan of any kind of prison reform that threatened the rigours of punishment. 'The modern idea is the protection of society,' according to the London *Advertiser* (22 January 1884). 'The criminal is punished, simply because such treatment may help to deter him and others like him from pursuing their evil courses.' The 'criminal classes' – a code phrase for vagabonds, tramps, the unemployed – deserved nothing better.[26]

Likewise, editors were fearful of disorder; even the hint of disorder sufficient to panic some nervous nellies – every public demonstration, including a religious parade, seemed a nascent riot. The preservation of order was vastly more important than the victory of any particular cause, be it the rights of labour or justice for the Métis. So *La Patrie* (28 March 1885) emphasized that it did not have 'la moindre sympathie' for the Métis uprising.[27] 'On whatever subjects men differed, they have agreed that the insurrection must be suppressed,' thought the Montreal *Herald* (19 May 1885), ' – that the national authority must be respected, – that the integrity of the country must be preserved, – that security for life and property must be guaranteed to every local subject.' Did all 'men' agree? Certainly all editors did, then and whenever the social peace was disturbed.

The last discipline, a discipline the press often found lacked sufficient force, was patriotism. Editors deemed this, really a social expression of man's altruistic instincts, essential to national order and good government: 'Le patriotisme, c'est l'attachement à son pays, c'est la préférence donnée aux intérêts généraux de la communauté, sur les intérêts individuels. C'est le principe de la charité appliqué au peuple. Dans toute société organisée, il est nécessaire que chaque individu sacrifie une part de sa liberté, de ses droits, de sa fortune. Sans cela, il n'y a pas d'association ou de gouvernement possibles' (*La Minerve*, 6 March 1866). What editors could not abide was a mood of indifference, a selfish fascination with personal gain, some finding this the besetting sin of the dominion's life. *L'Étendard* (7 April 1883) spoke out against the easy acceptance of dishonesty in high places by all too many people. The Victoria *Times* (3 November 1890) denounced the greed of the 'classes' whose gold bought and sold elections ('Dishonesty has ruined democracies; rum, never'). A distempered *La Presse* (30 October 1896) railed against 'l'ignorance et la vanité ... les plus nuisibles defauts de l'homme,' ruinous to 'les meilleurs projets, les plus belles entreprises,' even 'les partis politiques.' What was needed was a greater devotion to society, less to self. The Radical Ottawa *Journal* (20 September 1893), usually no great admirer of the governor-general, gave over an entire editorial to praise of Lord Aberdeen's comments on 'The Heritage of Service.' 'Do we not realize,' the explanation went, 'that it means not only service to one's home, one's family, one's business, but that it means free service to one's neighbours, to humanity?' Necessary to bring any lasting moral progress, it seemed, was a citizenry that took as much interest in public affairs, that recognized 'the dignity of politics' (Toronto *Globe*, 12 October 1885), as the editor did. The emphasis on patriotism, then, was sometimes flavoured with a bit of occupational vanity.

Anyway, the editors had found that terrible enemy (the requisite devil in any mythology) to justify their celebration of conformity: the spectre of anarchy. Around 1890, the daily press was filled with editorials entitled 'Anarchists in America,' 'Anarchist Outrages,' 'La guerre sociale,' or 'The Anarchists.'[28] Every paper called for the harshest measures possible to stamp out the nihilists, dynamiters, and assassins. In the words of the Hamilton *Spectator* (21 August

1886), the anarchists were the 'proved enemies of society.' Anarchy frightened not just because of the brutality of the terrorist, although *La Patrie* (17 January 1894) admitted 'nous sommes épouvantes de ces forfaits dont les auteurs ne respectent ni l'innocence, ni des lois.' The deeper anxiety grew out of the challenge that the anarchist posed to all the editors held dear. This the Winnipeg *Sun* (5 December 1887) made abundantly clear:

Anarchy ... means no government, no law, no courts, no validity to any contract, civil, commercial or matrimonial. This involves the extirpation of all the present responsibilities of men to each other, the wiping out of all industries which cannot be carried on without binding contracts, the destruction of the home, and a condition of affairs to [*sic*] which there shall be no schools, no religion, and no punishment for crime. This is the ideal condition to which anarchists would reduce the people. It is this chaotic, irresponsible, brutish system, without either human or divine authority, with no law to restrain or government to control and protect, that these ignorant malcontents would force upon the people, on the penalty of loss of life and property, in the place of their present institutions – a system with no other basis than the caprices, passions, physical powers and criminal impulses of men.

Could one imagine a more horrible fate than to live where man's bestial nature had been liberated from every constraint essential to a civilized existence? Anarchy was, in truth, liberty run wild.

THE GOSPEL OF HARMONY

A fair amount of space, editorials perhaps even more than news, dealt with the realities of disunity. Not that the dailies were champions of conflict per se. Just the opposite. Editorial pages were sprinkled with phrases such as 'live and let live,' 'le fair play' (a franchophone favourite), 'the mixed community,' 'harmonie' and 'equilibre,' 'mutual dependence.' The need to push the National Policy, for instance, led the Toronto *Mail* (29 April 1876) to recall to mind 'that mutual dependence which means mutual assistance, is the great social law – the principle which effectually binds men together in organized bodies.' In contrast, the London *Advertiser* (24 December 1884), upset by the precedent of the National Policy, warned: 'The chief source of danger arises from class legislation – class legislation demanded by powerful corporations seeking to establish monopolies, or by combined labour associations seriously interfering with the freedom of the labourer and his right to act alone and for himself.' But much later, and in defence of that strategy, *La Minerve* (4 June 1894) could affirm the duty of government 'd'équilibrer les privilèges et la protection nécessaires à chacun des éléments qui composent le corps social.' Underlying this apparent confusion was a common conception of the dominion as a congeries of interests and classes, races and creeds, sections and provinces, each striving for a place in the sun. The task was to weld this discordant gathering into a functioning whole, which was all the more difficult because the existence of these groups gave birth to much controversy. Around this purpose daily newspapers, not always with one voice though, wove a third mythology of nationhood which emphasized, above all, the virtues of harmony.

The most fundamental division, of course, was rooted in sex. That also proved the least worrisome. Yet what journalists liked to call a phenomenon of the age was the increasing entry of women into the broader society, into factory work as well as 'good works,' a movement loosely linked to a noisy agitation for women's rights. The editor did not approach the 'Women's Question' with an open mind. Sexism was rife: editors believed God had given the sexes different natures, and different spheres of activity suited to these natures. When the occasion demanded it, they could trot out some clichés that defined woman's lot:

If the women of all civilized countries are purer and more virtuous than the men, it is because all the laws of nature intended them to be so and because by reason of such natural forces they have not as a rule been brought within the range of the contaminating influences by which men are continually surrounded. (Moncton *Times*, 19 November 1883)

La volonté de Dieu ... lui a donné la sublime mission de créer des bases étables à la société, en élévant chrétiennement ses enfants. (*La Patrie*, 12 March 1887)

Nature has made them dissimilar ... Man, the rough and rude; woman, the gentle, modest and kind. (London *Free Press*, 1 March 1889)

Scripture does map out woman's sphere of life. That it makes her an inferior being by its assertion that she shall be subject to her husband and shall shine in the domestic circle cannot be pretended. On the contrary, it confers upon her a sacred place in which, through her exclusion from the hurly-burly of contention, she can easily exercise a gentle sway over the sterner sex, and an ennobling influence upon the race. (Toronto *Mail*, 12 May 1893)

This is lush prose indeed – the line of argument assumed woman was emphatically a moral being (and man a worldly being) whom 'the formations of custom'[29] decreed would be active in the home and devoted first to raising children.

The import of these myths, though, could be double-edged. The true chauvinists viewed any effort to equalize the sexes, especially woman's suffrage, as a threat to smear all women with 'a mannish tinge' (*Manitoba Free Press*, 21 February 1893), prophesying a gloomy future of unrestrained sexual competition that could not but result in broken homes, a struggle for jobs, even a debauched womanhood. Women's friends, by contrast, were much influenced by the idea of democracy: they saw equality as a measure of justice necessary to undo 'the exclusion of women' (Toronto *Globe*, 29 November 1884), the legacy of a benighted past, and to bolster 'le caractère moral' (*La Patrie*, 3 November 1885) in political life. Anyway, both camps admitted women had a crucial role mothering the nation, strengthening its moral fibre. A very traditional *Le Monde* (10 July 1897) published an article which called upon women to take up the task of 'la relèvement de la famille,' the 'devoir de patriotisme et de religion' in a time of moral turmoil. A more adventuresome *Mail and Empire* (30 June 1897), no admirer of feminists, urged an expanded definition of the woman's sphere carrying her beyond the home to confront vice. And a progressive-minded Charlottetown *Examiner* (6 February 1892) expected women would everywhere 'exert a refining and purifying influence – as she now invariably does in the all too narrow sphere of the home.' No wonder organized womanhood, notably that most respectable National Council of Women set up in the 1890s under the patronage of Lady Aberdeen (the governor-general's wife), received much kudos. Man's worldliness had to be balanced by woman's morality ('Legislation as at present conducted is as one-sided and unsatisfactory as bachelor housekeeping,' claimed the London *Advertiser*, 26 January 1891, a great friend of women). Woman, it seemed, should be man's helpmate (and few, indeed, were the editors who would give her a greater stature) in the community at large as well as in the family.

A good deal more troublesome, and certainly more frightening than any future battle of the sexes, was the immediate prospect of class warfare implicit in the rise of trade unions and farmers' organizations. In response newspapers elaborated arguments about how Capital and Labour, City and Country, were actually partners in the cause of Canadian progress.

Editorials on 'Capital and Labour' usually focused on the magic formula of growth. The essential platitude, reiterated by the *Daily Columbian* of New Westminster (4 August 1892), laid down that 'capital and labour are required to go hand in hand for the development of any country.' Editors went through intellectual contortions to demonstrate why this alliance was so natural. The Hamilton *Weekly Spectator* (30 September 1882) called capital 'stored up labour, just as the grain or the lump of coal is stored up sunshine.' Less poetic was the truism, voiced here by the Montreal *Star* (10 April 1886), that capital rendered labour 'possible,' saving people from a life of 'mere subsistence,' by massing funds for 'great enterprises.' Indeed, 'le développement, de plus en plus rapide, de la richesse,' according to *La Presse* (13 March 1896) was 'le seul moyen d'ameliorer le sort du grand nombre.' Even the Radical distrusted the idea of a redistribution of wealth, favouring levelling up rather than levelling down. Banish capital and you doomed labour; free capital and you enriched labour. 'L'affaiblessement de l'un produit l'affaiblessement de l'autre, de même la destruction du capital entraine la destruction du travail,' declared *Le Monde* (3 July 1886). 'Si au contraire, l'harmonie existe entre des deux agents de la prospérité, it en resuite un avantage pour les deux.' The upshot of this argument was a demand for mutual respect, the recognition of 'the rights of labour' and 'the rights of capital' by both parties. 'Labour has no right to coerce the action of one of its own order or by force to abridge any of the rights of capital,' in the view of the Toronto *Telegram* (17 July 1886), 'while capital must learn that human labourers cannot safely be treated as unthinking machines and they have a right to such compensation as will enable them to maintain themselves and family in comfort and afford opportunity for improvement and education.' Such respect would ensure that the progress of the community was never disturbed by an unnecessary recourse to 'the methods of war' – the strike and the lockout.

Editorials on 'City and Country' roamed further afield to show how central was the harmony of urban and rural Canada. A lingering ruralism did have some influence on press rhetoric. Newspapers were never skimpy in their praise of farming, 'the employment originally assigned man by his Creator' (Montreal *Witness*, 5 January 1878), 'le plus honourable, le plus rénumérateur [*sic*], le plus sûr de nos jours' (*La Presse*, 17 January 1890). And they occasionally admitted cities had earned a reputation as dens of iniquity, 'the general rallying ground of diabolism in its thousand and one shapes' (*Manitoba Free Press*, 17 February 1883). But, by and large, the press took a utilitarian approach to the countryside, its primary significance now as a hinterland of the metropolis. 'The cities are to the surrounding country what the heart is to the body – the centre of energy and life,' claimed the Halifax *Chronicle* (19 February 1874). The big cities, the Montreal *Star* (30 November 1880) reasoned, were the homes of learning and intelligence in a country, 'so they become the centres of its thought and sentiment, which sooner or later become the dominant ideas of the nation.' Whether heart or brain, the cities were the fount of national leadership. That presumption enabled many an editor (not all though) to accept the census reports showing the swelling of the city and the haemorrhaging of the countryside as simple evidence of progress, perhaps a result of the improved life of the city or the impact of farm technology. Back-to-the-land schemes were favoured because, among other happy consequences, 'la misère dans nos villes diminuera si elle ne disparait pas completement' (*La Minerve*, 8 January 1895), relegating the countryside to the status of a dumping ground for the unwanted population of the city. Even agriculture was treated more and more often as another industry, like mining or manufacturing. True, the importance of agriculture had become, thought *L'Étendard* (20 January 1883), 'une vérité banale.' 'Agriculture is the supreme industry of Canada,' exclaimed the London *Free Press* (26 July 1889). 'It lies as a substantial basis beneath all our enterprises. It is the national backbone.' The point was that 'de la prospérité de la compagne dépend la prospérité de la ville' (*La Patrie*, 7 October 1892). City and country constituted an organic whole, each consuming the goods the other produced ('Le manufacturier, l'artisan, le cultivateur, et un mot, tous les habitants sont livrés les uns aux autres; leurs intérêts sont communs')[30] which, by the way, justified the hectoring tone of some editorials urging the farmer to shed old ways, accept the lessons of scientific farming, and apply business principles to his work, all to heighten productivity. In short, there must always be an exchange of people, goods, and ideas between city and countryside. No wonder an observer in the Toronto *Week* (22 January 1892), an opinionated review, concluded that circulation was 'a law of health in the development of national brain and character.'

The most intractable controversies, the cause of interminable wrangling, resulted from efforts to build a nation-state that would surmount the divisions of section and race. Here, especially, newspapers played a contradictory role, the voice of parochial or ethnic dissent as well as the advocates of national harmony. That tedious battle over the exact structure of federalism, the respective powers of nation and province, saw Conservative organs campaign vigorously against the bane of 'sectionalism' while their Liberal rivals strove to crush out the spirit of 'centralism,' each proclaiming its devotion to Confederation. Even *Le Canadien* (30 October 1888), like all francophone dailies suspicious of an overbearing Ottawa, could charge: 'Sans un gouvernement central fort, sans un gouvernement canadien, dont l'autorité soit reconnue comme suprême, il n'y a pas de Canada.'[31] But the Liberal favoured instead the primacy of 'provincial rights' and 'l'autonomie des provinces.' 'The bond of Confederation must be one of good fellowship, freedom, and co-operation,' argued the Winnipeg *Sun* (14 February 1883). 'We are not to be welded into a solid unity by the sledge of despotism.' The discussions over tariffs, railways, steamship lines, port facilities, settlement and resource policies, any and every form of development, were invariably grounded in a fine appreciation of the balance of interests in the locality and the nation. What made the National Policy so grand a strategy for 'the unification and building-up of the Dominion,' mused the Ottawa *Citizen*

(10 March 1894), was the fact it harnessed the ambitions of centre and periphery, east and west to the cause of nationhood. What made 'le libre échange' so necessary, a Liberal paper such as *L'Électeur* (30 July 1887) might respond, was the fact it granted 'la faculté d'échanger sans entraves' to producers in every region to realize a profit on any market, thus forming a unity out of mutual satisfaction. The more sanguine editors were even able to make a virtue out of racial diversity. 'History teaches that the highest development of civilization comes not from the progressive march of an isolated race.' claimed an exuberant Halifax *Herald* (28 July 1881), 'but from the commingling of different peoples and the survival of such characteristics as go to make a great and highly civilized community.' Similarly, *Le Monde* (24 June 1893) repeated the tired cliché that 'une noble emulation entre les divers groupes nationaux devrait multiplier les ouevres et activer le progrès.' Such rhetoric, if it masked a fundamental divergence over the long-term goals of union, nonetheless served to give that pragmatic bargain of Confederation a higher meaning.

None of these myths should surprise. Newspapers of all stripes were normally committed to consensus, although the grievances of women or labour might seem compelling to some. Even when anger forced an editor to buckle on his armour to save the oppressed farmer or protect a province's rights, he cloaked his intransigence by damning some other interest, be that grasping industrialists or an imperial Ontario, for upsetting the balance of power. And, time and again, the press was filled with denunciations of extremism (the requisite devil in this mythology) because its expression threatened social peace and economic growth. Thus, whenever anyone raised the race or religious cry, many more editors responded by warning that a revival of past feuds could only engender a devastating civil strife that would die out over the tomb of Canada. That explains the abuse heaped on fervent nativists or overzealous *nationalistes*, the anglophone praise of the achievements and loyalty of French Canadians or the francophone celebration of the chivalry and enterprise of English Canadians. The gospel of harmony, at bottom, was merely a particular version of that 'moderatism' which has always been a standard pose of the popular press.[32]

THE ILLUSION OF SANITY

Few controversies, at first sight, seem so pointless, even fatuous, as what contemporaries called 'the Destiny Question.' The doctrine of nationalism laid down that every legitimate nationality must boast some unique destiny, and so editors were all too often carried away on flights of fancy about the Canadian future. Over the years, there was a progression of fads: first national independence, later a brand of continental union, and eventually a type of imperial association, any of which promised escape from an unfortunate colonial present. At bottom, then, these fads were rooted in malaise, occasionally in a sense of grievance that presumed some goal could not be realized within the constraints of the status quo. Their advocates fashioned myths which gave expression to assorted hopes, fears, and hatreds evident in the Canadian milieu, all in a vain endeavour to convert readers and leaders to the wisdom of a transformed country. It was in vain because, however marvellous the imaginary fate might seem to its advocates, even more doubters appeared to carp and criticize, explaining the follies of that fate and the virtues of the present. None of the debates was ever satisfactorily resolved, exhaustion or the arrival of something new marking an end to the earlier craze; the various definitions of Canada's destiny lacked that quality of urgent necessity which bolstered the other mythologies. Even so, 'the Destiny Debate' assisted the birth of an image of Canada as a haven of sanity in a world of turmoil, an image that during the 1890s won much favour with editors of all stripes.

First on the scene after Confederation was the notion of Independence. Early in 1869 a gaggle of newspapers – notably the Quebec *Chronicle* (Conservative), the new Montreal *Star* and *Le Pays* (both Radical), and the London *Free Press* (still Liberal) – flirted with the idea of Independence, usually linking it to some proposal for a North American *zollverein*. That little editorial flurry died out a few years later, really after the Treaty of Washington (accepted in 1872) had settled the causes of the Anglo-American discord which made the Canadian future seem uneasy. During the late 1870s and early 1880s, though, the idea of Independence regained favour, this time as part of the Radical vision of a democratic Canada sponsored by the people's journals and their sympathizers. Although this enthusiasm waned by the end of the decade, still the idea retained some currency among Liberals who desired Autonomy now and Independence later. ('Canada first! Le Canada avant tout. C'est la divise da [*sic*] M. Laurier,' announced a proud *L'Électeur*, 21 November 1896). Independence, after all, was a destiny admirably suited to the dogma of modernity.

Champions of Independence were, by and large, a confident lot, sure their scheme was the natural conclusion to Confederation. A chief enemy of the Canadian nationality, indeed to the Canadian democracy, was now the British tie (not necessarily Britain itself). Their Canada was 'a fireproof house,' protected by distance and disinterest from the 'inflammable' ambitions of European nations (though the most cautious suggested that Independence might be partnered with guaranteed neutrality). The Ottawa *Free Press* (5 November 1881) pointed out that 'only through England being engaged in foreign wars is their any likelihood of our suffering.' In particular, the British tie seemed the curse of Canadian-American relations. Time and again, British diplomats had sacrificed Canadian interest to secure an accord. ('Maine was ours, Oregon was ours, San Juan was ours, the fisheries were ours,' recalled an unhappy Toronto *Globe*, 23 April 1887. 'All are gone. The foundation of a Canadian nation has been given away piecemeal.') Besides, the tie appeared the only possible cause of a future clash with the otherwise peaceful Republic. ('If ever we are engaged in hostilities with our American neighbours,' claimed a naïve Toronto *News* on 24 June 1884, assuming Canadian innocence and American goodwill, 'it will be owing to our connection with England.') This sort of reasoning allowed a few committed editors to draw the conclusion that Canadian Independence was actually in the Empire's interest, because the American anglophobia born of Britain's presence in the New World would die away.

All the more galling was the fact that the tie perpetuated an unhealthy colonial mentality amongst the Canadian people. Nothing was 'more opposed to the development of Canadian manliness, more enervating to our nascent national life,' angrily declared the London *Advertiser* (29 February 1888), than 'the indiscriminate fawning imitation of everything English.' The champions of Independence were especially critical of the Loyalist myth, indeed claiming the United Empire Loyalists had been moral cowards, 'the gentry but not the flower of the colonies' (Winnipeg *Sun*, 22 August 1884), who to protect their property and positions had betrayed their country in its hour of need. What the dominion needed was a large dose of Canadianization, a campaign urged by Toronto's people's journals during the early 1880s, which required the elimination of the governor-general's little court, hiring preferences for the native-born (especially in the civil service and the universities), an end to 'title-hunting' among politicians. Anyway, the persistence of the British connection seemed an affront to 'Young Canada' (to use a favoured phrase), dangerous to its spirit as well as its interests. Far better to go alone, to follow the logic of nationality. Was it not 'a noble ambition to be your own master, and to be independent of everybody'? asked the Vancouver *World* (5 December 1891). These romantics variously promised that Independence would assure Canadian security and prosperity, end the threat of Annexation, and harmonize the interests of French and English. But the strongest argument for Independence, decided the Toronto *News* (29 June 1884), was 'the moral effect which it would have upon our national life in raising the entire tone of our politics, broadening our views, and imparting the self-reliance and determination which those who perpetually depend on others to rule and protect them can never attain.'

Continentalism was the near twin of Independence. Some editors saw Independence as a halfway house on the road to a kind of North American alliance, if not a continental union. Francophone 'nationalistes,' invariably in the Radical camp, had a definite hankering for Annexation, not surprising given their anglophobic and republican preferences. Anglophone Liberals were more likely to avoid any annexationist taint, touting instead the merits of a close economic alliance. In 1887 continentalism became a live issue as a result of the Commericial Union agitation begun by the maverick *Mail*. Bereft of an answer to the triumphant National Policy, the Liberal party and so its organs fathered that peculiar scheme of Unrestricted Reciprocity to solve Canada's ills and win national office.[33] The new panacea, however unlikely its acceptance in Washington, aptly suited a public mood of unease, even pessimism, fostered by retarded growth and sectional animosity. For the next four or five years, Liberal dailies and sundry allies elaborated a continentalist strategy of progress, especially economic growth, some few papers such as *La Patrie* going a step beyond to Annexation. Only after the Liberal convention of 1893, which turned the party away from Unrestricted Reciprocity, did the press debate subside.

Continentalism, in whatever form, rested upon the myth of the 'New World.' Europe, so it seemed, was a tired continent, marred by its feudal heritage and military ambitions, while North America was in the vanguard of progress, destined to supersede the Old World 'as the centre of civilization and political power of the world' (Halifax *Acadian Recorder*, 2 February 1880). This kind of isolationism made Britain appear something of an alien intruder; indeed *La Patrie* painted the picture of a perfidious Albion imbued by a desire to dominate the world. Only 'une ligne imaginaire' (*La Patrie*, 27 February 1891) divided Canadians and Americans since geography, economics, culture, and aspirations had made North America a single community. One of the best expositions of Liberal reasoning appeared in the Toronto *Globe* (17 July 1889), just after a severe crisis in Canadian-American relations:

> Providence has placed the United States and Canada side by side on this Continent. Each has a goodly heritage, and intends to occupy and make the most of it through all the future. Come what will, the two peoples are destined to be perpetual neighbors, and neighbors in closer relationship than any other nations under the sun. Their territories lie side by side for a larger extent than those of any other peoples, and throughout a large portion of that extent are separated only by an imaginary line. The two have also more in common than any other two neighboring nations. They are of common stock. They are heirs of a common and glorious history. They have the same civilization, the same literature, the same religion. At the bottom their institutions and their modes of thought are identical. Both pride themselves on their liberty, intelligence and enterprise, and the essential equality which is the birthrite of their citizenship. And, so far as Canada is concerned, the United States is not only her nearest but her only neighbor.

Continentalism really meant tying Canada's fortunes to the rising star of America's empire. Liberals dwelt on the apparent decline of Canadian agriculture or the rise of combines and monopolies or the hard times of the working men or the swollen national debt, all to demonstrate the failure of the National Policy. And Liberals assumed that, no matter what its social troubles, the United States could claim a dynamic, successful economy. What they argued, neatly turning the Conservative's home market thesis on its head, was that Canada and the United States constituted a single marketplace which politics had split asunder. 'In many respects there is no country possessed of such advantages as North America,' observed the Saint John *Telegraph* (11 November 1887) with glee. 'Within its bounds are to be found the greatest abundance of fertile soil, the greatest variety of natural products and of mineral wealth. Coal and iron, gold, silver and copper, salt and oil, are found beneath its soil. Above it is the luxuriant forest, the rich growth of wheat, corn and all fruits of the tropic and temperate zones.' Commercial Union or Unrestricted Reciprocity would cheapen prices for Canadian consumers, open huge markets for Canadian producers, and make the dominion the newest frontier of American capitalism. 'Only remove the customs houses,' enthused the *Manitoba Free Press* (17 August 1887), 'and the wave of prosperity and advancement which has been beating up against the 49th parallel for years must necessarily flow in upon the country.' Everyone would benefit; even industries would receive 'an impetus such as no tariff juggling could give them' (Toronto *Mail*, 15 February 1887). In fact, anglophone Liberals could claim their schemes would dispel class and sectional tensions, leaving people the 'leisure to cultivate generous feelings towards each other and loyalty to their common country' (*Manitoba Free Press*, 27 June 1884). Even *La Patrie* (18 April 1892) could employ the thesis of states' rights to argue annexation would make Quebec 'un Etat souverain, absolument libre de conduire ses affaires selon son bon plaisir.' The point was that continentalism amounted not to a formula for national suicide but to the means whereby Canadians or Canadiens might realize their legitimate aspirations.

Likewise, Imperialism appeared a means to an end, this time only the pan-Canadian nationality, of course, since no francophone editor could readily assent to so Anglo-Saxon a destiny. Domestic themes, Canadian exigencies, once more underlay the debate. Imperialism of any kind was a pleasing dream until the mid-1880s when some British leaders rediscovered the virtues of their colonial Empire. The new enthusiasm was bound to find an echo in English Canada. But more important, the swelling tide of continentalism inspired loyalists to reply with their own panacea, something called Imperial Federation. Supplementing all this was an outburst of jingoism, directed especially against the Americans, in Toronto's people's journals, which had discovered the appeal of super-patriotism and the like among lowbrow readers. The Conservative press in English Canada, now joined by a few Radicals, committed itself in principle to the notion of Imperial Unity. And during the 1890s this vague Imperialism, rarely any enthusiasm for Imperial Federation, became the prevailing version of Canada's destiny in press debate.

Imperialism rested upon a myth of the British Empire as the marvellous expression of the century's progress. No other state, rhapsodized the Saint John *Sun* (22 May 1880), had ever occupied so much territory or contained so many people – or used its power so wisely:

> British Colonies girdle the earth; over every eighth acre of the globe the Red Cross flag is waving; and our laws, languages and institutions are blessing nearly a quarter of the human family. Scattered over creation – on the continent of Europe, in the vast regions of Hindustan, in various parts of Africa, throughout Australasia, in South and Central America, and within 'This Canada of Ours,' the British race are working out important problems in science, literature and good government. On such an Empire the sun never before has shone, and over such extensive territories no one has ever swayed a sceptre ... Within its limits all climates are included, all races represented, and untold and imaginable wealth is contained. Our morning gun awakens to activity a slumbering world, while the sublime strains of our noble National Anthem, floating out upon the evening air, lull the nations to rest. And beneath the benign influences of British rule, liberty has been established, tyranny has ceased to exist, the moral, social and intellectual condition of the people has been promoted, and the desert has been made to rejoice and blossom as the rose.

History, race and culture, and technology had produced an Imperial nation with the potential to become 'the greatest secular agency for good now known to mankind.'[34]

That kind of moral idealism aside, Conservative or Radical enthusiasts of Empire were much more taken with the benefits Imperialism would bring the dominion. The jingoes in the people's press looked to Britain to humble the lordly Americans. (In the event of war, the Toronto *Telegram* of 12 July 1890 noted with obvious relish, 'the warships of our maternal ancestors would be blowing the seacoast cities of the United States off the earth, while Ontario on its own account would be taking Detroit and burning Buffalo, as it has done heretofore.') Editors in British Columbia, made uneasy by European and Russian exploits in the Pacific region, favoured the notion of an imperial *kriegsverein* which must protect the coastal province. (A united Empire, dreamed the

Vancouver *News-Advertiser* on 3 March 1889, would be 'an enemy too dangerous to provoke and an ally too important for any other people to wish to lose,' able 'to control the destinies of the world.') Most exciting of all, though, were the proposals for imperial preference or an imperial *zollverein*, often portrayed as little more than the National Policy writ large. Supposedly, an economic union would ensure Canadian farmers preference in the British market, turn the Canadian Pacific Railway into the chief trade route to Asia, and foster an influx of British settlers and capital.[35] Altogether, claimed an exuberant editor in the Toronto *News* (16 February 1891), imperial preference 'would make Canada the greatest country in the world.' The promise of an economic stimulus, so at least editors thought, was far more persuasive than any call to Canadians to act out a world role via the instrument of Empire.

Such a prosaic view of life also buoyed up the criticism of these grand schemes for a new destiny. Editors were forever calculating what any dramatic change in Canada's situation would cost. *La Minerve* (13 March 1894), for example, bluntly pointed out that an independent Canada would lack the means 'de soutenir efficacement notre honneur et notre dignité nationale,' especially if threatened by American pressure. Continentalism was no more pleasing because it would lead, in the words of *Le Monde* (17 March 1888), to 'une perte de $7,300,000 dans le revenu; le taxe directe' and 'une perturbation profonde dans la situation économique et industrielle du pays; la ruine de notre industrie manufacturière et la consécration définitive de la prédominance des grandes centres américains de distribution.' Mixing Independence and continentalism could produce only Annexation, the death of Canada and Quebec. Yet the tory invention of Imperial Federation, according to the Liberal, was equally unCanadian. 'Let Canadian mothers think of their sons drafted for the defence of sections of the Empire ... from the onslaught of the Zulus, Boers or Burmese,' commented the Montreal *Herald* (15 December 1892). Besides wasting Canadian men and money in far-off lands, Imperial Federation meant limiting Canada's own freedoms, a prospect which upset even 'Anglo' Conservatives. 'Is it not better to go on developing, consolidating and building up the country as we have it,' asked the Hamilton *Spectator* (13 May 1889), 'than to try a new venture in nation-building?'

Reasons might differ, but editors usually returned to the refrain that colonial status offered Canada the security necessary to prevent an American takeover and the self-government necessary to realize progress. In fact, this myth of protected self-governance, often buttressed with assorted references to history, proved the rock upon which all the romantic dreams were wrecked. 'With complete control of our affairs, as part of the empire,' believed the Vancouver *News-Advertiser* (1 July 1897), 'we are free from anxiety as to foes from without and can give all our attention to internal concerns.' Even a francophone could claim (in *Le Monde*, 21 November 1890) that 'les canadiens-français jouissent sous la protection de l'Angleterre de toutes les libertés qu'un peuple peut désirer.' Why embark on a new, unnecessary journey that might involve Canada in entanglements of no real interest or benefit?

Editors, at least since 1880, had come to specialize in a bleak picture of the outside world. These patriots did look on their respective mother countries, Britain or France, with favour. Although editors on the left might occasionally give voice to doubts about the wisdom of imperialist exploits in Africa or Asia, usually almost everyone else cheered on empire-builders such as Gordon and Rhodes (or in Quebec their French counterparts), enjoying a vicarious sense of pride in what seemed heroic endeavour. But they were also convinced the old lands were countries in crisis. An 'Anglo' Conservative, for instance, worried about the Radicalism which had turned the Liberal party into an anti-national force hostile to British power and British traditions. An 'Anglo' Liberal, in contrast, saw in conflict 'two Britains' (Toronto *Globe*, 23 February 1889), a Britain of privilege which for centuries had battened on a Britain of work, a legacy that in this democratic age meant a series of confrontations between the 'classes' and the 'masses.' Francophone editors discovered 'deux peuples, deux partis en France,' one Republican and the other Catholic. 'C'est la guerre civile à l'état latent' (*Le Monde*, 10 July 1897). The Conservative, whether ultramontane or partisan in his loyalties, lamented the destruction of the Old France and the pillaging of the church by the now-dominant liberals and anti-clericals. *La Patrie* of course, and *Le Monde* briefly in the mid-1890s, defended the forces of democracy who were striving to modernize a France endangered by the forces of reaction. (Neither paper, by the way, identified the Catholic church in France as the enemy.) What happened, then, was that editors employed their philosophical perspectives to illuminate events in the old lands, thereby giving their own disputes a higher significance.

Crises seemed even more acute in Europe and America, though. Now, admittedly, francophone editors spent more time worrying over Europe's condition than America's ills, whereas anglophone editors were much more fascinated with the American scene. Even so the diagnosis was the same. Europe was a continent on the verge of an upheaval. Its people were infected by the virus of revolution. 'Each nation seems to feel as if there was a volcano beneath its feet, whose rumblings are indicative of an approaching eruption,' contended the Montreal *Herald* (11 April 1883). More serious, its life was endangered by the habit of militarism. 'Aujourd'hui, l'Europe est un vaste camp retranché, les sommes fabuleuses sont perdues, les forces vives des nations sont paralysées et tout cela pour la préparation à la guerre' (*Le Monde*, 4 February 1896). The horrible prospect that Europe would dissolve into the flames of revolution or war was ever present. Likewise, editors (more Conservatives than Liberals) worried that the United States had entered upon an advanced state of moral and social decay. Witness the 'lynch law,' the spiralling rates of divorce and crime, political corruption, excessive wealth and grinding poverty, radical troubles, strikes, class tensions and sectional politics. Each editor might find a different cause: an unsound republicanism, the worship of the almighty dollar, the fetish of liberty, a swarm of undesirable immigrants, protection and plutocracy, and so on. Seemingly, the Canadian imagination ran free and wild when the troubles of the American giant were at issue – what might be threatening in Canada became debilitating south of the border.

These stereotypes of a world in turmoil provided the necessary backdrop to the myths of Canadian success and superiority editors relished. 'Abroad, all is confusion: doubt, rumours of war, military expeditions and the fever of military preparation,' asserted the Toronto *Mail* (30 September 1884). 'At home all is peace, progress, and prosperity.' True, Conservative dailies were most given to this kind of smugness – indeed, during the late 1880s and early 1890s, they employed a celebration of Canadian achievements to drum up support for the embattled National Policy. But a chauvinist tinge infected the rhetoric of editors in all camps. So the Toronto *Mail* (18 August 1880), then very loyalist, nonetheless concluded that in many ways, whether in its commitment to liberty and equality or in its Christian faith and good schools, Canada was 'far ahead of the old land.' Searching hard for something novel to say in honour of Dominion Day, the Toronto *Globe* (1 July 1889) noted how other countries had selected for their national emblems 'ravening beasts and dishonest birds of prey,' whereas Canada had adopted 'the honest, peaceable and industrious beaver,' worthy of its people's character. Even a Radical paper such as the Toronto *Telegram* (30 June 1897) could declare that Canadians 'are well fed and happy beyond any people on earth.' The banality, the blindness of such declarations might astonish. But sophistication counted little, ingenuity, cliché, and repetition a lot more. The press was only engaged in a normal task of mass communication, namely reconfirming the public's faith in its country's present. The welter of editorials embellished a vision of Canada as the Victorian commonwealth par excellence, its people enjoying a way of life nowhere surpassed. The result was the fixing in national thought of a definite Canadian identity that would last well into the coming century.

6

A fourth estate?

Always, journalists boasted a professional credo breathtaking in its sheer grandiloquence. They trotted it out at press banquets and the like, sometimes to meet the charges of an irate clergyman, sometimes to condemn their own practices, but usually just to reconfirm their inordinate sense of pride. Tradition and function gave this credo its force. In the past, proclaimed one apologist, the journalist 'had battled in the front rank of the great army of civil and religious liberty, and set the feet of multitudes over all the civilized world in the way of progress.' Nowadays, he continued, 'the press is giving a multitude of new voices to organized humanity, the power of articulate speech to the masses of the people, and far beyond all other agencies is fitting the nations for the parliament of man and the federation of the world.'[1] Clearly, the glory of the journalist rested on the presumption that he served, first of all, the public.

Was any of this windy rhetoric justified? In truth, the press was never just the independent champion of its readers, a fact that proved a source of some misgivings to high-minded journalists. Its autonomy was tainted by a need to serve 'the powers that be': financial and social pressures ensured newspapers would often side with the big battalions. And yet the press was a lot more than simply a mouthpiece of the Establishment. The press did indeed act as a fourth estate, standing midway between the people and their leaders, offering service and criticism to a collection of different constituencies. That made the press an important pillar of the open society. The journalist's credo had some basis in reality.

THE READER'S RIGHTS

A source of a good deal of woe in a publisher's life was the threat or reality of a libel action. In fact, the incidence of libel, if one can believe contemporary observations and later reminiscences, was truly extraordinary. People of high and low position were forever threatening to punish some offender against the canons of good taste, fair play, or truth. It all signified that the respectable citizen was very touchy about his or her name and the typical newspaper a bit too nonchalant about its practices.

The libel laws were a necessary mechanism of community control over an institution able to have a devastating effect on the reputation of the individual. Libel came in two forms: criminal libel regulated by the dominion's laws and civil libel determined by the varying laws of the provinces. Usually, the most distressing actions grew out of charges of criminal libel, which could result in fines, prison sentences, to say nothing of heavy legal expenses. A cause célèbre arose over an unfortunate article published in the Toronto *News* during the summer of 1885: the article implied that Montreal's 65th Battalion had proved unreliable in the recent Northwest fracas as a result of its sympathy for Louis Riel. That provoked a criminal charge against owner E.E. Sheppard, who after much delay (for a time he managed to avoid efforts to bring him to Montreal, the home of the injured party) was finally convicted and forced to pay a fine of $400 or $500.[2] He at least avoided imprisonment. Not so John Ellis, publisher of the Saint John *Globe*. In 1887 this violent Liberal partisan used his paper to denounce one Judge Tuck, who had prevented a recount of votes in a federal constituency. Now editorial criticism of the courts or its personnel was always a risky business: in 1883 the publisher of the Victoria *Standard* was compelled to pay $250 and costs for libelling a magistrate,[3] and in 1892 the publisher of *L'Électeur* was censured by two justices for his unwelcome views on their court.[4] It sometimes seemed an unwritten law popular with judges that their conduct was not open to newspaper scrutiny. Anyway, Ellis was hauled before the court on contempt charges, ordered to pay a fine of $200 and spend 30 days in jail, and left to cover lawyers' fees of $2,000 or $3,000.[5] Both trials, by the way, produced a lot of press comment, and in certain quarters Sheppard and Ellis emerged as martyrs in the same cause of press freedom.

Far more common, of course, were civil suits. At one point, the *Printer and Publisher* (January 1894) reported that *L'Électeur*, which appears to have been the most offensive and punished daily in the country, had 'twenty-five suits pending against it, the amounts aggregating $55,000.' Politicians were especially sensitive to any slight, real or imagined. An acrimonious article in the Moncton *Transcript* in 1892, overly critical of a tory MP, cost owner John Hawke $50 in damages.[6] Early in 1894, A.-R. Angers initiated an action for $25,000 against *L'Électeur* because the paper suggested he had accepted graft when he was Quebec's lieutenant-governor. The next year Angers won a judgement of $5,000, later reduced on appeal to $2,000 and costs (roughly another $2,000).[7]

Journalists themselves could be almost as thinskinned. In 1894 Berthiaume of *La Presse* threatened to sue *Le Monde* for $25,000 because it had disparaged his paper and questioned his circulation figures.[8] A.H. Scaife, editor of the weekly Victoria *Province*, began a libel action in 1895 against the Victoria *Colonist* as a result of an article entitled 'Journalistic Ruffianism.'[9] Business types, as befitted their sense of self-importance, were wont to demand huge sums to satisfy injured pride. Twice in 1884 the Toronto *Mail* discovered this passion: first J.A. Dixon, of a Montreal firm, claimed $50,000 (but, after all, the paper's news columns had purportedly accused him 'of having absconded, leaving a number of creditors, of having stolen money from his wife, of being a fugitive from justice, and being ruined by drink and bad company'!), and later L.-A. Sénécal, the notorious Quebec promoter of extravagant railways, gave notice of a suit for a whopping $250,000.[10] Usually, though, the plaintiff was a more ordinary soul after a modest recompense for an apparent slander. The Hamilton *Times* (9 January 1883) waxed indignant because an inaccurate report that a Mr and Mrs Robinson were not married had resulted in a verdict against the daily. P.D. Ross told in his reminiscences how the Montreal *Star* was sued in 1885 as a result of a sports item claiming an unspecified two men of a four-man rowing team were 'anything but respectable.' In separate trials the four victims each won their cases – but, strange as it may seem, the courts managed to award four different settlements, ranging from $1 to $500 plus assorted costs![11] And in 1894 Berthiaume was forced to pay $150 and costs to a lowly Charlotte Fullerton, because a bit of police news had tarnished her reputation as a trusted housekeeper.[12]

In fact, the press was rarely treated with undue severity by its victims or the courts. Most threatened libel actions resulted in little loss to publishers. Some cases avoided the courts altogether since the newspaper published a retraction, or even settled for a modest sum. A timely 'explanation' saved Thomas Bell, publisher of the Winnipeg *Nor'Wester*, from trial on charges of criminal libel in 1895 arising from his claim that the Winnipeg *Tribune* dealt in 'false news.'[13] That same year the Brantford *Courier* settled out of court a libel action with a Mrs Beaton, accused of murder and immorality, for $100.[14] Besides, when a case did go to court, the newspaper had a fair chance of winning over a judge and jury as long as it could prove that the item at issue was substantially true, or at least fair comment, and that it was printed without any malice to serve the public interest. So in 1880 the Toronto *Globe* won its case against Patrick Boyle (another journalist), upset by a charge of corrupt dealings, because the paper established that he had been implicated, indirectly at least, in a shady bargain to rig the award of a government printing contract to another firm.[15] And even if the court ruled against a publisher, the damages levied were often minimal. In

1880 the Cobourg Assizes gave W.T.R. Preston of the Port Hope *News* a judgment of $25 against C.W. Mitchell of the Ottawa *Free Press*.[16] In 1894 one Dr Leonard, accused by *La Presse* of causing the death of a child, could secure only nominal damages, which amounted to $100 plus $65.33 in costs and a retraction already offered by Berthiaume.[17] No wonder Ross was able to boast later that he never lost a libel suit (though he did win one in 1895 against an alderman who had claimed in print that the *Journal* 'prostituted itself at 10 cents a line').[18] The latitude allowed the erring journalist was considerable.

Even so, by the 1890s publishers seemed fed up with their lot. The Canadian Press Association went to great pains to investigate libel and to lobby for changes in the federal and Ontario laws. John King acted as the association's libel specialist, advising single papers plus the whole membership on the proper way to meet, better yet to escape, the threat of libel. In Quebec, where the law of libel did not even 'recognize the existence of newspapers as such,' according to the *Printer and Publisher* (January 1894), francophone and anglophone journalists joined forces to urge reforms that would give the press rights well-established in Ontario or Britain, namely to report without fear a public meeting and to make fair comment on issues of public import. Indeed, throughout the decade the *Printer and Publisher* focused on libel actions across the country, eager to push journalists to demand that legislatures bring improvements.

The libel laws, however justified in principle, seemed both an affront as well as a danger to a free press, and so to the new democracy. Newspapers were forever claiming the laws and the courts had fostered a new business of 'trafficking in libel actions,' another 'branch of the blackmailing industry.'[19] 'Everybody who knows anything about the subject,' grumbled the Toronto *Mail* (18 April 1894), 'knows that nine out of ten of the libel suits begun against newspapers are the result of a temporary partnership struck up between 'shyster' limbs of the law and citizens whose antecedents are more or less shady.' Worse yet, the libel laws were used to harass an outspoken press. That charge was not without cause. In March 1889 the Jesuits entered a suit for criminal libel, claiming damages of $50,000, against the Toronto *Mail* to bring this nativist champion to account for its assorted attacks on the order.[20] In the summer of 1893, the provincial ministers in Quebec took out seven libel actions over an article published by *La Patrie*, a move which could only appear an attempt to punish that fiery opposition organ.[21] In November 1898 the *Printer and Publisher* reported a series of libel actions had been entered or threatened by the chief of police, the superintendent of waterworks, and some aldermen against the Montreal *Herald*, then engaged in a furious crusade against the old bugbear of municipal corruption. The spectre of libel, feared *Le Monde* (23 May 1893), meant 'la liberté de la presse n'existe que de nom,' since journalists could not disclose 'les coulisses des scandales' they had uncovered. That was an outrage – for 'baillonez les journaux ou faites les disparaître,' warned *Le Monde* (11 July 1893) over the *La Patrie* actions, 'et le public aura perdu le plus forte garantie de liberté et de justice.' In press circles, it was an article of faith that 'a few and untrammelled press is a necessity of the commonwealth. Disabilities laid upon it are injurious to the people at large, and all the libels that it has ever published are but as the dust of the balance against the advantages that a free expression of opinion has placed at the disposal of the public.'[22] In short, press apologists argued the virtues of the collective right of the public to know as against the individual right of every citizen to privacy. No code of ethics, imposed from without or within the profession, asserted the Montreal *Herald*, could absolve the press from 'its right and duty to tell its readers everything that may have happened and transpired.'[23]

That kind of reasoning reflected the ways in which newspapers thought they served their readers. According to *La Presse* (21 February 1897), at the time upset by a lost libel suit, the publisher had a 'mandat de défenseur des intérêts du peuple.' Occasionally, dailies would refer to themselves as 'the public prints,'[24] a suggestive and self-indulgent nickname. 'Newspapers are established as business enterprises, for the circulation of news and the protection of the interests of the whole public,' mused the Montreal *Star* (23 August 1877). 'When a journal ceases to represent the public, then it loses its value.' The newcomer to the press was always loud in his promises of fearless service. So the boast of A.S. Woodburn, founder of the Ottawa *Journal*: 'Whatever may be its faults THE EVENING JOURNAL will certainly not be the organ of any clique, party, or denomination; it will give the news of the day regardless of its effect upon either friend or foe; it will comment fearlessly upon passing events in the interest of law, order and progress, and will not refrain from just and temperate criticism in order either to benefit or injure any race, party, or denomination' ('Prospectus,' 10 December 1885).

Journalists made much of the accessibility of the newspaper to the public. 'An editor's office is common property to the public,' recalled Sidney Bellingham, onetime publisher of the Montreal *Daily News*. 'Strangers come and go, each in their several quests.'[25] The chronicler of the *Telegram*'s story claimed that 'all classes and conditions of men' came to the editorial room to plead for one favour or another, 'and the case of each is treated with the utmost impartiality.'[26] *La Presse* (12 May 1894) organized a 'bureau de travail' where the unemployed could publicize their availability. Another people's paper, the Toronto *News* (16 August 1899), had arranged a special information service which contained, presumably among much else, a list of boarding houses and furnished rooms in the city. Indeed, dealing with the public could be a frustrating and time-consuming business, or so C.S. Clark argued. A host of letter writers, clergymen, snobs, ordinary advertisers, and on and on expected the newspaper to satisfy their whims, no matter how ridiculous.[27]

More telling, though, was the actual record of the enthusiasms which captured the fancy of the daily press. First, newspapers were great boosters, of their cities and provinces. No place seemed better or brighter than the home of the readers: time and again, editorial space was devoted to touting the 'intelligence' of Winnipeg (*Manitoba Free Press*, 7 July 1880), the 'solid and enduring nature' of Toronto's growth (Toronto *Mail*, 19 November 1886), the fact that little was needed 'to make Ontario an ideal earthly home' (Toronto *Telegram*, 14 August 1889), or 'un bel avenir pour Québec,' here the city not the province (*L'Électeur*, 21 March 1890). Likewise, rival cities were the butt of ridicule and abuse: the Hamilton *Herald* (12 June 1890) gleefully called Toronto 'the laughing stock of the province,' 'a city boomed to death' that would last as 'but a suburb to be absorbed by a great city [no doubt Hamilton] in its far-reaching development.' Social institutions, notably charities, were usually applauded because their good works served to bind the community. Assorted schemes for civic improvement and the like, say a public library, normally won press support. A proposal to put up a new YMCA building in London, for instance, led the *Advertiser* (8 March 1893) to reflect that it was 'impossible to over-estimate the importance of surrounding our young men with the best influences along lines touching their physical, mental and moral development.' And newspapers often elected themselves champions of a cause that promised to boost their homes: in October 1893 the Quebec *Telegraph* began a campaign to inspire a winter carnival 'in order to benefit local trade and afford employment to the unemployed.'[28] But, above all, newspapers were typically builders of pride and confidence. The Saturday edition of *Le Monde* (24 June 1893) was a 16-page extravaganza, 'un hommage à la nationalité,' which celebrated the French-Canadian experience in honour of St-Jean-Baptiste Day. The *Printer and Publisher* (June 1895) gave generous praise to the *Mail and Empire* because of its determined Canada-boosting, necessary to give the country 'confidence in herself.' Chauvinism, apparently, was the proper mood for a patriotic press.

The other side of the coin was the newspaper-turned-censurer. People's journals, especially, were ever alert to the scent of immorality or privilege in high places, ready to condemn any threat to the public interest. In December 1886, for example, *La Presse* was an angry crusader for civic reform, convinced that Montreal's government and charter desperately needed change and deeply suspicious of 'un job de $37,000' involving paving contracts and suggestions of aldermanic impropriety. In a different vein, the Toronto *Star* (22 September

1894) carried a two-and-a-half-column 'Story of the Medical Society' which disclosed how this closed corporation enjoyed privileges that allowed it to control the life of doctors and exploit the public. Sometimes, a paper would discover a grand evil demanding immediate remedy – the Toronto *News* (11 March 1885) noted how 'in a series of articles' it had demonstrated that the police force 'from the Chief's office down was rotten to the core.' Sometimes, a paper would scold the public – *Le Monde* (23 May 1893), angered by the corruption of Montreal politics, called for an end to voter apathy and a wave of indignation to sweep the bad men out of office. Similarly, the Montreal *Herald* (4 July 1890) took both the Quebec public and the provincial government to task for allowing the continuance of what the paper called the barbaric treatment of the insane at the Longue Pointe Asylum. The newspaper as censurer was a moral creature, full of righteousness. Its crusades did not threaten the social fabric but rather employed the prevailing myths to condemn people, practices, or institutions that hindered the progress of the city or the country.

Booster or censurer, the daily newspaper bowed before the great god of public opinion. 'The press, after all, but reproduces the thoughts, and gives expression to the opinions, feelings, aspirations, and even passions of the community,' claimed S.P. Day in 1864. This English visitor was merely explaining how the scurrilous tone of much press comment reflected, naturally if unhappily, 'the elements of discord' that troubled colonial life.[29] Publishers, successful ones anyway, were well aware of this need to act as instruments of the public will: in 1871 Thomas White of the Montreal *Gazette* explained to his political master, John A. Macdonald, that the restive temper of the anglophone community compelled him 'in the Commercial interest of the Gazette ... to take a course somewhat different from what my own desires would have led me to.'[30] It was the belief in the ultimate sovereignty of the reader which led the Montreal *Herald* to declare each newspaper 'a class unto itself,' bound only by 'the tastes and requirements of its readers' as well as 'the well defined limitations of the Statute book.'[31] And it was this same sovereignty, argued the *Printer and Publisher* (October 1893), which determined the quality of journalism:

The mass of mankind, for whom newspapers are written, are neither learned nor judicious; the most that can be expected of them is that they will move on a deadlevel of mediocrity. To influence them and to command their support, a public journal must not be very much better or very much worse than they are. If it falls below them in intelligence, they will despise is [*sic*]; if it soars too far above them, they will ignore it as beyond their comprehension ... No conscientious journalist will abet that which principle condemns as wrong. But if he is wise, he will couch his condemnation of popular errors in such a manner as not to alienate his readers or to provoke them to reject his teachings altogether. If he runs amuck at the public, he will simply sacrifice any influence he might have exercised. He must show that he differs in opinion from the rank and file of his readers without slapping them in the face.

The appeal to public opinion, to the readers' tastes, had and would serve journalism as a refuge against attacks and a weapon against pressures.

THE CLERGY'S RIVALRY

One such pressure came from clergymen. That should not be a surprise. Church and press were engaged, in some ways, in a struggle for the hearts and minds of the public. Each authority boasted a degree of moral significance. Besides, clergymen, once virtually the clerisy of the colonies, now discovered their erstwhile pre-eminence endangered, if not usurped, by the upstart intelligentsia of journalists. Wasn't some kind of occupational rivalry likely? But here, at least, the experience in Anglo-Protestant Canada differed markedly from that in French and Catholic Canada.

In Protestant Canada, the facts of life might suggest the church had already lost out. 'The press represents the people more truly than does the pulpit, and of the two the former probably exerts the more powerful influence,' affirmed a smug Hamilton *Herald* (26 April 1890). 'It talks to a much larger constituency and it talks daily and without cessation.' Churchmen could not really deny this. Indeed, a Reverend Dr Laidlaw admitted that in practice 'the press is far more extensively and continuously engaged in the work of preaching than the pulpit is.'[32] The social outreach of the daily newspaper, added Reverend Robert Campbell, put the 'press, as a means of shaping the views of the great mass of people, far beyond the pulpit and the platform.'[33]

The Protestant churches, their power hobbled by denominational divisions and political traditions, lacked the clout to effectively discipline or censor the press. That fact did not stop clergymen from lecturing the press on its social responsibilities, though. For the press, as Campbell emphasized, was not 'an unmixed good': 'it is a potent engine of destruction as well as salvation.'[34] Clerics, still very much the guardians of the nation's morality, were wont to criticize the press when it failed to act in accord with the designs of a Victorian God. The difficulty lay in the commercial side of journalism. Business considerations all too often overrode the dictates of morality. Laidlaw noted that publishers were easily tempted 'to consult the tastes and wishes of the people rather than the oracles of infinite wisdom.'[35] Campbell feared 'the desire to obtain a large circulation and so win wealth and power by pandering, it may be, to vicious tastes.'[36] The *Printer and Publisher* (June 1895) reported that an anonymous speaker at the meetings of the Toronto Ministerial Association had 'recently remarked that the newspapers are destroying the religion of the young men ... by printing so many columns of sporting and similar matter.' In particular, clerics concentrated on 'the bane of sensationalism' which threatened to convert the daily into an instrument of evil. That penchant for the lush details of crime and scandal led A.T. Drummond, a Presbyterian layman, to wonder whether 'Our American Newspapers Are Degenerating?'[37] He and his ilk urged upon publishers the virtues of self-censorship to ensure that news and comment worked to uplift the public. 'Every journal, whatever its creed or politics may be,' declared Reverend E.H. Dewart, editor of the *Christian Guardian*, 'should be in an important sense "a preacher of righteousness and truth."'[38] 'Let pulpit, platform and press join hands in advocating all that is true and pure and good,' concluded Campbell, 'and then shall they together prove "mighty through God to the pulling down of strongholds."'[39] This ritual of argument, whether lay or clerical, was at bottom part of an effort to get journalists to admit the moral superiority of the churches.

Uneasy best describes the response of the journalist. The typical editor did accept the prevailing ideal of a moral or family newspaper, able to work as an agent of righteousness in the community. What did this ideal require? It required 'the inculcation of all the domestic, social and commercial virtues; the diffusion of useful knowledge; the cultivation of the mental and moral faculties; the encouragement of all that is right, and the rebuke of all that is wrong,' claimed the London *Advertiser* (14 January 1865). That would make the newspaper 'a sort of oracle, or at least a valued mentor and friend, whose visit will always be prized.' More to the point it would ensure the newspaper became, in the words of the Toronto *Leader* (7 November 1871), 'a source for the elevation of a country's morals,' instead of 'a source of degradation and licentiousness.' Time and again, editorials condemned the example of the American press, 'the ever-ready receptacle of social scandal' (Quebec *Chronicle*, 13 March 1866), always 'pandering to the morbid interest exhibited by some minds for loathsome details of indecency and lust' (Montreal *Star*, 14 August 1874), which had fostered licence not liberty in the Republic. The very power of the newspaper, the fact that it was sometimes 'the sole medium of communications' in a household, argued the Toronto *Telegram* (25 January 1881), meant it was 'highly important the tone of the public press should be as nearly upto the ideal standard as possible.' For 'while no sensible newspaper pretends to dictate to people what to believe or to receive,' asserted the *Mail and Empire* (8 June 1897), 'the tone, the nature of the information supplied, the opinions advanced, combine to affect character, and this combination can very readily affect it for evil.' Nearly all kinds of anglophone newspapers, whether people's or quality, had long agreed in public with the clergy's dicta.

Journalists could not deny, however, that the American disease had spread north. Sensationalism, in one form or another, was an inevitable result of the search for popularity. 'This passion,' lamented Thomas White of the Montreal *Gazette* in 1883, 'is so intense that in the effort to minister to it nothing is sacred.' He singled out 'the interviewing system' for abuse: 'Even the sanctity of [the] home is invaded, and the family skeletons dragged from their cupboards, and dished up in spiciest form to minister to the prurient tastes of the public.'[40] The Toronto *Week* (31 October 1890) took issue with the zealous reporting of murders and the like, since all too often this glorified the deed and made the criminal a celebrity. In 1900 Gordon Waldron of the Toronto *Weekly Sun* denounced an assortment of ills, some sensational and some just plain immoral: the prevalence of 'the foulest and filthiest advertisements,' the publication of American 'racing news,' the appearance of society columns filled with tainted gossip, and the flattering of 'literary charlatanism' in book review columns. A bit less fanciful was his charge that 'false headlines and the garbling and distortion of news,' designed to create a sensation, had become much too familiar in the Canadian press.[41] Just as bad, it seemed to one J.R. Bone, were the expression of 'jingoism and flag-waving' which blossomed forth in the press during the early stages of the Boer War.[42] Such practices filled Joe Clark, another Toronto journalist, with gloom. "The tendency of the time is downward,' he wrote in 1896, 'for while the daily press, conscious of its unworthiness, puts on a pretense of increased righteousness, its practices are constantly growing more indefensible and its influence more baneful.'[43]

Not even the quality newspaper could resist all temptation. In the late autumn of 1890, for instance, the Toronto *Mail* began publishing in instalments the autobiography of Reginald Birchall, an action which earned the paper the sobriquet 'the scarlet woman of journalism.'[44] Birchall was a young Englishman of gentlemanly airs, educated at Oxford in fact, who reputedly enticed fellow-countrymen to Canada where he murdered them for their start-up money. The Birchall case had excited Ontario readers, and boosted circulations, for months. The *Mail*, presumably, hoped to scoop rivals by exploiting the public's fascination with the details of Birchall's life and crimes. Faced by mounting criticism from local clerics, the *Mail* (8 November 1890) offered in defence a coyly argued editorial entitled 'The Sermon of Birchall's Life.' Therein, an editor claimed that the autobiography was published in the public interest, out of a sense of moral duty, to alert people to the pitfalls of life. 'It is probable that none of us can afford to decline to receive lessons as to the paramount necessity of living a godly, righteous, and sober life, come they from the pulpit of the parson or the cell of the condemned man.' That kind of hypocrisy was a common ploy of the distressed sensation-monger. Publishers could mask nearly every sin by invoking the sacred right of the public to know. Indeed, according to the Hamilton *Herald* (26 April 1890), the pulpit would be a much more effective tool of Good should it emulate 'the newspaper idea in waging war against existing abuses.'

Even so, no yellow press ever developed in English Canada. The fever of sensationalism was restricted by the fact that the notion of a 'moral' journalism found much favour with the public – and the profession. In 1896 James Brierley, soon to be publisher of the Montreal *Herald*, emphasized that the Canadian population could boast a 'higher average morality and intelligence,' better yet that Canadian cities lacked 'the extremes of morality and depravity, of culture and ignorance' which 'jostle each other on the street' in the Republic.[45] There was an element of truth in this patriotic guff: the market for a thorough-going yellow journalism was too small in a land where the moral conventions of Protestantism had such sway. Sensation-mongering was closely associated with newcomers, such as the evening editions of the Montreal *Herald* (1894)[46] and the Ottawa *Citizen* (1898),[47] intent on making a splash. Success and profit, at bottom, lay in winning the loyalties of a broad, bourgeois public. So the quality papers were normally paragons of Victorian virtue. And the people's journals, once they began to prosper, restrained their earlier exuberance, the Toronto *Telegram* in particular earning a reputation as a family newspaper. It was not hard for most journalists, then, to convince themselves that the record of the press, allowing for a few exceptions, had remained 'essentially clean.'[48] Or, as E.J.B. Pense of the Kingston *Whig* put it in 1899, 'Canadian journals are household journals, free visitors by right of existence to homes and firesides.'[49] The search for popularity had apparently left intact the moral force of the press, whatever the views of jaundiced clerics.

Journalists returned the favour: the daily press in English Canada was throughout a critic – and some papers were acerbic – of the performance of the clergy. The journalist readily admitted the enormous social importance of the churches, an inevitable corollary of the press's enthusiasm for Christianity. 'The clergy are a moral police force,' argued the Ottawa *Times* (11 February 1870), 'who keep the people in the way of doing right, by constantly keeping before human nature the duties which man owes to his Maker and to himself.' But the churches' power was limited by the ideas of liberty and democracy. Almost all anglophone dailies, even in the Conservative camp, accepted the notion of some necessary separation of church and state. ('The mixing of church and state has been productive of great evil in the past, and the spirit of the age is averse to any further connection between the two.')[50] Occasionally, a commitment to 'Equal Rights' would lead some editor to denounce the persistence of tax exemptions for church property, a species of favouritism which cost the ordinary taxpayer much money. More often, editors grew distressed over the clergy's penchant for moral regulation, notably sabbatarian laws, although these measures also won much support in the press. The battle over Sunday streetcars in Toronto during the 1890s sparked an extraordinary controversy, the *World* in particular filling its editorial columns with denunciations of Methodist tyranny. What most distressed, of course, was the way Catholic prelates routinely interfered with the secular pursuits of their congregations. Clerical politicking, bans on newspapers, even separate schools could easily appear dangerous infringements of 'the ordinary principles of liberty,'[51] a view which fuelled the fires of nativism in Ontario and elsewhere. The burden of press criticism was that the churches should confine themselves strictly to the spiritual dimension of Canadian life.

Journalists went a step further and questioned whether the church was fulfilling its social mission. The reasons varied. The Hamilton *Herald* (21 December 1889) took to task 'the evangelists' trade': these 'fakirs' did little more than work up a great 'excitement' and gain 'notoriety,' with fanatical outbursts that hardly benefitted faith or morality. That was the clerical brand of sensationalism. The Toronto *Globe* (8 April 1887) feared that the Protestant churches had become 'too comfortable, too decorous, too self-satisfied, too much inclined to rest and be thankful,' out of sympathy with the 'masses.' And yet the overriding duty of the churches was to Christianize the new democracy, else the modern world would suffer 'another repetition of the decay and ruin of civilization through the ignorance and corruption of the great body of the people.' The Halifax *Herald* (22 June 1892) worried that 'the clergy by reason of their habits of life and thought are year by year becoming more removed form the people.' The sad consequences was a decline of religious worship 'into a cold formalism from which the life and spirit is departing.' It was the clergy's duty to 'become more democratic in their sympathies,' to modernize their approach so that 'the old truths' could be 'differently applied to meet the needs of mankind in this last half of the nineteenth century.'

A special favourite of journalists was the cause of Protestant union. This ecumenism was, of course, a direct challenge to a clergy whose life was bound up in the reality of denominationalism. Many, though by no means all, editors equated denominationalism with the old hatreds and feuds that had blighted the Protestant past. An embattled faith could no longer afford the luxury of dissension amongst its followers: the various churchmen wasted too much energy (and money) defending their own narrow preserves. So the Montreal *Gazette* (25 November 1870) yearned for 'the removal of the disunion which now paralyses so much Christian energy and usefulness, weakening, and often defeating the contest of the Church against the common enemies, against ignorance and irreligion, against intemperance, idleness and crime.' In contrast, some kind of Protestant brotherhood, maybe a Christian alliance, mused idealists, would raise the stature of the faith and convert the church into a formidable foe of the materialism which afflicted modern life. It all amounted to a call for the clergy to mend their ways, else lose the mantle of moral leadership. The anglophone journalist, at least, worried little about urging reform on his moral betters.

His brother in French Canada felt differently. There, the daily press lived very much in the shadow of a powerful church. Catholic bishops were jealous of their prerogatives, their self-proclaimed right 'd'enseigneur, de commander, de juger' their flock,[52] in order to ensure the integrity of the faith and the authority of the church. These bishops were well aware, as Mgr Thomas (bishop of Ottawa) put it in 1883, that the press was 'une force immense dans nos sociétés modernes'[53]; Bishop Bruchesi, years later, claimed that 'dans l'organisation actuelle de la société la presse joue un rôle prépondérant.'[54] The prelates carefully watched over the press to ensure that it worked in the right way. Bishop Thomas called the press an 'admirable institution' when it strove 'd'éclairer toutes les classes sur leurs devoirs et leurs droits réels et de les encourager ainsi à la pratique de la morale chrétienne.' But he condemned that press when it deigned to question the church, or remained silent on matters of import to Catholics, or indulged in sensationalism whether by publishing trashy novels or salacious news, all of which threatened the cause of moral progress. Had not Pope Leo XIII himself declared in 1879 that the daily press was 'une des causes principales du déluge de maux qui nous inonde et du misérable état auxquel est réduite la société'?[55] No unlimited freedom of the press could exist: it was the duty of journalists to accept 'la soumission et l'obéissance aux évêques,'[56] just as it was the duty of the bishops 'd'interdire même la lecture des journaux qu'ils jugent dommageables aux intérêts' of the church.[57]

Journalists found it difficult, at times, to conform to the clergy's vision of 'la bonne presse.' Even the ultramontane editor, sometimes a recipient of clerical patronage, had his difficulties. Over the years, Léger Brousseau, owner of *Le Courrier du Canada*, was the unlucky target of many missives from clerical subscribers suggesting what news to select or editors to employ.[58] In 1876 Joseph-Israel Tarte, then in his 'ultra' phase, clashed with Archbishop Taschereau of Quebec because of *Le Canadien*'s attacks on the University of Laval.[59] In 1882 Frédéric Houde resigned from *Le Monde* because his editorials critical of Taschereau won the censure of Bishop Fabre of Montreal.[60] That zealot F.-X.-A. Trudel had to suffer in 1889 when the same Fabre sent a circular letter around the diocese warning against the disobedience and politics of *L'Étendard*.[61]

The ordinary publisher or editor took umbrage at efforts, usually by lay ultramontanes, to convert his newspaper into a truly Catholic organ. A Conservative daily such as *La Minerve*, often blamed because it put party before church, replied by damning ultramontanes rivals, be that *Le Nouveau Monde* in the 1870s or *L'Étendard* in the 1880s, as factional rags that only fostered dissension in the church and the community.[62] A people's journal such as *La Presse*, often attacked for its ready publication of crime and fiction, responded by pointing out that its editors merely tried to meet public demand.[63] The demise of *L'Étendard* provoked *Le Monde* (29 May 1893) to declare that publishing a modicum of sensation was 'une question de vie ou de mort' for the modern daily. A little later, *Le Monde* (17 June 1893) followed up with a full-blown assault on the ideal of a Catholic organ. Such a strange daily would live in a straitjacket, forced to suppress news (notably about crime and Protestants!), never able to appeal to women because of its melancholy, able to win only a minute highbrow public with articles 'naturellement longs, dogmatiques, bourrer de citations et incompréhensibles pour la masse des lecteurs.' That was a formula for disaster: the social outreach of journalism had made nonsense of the dreams of high-minded ultramontanes.

Besides, where was the cause sufficient to justify the birth of 'une bonne presse?' That old rouge spirit of resistance did linger on in press circles, at least among Liberals. The church's displeasure over the apparent anti-clericalism of *Le Pays* and *Le Bien Public* contributed to their respective deaths in 1871 and 1876. Throughout the 1880s and the 1890s, Beaugrand's editors at *La Patrie*, if respectful of the church's moral authority, nonetheless claimed the right to judge secular questions free of all controls by clerics and damned any interference in press affairs as a species of ecclesiastical tyranny.[64] But elsewhere submission was the order of the day. Typical was the claim in *La Minerve* (10 October 1888) that 'en matière religieuse il a toujours été ... exclusivement catholique, c'est-à-dire soumis à l'autorité suprême du Souverain Pontife et à celle de l'épiscopat qui a reçu du Vicaire de Jésus-Christ, la mission de gouverner l'Eglise locale.' Party organs, whether Liberal or Conservative, normally vied with each other to prove their loyalty and to employ the religious cry against a rival: so *L'Électeur* (2 April 1889) waxed indignant over supposed attacks on the Jesuits and the pope in the Conservative *Le Canadien*. Even the slightly yellow *La Presse* (10 August 1896) boasted that it was 'un journal catholique,' inspired by the 'admirables encycliques de Sa Sainteté Léon XIII.' Some years later, the paper publically apologized, and temporarily dismissed two journalists, because a piece of illustrated sensation had excited the ire of Bishop Bruchesi of Montreal.[65] Always, Berthiaume tried to balance crime and scandal with effusive piety and moral homilies. When five bishops published a pastoral letter late in 1896 condemning *L'Électeur* because of its 'idées malsaines et articles perfides,'[66] Pacaud immediately surrendered, changing the paper's name to *Le Soleil* to shake off the now regrettable past. And the sale of *La Patrie* early in 1897 to the Tarte brothers signalled the disappearance of the last important voice of rouge intransigence. The new editor, Henri Bourassa, promised devotion to Catholicism and obedience to church discipline.[67] No wonder a perceptive visitor from France, André Siegfried, concluded early in the new century that freedom of the press was something of a dream in Quebec. 'The bishops, with their power of condemnation, are able to exercise almost complete control,' he wrote. 'Condemnation from the pulpit results in a decrease of sales at once. Should this not suffice, the confessional does the rest. Editors know they can resist for two or three months, but not more. The Church always wins in the end.'[68]

The upshot was that the daily press had become a champion and, in some ways, an instrument of the social dominance of the church. Dailies avoided, whenever possible, the knotty issue of church and state, emphasizing instead the virtues of a status quo that rested on the harmony rather than the separation of the two authorities. Any focus on the church's affairs was normally respectful. The *mandements* of bishops and the views of clerics on social questions found an easy entry into newspaper columns (excepting *La Patrie*'s). Indeed, newspapers turned to praise, cultivating the myth of a patriotic clergy. According to *Le Canadien* (5 August 1880), 'le clergé fut le fondateur, le pére de la nation canadienne-française.'[69] In the same vein, *L'Électeur* (11 April 1889) claimed that it had always recognized 'la part important qu'a prise notre clergé à notre existence nationale, son action si visible dans tout le cours de notre histoire.' And *La Minerve* (1 September 1898) stressed that the priests had propagated 'le culte de notre langue et l'amour du sol canadien.'[70] It was all striking evidence of the deep-rooted Catholicism of the populace – the press had to celebrate the clergy because most readers would not countenance indifference or rebellion.

THE BUSINESSMAN'S INFLUENCE

Late in 1899 Willison gave a speech on 'Journalism' to the Political Science Club of the University of Toronto. Much of his address dwelt on the strengths and weaknesses of the Canadian press, the ideals of journalism, and the perils of sensationalism and political passions. But what he singled out as 'more ominous and dangerous' to a free press was 'the growing power of corporations and the influence of great aggregations of capital in a few hands.' He thought that business enterprises might attempt to use their money to secure a stranglehold on the press, which he emphasized could have 'no mission in the world worth filling except as the articulate voice of the plain, unorganized and unsubsidized people.' But don't worry too much, he added, since there was 'no reason to conclude that the corporations have a dominating voice in the press or in the public life of Canada.' At bottom, then, Willison's warning was merely a rhetorical device to show democracy and its partner, a free press, were safe and sound in Canada.[71]

In fact the evidence, even if incomplete, shows the connections between businessmen and journalists were sufficiently cosy to compromise the independence of the press. Each had something the other needed: businessmen the money, journalists publicity. Some kind of trade-off was well-nigh inevitable. Occasionally, wealthy capitalists, especially railway promoters, invested in newspapers to drum up public support, and thus public monies, for their own projects (one of the reasons, by the way, F.-X.-A. Trudel felt the founding of *L'Étendard*, never the businessman's toady, was so necessary).[72] Around 1871, John Sheddon, involved in assorted railway schemes in Ontario, acquired a $5,000 mortgage on the Toronto *Telegraph*, which naturally favoured his plans for public assistance.[73] At the same time, Hugh Allan (perhaps the country's wealthiest man) held some of the debts of the Montreal *Gazette* and *La Minerve*, both supporters of his Northern Colonization Railway. Eventually, he and his associates, it would seem, agreed to compensate the White brothers, owners of the *Gazette*, at their request for the paper's advocacy of the Pacific railway scheme.[74] During the 1880s rumour had it that L.-A. Sénécal invested sums in assorted dailies, including *Le Monde* and later *La Presse*. So too did the Canadian Pacific Railway, which held shares for a time in the Montreal *Herald* and the *Manitoba Press*, once critics of the company. In 1888 an agreement was drawn up between W.F. Luxton and Donald Smith, a CPR stockholder and director, which effectually transferred control to the company.[75] In 1893 an exasperated William Van Horne, the company's general manager, tossed a recalcitrant Luxton out of the editorial chair to make way for Molyneux St John, recently the chief of the CPR's advertising department.[76] During the mid-1890s C.E.L. Porteous, business manager of Toronto's streetcar company, pursued a different tactic: buy not the newspaper, only its views.[77] He did apparently co-sign a bank note for W.F. Maclean to keep the *World* afloat.[78] And Porteous paid E.E. Sheppard $600 late in 1896 for the services of the *Star* and *Saturday Night*, F. Nicholls $3,700 early in 1898 again for the *Star*.[79] Such arrangements were usually temporary and secret, worthwhile only as long as readers were unaware their newspaper's views had been 'bought.'

Some bonds were more permanent, however. A few of the leading newspaper owners were capitalists in their own right: the Riordon brothers (Toronto *Mail*, acquired 1877), Robert Jaffray (Toronto *Globe*, 1888), Frederic Nicholls

(Toronto *Star*, 1895), or B.F. Pearson (Halifax *Chronicle* and *Echo*, 1899). The Victoria *Colonist* proved so servile to the interests of its part owner, James Dunsmuir of mining fame, that a rival dubbed the paper 'the Daily Dunsmuir.'[80] And since many a newspaper lived so close to the edge of bankruptcy, it paid publishers or managers to cement friendships with possible sources of money. In 1877 Thomas Patteson of the Toronto *Mail* virtually promised the Merchant's Bank favourable treatment if only the bank would grant his faltering paper a new line of credit.[81] In his reminiscences P.D. Ross, readily admitted his debt to Charles Magee, president of the Bank of Ottawa, who in 1891 arranged the financing necessary for Ross's takeover of the Ottawa *Journal*.[82]

However, the chief connection was undeniably advertising, now that ad revenues had become the grand source of operating funds. Sometimes advertisers did try to use their clout to exact a favourable coverage or to veto an unwelcome opinion. The *Printer and Publisher* (May 1899) reported that the Grand Trunk Railway, soon followed by the Richelieu and Ontario Navigation Co, was adding to its advertising contracts the clause that they were void 'if the paper "unfairly or unjustly criticized" the railway.' The next year the *Printer and Publisher* (March 1900) noted the excitement caused by the fact that Henry Morgan and Co, a Montreal department store, had cancelled its ads with the *Star* and *La Patrie* because they had refused to heed a request to cease agitating the race question. Usually, such blatant interference was not necessary to secure a friendly press. The dependence of big city papers on department store ads, for instance, probably had much to do with their lack of sympathy for the efforts of small merchants to restrict the growth of the new retail monsters.[83] Indeed, a writer in the *Printer and Publisher* (August 1893) thought an editor was 'careful to say nothing which his advertisers will not like.' Perhaps this was an exaggeration, yet the lush growth of advertising had clearly lessened the importance of the reader and enhanced the importance of business.[84]

Daily newspapers, especially in the Radical camp, often had harsh words for individual companies and even industries. Partly the criticism reflected the increasing acceptance of the idea of democracy, but equally it grew out of the necessity to voice the resentments of the masses. That old standby of Reform days, the anti-monopoly cry, was given new force after 1880. What frightened many an editor was the birth of Big Business – the assorted civic utilities, the huge railway corporations, and the industrial combines, all of which could be cast in the guise of monopolies. Much was made of the 'fact' that these monopolies had corrupted municipal councils, provincial legislatures, even Parliament in their search for franchises, land grants, subsidies, or tariffs. Even more general, though, was the assumption that the monopolies had managed to exact gross profits out of the hapless consumer. 'What is certain is that capital is an enormous power in the world, and that it is daily becoming a greater power,' worried an editor in the Montreal *Star* (20 July 1881). 'It is a power so great that people feel that there is a danger in leaving it to exert its full force unchecked.' So it seemed 'the question of the future is how, without unduly interfering with individual liberty, we may ensure that capital shall be what it ought to be, an aid to civilization and a source of benefit to the world at large, to all who have helped to produce it, not to those only in whose hands it may happen to be held.'

The gas company and the street railway were targets for an excessive amount of abuse because their monopoly affected so immediately the pocketbooks of readers. Fiery editorials charged the gas company held Toronto in 'a vice-like grip' (Toronto *World*, 19 March 1894), or lamented 'the big profit' everyone knew utility enterpreneurs made (Toronto *Star*, 7 February 1895), or called upon Montrealers to avoid becoming 'esclaves du monopole' (*Le Monde*, 7 May 1895). Service was never good enough, especially in the suburbs and the poorer districts, yet costs were always too high. That civic watchdog *La Presse* (23 July 1895) demanded that the gas company live up to its contract by servicing 'les quartiers populeux' with cheap gas. How to force compliance? Sometimes an editor, such as that of *L'Électeur* (19 February 1890), infuriated by 'les exactions réellement intolerables des compagnes du gaz de Québec et de Montréal,' hoped the legislature would charter competition. More often, editors railed at the city council to police the performance of utilities and maintain control of city streets. One or two dailies, notably the Toronto *World*, flirted with the notion of 'municipal socialism,' a civic takeover of all utilities. Whatever the scheme, here the news as well as the views of the daily press did display a definite suspicion of corporate practice and power.

Likewise, there were always newspapers which looked askance at the political and economic power of the railway and mining companies. In 1880 and 1881, of course, Liberal dailies across Canada worked themselves up into a frenzy of excitement over the newest monstrosity, the Canadian Pacific Railway, created by the Ottawa government. A little later the Toronto *World* became hysterical over the prospect of a 'railway fusion' in Ontario that would leave the province's arteries in the hands of the Grand Trunk. Immediately, the new *L'Étendard* focused on the nefarious dealings and unrestrained powers of L.-A. Sénécal. The Winnipeg *Sun* never seemed to tire of abusing the CPR for oppressing the farmers and slowing western growth. The Victoria *Times* during the late 1880s and early 1890s was a great critic of the Dunsmuirs. What were the remedies? Sheer the corporations of their privileges, sponsor new railways (the cry 'free railways' rivalled 'free trade' among Manitoba Liberals in the 1880s), set up a railway commission to regulate rates, perhaps even nationalize the railways. Much of this amounted to little more than letting off steam, though: most editors were leary of any dramatic assault on the rights of Capital.

Manufacturers received their share of vilification, especially after editors discovered in the late 1880s the existence of industrial combines in sugar refining, textiles, agricultural machinery, and on and on. 'The only thing left untrammelled appears to be the free air of Heaven,' lamented the Conservative Ottawa *Citizen* (18 May 1888); 'from the cradle to the grave these commercial harpies appear to have encircled poor humanity.' Combines were really little more than temporary, often ineffective, price-fixing arrangements among manufacturers in some line of business. But they appeared so dangerous because they snuffed out, in the words of the Charlottetown *Examiner* (2 March 1888), 'the wholesome spirit of competition, which was at once the life of trade and the consumer's safeguard.' Conservative editors hoped that a bit of fiddling with the tariff would undo the harm; Liberal editors recommended the more drastic measure of the free trade or tariff reform to free the marketplace. Either way, the key again was to reinvigourate that competition which, ironically, had given birth to the combines.

That said, the Labour and Farm challenges to the rise of Big Business won a very mixed response from the press. A Radical daily, of course, was always ready to extend a helping hand to the oppressed masses. Liberal dailies, too, would take up the causes of the workingman or the farmer to assist the assault on Conservative rule. In principle at least, editors by the mid-1880s were prepared to accord Labour and Farm the right to organize in trade unions and agricultural associations, thereby to protect class interests against the workings of the free market. The Toronto *World* (11 March 1886), for instance, bluntly told employers they were 'very far wrong indeed if they think they can continue to ignore the men's unions, and refuse to recognize them.' The Winnipeg *Sun* and later on the Winnipeg *Tribune* were forever urging on Manitoba's farmers the wisdom of solidarity – 'Organization is the only means by which their voice can be heard,' said the *Tribune* on 1 March 1890. The people's journals and the Liberal press in central Canada during the mid-1880s joined forces to question the Macdonald government's practice of assisted immigration, which lowered wages by bringing to Canada British workingmen to compete for jobs. Around the same time, the Winnipeg dailies (briefly even the Conservative *Times*) led the weekly press of the prairies in a series of crusades against eastern business interests, banks as well as Ontario manufacturers and the CPR, which purportedly blocked the farmer's route to prosperity. During the 1890s most British Columbia dailies, notably the Victoria *Times*, backed labour's demands to halt, hopefully reverse, the flow of Asian immigration, a campaign that induced editors to elaborate a racist doctrine of white supremacy. (In 1896 William Van Horne was sufficiently upset by the clamour over the Yellow Peril, so threatening to the CPR's source of cheap labour, that he wrote long letters to both John McLagan of the Vancouver *World* and Willison of the *Globe.*)[85]

Labour and Farm militants might be forgiven, however, if they found press rhetoric rang a bit hollow whenever there was a crisis. Commitment to the gospel of harmony usually overrode sympathy for the underdog. Farm organizations that moved beyond the issue of rural improvement into the realms of commerce or politics soon came in for much criticism. The London *Advertiser* (7 March 1874), for example, warned the Grange (then on the march in Ontario) that there was 'no call here for any crusade against railroad men or politicians; produce dealers or manufacturers, no necessity of any rallying cry of class against class.' That was mild compared to the denunciations in the early 1890s of the Patrons of Industry who tried to use co-operatives and independent politics to foil the advance of urban power. Likewise, unions noted for their militancy could expect little press affection, especially from Conservatives. *La Minerve* (11 January 1895) editorialized against the American internationals whose control over Quebec's trades amounted to 'une espèce d'annexion sociale.'

Industrial disputes were a marvelous test case because here the interests of Capital and Labour came into obvious, sometimes violent conflict. Editors did not like strikes: the Saint John *Telegraph* (7 September 1893), voicing only the common wisdom, warned that strikes were 'ruinous to the workmen, injurious to the employer, and detrimental to the best interests of the country.' Not only the Victoria *Colonist*, very much the business servant, but also the Vancouver *World*, then vaguely Radical, saw the labour troubles at the Dunsmuirs' Wellington collieries in the summer of 1890 as an assault on the rights of property, requiring the presence of the militia. The Charlottetown *Guardian* (22 November 1894) lamented that it had stood almost alone among Maritime newspapers in its sympathy for the efforts of the American Railway Union 'to rescue Pullman's serfs' – and it felt that strikes or lockouts were legitimate only as 'last resorts.' The great concern of *La Patrie* (5 July 1894) was that these American troubles not spread to Montreal: that would mean 'une ruine pour notre cité.' Even *La Presse* (30 January 1895) argued that 'les grèves se terminent rarement au profit des ouvriers.' So it normally lent support to any efforts to avoid an industrial dispute through arbitration and the like. Newspapers, then, tended to blame strikes on labour, to worry about law and order and industrial progress, to urge social peace, whatever the merits of a union's case.

The fact was that journalists worshipped at the altar of capitalism. The news and views of the daily newspaper, in French as well as English Canada, bespoke this enthuasiasm. Even the Toronto *Telegram* (4 July 1885), for instance, carried on page three a report of the annual meeting of the Imperial Bank of Canada. *La Patrie* (23 March 1887) not only published the annual report of Sun Life but also offered an editorial praising this noble company for its endeavours on behalf of Canada. The Victoria *Times* (18 June 1887) actually found occasion to praise a Dunsmuir for 'his enterprise and shrewdness as a business man' and 'his public spirit as a citizen.' The Hamilton *Herald* (19 November 1890) yearned for the appearance of 'a dozen business men' to take charge of the troubled affairs of the city. In a column devoted to recognizing worthy souls, 'Galerie contemporaine,' *La Presse* (2 April 1893) published (complete with portrait) an effusive appraisal of the career of J.S. Bousquet, manager of the Banque du Peuple. Note that all of these papers had solid credentials as Radical spokesmen.

What justified this celebration? Journalists viewed nearly every sign of business activity as proof of the country's progress. Take the railways. 'The number and quality of the railways of any country may be viewed as a criterion of the state of its civilization,' reasoned the Ottawa *Citizen* (11 January 1878). 'They are to the body politic what veins and arteries are to the body physical, for through them flow the agricultural produce, the manufacturing industries, the sources of commerce – the life blood of the state.' This was why *Le Monde* (24 March 1896) was able stoutly to defend public aid to railway promoters – railways were 'la condition première du progrès matériel dans un pays.' Then there was manufacturing. 'The successful establishment of a new sugar refinery, a new cotton mill, a new woolen mill, does not mean the making of one man's fortune,' the Toronto *Mail* (23 November 1881) claimed. 'It means the employment of many men's capital; the employment of many men's labour; the saving of many thousands of men to our population; the setting free of a stream of advantage which flows beneficently past the doors of the poor for their use, if they have the industry to take advantage of it.' That refrain was repeated not just by Conservatives eager to defend the National Policy but also by any local booster who wished to attract new industry with some special privilege. Even banks had their champions. *Le Monde* (19 September 1884) called upon French Canadians to organize a powerful financial institution to give aid 'au progrès industriel, agricole, et mercantile du pays.' Indeed, *La Presse* (20 July 1895) found itself in an embarrassing situation because it had touted the merits of the Banque du Peuple three days before it closed its doors.

The rest of the answer lay in the myth of the businessman as hero. Newspapers were forever propagating this myth. The 'pluck and resolution' of the CPR managers, declared the Montreal *Herald* (11 May 1883), proved 'that all things are possible to the clear headed, stout hearted, resolute man of action.' Beaugrand of *La Patrie*, once so critical of the CPR, was eventually (25 March 1887) moved to pay 'un juste tribut d'admiration à l'intelligence financière, à l'energie, à largeur de vues, à l'administration prudent, au dévouement continuel et par dessus tout, aux sentiments patriotiques' of George Stephen, Donald Smith, William Van Horne, and their ilk. In a more general vein, the Toronto *Mail* (10 October 1894) found space to praise the lowly storekeeper, then being abused by the Patrons of Industry, because these merchants had proved 'a veritable tower of strength to the settlers,' doing 'their part in building up Canada.' Such declarations rested on the assumption, often expressed in editorials critical of socialism and the like, that businessmen somehow energized the country's life. The 'man who makes food cheaper by opening up new lines of communication, and by co-ordinating various systems of industry as to economize labour is a benefactor of society' (Montreal *Star*, 21 March 1881). Kill off the capitalists, 'and that would mean [an] end to all great enterprises, an end to construction of railways and telegraph lines, an end to the establishment of manufactories, an end to all projects in which capital had to be invested' (Toronto *Telegram*, 3 December 1883). The grand captains of industry and the railway builders had emerged as the 'véritables paladins au progrès' (*Le Journal*, 6 December 1902).[86]

This enthusiam for capitalism enabled journalists to come to terms with Big Business. The Fredericton *Gleaner* (23 July 1890), for example, welcomed the transfer of the New Brunswick Railway to the CPR: that might create 'a virtual monopoly,' but hopefully it would also ensure a great increase in the commercial traffic going through the city. Likewise, the Halifax *Chronicle* (5 April 1893), in times past a critic of most combines, nonetheless argued the legitimacy of 'a union of capital to carry forward great undertakings.' Sometimes the dawning age of the corporation seemed a cause for celebration. 'A few great trusts will hereafter do the work of manufacturing, handling and transporting that is now performed by hundreds of small companies or individuals,' predicted the Toronto *News* (4 August 1894). 'This will certainly cheapen the cost of these services, but it will not reduce the amount of employment afforded.' Indeed, *La Presse* (7 July 1902) found cause only for admiration in the way science, invention, and organization had given birth to 'l'industrie organisée,' the new corporate giants.[87]

Whatever the force of the anti-monopoly cry, the daily press had worked to foster a climate of opinion favourable to business interests. Usually, a man could count on some press support, purchased or voluntary, when requesting a favour from government. Usually, the same businessman could also count on at least a modicum of sympathy from a journalist or two should his enterprises become a target of public criticism. Invariably the press displayed a deep respect for the rights of property ('le base de nos lois civiles')[88] which hobbled any schemes to regulate the behaviour of – to say nothing of despoiling – any businessman, whether a 'good corporate citizen' or a 'robber baron.' Journalists were by no means simply the servants of business; they were, though, more often fans than critics of private companies and business practices.

THE POLITICIAN'S DOMINION

Neither the cleric nor the businessman could lay claim to the type of influence over the press enjoyed by the politician. Journalism and party seemed inextricably linked – by tradition and necessity.[89] True, that once prominent hybrid, the newspaperman-cum-politician, had become a much less common breed after Confederation because both party politics and daily journalism, at the top anyway, required full-timers. But the typical publisher or editor remained addicted to playing politics, for him a grand sport that added spice to life and gave significance to his calling. ('The game of politics is a great game,' mused Willison; 'it is played with men as the standing figures on the board, and it is full of joy to the journalist who loves his work, his country and his kind.')[90] Besides, the results of the game often gave him, or at least his newspaper, sustenance in the form of readers, subsidies, and patronage. The typical politician saw newspapers as essential vehicles of publicity, indeed a surrogate for organization, which could confound foes, strengthen party discipline and morale, and educate electors. (So Laurier claimed, 'the publication of a newspaper is a very great advantage always for the prosperity and well-doing of a political party.')[91] He was, then, quite prepared to reward friendly journalists and to punish the disloyal or hostile.

The resulting marriage, however, was at times a stormy one. That old question of dominace could easily cause trouble: politicians naturally assumed they were the masters, journalists their servants, a presumption that not every editor or publisher would stomach. The party chieftains had difficulty realizing that their reputed organs must curry favour with a wide range of readers, and this meant these dailies had to be more than just the mouthpieces of a party. Put another way, the publisher and editor was forced by the logic of mass communication to carry news or advocate views, perhaps highlight stories, that might be harmful to the best interests of the party. More important, the politician and the journalist had differing views of politics. The bias of the politician made him see politics as a contest between two teams intent on winning office; the bias of the journalist made him see politics as a war of ideas in which right must triumph. Is it any wonder the politician's hold over the press was challenged,, even by faithful journalists? Sometimes, events seemed to promise a renewal of the struggle for a free press, this time against the mastery of party instead of government.

The cause of freedom, however, got sidetracked because of the outbreak of a civil war of sorts between party newspapers, albeit Conservative and Liberal rivals, and a motley crew of self-styled independents and mavericks (Figure 2). The economics of journalism underlay the conflict. One route to commercial success, at first it seemed the only route, required a party label to attract a loyal readership. (Hector Charlesworth noted of his grandmother, 'She was a staunch Tory, and every day read the *Mail* ... from the first column to the last.')[92] This maxim made each city, eventually from Halifax to Victoria, the site of at least one Conservative and one Liberal daily. The balance of forces between the two camps remained roughly equal, sometimes the Liberals ahead, sometimes the Conservatives, winning more readers, until the late 1890s when the defection or death of old Conservative warriors (especially in Quebec) plus the political dominance of the Liberal party in Ottawa and the provinces gave the Liberal press a definite edge. Still the Liberal achievement was eclipsed by the triumph of the 'Independents.' After the mid-1860s the sectarian papers, even more the people's journals, pioneered a new strategy of non-partisan politics to win a mass readership irrespective of people's political preferences. The circulation of the so-called independent press zoomed upwards in the 1880s, due not only to the appeal of popular journalism but also to a few converts from the ranks of the party press as well. Although the most prominent independents were located in the big cities of central Canada, notably Toronto, before long maverick dailies and non-partisan newcomers had appeared across the land, even in some small towns. Yet the challengers did not sweep aside their party rivals: in 1900 the party press claimed 77 dailies, boasting a combined circulation of 660,699 (or 53 per cent of the total daily and weekly circulations of the daily press), while the independent press had a mere 37 champions, though with a combined circulation of 572,461 (or 46 per cent of the total).

The civil war, of course, was waged on the editorial pages. Controversy revolved around the propriety of any link between party and press, given the common assumption that the newspaper moulded public opinion. The self-styled independents argued that the fettered journalism of a party organ could never benefit the public. 'The primary object of such a journal is not to serve the interests of the public at large,' asserted the Toronto *Telegram* (15 May 1876), 'but to promote the policy of a particular faction.' Indeed, 'the party organs ... do nothing but defend their own and abuse the other,' agreed the Toronto *World* (7 April 1884). That made the party paper, in the words of a newly intransigent *Monde* (15 October 1892), 'l'ennemi du bon gouvernement et l'ennemi des gouvernés.' Its apologies for the misdeeds of friends and assaults on the virtue of rivals could not but threaten the new democracy: 'Thus the public mind has been debauched, the proprieties of life outraged, the self-respect of voters ruined, and the parliaments of Canada made the stamping ground of monied adventurers and political sharks' (Toronto *News*, 29

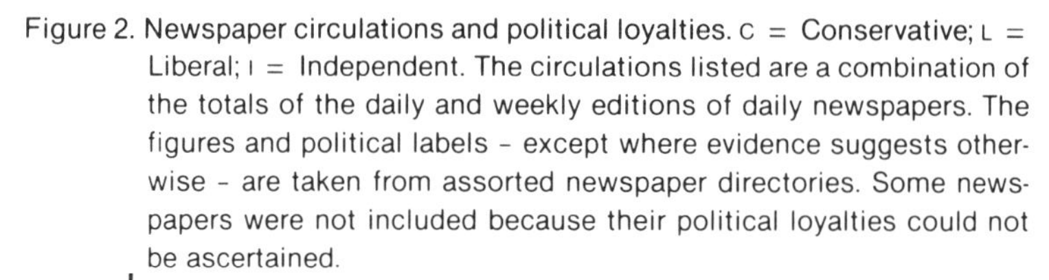

Figure 2. Newspaper circulations and political loyalties. C = Conservative; L = Liberal; I = Independent. The circulations listed are a combination of the totals of the daily and weekly editions of daily newspapers. The figures and political labels - except where evidence suggests otherwise - are taken from assorted newspaper directories. Some newspapers were not included because their political loyalties could not be ascertained.

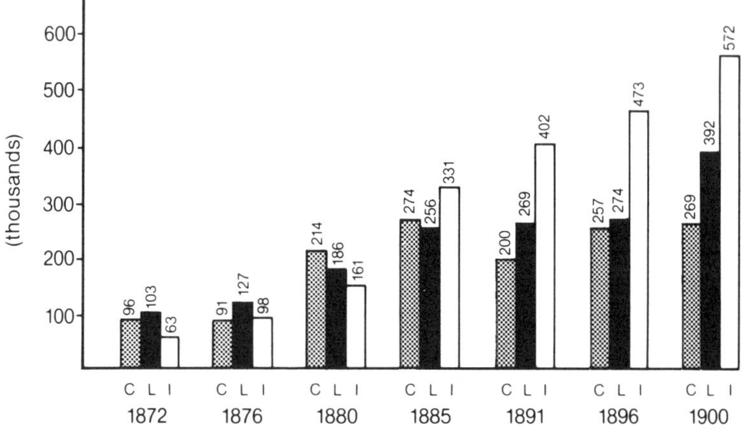

September 1883). The party organ betrayed the newspaper's mission to voice the popular will and to uplift public opinion.

Contrast this invective with the self-praise of the independent press. 'An independent press desires above all things the good of the country for which it denies itself the temporary benefits which partisanship gives,' claimed a smug Montreal *Star* (5 July 1882), 'and it desires to do full justice to men and measures of all parties.' This gave the independent press a special role in political life: not just to tell 'the truth about the affairs of the country and about political doings' (Montreal *Star*, 16 April 1886), but to protect 'popular rights' (Toronto *News*, 14 May 1885) againt any infringement. Early on, when it was hardly independent in any real sense, *La Presse* (3 September 1886) maintained that such papers were 'les intermédiaires utiles entre la certitude aveugle du ministériel et la scepticisme de l'oppositioniste.' An independent press acted as 'la soupape de sûreté, ouverte à tous les doutes, à toutes les répugnances, à tous les mécontentements, à tous les courants souterrains' which might otherwise never find a voice until the political fabric was shattered by public anger. Likewise, *Le Monde* (15 October 1892) claimed that the 'liberté de pensée, de parole et d'action' of the independent dailies made them great 'reformateurs,' in the words of Charles Dana 'daily humanitarians and utilitarians.' In short, the independent press was nothing less than the true voice of the Canadian democracy.

The party press, if thrown on the defensive, responded in kind. Much was made of the need for a 'strong and forceful' public opinion, the result of views 'arrived at by conviction,' not 'simply parrot-like repetition of the opinions of the predominant mob.'[93] That was the task of the newspaper – not just any newspaper but one which, announced Edmond Larrau in *La Patrie* (25 February 1882), 'représente une idée; une idée qui est le partage d'un group, d'une dénomination politique, d'une classe dans la société.' So when *La Minerve* enjoyed a brief renaissance in 1898, there came the proud proclamation that it was 'un journal conservateur, fidèle à son passé et respectueux des grandes traditions politiques du parti de Lafontaine, de Morin et de Cartier.'[94]

The trouble with the independent press, it seemed, was that these papers represented nothing. 'The so-called independent journalist is a man who has a whole wardrobe of neatly made convictions,' asserted the Hamilton *Spectator* (10 January 1887), 'which he changes to suit the weather, the fashion, or, mayhap, the condition of his purse.' He could exercise no lasting influence over public or party. Indeed, the London *Advertiser* (26 October 1874) once claimed 'the demands of our institutions require that the great newspapers shall take side with one party or the other,' so entrenched was party in the Canadian constitution. That was why the revitalized *La Minerve* (1 September 1898) could think its rebirth meant a return to 'sa place au conseil de la nation.'

The demands of party journalism by no means required servility. 'It is his highest duty to elevate the ideas and the tone of his party and to guide it in the ways of progress and purity,' the Montreal *Herald* (8 May 1879) said of the party journalist. 'The plain duty of the journal, in giving its opinion on political matters,' the Toronto *Globe* (3 February 1888) charged in its own defence, 'is simply to express what it believes would conduce most to the public interest.' Apologists had squared the circle, arguing the organ could serve the public as well as the party. Their reasoning assumed that any devotion to party, 'la cause commune,'[95] grew out of principle not payment. Such fealty, held the true believer, merely gave substance to the journalist's mission to lead the public in the ways of righteousness.

A good deal of the rhetoric in support of party journalism was specious. Apologists failed to admit the extent of the connections between party and press. All kinds of money was funnelled into the upkeep of needy papers. An unhappy Maurice Laframboise, who may have lost $30,000 trying to sustain Montreal's *Le National* (1872–79), admitted that in French Canada it was impossible to assure newspapers 'une existence exempte de profonder perturbations sans l'aide généreuse et persistante d'amis dévoués, sans de puissantes contributions de la part du parti dont ils partagent les vues et défendent les intérêts.'[96] The Ottawa *Times* in the early 1870s was something of a ministerial organ, changing hands when the government at Ottawa changed. Conservative monies started, and for a time sustained, the Toronto *Mail* and later the Toronto *Empire*. L.-A. Sénécal apparently funded the short-lived Quebec *Times* (November 1881–January 1882) to reach the English-speaking electorate on behalf of Chapleau's election campaign.[97] He performed a similar function, though the results were more lasting, in the founding of *La Presse*. Rumour had it that when the CPR set out to buy control of the Toronto *Globe* in 1882, Ontario Liberals moved swiftly to organize a purchase by wealthy friends, among them Robert Jaffray and George Cox, of Mrs George Brown's holdings.[98] Clifford Sifton, in his own right, invested in the Brandon *Sun* and the *Manitoba Free Press*, though he tried in vain to hide his ownership. In September 1895 the *Printer and Publisher* reported that *La Minerve* was 'controlled financially' by J.-P. Caron, a leading Conservative, and that 'a controlling interest' in *Le Monde* had been acquired by another Conservative, J.-A. Ouimet. In 1899 George Cox, now a senator, arranged a consortium of wealthy friends to buy and revitalize the Toronto *Star* in the Liberal interest. Quebec's Conservatives were able to go to J.D.R. Forget, a grand financier, to fund the waning *Le Journal* of Montreal (1899–1905).

Victory at the polls signalled to loyal publishers that they would receive a share of government patronage, mainly advertising or printing contracts. The origins of the practice went back to the early days of journalism, though only after mid-century did newspaper subsidies consume large sums of public money.[99] Party chieftains took great care to reward the faithful with government contracts: at least as early as 1876, the Ottawa government had an official list for departments which designated the newspapers deserving business, a list periodically updated and always revised when office changed hands. Equally, party journalists assumed that compensation for past services, and future exertions, was their due: in the 1870s James Moylan, admittedly the proprietor of an Irish-Canadian weekly, regularly published official announcements without approval but submitted bills to departments anyway, a practice to which Macdonald gave his blessing.[100]

The actual amounts of money involved could sometimes be sizeable. According to *La Patrie* (30 March 1897), the Quebec government bestowed around $10,000 on *L'Événement* and another $19,000 on *La Minerve* in the single year 1895–96. But it was the federal government which had the most funds to disburse. The auditor general's reports during the 1890s can be used to compare the practices of Conservative and Liberal office-holders, each over a five-year period (Table 30). There was not too much difference in purpose or habit, whatever the claims otherwise. Ottawa gave the press contracts worth roughly $125,000 in 1890–91, rising to $172,500 ten years later. Although the monies were shared among a wide range of journals, the largest sums usually went to big-city dailies. In 1895–96, for instance, the Belleville *Intelligencer*, a daily closely associated with Prime Minister Mackenzie Bowell, received $159.85 in advertising, whereas the Montreal *Gazette* got $1,057.27. The most lavish contracts came from printing, not advertising. So the Moncton *Times* earned $81,650.18 from job printing in the Conservative years, much of this probably for the purposes of the government-owned Intercolonial Railway. Of the $97,796.57 the Laurier government gave the troubled Montreal *Herald*, $86,590.31 arose out of printing jobs – indeed in 1900–01 the lucky company won almost $50,000 in such contracts alone. Party favouritism was obvious. Why else would the Conservative *Sun* of Saint John receive $54,853.28 in the early 1890s and the rival *Telegraph* $45,548.65 during the Liberal years? The major organs were handsomely rewarded: the $12,696.60 the *Empire* (and later the *Mail and Empire*) garnered from government advertising in the Conservative years was matched by the $12,276.35 the *Globe* acquired in the Liberal years. The Conservative régimes seemed a bit niggardly in their treatment of francophone organs, by comparison with anglophone dailies (perhaps Quebec's Conservative governments looked after the former?), but the Laurier government remedied that (witness the $10,177.10 for *La Patrie* and the $11,297.25 for *L'Électeur*/*Le Soleil*). Maritime dailies did especially well out of printing contracts, the central Canadian faithful earned their subsidies mostly in advertising contracts (the Montreal *Herald* was an outrageous exception), and the prairie and Pacific organs had to make do with modest sums from both sources. Largely left off the lists were the independent or maverick papers – as long as they remained such. The Toronto *News* and especially the *Telegram* received negligible contracts over the course of the decade. Even the Montreal *Star* and *La Presse* got very little, given their huge circulations. But a switch in loyalties earned decent subsidies for two 'independents,' the Toronto *Star* and the Hamilton *Herald*, in the Liberal years.

Did any of this matter? Observed the Hamilton *Spectator* (9 January 1882): 'The fact is no journal of standing of either party looks upon its government patronage as being of importance to it. Every such journal has scores of private patrons whose account is vastly greater with it than that of the Gouvernment ... If there is any want of independence in the Canadian press it is not because of the money it receives from the Canadian Government.' True enough, the annual sums bestowed upon a newspaper usually constituted only a small portion (less than 5 per cent?) of total revenues. And yet opposition or independent papers

TABLE 30

Selected newspapers and federal patronage 1891–1901 (in dollars)

	Conservative years (July 1891–June 1896)	Liberal years (July 1896–June 1901)
HALIFAX		
Herald	33,951.75	1,152.73*
Chronicle	38.00	27,811.31
SAINT JOHN		
Sun	54,853.28	1,215.56*
Telegraph	–	45,548.65
QUEBEC		
Chronicle	14,672.49	555.83*
Telegraph	45.20	10,478.29
L'Événement	2,016.03	120.10*
L'Électeur/Soleil	17.70	11,297.25
MONTREAL		
Gazette	12,149.50	698.09*
Star	2,020.79	754.63*
Herald	105.83	97,796.57
Witness	41.13	6,196.36
Minerve	2,869.16	203.30*
Le Monde	1,599.18	203.52
La Presse	2,166.81	50.74
La Patrie	4.20	10,177.70
OTTAWA		
Citizen	4,648.29	336.79
Journal	1,331.16	2,040.24
Free Press	269.25	5,505.76
TORONTO		
Mail	418.10	
Empire	9,707.31	
Mail and Empire	2,989.29	983.41*
World	4,546.04	83.30
Telegram	67.84	5.80
News	132.30	21.45
Star	504.40	5,367.73
Globe	80.40	12,276.35
HAMILTON		
Spectator	4,742.66	565.30*
Herald	847.10	2,173.45
Times	–	5,037.95
LONDON		
Free Press	2,885.74	364.60*
News		392.40
Advertiser	7.00	3,590.66

TABLE 30 continued

	Conservative years (July 1891–June 1896)	Liberal years (July 1896–June 1901)
WINNIPEG		
Manitoba Free Press	1,329.55	2,503.52
Nor'Wester/Telegram	1,118.82	13.50*
Tribune	54.45	1,038.47
VANCOUVER		
News-Advertiser	580.55	189.60
World	42.05	1,685.05
VICTORIA		
Colonist	1,407.90	109.70
Times	37.25	786.05

* All or a large part of this patronage was received in 1896–97.

loved to disclose the subsidies paid to ministerial organs to prove their venality. An irate *La Patrie* (20 August 1879) carried a list of supposed Liberal papers—'Les Vendus' it called them – which had apparently been bought off by Chapleau and Sénécal. Likewise, a self-righteous Toronto *Globe* (19 May 1885), though the recipient of monies from the Ontario government, published a list of Conservative dailies and their earnings under the suggestive title 'They Don't Count.'[101] The publication in 1899 of the news that the Montreal *Witness* had received a paltry $694 from the Laurier government, while much larger sums went to more reliable organs, so frightened the Dougalls they planned an editorial explaining the money meant no loss of independence.[102] In 1901 Willison estimated that 'within the last five years between three and four hundred thousand dollars of party money,' by which he meant mostly patronage money, 'has been put into Liberal papers in Canada.'[103] In short government 'pap' did matter. The money was welcome: it could make a difference in the profit-and-loss statements of lucky publishers, even if it was rarely the means of economic salvation it had been for the feeble papers of the 1850s and 1860s. Acceptance did indicate some sort of bond. Politicians did not give patronage out of the goodness of their hearts.

Finally, politicians could bestow upon journalists all sorts of favours. In 1872 Isaac Buchanan, a leading Hamilton Conservative, urged upon Thomas Patteson the wisdom of hiring a stalwart protectionist, such as John McLean, to aid the forthcoming *Mail*.[104] Party organizers were sometimes set to work as circulation boosters, a practice which apparently helped the weekly *Mail* reach quickly a fair-sized readership in rural Ontario. Quebec's government railway in the 1870s, the Quebec, Montreal, Ottawa and Occidental Railway, offered printing and advertising contracts to *La Minerve*, *Le Canadien*, the Montreal *Gazette*, and *Le Nouveau Monde* – in fact the railway commission's Montreal office was owned by Alphonse Desjardins of *Le Nouveau Monde*.[105] When Martin Griffin, the *Mail*'s editor, accepted the post of parliamentary librarian at Ottawa in 1885, he was merely following in the footsteps of many a loyal journalist who found peace and comfort in the provincial or federal civil service. Government departments typically preferred to release news first to representatives of friendly journals, a habit which caused J.E.B. McCready (the *Globe*'s correspondent in the 1880s) a lot of trouble.[106] The *Monetary Times* (21 August 1891) reported a peculiar arrangement whereby half the profits resulting from a paper contract between the New England Paper Co and the Ottawa government 'should be applied towards the extinction of a debt due by *La Presse* newspaper, though the agreement does not appear to have been carried into effect.' In 1897 William Templeman of the Victoria *Times* was called to the Senate, like many a publisher before and after. In 1901 Laurier helped to persuade Toronto moneymen to lend Berthiaume some $300,000 to consolidate his paper's debts.[107] Sufficient evidence has come to light, then, to show that the happiness of a journalist, be he reporter or publisher, could depend upon the assistance of friendly politicians.

What services did the journalist offer in return? First, the party organ acted as a newsletter, publishing news and views about friends or foes – necessary to keep partisans abreast of what was happening within the party, what conspiracies the other side had concocted, where politics was going. During any election campaign that information was vital to victory, the news because it enabled a quick response to, say, an enemy gambit and the views because they could be used by local candidates on the hustings to win over voters.

Second, the organ was a devout booster of the party leader, the rank and file, and their cause. Always, the journalist should strive to bolster morale: 'Say something to encourage our people and inspire them to work,' A.S. Hardy (premier of Ontario) urged Willison in the midst of the provincial election campaign of 1898.[108] In victory the organ gloated, telling all readers right had triumphed[109]; in defeat the organ counselled courage and perseverance, sure evil would fail in the end.[110] The party leader, whoever he might be, was the recipient of constant adulation, his ego often stroked with detailed reports of his comings and goings plus effusive editorials praising his works. The virtues of the party's policies were repeated ad nauseam and its traditions reinterpreted to suit circumstances, which gave both parties an important intellectual gloss. Best of all, the boosterism of the party journalist meant that the party could always count on powerful champions, no matter how gross the actions of leaders or followers, an attribute of political life especially striking when the Pacific Scandal and other such news of corruption surfaced. (Defending the party might produce some extraordinary editorials – a classic instance was *La Minerve*'s efforts to calm French-Canadian anger over the Riel execution late in November 1885 – as editors scrambled to explain away what seemed patently unacceptable to the public.)

Third, the organ served as a censurer – of the enemy mostly. 'Bite someone or something occasionally just to show that you want to hurt somebody now and then,' was another of Hardy's maxims.[111] Sometimes the enemy was within, as in the case of D'Alton McCarthy (the renegade Conservative) whose support for Tariff Reform led the Toronto *Empire* to read him out of the party late in 1892. Much more often, though, abuse and ridicule were showered on the opposing leader (Macdonald was stereotyped a corruptionist, Blake a moral coward)[112] and his policies or views, always dangerous to the public interest. Indeed, the chief editorial focus of the major organs was normally on the manifold sins of the enemy. All in all, a network of newspapers seemed essential to give the party substance, to make it a community of ideas and interests as well as a formidable foe able to complete in the game of politics.

No wonder politicians occasionally cracked the whip. A misbehaving journalist could not be allowed to get off scot-free. In 1892 leading Liberals, primarily Oliver Mowat (premier of Ontario), engineered the removal of Edward Farrer, of annexationist fame, from his editorial chair at the *Globe*. An erring newspaper soon found its patronage cut off. Chapleau withdrew provincial patronage from Tarte's *Le Canadien* early in 1882 because of the paper's ultramontane leanings; the dispute ended amicably a year later when Tarte returned to the party fold.[113] The Toronto *Mail*, while Conservative the beneficiary of hefty advertising contracts, lost these in the late 1880s and early 1890s during its years of mugwumpery. In 1891 Mercier's men threatened disaster for Quebec City's *La Justice*: unless it submitted to the *parti national*, the paper would lose its right to publish on *L'Électeur*'s printing presses.[114]

Sometimes a politician actually sponsored a newcomer to challenge or replace an erstwhile friend. Macdonald did this three times in Toronto: the *Atlas* (1858), the *Mail* (1872), and the *Empire* (1888). In 1883 Mercier and his cohorts launched Montreal's *Le Temps* because *La Patrie* refused to accept Mercier's leadership – Beaugrand's surrender was soon followed by the death of *Le Temps*.[115] Late in 1895, Laurier and other Liberal chieftains appear to have inspired the birth of Montreal's *La Bataille*, again to argue properly the Liberal case, moderate to the core, when *La Patrie* would not.[116]

The actual management of the views and news of the press required close attention. Now and then, the politicians themselves acted as directors to censor the opinions of an organ: Laurier served for a brief time at *L'Électeur* in the early 1880s and G.W. Ross (eventually a Liberal premier of Ontario) did the same at the *Globe* during the next decade. Mostly, though, the politician stayed away from direct involvement but devoted much time to guiding his favourite organs. Macdonald was a master of this art. His correspondence is full of letters pertinent to the problems of press management. Once, while in Washington to assist in the negotiation of an Anglo-American accord, he sent off a letter to a crony urging him to arrange with 'the friendly newspapers' a trap for Brown and the Liberals in the forthcoming debate over the agreement.[117] In 1872 he was in constant communication with T.C. Patteson over matters large and small, both the handling of the National Policy and the hiring of assorted journalists. Throughout the mid-1870s, he and Thomas White exchanged letters on the *Gazette* and the Montreal scene. In 1886 Macdonald tried in vain to curtail the anti-Catholic 'incendiarism' of the *Mail* under the management of C.W. Bunting and Edward Farrer.[118] So it went. Even a devoted tactician such as Macdonald must have found the task of guiding his newspapers, at times, a tedious chore.

Willison's correspondence of the 1890s sheds light on the problem from the journalist's point of view. Because Willison was editor of the country's premier Liberal organ, he received guidance from everywhere. Sometimes the matter was important: during 1895 and 1896 J.D. Cameron, Manitoba's provincial secretary, pressured Willison to ensure the *Globe* did not compromise Manitoba's stand on public schools. Often the matter was very minor: late in 1897 Richard Cartwright (a federal minister) asked for an editorial which would sooth Lord Strathcona (Donald Smith, the CPR magnate) who was angry at some reflections on himself in an earlier *Globe*. Willison, of course, had many more dealings with the party leaders. Laurier's letters, as befitted a man who had taken up Macdonald's mantle, were a judicious blend of praise and understanding but always loaded with suggestions and sometimes mild complaint when the *Globe* seemed at odds with the party good. Only rarely were his missives full of iron when Willison proved too presumptuous. The issues discussed could be weighty, pertaining to the tariff, racial discord, party unity, and the like. There was, at times, a real exchange of views between the two men. By contrast, the letters of A.S. Hardy were full of niggling advice and much criticism, clearly reflecting the belief that the *Globe* was not fulfilling its tasks as a party organ. Hardy even took it upon himself to question the *Globe*'s style of reporting![119] In both cases, of course, the party leader was the master and Willison the servant. Willison might disagree, and a compromise might be arranged, but he clearly was not his own man. The duty of the party journalist was, at bottom, to obey.

This duty could become very irksome. Even the long-suffering Patteson once exploded. In May 1875 he received a remonstrance from Cobourg's Conservatives, who felt slighted because a full report of a local banquet had not appeared in the *Mail*. That was too much. Patteson had printed for private distribution a long letter explaining the difficulties of running an effective party organ. He specifically repudiated 'the right of any section of the Liberal-Conservative party to interfere with the management of this newspaper, or to dictate what should receive preference among the many things *all* of which it is impossible to publish.' He satirized the presumption that 'it is a very easy task to run a paper, to please everybody bent on self-glorification and to do justice alike to all Conservatives,' an especially quarrelsome bunch it seemed. Sadly, he concluded that it was his lot in life to 'offend a larger or smaller number of persons every day, and bear the brunt of it in addition to the other labours devolving on him.' All this he did for 'an inadequate salary.'[120]

The more sensitive Willison eventually, if briefly, broke free from party fetters. The *Globe*'s success had made him a person of some influence in party councils. But throughout the 1890s he had tried to turn the *Globe* into a more impartial, and complete, record of politics, though still very Liberal in its views. That course might win him kudos from other journalists, but not from politicians however (and notably Premier Hardy). What seemed a crescendo of party criticism, a persistent desire to reincarnate Brown's *Globe*, exasperated Willison and offended his sense of amour propre. 'Personally I resent the assumption of every Liberal politician that I am his hired man, that he has the right to dictate or shape my course as a journalist,' he wrote angrily to Clifford Sifton in 1901. 'I claim as much freedom as any other Liberal.'[121] Partly, the outburst grew out of Willison's conviction that he deserved gratitude, not criticism: Willison was addicted to adulation. Partly, too, it reflected a disdain for the abilities of the little men who always carped: Willison was something of an intellectual snob. Most of all, though, it was the cry of a man who loved his profession and found he could not realize his ideal journalism in a party context. Little wonder that late in 1902 he resigned from the *Globe* to seize the opportunity offered by Joseph Flavelle to edit an avowedly independent Toronto *News*. Willison swiftly became the scourge of what he called 'the theory of hereditary partisanship, and the remarkable notion that loyalty to a party leader is as sacred an obligation as loyalty to king and country.'[122] The ultimate irony, of course, was that the *News* experiment proved an expensive flop, the paper soon falling into Conservative hands and Willison returning to the ranks of party journalists but now on the other side of the fence.

Willison's experiences were not altogether unique. There were some journalists loyal to a fault. Witness Ernest Pacaud, publisher of *L'Électeur*, which aptly lived up to its boast as the 'Organe des Libéraux du district de Québec,' or David Creighton, manager of the Toronto *Empire*, which came to represent to contemporaries the acme of party journalism. Yet no matter how extensive the connections between party and press, politicians were never able to turn journalists as a group into their docile tools. Journalists did dissent and occasionally 'kick over the traces,' whether moved by principle, profit, or plain crochetyness.

Take first the example of the independent dailies. Their support for any politician or party was always qualified by the notion that the press must be a tribune of the public and so an adversary of the powerful. The intransigent Protestant moralism of the Montreal *Witness* ensured it would remain an ally of dubious merit, often full of bile, for the Liberal party in Catholic Quebec. After 1878 Graham's *Star* combined strong support of the Conservative cause at election time with sometimes harsh criticism of Conservative practices between elections. Robertson's *Telegram* may have moved into the Conservative camp by the late 1880s, but the paper's jingoism and nativism made it a constant nag, no doubt something of a thorn in the side of Macdonald and his successors. Maclean's *World* flirted first with Blake's Liberals, later with Macdonald's Conservatives (where the money was), yet never gave up its freedom to argue eccentric causes. The Toronto *Mail*'s effort to voice the revolt of the 'classes' turned it into a critic of nearly every politician. Likewise, *L'Étendard*'s ultramontane fervour, at least during most of the 1880s, meant that it would never wholly trust any political figure or anything as secular as a party. In 1893 and 1894, *Le Monde*'s devotion to the ideas of democracy and nationality brought it into sympathy with Mercier, a by then discredited politican whose corrupt practices were condemned by both parties (though the paper continued to receive federal advertising contracts throughout). The declared independence of these dailies, then, did have some substance, if not always as much as they might boast.

Equally important was a persistent factionalism in the ranks of the rest of the press, outside of the thoroughly disciplined organs that is. Factionalism was an ever-present reality of party journalism in French Quebec, really a reflection of that penchant for feuding common among French-Canadian politicians. Around 1880 Tarte's ultramontanism, for instance, made *Le Canadien* a critic of the opportunist views of the dominant Chapleau faction in the provincial Conservative party. In 1886 *La Presse*, though supposedly in Conservative hands, flirted for a time with Mercier's *parti national*, perhaps to ensure a refuge for Chapleau should he decide that events warranted leaving the Macdonald cabinet over the Riel execution. During the late 1880s, Quebec's *La Justice* voiced the aims of the so-called Conservative-Nationalists who were sometimes uneasy members of Mercier's Liberal-dominated coalition government. In 1896 *La Presse*, on the verge of independence, became a severe critic of 'la faction ultra-tory' of Ontario's Conservative party, since its nativism imperilled Confederation. Off and on, Beaugrand's *La Patrie* was at loggerheads with Liberal chieftains at home and in Ottawa because of the newspaper's yearning for the old rouge causes of separation of church and state or annexation to the United States.

But there were also many mavericks in the less heated politics of English Canada. A disgruntled Toronto *Leader*, feeling abandoned by its tory friends in the mid-1870s, challenged the alliance of Catholic Quebec and Orange Ontario on which the Conservative party still counted for success. During the early 1880s, the Conservative Quebec *Chronicle* strenuously objected to the pro-Montreal bias of the province's Conservative governments. At the end of the decade, the Ottawa *Citizen* (influenced by the fact that Catholics were a significant local force) rejected the nativist views of the provincial Conservatives, under William Meredith, who were trying to ride into office on the Protestant horse. The Winnipeg press was especially prone to breakaways: the *Times*, a Conservative organ, was much upset with the Macdonald government in 1883 because of its new tariff on agricultural implements; the *Manitoba Free Press* split with the Liberal Greenway government in the late 1880s over its railway policies; the *Tribune*, very Liberal in provincial politics, never quite trusted a federal party led by the French-Canadian Laurier and controlled by Ontario men. And in British Columbia, where party politics was not properly introduced into the local scene until the late 1890s, newspapers could shift, apparently at leisure, from one group of politicians to another.

Far more threatening to the party's rule, though, were the new conventions of journalism fostered by the maturing of the daily press. The purblind partisanship of days gone by no longer fitted the dignity of so vigorous a fourth estate, a point reiterated by the *Printer and Publisher*. 'Many a bright man has had his patriotism crushed to powder by the stern onslaughts of a press dominated by party feelings and prejudices,' it told journalists. That was a disgrace to 'modern newspaperdom.'[123] Besides, 'the tendency of politicians (both sides) was to make use of the press without adequate return,' the journal warned.[124] Better to deal with politicians in the same fashion as any other supplicants for press publicity. Usually, Willison is credited with leading the daily press toward a more impartial style of political reporting, though in fact other publishers and editors were also moving in the 1890s to free their news columns of blatant bias. Indeed, even on the editorial pages, the public men of the 1890s were more likely than their predecessors has been to receive fair treatment. The failure of outright organs such as the Toronto *Empire* and *La Minerve* was taken as proof that the party-dominated daily had gone for good (which, by the way, was not correct). The public and the advertiser expected the newspaper to espouse the ideal of community service, not just party service. A few dailies actually experimented with political neutrality: during the federal election campaign of 1900, for example, the Ottawa *Journal* opened a column to Conservatives and Liberals, reserving the editorial page for criticism of instances of excessive partisanship and eventually (on 6 November 1900) admitted its inability to make a clear choice between the combatants. The business imperative balanced the dictates of party fealty, a change which Walter Nichol of the Vancouver *Province* praised as a laudable feature of the modern age.[125] That was the key. The politician, whatever his influence over individual journalists, could not fully control what was now an industry.

Not surprisingly, the very institution of party did come under attack in the press. During the late 1870s and early 1880s, the anti-party cause was a prominent aspect of the Radicalism sponsored by the people's journals of English Canada. Less often, the occasional *nationaliste* paper in French Canada, say *L'Union Nationale* in the late 1860s or *Le Monde* in the mid-1890s, would provide a reasoned critique of the party system. Any newspaper declaration of independence, of course, produced an obligatory denunciation of the evils of partyism. Critics charged that parties lacked any firm grounding in principle and were held together only by a lust for the spoils of office: the result was the dominance of 'machine' politicians, corruption in high places, needless appeals to racial and sectarian animosities, and on and on. The litany of sins placed at the door of party conveyed the impression that it was, in fact, the enemy of all things good. Remedies varied: an organization of independent voters (Montreal *Star*), electing every official in sight (Toronto *News*), a political realignment (Winnipeg *Sun*), a new party (Farrer's *Mail*). The common hope was to destroy partyism, 'the madness of the many for the gain of the few' (Toronto *Telegram*, 29 January 1887). None of the remedies proved especially practical, though. Indeed, the experience of third parties such as the Equal Rights Association or the Patrons of Industry suggested that things were better left as they were. That accounted for the declining vigour of the anti-party cause during the 1890s, even among the self-declared independents. The rhetoric of anti-partyism remained useful as a means of expressing indignation, not fostering change.

Besides, the stream of abuse had elicited an even more convincing defence of the party system from Liberal and Conservative apologists. Whatever the ills of partyism, parties were vital instruments of political organization, necessary else government would become the plaything of transient factions. (A party 'includes a leader who must be a superior man; a following of trained intelligences which in turn lead the people; defined principles; a well understood plan of progress; and all combined for the good of the country according to the principles accepted as the best.')[126] Besides, the two-party system had history and nature behind its existence. The Liberal-Conservative dichotomy was entrenched in the British constitution and its Canadian offshoot. That opposition was 'an expression of human character,' a conflict rooted in 'human nature' between those who yearned for change and those who wished to preserve.[127] The editorial pages of party dailies, sometimes independent papers as well, often reflected on the special attributes of the two parties. So the Conservative apologist made much of the claim that his was a party tradition and progress and patriotism locked in combat with an enemy which was dangerously radical, too parochial, pro-American but anti-national, even irreligious. His Liberal foe replied that his was the party of liberty, always on the side of reform, menaced by a tory enemy imbued with the spirit of reaction and bent on creating privileges. The variations in this imagery were legion. But, always, the apologist linked his celebration of his party with a dark picture of the enemy. That publicity gave the two-party system a solid foundation in myth essential to its survival in the new democracy. Here again the daily press had played a central role in legitimizing the patterns of authority.

7

Conclusion

In 1901 S.D. Scott delivered a curious paper entitled 'The Newspaper of 1950' to his colleagues and friends at the annual meeting of the Canadian Press Association.[1] Scott was no novice: educated at university, earning an MA from Mount Allison, he quickly found his true vocation in journalism and became in 1885 editor-in-chief of the Conservative Saint John *Sun* where, purportedly, he distinguished himself as a masterful writer of political 'leaders.'[2] Scott's essay was as much a commentary on what had happened as speculation on what the future would bring. After all, his and the preceding generation of journalists had lived through a time of astonishing changes. Would this progress end with the century just past? Scott turned first to the phenomenon of technological dependence: the modern newspaper was emphatically an offshoot of the industrial machine – rapid printing, cheap paper, the linotype, railways and telegraphs, now photoengraving. He expected, too, that 'the enormous increase of readers' would continue unabated, especially as the daily newspaper intruded further into the countryside. And he foresaw the enhanced importance of advertising ('the time may be coming when ... the literary contributor will ask to have his treatise placed next to good advertising matter'!) which had already made newspapers cheap by ensuring 'the subscriber now gets his paper for a fraction of the cost of production.' Not that the business imperative would turn the newspaper into merely another commodity like 'a gallon of oil' or 'steel rails.' Scott explicitly denied what he called Alfred Harmsworth's prophecy of the 'simultaneous newspaper,' a series of clones manufactured by 'a combination of capital and enterprise, such as that of the Standard Oil Co.' The typical newspaper would remain a product of 'intellectual and moral forces,' never for sale to the highest bidder, boasting 'a character and disposition appealing to a certain constituency of readers.' Indeed, he predicted that the number of newspapers and their 'individuality' would increase during the next century.

Naturally, he concluded his brief exposition with the ritual hope the newspaper of 1950 would be 'a power for righteousness.'

Scott's sanguine views, his celebration of past changes and prediction that things could only get better, showed the impact of a particular theory about the nature of a free press. The prevailing ideals of journalism were enshrined in what has since come to be known as 'libertarianism.' This theory owed much to an assortment of liberal thinkers in Britain, running from John Milton to John Stuart Mill, who had been fascinated by the need for intellectual liberty and free discussion. The theory stressed the virtues of many voices, many views, a rich variety of independent papers searching for Truth in an open marketplace of ideas.[3] Journalists in Canada, as elsewhere, paid at least lip service to such presumptions. That grand moralist and sometime journalist, Goldwin Smith, made much of these at a press banquet held in his honour in 1881. (The fact that Smith was engaged in a feud with a few brother journalists, nothing new to him, only gave his words an added bite.) He emphasized his fear not 'that the press should be wanting in power, but that its independence may be impaired,' presumably by the predominance of a couple of great organs such as the *Mail* and the *Globe* of Toronto. He knew 'of no better guarantee of a country's political future than the existence of multiplied centres of opinion.' And he went on to proclaim that 'liberty of thought' must be 'the palladium of our profession,' by which he hoped to assert the necessity of publishing 'heterodox views.'[4] The point was that only a thoroughly free press could protect popular liberties and advance the country's progress.

Did newspaperdom live up to these golden ideals? The libertarian dream of a free press did, in some ways, fit the realities of popular journalism during its years of adolescence. The rapidly expanding audience for the daily newspaper established the cultural preconditions for a lush variety of competitors. Over the course of the previous 50 years, there had been a marvellous array of newspaper titles, time and again some hopeful launching a newcomer in an already cluttered market. If most did not last, at least for very long, there remained into the 1890s a sufficient number of rivals to fuel an orgy of competition, even in the Toronto and Montreal markets. Survival and success depended, at bottom, on the publishers' willingness to cater to the tastes and prejudices of assorted constituencies, mostly inside but sometimes outside the cities. Competition spawned an era of experimentation, a press made up of journals of opinion, party organs and mavericks, sectarian warriors and independents, people's versus quality dailies, as publishers tried different formulas to win fame and fortune. Competition invigorated that lust for controversy out of which was born three different perspectives on life and affairs, more than enough to fashion a vigorous press debate. And competition ensured the persistence of eccentricity in press ranks, since a publisher or editor had to highlight his daily's character to secure the loyalty of readers. The result was newspapers that acted as censurers as well as boosters in the social and political arenas. The very workings of the marketplace, in short, bolstered what could pass for a 'free press.'

Nothing is perfect though. John Stuart Mill's famous celebration of 'diversity of opinion,' the grand key to Truth, could not rely upon a press that was, at best, only a mechanism of bourgeois liberty.[5] Whatever the vigour of competition, a successful entry into the ranks of daily journalism became more and more difficult as time wore on because of the growing expense of running a newspaper. By the end of the century, the market in places such as Halifax, Quebec City, English Montreal, Ottawa, Toronto, Hamilton, London, and Winnipeg was effectively closed to newcomers (which accounts for the premium on the value of established dailies). Most of the papers that would still flourish in 1950, to use Scott's year, already existed, even in the smaller cities. The increasing dependence on advertising revenues meant that survivors must offer much the same kinds of material to win an audience attractive to advertisers. The leading newspapers of Toronto and Montreal did exercise an important influence over the views of dailies in the hinterland. Everywhere, the daily press was conditioned by the twin biases of class and locale, speaking first the ambitions of the urban middle class, which meant it could hardly reflect the society as a whole. Undeniably, journalists did serve the needs, usually forward the aims, of church, business, and party. Even the Radicalism of the people's journals was a trifle suspect – a commercial version of the resentment of the 'masses', highly saleable but substantially in agreement with the values of the establishment. And the very myth-making of newspapers showed that no matter how diverse the particulars of their views, still the press was a social authority working on behalf of consensus.

Especially striking was the vigour with which the daily press played out its role, in Scott's words, as 'a power for righteousness.' Journalists were forever passing judgments on people or events. That habit was most apparent, of course, whenever an editor turned his eye on the political arena to find some new sign of the enemy's villainy. During the fall of 1899, for instance, the Montreal *Star* launched its most 'manly' crusade against the 'cowardice' of the Laurier government, which refused for a time to sponsor any official Canadian involvement in the Boer War. But evidence of this kind of zeal could also be found in the routine news on the front pages of newspapers. So the reporters of *La Presse* (31 July 1895) readily identified one Azarie Gauthier as 'le meutrier' and 'l'assassin' in a sensational local murder case, long before any trial. Someone on the staff of the *Manitoba Free Press* (10 May 1899) determined guilt by placing the headline

'Strikers Use Dynamite' over a report on an attempt to blow up a streetcar in Duluth, where the employees of the street railway company were on strike. These judgments suggest that the journalists saw themselves as important agents in a very moral universe. Editors and reporters employed the language of morality to explain events and to speed understanding: they assumed that happenings could be classified right or wrong, that there were virtue and vice, fair as well as foul play, truth and falsehood.[6] The news of the world, whether at home or abroad, was replete with lessons about life which the press was duty-bound to elaborate. It was the emphatic moralism of the daily press which best justified its title of a Victorian authority.

How much independent power could the journalist exercise over the course of events? Certainly, there were instances where a daily seemed able to work a significant change in the way things were. An intransigent Toronto *Mail* managed to excite so much interest among Ontarians first in Commercial Union in 1887 and two years later in the disallowance of Quebec's Jesuits' Estates Act that both became, briefly, the leading political issues. The Montreal *Star*'s campaign of 1899 was credited, then and later, with driving the Laurier government into the Boer War. A collective agitation such as the people's dailies mounted on behalf of urban reform undeniably gave this cause an increasing priority in civic affairs. The emphasis upon class harmony common in the rhetoric of all dailies popularized a myth that labour militants found difficult to dispel.

But there were also instances where events denied the power of the press. Riding the Protestant horse in the mid-1870s did not save the waning Toronto *Leader* or spark a major assault on Quebec's church. *L'Étendard*'s angry treatment of Sénécal hardly spelled the downfall of his power or reputation. The revolt against party, touted by most people's journals at some time or other, did not shake the foundations of the two-party system. The journalist's disdain (in English Canada) for denominationalism did not produce a great wave of Protestant ecumenicism.

In fact, the success or failure of any novel campaign rested upon the response of other papers and institutions. The *Mail* could work up a furore over Commercial Union in 1887 because farm organizations were sympathetic and the Liberal party felt a desperate need for an appealing policy[7]; and the paper succeeded again in 1889 because a collection of clerical and political leaders soon created the Equal Rights Association to give body to the anti-Jesuit cause.[8] During its Boer War crusade the Montreal *Star* won growing support among Conservative and independent papers elsewhere, that important echo effect, sufficient to mobilize public sentiment and frighten Liberal editors and politicians alike.[9] Urban reform and class harmony, most especially class harmony, were goals which found favour with many institutions and much of the establishment.

Abusing Sénécal, however, would not work unless the whole of the press joined in the game – and the Conservative papers were not interested. The revolt against party or the criticism of denominationalism both clashed with the vested interests of powerful institutions whose legitimacy was rooted in popular sentiment. A newspaper acting in concert with its fellow could be a powerful force; a newspaper in isolation, particularly in pursuit of some impossible target, was bound to be unable to effect change. The very rivalry among newspapers prevented the emergence of some sort of tyranny of the press. Even united the press could usually work its will only when allied to some outside agency – which always fostered suspicions about who was leading whom. The power of the press grew more out of its cultural significance than its supposed independence.

The popular press had prospered because it met new social needs born out of the sweep of modernity. The emerging bourgeois democracy required an increasing level of mass involvement in the daily round of life. People at the top, notably in politics and business, had to be able to communicate with the publics below. Likewise, these publics needed some agency to voice their concerns and so influence the establishment. But, most important, the emerging society demanded a citizenry with sufficient knowledge to make reasonable decisions about how to vote, what to buy, where to invest, how to find jobs, even what to believe. Older institutions such as the church or the school could not adequately serve all these ends. The popular press could.[10] It commanded the power to transmit facts, ideas, and fantasy to so much of the citizenry.

According to James Curran, a student of British journalism, historians have identified a plethora of roles for newspapers: 'agencies of social reform, forums for the exchange of ideas, purveyors of public information, checks on government abuse, sources of diversion and entertainment, the personal platforms of politician-proprietors, sources of cultural debasement, and so on.' Curran preferred the description of the press as 'an agency of social control.'[11] And why not add 'a means of social liberation' or 'a source of cultural uplift' as well? All apply. The messages of the daily press touched upon so many aspects of life. 'Into what domain of thought or activity has the daily press not intruded itself?' wondered H.H.U. Colquhoun.[12] 'In this modern age,' Laurier claimed in 1901, 'the press seems to be essential to the success of everything which requires exertion.'[13] The expansion of a national party system would have proved much more difficult without the welcome assistance of daily papers. The swift rise of the department stores, as their owners realized, depended heavily upon the medium of newspaper advertising. The brand-name manufacturers of the 1880s and 1890s would not have been able to organize new markets so readily without the reach of the press. In short, the effective integration of a transcontinental community necessitated a popular press which could supply information to, and fashion myths for, a mass audience. Perhaps it was not essential to the success of everything; it was, however, vital to the forces which were changing Canadian life.

This press was very much a child of the times. Media of any sort are extremely sensitive to shifts in their milieu, no doubt because they occupy a central social position servicing other institutions as well as the public at large. The future brought changes that would have upset Scott. The arrival of new media, notably broadcasting, ended the primacy enjoyed by the daily press in the field of mass communication. The growing preference of the mass public for news, not opinions, crippled the role that papers had played as key actors in the national debate. The number of newspapers reached a peak around the Great War and fell off dramatically in the next three decades, competition declined rapidly in the 1920s when the newspaper industry consolidated itself into an oligopoly, and the chain newspaper as well as the monopoly newspaper became all too common. The ideal of community service sapped even the Radical fervour of the old people's journals, the new mythologies of affluence overwhelmed the Victorian ethos, and the dictates of party fealty lost out completely to the business imperative. These mutations made a mockery of libertarian dreams. The newspaper of 1950 was closer to Harmsworth's forbidding prophecy than Scott's more hopeful vision. By this time, the press was much more an agency of social control, of conformity not novelty, than it had been in the heady days of expansion and competition.[14]

The crisis, the demise of the classic 'free press,' was hardly unique to Canada. The libertarian dilemma applied in Britain, France, and America, though of course the story differed in each land.[15] Part of the trouble was that the 'free press' could not survive the triumph of industrial capitalism, even if libertarian notions did persist to justify its corporate successor. (That irony the Special Senate Committee on Mass Media discovered in its investigation of the views of Canadian publishers in 1969 and 1970.)[16] Further, the press's role as a catalyst of change was in some measure a function of the novelty of mass communications. The maturing of the daily newspaper mightily enhanced the power of the printed word, making possible a variety of things from mass consumption to mass politics. The galvanizing effects of the daily were bound to decline as social conventions and institutions adjusted to its presence. Finally, the routines of the affluent society do not require a 'free press,' whatever compelling needs that society has for the newspaper industry and the rest of the multimedia. New idealists have given birth to a different vision of journalism, the social responsibility theory, which asserts that media must conform to the ideals of objectivity and balance, indeed become a sort of utility dispensing the truth about society.[17] It is all a far cry from the world in which Scott and his listeners lived.

APPENDIX

Leading daily newspapers 1870–1900

This checklist details some basic information about the most important daily newspapers in Canada's cities during the era when popular journalism emerged as the major force in newspaperdom. The checklist is not comprehensive or always complete, since certain data were not available for each daily. It is arranged by city and by title. Each listing may contain as many as four separate entries:
the date of appearance and/or disappearance if either occurred during the three decades;
the key figure in the determination of a newspaper's policy, an editor, manager, publisher, or a combination of these ('publisher' does not necessarily indicate full ownership);
a description of the philosophical perspectives and political loyalties of the paper over time, with the declared political loyalty of every surviving newspaper in 1901 given as C (Conservative), L (Liberal), or I (Independent);
the combined circulations of all editions, weekly as well as daily, for specific dates (significant discrepancies between McKim's and Ayer's directories of 1901 have been noted).

HALIFAX

Acadian Recorder Blackadar Brothers (publishers), J.W. Longley 1873–87 (editor). Liberal (definite Radical tendencies under the guidance of Longley, but generally loyal to the Liberal party); L (1901). 1,595 (1872), 2,775 (1880), 4,750 (1891), 4,000 (1900).

Chronicle Annand family (publishers), W.S. Fielding 1875–84 (editor). Liberal (a party organ); L (1901). 6,230 (1872), 11,200 (1880), 9,000 (1891), 20,500 (1900) (Ayer's lists only 7,175, but this is unchanged from the 1898 figure and does not include the *Echo*); figures include circulations of first the *Citizen* and later the *Echo*.

Herald (1875–) J.J. Stewart (publisher), William Dennis 1883– (news editor, eventually managing editor). Conservative (a party organ); C (1901). 12,500 (1880), 14,000 (1891), 17,094 (1900); figures include the circulation of the *Mail*.

HAMILTON

Herald (1889–) Harris brothers (publishers). Radical (party loyalties unclear); I (1901). 9,500 (1891), 6,000 (1900).

Spectator William Southam 1877– (joint publisher). Conservative (a party organ); C (1901). 7,350 (1872), 12,200 (1880), 17,500 (1891), 14,453 (1900).

Times H.F. Gardiner 1880–1903 (editor). Radical Liberal 1878–96 (a party organ); L (1901). 4,130 (1872), 9,100 (1880), 16,000 (1891), 8,750 (1900) (Ayer's lists a combined circulation of 14,500).

LONDON

Advertiser John Cameron (publisher). Liberal (a party organ); L (1901). 10,600 (1872), 26,300 (1880), 28,500 (1891), 15,688 (1901) (Ayer's gives a weekly circulation of 21,000 – unchanged from 1898 – and McKim's a mere 7,000).

Free Press Blackburn family (publishers). Conservative (a party organ); C (1901). 2,540 (1872), 14,500 (1880), 23,750 (1891), 17,000 (1900) (Ayer's lists 12,000 as the weekly circulation. I have selected McKim's figure of 4,500).

News (1896–) C.B. Keenleyside (editor/publisher). I (1901). 8,249 (1900).

MONTREAL

L'Étendard (1883–93) F.-X.-A. Trudel 1883–90 (director). Conservative (ultramontane maverick, which welcomed H. Mercier's *parti national*). 9,096 (1883), 14,500 (1891).

Gazette White Brothers (publishers). Conservative (a party organ); C (1901). 7,450 (1872), 10,000 (1880), 12,171 (1891), 15,555 (1900).

Herald Edward G. Penny 1861–81 (editor/publisher), Peter Mitchell 1885–92 (director), James Brierley 1897– (publisher). Liberal until 1885; Radical 1885–92 (ready to support policies rather than parties, though more or less Liberal); Liberal 1892– (a party organ); L (1901). 10,900 (1872), 10,000 (1880), 7,500 (1891), 22,500 (1901) McKim's directory lists daily circulation at 18,000, Ayer's at 6,500 (unchanged from 1898).

La Minerve (–1899) C.-A. Dansereau 1871–80 (editor / publisher), Joseph Tassé 1880–95 (editor). Conservative (a party organ). 9,950 (1872), 9,000 (1880), 11,000 (1891).

Le Nouveau Monde/Le Monde (1867–97) A wide variety of editors and publishers. Conservative 1867–92 (ultramontane variety 1867–82; thereafter a party organ); Radical 1892–95 (espoused political independence and sympathized with the nationalism of H. Mercier); Conservative 1896–97 (a party organ). 3,950 (1972), 14,550 (1880), 19,250 (1891), 16,000 (1896).

La Patrie (1879–) Honoré Beaugrand 1879–97 (publisher), J.-I. Tarte 1897– (his sons were the paper's owners). Radical Liberal 1879–97 (always something of a maverick); Liberal 1897– (a party organ); L (1901). 7,000 (1880), 13,000 (1891), 52,488 (1900).

Post (1878–88) ?. Conservative (an Irish-Canadian daily, but apparently very much a party organ as well). 12,000 (1880).

La Presse (1884–) T. Berthiaume 1889– (publisher). Radical (a maverick, briefly favouring Mercier in 1886, swinging over to the Conservative camp from 1887 to 1896, then moving on to the Liberal camp); I (1901). 13,090 (1885), 26,543 (1891), 104,192 (1900).

Star (1869–) Hugh Graham (publisher). Radical (a maverick, Conservative-leaning after 1878); I (1901). 15,600 (1872), 64,850 (1880), 101,460 (1891), 175,378 (1900).

Witness Dougall family (publishers). Radical Liberal (a maverick, with eccentric ultra-Protestant views); I (1901). 23,100 (1872), 42,542 (1880), 46,140 (1891), 39,250 (1900).

OTTAWA

Citizen C.H. Mackintosh 1874–92 (editor/publisher), Shannon brothers 1892–97 (publishers), Southam family 1897– (publishers). Conservative (a party organ), C (1901). 3,010 (1872), 3,900 (1880), 6,000 (1891), 12,560 (1900).

Free Press (1869–) C.W. Mitchell (editor/publisher). Radical Liberal 1878–96 (a party organ); L (1901). 3,105 (1872), 11,500 (1880), 9,250 (1891), 11,800 (1900).

Journal (1885–) P.D. Ross 1887– (publisher). Radical (a maverick: favoured the Equal Rights Association 1889–90, leaned both to the Conservatives and the Liberals in the 1890s, studiously neutral in the election of 1900), I (1901). 8,750 (1891), 14,218 (1900).

QUEBEC

Le Canadien (–1893; moved to Montreal in 1891) J.-I. Tarte 1874–93 (though L.-J. Demers was editor/publisher throughout most of the 1880s). Conservative (ultramontane maverick 1875–81; Chapleauiste organ 1881–91); Liberal 1891–93. 9,000 (1880), 14,500 (1891).

Chronicle J.J. Foote 1863–97 (editor/publisher). Conservative (a party organ, though given to some bursts of independence in provincial politics); C (1901). 3,400 (1872), 3,000 (1880), 3,500 (1891), 5,600 (1900).

Le Courrier du Canada (–1901) T. Chapais 1884–1901 (editor). Conservative (ultramontane variety). 3,000 (1880), 2,750 (1891), 3,081 (1898).

L'Électeur/Le Soleil (1880–) E. Pacaud 1880–1903 (editor/publisher). Liberal (a party organ); L (1901). 3,980 (1880), 10,000 (1891), 17,700 (1901).

L'Événement (1867–) Hector Fabre 1867–75 (editor/publisher), L.-J. Demers 1883–1902 (publisher). Liberal at least into the mid-1880s (something of a maverick); Conservative by the late 1890s (still a maverick though); C (1901). 3,300 (1872), 7,800 (1880), 7,000 (1891), 7,500 (1901) (Ayer's estimate of joint circulation 21,680).

Le Journal de Québec (–1889) Joseph Cauchon –1875 (editor). Conservative until 1872; Liberal 1872–79; Conservative 1880–89. 2,160 (1872), 1,050 (1880).

Mercury G.T. Cary 1855–90 (editor/publisher), W.J. Maguire 1890–98 (editor/publisher), George Stewart 1898–1902 (editor/publisher). Eccentric (under Cary the paper perpetuated the idiosyncratic style of an earlier generation of journalism); Conservative 1890–98; Liberal 1898– ; L (1901). 800 (1872), 1,015 (1883), 1,250 (1891), 750 (1900) (Ayer's estimate of circulation: 3,000).

Telegraph (1875–) Carrel family (publishers). Radical Conservative at first, swinging toward the Liberal party in the 1890s; I (1901). 4,000 (1880), 6,000 (1891), 6,700 (1900).

SAINT JOHN

Gazette (1888–) ?. I (1901). 3,500 (1891), 4,500 (1900).

Globe J.V. Ellis (editor/publisher). Liberal (a party organ); L (1901). 3,110 (1872), 5,400 (1880), 5,441 (1891), 5,500 (1,900).

News (–1884) Edward Willis 1863–83? (editor/publisher). Ministerial (Conservative when Macdonald in power, Liberal during the Mackenzie Government). 9,100 (1872), 6,800 (1880).

Sun (1878–) S.D. Scott 1885– (editor). Conservative (a party organ); C (1901). 4,300 (1880), 9,250 (1891), 11,451 (1900).

Telegraph William Elder 1870–? (publisher). Liberal; L (1901). 12,000 (1872), 9,500 (1880), 13,250 (1891), 11,750 (1900).

TORONTO

Empire (1887–95) David Creighton (manager). Conservative (a party organ). 29,000 (1891).

Globe George Brown 1844–80 (publisher), Gordon Brown, 1880–82 (editor), John Cameron 1882–90 (editor), Edward Farrer 1890–92 (joint editor), J.S. Willison 1890–1902 (first joint, then sole editor). Liberal (a party organ); L (1901). 45,000 (1872), 57,000 (1880), 46,450 (1891), 69,545 (1900).

Leader (–1878) James Beaty (publisher). Conservative until 1872 (a party organ), thereafter increasingly eccentric. 9,710 (1872).

Mail/Mail and Empire (1872–) T.C. Patteson 1872–77 (manager), C.W. Bunting 1877–96 (manager), Edward Farrer 1885–90 (editor), Riordon family 1877– (publishers). Conservative 1872–85 (a party organ); Radical 1885–95 (at first an intransigent independent, but by the mid-1890s moving back into the Conservative fold); Conservative 1895– (a party organ); C (1901). 17,500 (1872), 69,558 (1880), 62,010 (1891), 61,722 (1900).

News (1881–) E.E. Sheppard 1883–87 (publisher), Riordon family 1881–83 and 1887– (publishers), William Douglas 1890?–1902 (manager). Conservative 1881–83; Radical 1883–87 (a maverick, flinging curses at both parties and sponsoring democratic republicanism); Radical Conservative 1887–96; I (1901). 17,489 (1883), 31,500 (1891), 30,000 (1900).

Star (1892–) E.E. Sheppard 1895–97 (editor, nominal publisher). Radical 1892–99 (a maverick: briefly a labour advocate, supporter of the Patrons of Industry, moving under Sheppard to support dissident Conservatives and the Liberals after Laurier's victory); Radical Liberal 1899– (a party organ); L (1901). 16,613 (1901).

Telegram (1876–) John Ross Robertson (publisher). Radical (a maverick, Conservative leaning after 1886); I (1901). 14,000 (1880), 21,695 (1891), 25,144 (1901).

World (1880–) William Maclean (publisher). Radical (a maverick: Liberal leaning up to 1886, thereafter Conservative in loyalties and sometimes very servile); I (1901). 8,000 (1880), 11,500 (1891), 34,243 (1900).

VANCOUVER

News-Advertiser (1886–) F. Carter Cotton (editor/publisher). Radical Conservative (more and more a party organ); C (1901). 3,500 (1891), 3,700 (1900).

Province (1898–) W.C. Nichol (editor, soon publisher). L (1901). 9,835 (1900).

World (1888–) John McLagan (editor/publisher). Conservative 1889–92 (a maverick); Liberal 1893– (a maverick); L (1901). 5,000 (1891), 14,039 (1900).

VICTORIA

Colonist D.W. Higgins 1869–86 (publisher). Conservative (a maverick, devoted to provincial interests, to 1886; thereafter a party organ); C (1901). 1,480 (1872), 1,450 (1880), 3,750 (1891), 5,500 (1900).

Times (1884–) W. Templeman (editor/publisher). Radical Liberal (a party organ); L (1901). 4,000 (1891), 5,250 (1900).

WINNIPEG

Manitoba Free Press (1873–) W.F. Luxton 1873–93 (editor/publisher), William Van Horne 1890–? (because of the Canadian Pacific Railway's investment in the newspaper), Clifford Sifton 1898– (publisher). Liberal 1873–88 (became a party organ); eccentric 1888–98 (pursued a variable course, though a ministerialist bias, likely because of CPR investment); Liberal 1898– (a party organ); L (1901). 4,050 (1880), 14,713 (1891), 24,839 (1900).

Nor'Wester/Telegram (1894–) William Luxton 1894 (founder). Conservative (a maverick becoming an organ); C (1901). 10,303 (1900).

Tribune (1890–) R.L. Richardson (publisher). Radical Liberal 1890–96 (a provincial party organ); Radical 1897– (a maverick moving toward independence because of the Richardson/Sifton feud); I (1901). 6,750 (1891), 20,466 (1900).

Notes

A NOTE ON SOURCES

It would require many pages to list all the sources I have consulted in the course of preparing this account. The single most important sources, the daily newspapers themselves, are obvious. The other important material I have identified either in the notes or in the text. Two abbreviations for publications are used in these notes: *CHR* for *Canadian Historical Review* and *P&P* for *Canadian Printer and Publisher.*

INTRODUCTION

1 Newspaper sold on the trains as well. One traveller in the 1860s noted what he took to be a peculiar kind of Canadian entrepreneur, the 'car-boy,' who sold at a high price copies of newspapers to bored passengers (David Macrea, *How Things Are in America: From Notes of Travel in Canada and the United States, in the Year 1867–68*, a collection of letters published by the Glasgow *Weekly Herald*).
2 S. Moodie, *Mark Hurdlestone, The Gold Worshipper* (London 1853), I, xx–xxii as cited in J.J. Talman, 'Three Scottish-Canadian Newspaper Editor Poets,' *CHR*, 28 (1947) 166.
3 The circulation figure is merely a composite of the estimates listed in Geo. P. Rowell and Co.'s *American Newspaper Directory* (1873), 225–35. It seems likely that journals were missed and circulations inflated, so the figure itself is only a guess. The 1871 Census of Canada lists some 622,719 families in the dominion. Excluded from these figures are Prince Edward Island, Manitoba and the Northwest Territories, and British Columbia.
4 Canada, Department of Agriculture, *The Statistical Year-Book of Canada* (1901), 439.
5 A. McKim's *The Canadian Newspaper Directory* (1899), 221–5.

6 *La Presse*, 17 November 1884, 2.

7 John King, 'The Newspaper Press and the Law of Libel,' *Canadian Monthly and National Review*, 8 (November 1875) 394. King was a lawyer who specialized in newspaper libel cases. He is perhaps better known as the father of William Lyon Mackenzie King.

8 J.T. Clark, 'The Daily Newspaper,' *Canadian Magazine*, 7 (June 1896) 101. Clark worked in Toronto, with *Saturday Night* and the *Star*.

9 Cited in *P&P* (March 1894) 11.

10 *Modernization* is a term full of ambiguities. It is used here to suggest a society undergoing extensive social change because of the application of industrial technology to extend man's command over his environment. Readers interested in a more elaborate definition should consult C.E. Black's *The Dynamics of Modernization. A Study in Comparative History* (New York 1967). Some of the difficulties with the term are outlined in Richard Bendix, 'Tradition and Modernity Reconsidered,' *Comparative Studies in Society and History*, 9 (1966–67) 292–346; and Dean C. Tipps, 'Modernization Theory and the Comparative Study of Societies: A Critical Perspective,' ibid, 15 (1973) 199–226. For a thorough-going analysis of modernization 'at work' which by the way does consider the press, see Eugen Weber, *Peasants into Frenchmen. The Modernization of Rural France 1870–1914* (Stanford 1976).

11 This definition is derived from Denis McQuail's account in *Towards a Sociology of Mass Communications* (New York 1969), 7-11. McQuail's book is an excellent introduction to the study of mass communication.

12 I selected the press of 11 cities for close attention: Halifax, Saint John, Quebec, Montreal, Ottawa, Toronto, Hamilton, London, Winnipeg, Vancouver, and Victoria. I supplemented this with surveys of some newspapers in less prominent Maritime and western centres, such as North Sydney, Moncton, Fredericton, Charlottetown, Brandon, Regina, Calgary, Edmonton, New Westminster, and Nanaimo.

13 The count of Canadian families is taken from census figures of 1871, 1881, 1891, and 1901. The circulation totals are from assorted newspaper directories: Rowell's 1873 and 1877; Ayer's 1881, 1886, 1897, and 1901; and McKim's 1892 and 1901. In every case the directories counted totals from a period in the preceding year.

14 One source must be singled out for special mention: André Beaulieu and Jean Hamelin's annotated bibliography, *La Presse québécoise des origines à nos jours* (Quebec 1973–77). The first three volumes cover almost all the nineteenth century and deliver a wealth of facts about journalism, francophone and anglophone, in the province.

15 If the reader prefers to form his own judgment about the merits of what is occasionally called 'Canadian communications theory,' he can select from a

number of sources. There are, of course, Innis's two major works: *The Bias of Communication* (Toronto 1951) or *Empire and Communications* (Toronto 1972). For an explanation of Innis's views, necessary because his reasoning was so opaque at times, read Robin Neill's *A New Theory of Value. The Canadian Economics of H.A. Innis* (Toronto 1972), especially 82–105. Marshall McLuhan might best be approached by reading *Understanding Media: The Extensions of Man* (New York 1964) and *The Gutenberg Galaxy: The Making of Typographic Man* (Toronto 1972).

16 'The Structure and Function of Communications in Society,' in Lymon Bryson, editor, *The Communication of ideas* (New York 1948) 37–51.

17 See particularly his 'Technology and Public Opinion in the United States? *Canadian Journal of Economics and Political Science*, 17 (February 1951) 1–24, for an example of his approach at its best.

18 *The English Common Reader. A Social History of the Mass Reading Public, 1800–1900* (Chicago 1957).

19 For such studies which cover the nineteenth-century press, see Alan Lee, *The Origins of the Popular Press 1855–1914* (London 1976), a superb account of English journalism; Theodore Zeldin's 'Newspapers and Corruption' in his *France 1848–1945. Volume 2: Intellect, Taste and Anxiety* (Oxford 1977), 492–573; and Robert Keyserlingk, *Media Manipulation. A Study of the Press and Bismarck in Imperial Germany* (Montreal 1977).

20 This comment arises from Alan Lee's cogent critique of approaches that worry too much about 'impact.' Lee, *Origin*, 17–19.

21 That assumption afflicts the 'gee whiz' variety of popular biography – see W.A. Swanberg's *Citizen Hearst. A Biography of William Randolph Hearst* (New York 1961).

22 This is particularly obvious in the appraisals of the modern media by radical scholars – witness C. Wright Mills's 'Mass Society' in his *The Power Elite* (New York 1959), 298–324; J. Porter, 'The Ideological System: The Mass Media,' in his *The Vertical Mosaic. An Analysis of Social Class and Power in Canada* (Toronto 1965), 459–90; and Wallace Clement's chapters on the media in *The Canadian Corporate Elite. An Analysis of Economic Power* (Toronto 1975), 270–343.

23 Perhaps that is because the authors feel obliged to furnish so much detail on newspapers and journalists. See, for instance, Frank Luther Mott's *American Journalism* (New York 1962), a very useful work which nonetheless clearly shows the weaknesses of an older tradition of newspaper history.

24 This has given rise to another approach, the so-called 'uses and gratifications' theory; See W. Phillips Davison, James Boylan, and Frederick T.C. Yu, *Mass Media. Systems and Effects* (New York 1976), 131–57.

25 The phenomenon of 'taste publics' has received attention from students of leisure; Kenneth Roberts, *Leisure* (London 1970).

26 John Fisher and John Hartley, *Reading Television* (London 1978), conclude television is the 'bard' of modern times. Of course, such endeavours proved popular with literary critics and historians even before the fad of structuralism hit the academic world – witness Richard Hoggart, *The Uses of Literacy* (Harmondsworth 1957), on print media and working-class culture in Britain, or Raymond Williams, *Communications* (Harmondsworth 1968) on the British scene.
27 Sorting through a welter of rhetoric in search of patterns of ideas and the like is hardly without precedent. See Robert Kelley, *The Transatlantic Persuasion. The Liberal-Democratic Mind in the Age of Gladstone* (New York 1969) and John Cawelti, *Adventure, Mystery, and Romance. Formula Stories as Art and Popular Culture* (Chicago 1976).
28 The literature on 'effects' is mammoth. Joseph T. Klapper in *The Effects of Mass Communication* (Glencoe 1960) supplies an especially thorough analysis of the short-term impact of media upon their audiences. Paul Lazarsfeld and Robert Merton, 'Mass Communication, Popular Taste and Organized Social Action,' in Bernard Rosenberg and David Manning White, editors, *Mass Culture. The Popular Arts in America* (New York 1957), 147–73, though emphasizing the limits upon media influence, do survey the variety of specific effects. See also section 10, 'The Effects of Mass Media' in Charles S. Steinberg, editor, *Mass Media and Communication* (New York 1967), 411–89, and Steven H. Chaffee and Michael Petrick, *Using the Mass Media, Communication Problems in American Society* (New York 1975), 169–252. There is an excellent treatment of the media and the process of legitimation in Ralph Miliband's *The State in Capitalist Society* (London 1969).
29 For a good discussion of the dependency effect, see Melvin L. De Fleur and Sandra Ball-Rokeach, *Theories of Mass Communication*, third edition (New York 1975), 255–80.
30 The literature on the modernization of the Third World has highlighted, perhaps unduly, the crucial importance of mass communication. See, in particular, Wilbur Schramm, *Mass Media and National Development. The Role of Information in the Developing Countries* (Stanford 1975), 37–45.

CHAPTER ONE / THE PREREQUISITES OF MASS COMMUNICATION

1 See, for instance, Michael Schudson, *Discovering the News. A Social History of American Newspapers* (New York 1978), 31–50.
2 See Raymond Williams, *Marxism and Literature* (Oxford 1977), for a lengthy discussion of the relationship among society, the economy, and culture.
3 George Nader, *Cities of Canada. Volume I: Theoretical, Historical and Planning Perspectives* (Toronto 1975), 2–39.

4 M.C. Urquhart and K.A.H. Buckley, editors, *Historical Statistics of Canada* (Toronto 1965), Series A254, 23.
5 Robert Jones, *History of Agriculture in Ontario 1613–1800* (Toronto 1977), 198–9.
6 Michael Cross, 'The Lumber Community of Upper Canada, 1815–1867,' in J.M. Bumstead, editor, *Canadian History before Confederation. Essays and Interpretations* (Georgetown, Ontario, 1972), 308–29.
7 George Nader, *Cities of Canada. Volume II: Profiles of Fifteen Metropolitan Centres* (Toronto 1976), 247.
8 H.V. Nelles has written an excellent introduction for the reprint (Toronto 1972) of this pamphlet, exploring the variety of ideas that underlay the railway craze.
9 Nader, *Cities of Canada*, II, 247.
10 Ibid, 379.
11 See J.M.S. Careless, 'The Business Community in the Early Development of Victoria, British Columbia,' in David Macmillan, editor, *Canadian Business History. Selected Studies, 1497–1971* (Toronto 1972), 104–23; and J.M.S. Carless, 'Aspects of Urban Life in the West,' in A.W. Rasporich and H.C. Klassen, editors, *Prairie Perspectives 2* (Toronto 1972), 25–39.
12 Statistics on railway mileage, freight, and investment are from Urquhart and Buckley, *Historical Statistics of Canada*, Series S28, 528; Series S45, 529; and Series S1, 526.
13 John Cooper, *Montreal. A Brief History* (Montreal 1969), 29.
14 Urquhart and Buckley, *Historical Statistics of Canada*, Series E218, 141.
15 Nader, *Cities of Canada*, II, 89–90.
16 T.W. Acheson, 'The National Policy and the Industrialization of the Maritimes, 1880–1910,' in Gilbert Stelter and Alan Artibise, editors, *The Canadian City. Essays in Urban History* (Toronto 1977), 94–103.
17 Peter Goheen, *Victorian Toronto 1850 to 1900* (Chicago 1970), 64–70.
18 See David Gagan, 'Land, Population and Social Change: The "Critical Years" in Rural Canada West,' *CHR*, 59 (September 1978) 293–318.
19 T.W. Acheson has estimated that 'about three quarters of the migrants [from Charlotte County] moved to the United States, particularly to Massachusetts and Minnesota'; 'A Study in the Historical Demography of a Loyalist County,' in Michiel Horn and Ronald Sabourin, editors, *Studies in Canadian Social History* (Toronto 1974), 93.
20 Goheen, *Victorian Toronto*, 76.
21 Careless used this term with particular reference to railways – see 'The Rise of Cities in Canada before 1914,' Canadian Historical Association Booklet no. 32 (1978).
22 *Toronto Past and Present until 1882* (Toronto 1970), 59.

23 Michael Bliss, *A Canadian Millionaire. The Life and Business Times of Sir Joseph Flavelle, Bart. 1858–1937* (Toronto 1978), especially 27–82.
24 By 1880 Montreal's tonnage had reached 600,000 and Quebec's 555,000, and the balance shifted even more dramatically over the course of the next decade (Nader, *Cities of Canada*, I 178–9).
25 For instance, William Muir, a Montreal clothing dealer, told a parliamentary committee in 1874; 'Not less than one-third of my own trade is with Nova Scotia and New Brunswick'; cited in P.B. Waite, *Canada 1874–1896. Arduous Destiny* (Toronto 1971), 8.
26 The Census of 1901 showed Montreal and environs with a capital investment in manufacturing of $68,400,000 and an output of $81,200,000 and Toronto with $53,300,000 and $60,400,000 respectively.
27 Acheson, 'The National Policy and the Industrialization of the Maritimes,' 103–15.
28 Tom Naylor, *The History of Canadian Business 1867–1914. Volume I: The Banks and Finance Capital* (Toronto 1975), 97.
29 Jacob Spelt, *Urban Development in South-Central Ontario* (Toronto 1972), 139.
30 *The City below The Hill* (Toronto 1972), 6. The book was a collection of articles first presented in the Montreal *Star* and in 1897 published as a book. In 1888 A.-B. Routhier (*Québec et Lévis à l'aurore du XXe siècle*) had noted a similar kind of segregation in the landscape of Quebec – see his comments in Noël Bélanger et al, *Les Travailleurs québécois 1851–1896* (Quebec 1973), 46.
31 Gregory Kealey, 'The Orange Order in Toronto: Religious Riot and the Working Class,' in G.S. Kealey and Peter Warrian, editors, *Essays in Canadian Working Class History* (Toronto 1976), 31–2.
32 Michael Katz, *The People of Hamilton, Canada West. Family and Class in a Mid-Nineteenth Century City* (Cambridge, Mass., 1975), 94–175.
33 Ames, *The City below The Hill*, 74–5.
34 Cited in Christopher Armstrong and H.V. Nelles, *The Revenge of the Methodist Bicycle Club. Sunday Streetcars and Municipal Reform in Toronto, 1888–1897* (Toronto 1977), 5 and 183.
35 Greg Kealey, editor, *Canada Investigates Industrialism* (Toronto 1973), 267–8.
36 See C.S. Clark, *Of Toronto the Good* (Toronto 1970), a reprint of an 1898 book, and Susan Houston, 'Victorian Origins of Juvenile Delinquency: A Canadian Experience,' in Michael Katz and Paul Mattingly, editors, *Education and Social Change: Themes from Ontario's Past* (New York 1975), 83–109.
37 Desmond Morton, *Mayor Howland. The Citizen's Candidate* (Toronto 1973), 5.
38 See Michael Bliss, 'The Protective Impulse: An Approach to the Social History of Oliver Mowat's Ontario' in Donald Swainson, editor, *Oliver Mowat's Ontario* (Toronto 1972), 174–88. Bliss concentrates on the efforts to control market forces.

39 People were missed – so Toronto's workforce appears larger than Montreal's in 1851! Murky census definitions make the white collar/blue collar distinction especially suspicious in 1851 and 1881. Employees and employers were lumped together in some pursuits. People, how many cannot be guessed, had multiple occupations, and this was never acknowledged by census-takers. Finally, since the census of 1901 is deficient in occupational data, I was forced to use 1911 figures which are skewed by the so-called economic boom of the Laurier years.

40 See 'Graphique I' in Bélanger, *Les Travailleurs québécois*, 36.

41 Paul Rutherford, 'A Portrait of Alienation in Victorian Canada: The *Private Memoranda* of P.S. Hamilton,' *Journal of Canadian Studies*, 12 (summer 1977) 12–23.

42 Katz, *The People of Hamilton, Canada West*, 195. Katz has developed this theme of the uneasy class very effectively in his chapter 'The Entrepreneurial Class,' 1976–208.

43 There is room for much debate over this issue of the worker's situation, as well as over one appropriate definition of poverty. Ames estimated that the poverty line stood at a family income of $5 a week. He defined poverty as absolute deprivation. Both Terry Copp and Michael Piva have set that line at $9.64 (Montreal) and $9.48 (Toronto) respectively. They use an arbitrary definition of poverty based upon the Department of Labour's typical budget for a family of five (computed back from 1926 and 1921 respectively) to ensure a minimum standard of health and decency. See Copp, *The Anatomy of Poverty. The Condition of the Working Class in Montreal, 1897–1929* (Toronto 1974) and Piva, *The Condition of the Working Class in Toronto – 1900–1921* (Ottawa 1979). Unfortunately, the Copp-Piva argument requires acceptance of a definition of poverty which suits the present day, not the late nineteenth century. Further, it requires judgments about the worker's actual style of life when fragmentary evidence about consumption, diet, rentals, amusements, and so on suggest a modest degree of discretionary income on the part of many a working-class family.

44 This has been calculated from data in the Census of 1901, volume 3, table XX. Note that it includes all employees, white- as well as blue-collar, which makes the actual figures misleading as a guide to workers' salaries. Further, the 1901 data excludes most workers in small shops. The size of the increase, however, is an important indicator of change over time.

45 For an analysis of this process in the American context, see Herbert Gutman, *Work, Culture and Society in Industrializing America. Essays in American Working-Class and Social History* (New York 1977), 32–66. For a Canadian instance, see Wayne Roberts, 'The Last Artisans: Toronto Printers, 1896–1914,' in Kealey and Warrian, *Essays in Canadian Working Class History*, 125–42.

46 See Fernand Harvey, *Révolution industrielle et travailleurs. Une enquête sur les rapports entre le capital et le travail au Québec à la fin du 19e siècle* (Montreal 1978), 95–126.
47 Kealey, *Canada Investigates Industrialism*, 328.
48 For an impression of working-class life, admittedly fragmentary and overly dramatic, see Gregory S. Kealey, 'Hogtown. Working Class Toronto at the Turn of the Century' (Toronto 1974).
49 G.S. Kealey, 'Artisans Respond to Industrialism: Shoemakers, Shoe Factories and the Knights of St. Crispin in Toronto,' Canadian Historical Association, *Historical Papers 1973*, 137–57.
50 See Paul Larocque's chapter, 'Les Grèves,' in Bélanger, *Les Travailleurs québécois*, 113–49, for a lengthy analysis of strikes in Quebec.
51 Steven Langdon, 'The Emergence of the Canadian Working-Class Movement, 1845–75,' *Journal of Canadian Studies* (May 1973) 3–13 and (August 1973) 8–26. Langdon, unfortunately, confuses class and fraternal solidarity, so finding a vigorous class consciousness which did not exist.
52 Ian McKay, 'Capital and Labour in the Halifax Baking and Confectionery Industry during the Last Half of the Nineteenth Century,' *Labour/Le Travailleur*, 3 (1978) 63–108.
53 The Brotherhood of Locomotive Engineers was an excellent example of a union practising this tactic of accommodation. See Desmond Morton, 'Taking on the Grand Trunk: The Locomotive Engineers Strike of 1876–7,' *Labour/Le Travailleur*, 2 (1977) 5–34. For a more general discussion of the labour aristocracy, see Robert Gray, 'The Labour Aristocracy in the Victorian Class Structure,' in Frank Parkin, editor, *The Social Analysis of Class Structure* (London 1974), 19–38.
54 Ramsay Cook, 'Henry George and the Poverty of Canadian Progress,' Canadian Historical Association, *Historical Papers 1977*, 143–56.
55 Frank Watt, 'Literature of Protest,' in C.F. Klinck, editor, *Literary History of Canada. Canadian Literature in English* (Toronto 1966), 457–73.
56 Bélanger, *Les Travailleurs québécois*, 144.
57 Bryan Palmer, ' "Give us the road and we will run it": The Social and Cultural Matrix of an Emerging Labour Movement,' Kealey and Warrian, *Essays in Canadian Working Class History*, 116.
58 Ibid, 106–24, and Morton, *Mayor Howland*, 43–56.
59 On the suspicion of workers' institutions in general, see Noel Bélanger and Jean-Guy Lalande, 'Les Réactions devant la montée ouvrière,' in Bélanger, *Les Travailleurs québécois*, 151–92.
60 There is now an extensive literature on urban reform. Two different approaches to the issue can be sampled in Stelter and Artibise, *The Canadian City*: Paul

Rutherford, 'Tomorrow's Metropolis: The Urban Reform Movement in Canada, 1880–1920' (368–92) and John Weaver, '"Tomorrow's Metropolis" Revisited: A Critical Assessment of Urban Reform Reform in Canada, 1890–1920' (393–418).

61 His fame is briefly discussed in Jack Batten, *Canada Moves Westward 1880/1890* (Toronto 1977), 29–30.

62 Alan Metcalfe, 'The Evolution of Organized Physical Recreation in Montreal, 1840–1895,' *Histoire Sociale/Social History*, 11 (May 1978) 161–4.

63 Ramsay Cook and Wendy Mitchinson, editors, *The Proper Sphere. Woman's Place in Canadian Society* (Toronto 1976), 182–3. The Phelps article appeared in B.F. Austin's *Woman: Her Character, Culture and Calling*, published in 1890.

64 P.B. Waite, 'Sir Oliver Mowat's Canada: Reflections on an Un-Victorian Society,' in Swainson, *Oliver Mowat's Ontario*, 20.

65 See the fascinating account of this affair in Armstrong and Nelles, *The Revenge of the Methodist Bicycle Company*.

66 There remains doubt over exactly what the downtown in real wages (1900–20) meant to the various segments of the working classes. One view has been ably put forward by Copp's *The Anatomy of Poverty* and Piva's *The Condition of the Working Class in Toronto*.

67 Katz, *The People of Hamilton, Canada West*, 3–4.

68 Batten, *Canada Moves Westward*, 25–7.

69 Michael Cross, editor, *The Workingman in the Nineteenth Century* (Oxford 1974), 226.

70 Metcalfe, 'Physical Recreation in Montreal,' 151.

71 S.F. Wise, 'Sport and Class Values in Old Ontario and Quebec,' in W.H. Heick and Roger Graham, editors, *His Own Man. Essays in Honour of Arthur Reginald Masden Lower* (Montreal 1974), 93-117.

72 Cited in J. Donald Wilson, 'The Ryerson Years in Canada West,' in J.D. Wilson, R.M. Stamp, and L.-P. Audet, editors, *Canadian Education: A History* (Scarborough 1970), 217.

73 Cited in Neil Sutherland, *Children in English-Canadian Society. Framing the Twentieth-Century Consensus* (Toronto 1976), 180.

74 See Alison Prentice, *The School Promoters. Education and Social Class in Mid-Nineteenth Century Upper Canada* (Toronto 1977) for a lengthy analysis of the views and practices of this group.

75 In *La Science sociale suivant la méthode d'observation*, 23 (June 1897) 441–79, 24 (November 1897) 356–90, 25 (June 1898) 488–522.

76 The description of the so-called modern personality derives in part from Kenneth Lockridge, *Literacy in Colonial New England. An Enquiry into the Social Context of Literacy in the Early Modern West* (New York 1974), 27–9.

77 See ibid, 36–7 especially, for a cogent analysis of the limits to the significance of literacy per se.
78 Jack Goody, 'Introduction,' in Jack Goody, editor, *Literacy in Traditional Societies* (Cambridge 1968), 1.
79 Lawrence Stone, 'Literacy and Education in England 1640–1900,' *Past and Present*, no. 42 (February 1969) 69–139.
80 The head of the household was supposed to attest accurately (under threat of legal sanctions) to the literacy of his family. Given the survey was new and the technique indirect, I have doubts about this accuracy, especially when the facts are compared with the 1871 data. Harvey Graff, however, feels otherwise, and he has analysed a small portion of the manuscript census in depth. See his 'Towards a Meaning of Literacy: Literacy and Social Structure in Hamilton, Ontario, 1861,' in Katz and Mattingly, *Education and Social Change*, especially 251-6, as well as 'Literacy and Social Structure in the Nineteenth-Century City,' (PhD thesis, University of Toronto, 1975), and *The Literacy Myth. Literacy and Social Structure in the Nineteenth-Century City* (New York 1979).
81 Though the earlier indirect 'test,' dependent on the honour of the respondent, remained in use then and later.
82 All these figures are estimates, derived from Carlo Cipolla, *Literacy and Development in the West* (Harmondsworth 1969) and Stone, 'Literacy and Education in England.'
83 The attendance includes primary and secondary schools. The material on provincial totals is drawn from Urquhart and Buckley, *Historical Statistics of Canada*, Series V5–6 and V11–12, 587–9.
84 Susan Houston, 'School Reform and Education: The Issue of Compulsory Schooling, Toronto, 1851–71,' and Ian Davey, 'The Rhythm of Work and the Rhythm of School,' both in Neil McDonald and Alf Chaiton, editors, *Egerton Ryerson and His Times* (Toronto 1978), 221–76.
85 Data from Urquhart and Buckley, *Historical Statistics of Canada*, Series A5–8, 14, and Series V71–74, 594.
86 There were some exceptions. Harvey Graff, 'Literacy and Social Structure in Elgin County, Canada West: 1861,' *Histoire Sociale/Social History*, 6 (April 1973), 45–6, finds that Elgin's rate of semi-literacy was higher than that of Toronto, Hamilton, Kingston, or London. Unfortunately, this finding rests on the somewhat dubious census of 1861 plus the less satisfactory standard of reading only.
87 Allan Greer, 'The Pattern of Literacy in Quebec, 1745–1899,' *Histoire Sociale/Social History*, 9 (November 1978) 302–3.
88 Simple proximity is of some importance to the success of schooling, especially given the severity of Canada's winter. Besides, Lockridge has ably argued that

'social concentration' by itself fosters a rise in a population's literacy – see *Literacy in Colonial New England*, 62–71.

89 See Greer, 'The Pattern of Literacy in Quebec,' 329–30 for a brief comment on the 'metropolitan effect' of Montreal and Quebec.

90 This is unproven though. There is still doubt among historians whether the process of immigration 'selects' the more literate among a given population.

91 This has been amply demonstrated by Lockridge, *Literacy in Colonial New England*, and see especially 97–101 for a general consideration of the importance of Protestantism in Europe and America.

92 R.D. Gidney, 'Elementary Education in Upper Canada: A Reassessment,' in Katz and Mattingly, *Education and Social Change*, 3–26.

93 André Labarrère-Paule, *Les Instituteurs laïques au Canada français 1836–1900* (Quebec 1965), 466.

94 That, of course, is an interesting but as yet unproven assertion. We know very little about the typical upbringing of children anywhere in Victorian Canada. See Gérin's second article for a lengthy description of child-rearing in Canada.

95 Labarrère-Paule, *Les Instituteurs laïques*, 438.

96 Ibid, 424.

97 See Susan Houston, 'Politics, Schools, and Social Change in Upper Canada,' in Katz and Mattingly, *Education and Social Change*, 28–56.

98 Michael Katz, 'Who Went to School?,' in ibid, 271–93.

99 Davey, 'The Rhythm of Work and the Rhythm of School.'

100 Sutherland, *Children in English-Canadian Society*, 160.

101 Ibid, 178-81.

102 Mulvany, *Toronto Past and Present*, 85.

103 [S.P. May], 'Report on Mechanics Institutes,' Ontario, House of Assembly, *Sessional Papers*, 1881, no. 46, 61.

104 Harvey Graff, 'The Reality behind the Rhetoric: The Social and Economic Meanings of Literacy in the Mid-Nineteenth Century: The Example of Literacy and Criminality,' McDonald and Chaiton, *Egerton Ryerson and His Times*, 204. Of course, the 'crime-control industry' largely uncovered criminals who were unable to function properly in society, and illiteracy or semi-literacy (in Ontario anyway) was one cause and one sign of social maladjustment.

105 Kealey, *Canada Investigates Industrialism*, 273–4. See also Harvey, *Révolution industrielle et travailleurs*, 181–7.

106 Harvey Graff, 'Respected and Profitable Labour: Literacy, Jobs and the Working Class in the Nineteenth Century,' in Kealey and Warrian, *Essays in Canadian Working Class History*, 73.

107 James Douglas, 'The Intellectual Progress of Canada during the Last Fifty Years, and the Present State of Its Literature,' *Canadian Monthly and National Review*, 7 (June 1875) 471.

108 Bélanger, *Les Travailleurs québécois*, 65–6.
109 *Le Pays*, 13 February 1871, 2.
110 J.F. Hogan, *The Sister Dominions through Canada to Australia by the New Imperial Highway* (London 1896), 73–4.
111 Allan Smith, 'The Imported Image: American Publications and American Ideas in the Evolution of the English Canadian Mind 1820–1900,' PhD thesis, University of Toronto, 1971, 71–4.
112 Douglas, 'The Intellectual Progress of Canada,' 471.
113 Douglas Lochhhead, 'John Ross Robertson, Uncommon Publisher for the Common Reader: His First Years as a Toronto Book Publisher,' *Journal of Canadian Studies*, 11 (May 1976) 19–26.
114 'Report on Mechanics Institutes,' 181.
115 Douglas, 'The Intellectual Progress of Canada,' 472.
116 Thomas Conant, *Life in Canada* (Toronto 1903), 230.

CHAPTER TWO / THE MAKING OF THE DAILY PRESS

1 19 September 1839.
2 E.G. Firth, *Early Toronto Newspapers, 1793–1867* (Toronto 1955), 13–14.
3 W. Meikle, *The Canadian Newspaper Directory* (Toronto 1858).
4 J.-P. Bernard, *Les Rouges. Libéralisme, nationalisme et anticléricalisme au milieu du XIXe siècle*, (Quebec 1971), 50.
5 I.L. Bird, *The Englishwoman in Canada* (Madison 1966), 317.
6 Meikle, *The Canadian Newspaper Directory*, A.
7 Cited in J.H. Talman, 'Three Scottish-Canadian Newspaper Editor Poets,' *CHR*, 28 (1947), 166.
8 Much of the detailed information in the following four paragraphs comes from J.M.S. Careless's superlative two-volume biography, *George Brown of the Globe* (Toronto 1959 and 1963).
9 Geo. P. Rowell and Co.'s *American Newspaper Directory*, 1873, 232.
10 A comparison of the morning and evening *Globe* in 1861 and 1868 suggests that most of the reading and advertising material was exactly the same, if occasionally rearranged. By November 1868, though, the inside pages of the evening *Globe* were duplicates of the morning paper.
11 For a description of advances in print technology see [Robert Hoe], *A Short History of the Printing Press* (New York 1902).
12 Early Handwritten Credit Reporting Ledgers of the Mercantile Agency, vol. 26, 323, Dun and Bradstreet Collection, Baker Library, Harvard University.
13 *Monetary Times*, 2 December 1892, 643.
14 J.J. Talman, 'The Newspaper Press of Canada West, 1850-60,' *Transactions of the Royal Society of Canada*, series 3, 33 (1939) section 2, 154.

15 Macrae, *How Things Are in America* (n.p. 1867–68).
16 Dun and Bradstreet Collection, vol. 26, 336.
17 Reprint Toronto 1968, 215. Meikle, however, puts the *Colonist*'s total circulation at 13,500 in late 1857 (14–15).
18 Dun and Bradstreet Collection, vol. 9, 295.
19 Claimed, in February and March 1870, daily 16,198 and weekly 27,181 – see Ron Poulton, *The Paper Tyrant. John Ross Robertson of the Toronto Telegram* (Toronto 1971), 34. One-half may be closer to the truth.
20 See the lead editorial on 1 May 1854 in the *Gazette*.
21 Published in Meikle, *The Canadian Newspaper Directory*, 58–9.
22 Press comments in Halifax *Express*, 6 July 1864.
23 'By a Member of the Fourth Estate,' 'The Press of Ontario,' *New Dominion Monthly* (February 1872) 66.
24 R. Mahaffy, 'Ottawa Journalism 1860 to 1870,' *Ontario History*, 42 (1950) 210.
25 Rowell's 1873 and McKim's 1892. The count of actual dailies in existence was for the year of publication.
26 The *Daily News* was not available for analysis. *L'Ordre*, on the verge of extinction, proved a very eccentric sheet. It supplied the least information, some 5,299 lines that week, little telegraphic news or business information, but much advertising (64.5 per cent) and entertainment (7.7 per cent). Its particular interests were the plight of France and the cultural and community life of Quebec, to which it devoted long essays and reports.
28 'The Daily Newspaper: The History of Its Production and Distribution,' reprinted from the *New Dominion Monthly* (1878) 28.
29 Undated letter of information, Dougall Papers, Public Archives of Canada.
30 15 February 1871.
31 Paul Rutherford, 'The People's Press: The Emergence of the New Journalism in Canada, 1869–1899,' *CHR*, 56 (June 1975) 167–91.
32 Quoted in P.D. Ross, *Retrospects of a Newspaper Person* (Toronto 1931), 2. Supposedly, Graham said much the same thing to the young J.W. Dafoe – see Murray Donnelly, *Dafoe of the Free Press* (Toronto 1968), 12.
33 The *Star* was then four pages long, with 28 columns, and cost $2.50 a year.
34 Montreal *Star, A Souvenir of Canada's Greatest Newspapers*, n.d., 29. The web press worked from a continuous roll of paper an printed both sides of a sheet (hence 'perfected').
35 'A Clever Newspaper Artist,' *P&P* (July 1900) 1.
36 A *Souvenir of Canada's Greatest Newspapers*, 29. The stereotype process involved the creation of a special plate, upon which the reading and editorial matter was reproduced, which could be attached to the press. The process eliminated the need to place type in special frames called 'turtles' around the cylinder and allowed two presses to run off duplicate plates, thus speeding up production.

37 George Murray, 'A Notable Journalistic Career,' *Canadian Magazine*, 32 (1908–09) 418.
38 A.R. Carman, 'Our All-Canadian Peer,' *Canadian Magazine*, 48 (1917) 502.
39 'Historical Sketch of the Montreal Star,' in J.C. Hopkins, 'Special Historical Supplement,' *Canadian Annual Review of Public Affairs*, 10: 1910 (Toronto 1911) 85.
40 Ibid, 85–6.
41 A.H.U. Colquhoun, 'The Man Who Made the Montreal Star,' *P&P* (April 1895) 7.
42 Outside Canada, other pioneers such as Millard and *Le Petit Journal* (1863), Pulitzer and the New York *World* (1883), or Harmsworth and the London *Daily Mail* (1896) experimented with their own brands of what was condemned (first by Matthew Arnold) as the 'New Journalism.' See Lee, *The Origins of the Popular Press* (London 1976) 118. There is also an excellent study of Pulitzer's early techniques in George Jeurgens, *Joseph Pulitzer and the New York World* (Princeton 1966).
43 'The Evening Telegram,' A *Story of the Years*, 1889, 8.
44 Ibid, 9.
45 Mulvany, *Toronto Past and Present* (Toronto 1970), 193.
46 Poulton, *The Paper Tyrant*, 72.
47 Mulvany, *Toronto Past and Present*, 194.
48 Hector Charlesworth, *Candid Chronicles* (Toronto 1925), 75–9.
49 For instance, this diatribe (24 December 1883) on the efforts of English aristocrats to acquire huge land holdings on the prairies: 'It's a big scheme, / And shows that the British aristocrat / has a great head, / And is not such a fool as he looks. / But there is just one little factor left / out of the calculation / Which bids fair to knock the whole / business endways. / And that is: – The Democratic spirit of the people of / America, / Who will not tolerate any nonsense of / the kind.'
50 Beaulieu and Hamelin, *La Presse québécoise*, vol. 2, 232–3.
51 N.F. Davin, 'The London and Canadian Press,' *Canadian Monthly and National Review*, 5 (February 1874) 118-28.
52 Careless, *Brown of the Globe*, vol. 2, 340. Brown could absorb the mailing costs because of new lower postal rates.
53 See the *Globe*'s own puff on 15 April 1880.
54 The examples are taken from a 12-page issue of Tuesday, 24 August 1880.
55 The two examples are taken from the Saturday edition, 4 February 1888.
56 Including its proprietor, Robert Jaffray. On 20 March 1889, he wrote to Edward Blake, 'I don't think you can be aware on the desperate struggle the Globe is having to maintain its Protestant and liberal readers'; cited in R. Clippingdale,

'J.S. Willison, Political Journalist from Liberalism to Independence,' PhD thesis, University of Toronto, 1970, 55–6.

57 T.C. Patteson papers, Box 3, envelope 2, Ontario Archives.

58 Ibid.

59 Charlesworth, *Candid Chronicles*, 75.

60 Toronto *Mail*, 2 August 1880.

61 It is possible the *Mail*'s daily circulation had begun to slip back because of the aggressive competition of the *Telegram* and the *News*.

62 J.S. Willison, *Reminiscences Political and Personal* (Toronto 1919), 119.

63 London *Advertiser*: 6,000 daily and 28,125 weekly in 1883, around 6,000 daily and over 22,500 weekly in 1889. London *Free Press*: 8,800 daily and 20,300 weekly in 1883, around 8,000 daily and over 15,000 weekly in 1889.

64 Cited in Brian Young, *Promoters and Politicians. The North-Shore Railways in the History of Quebec 1854–85* (Toronto 1978), 24.

65 Cited in Ralph Heintzman, 'The Struggle for Life. The French Daily Press of Montreal and the Problems of Economic Growth in the Age of Laurier' PhD thesis, York University, 1977, 19, note 1.

66 The source of the assorted circulation statistics used in the text and the tables are based upon a range of newspaper directories: Geo. P. Rowell and Co.'s *American Newspaper Directory*, 1873, 1877, 1879, and 1890; Edwin Alden and Bro.'s *American Newspaper Catalogue*, 1883; N.W. Ayer and Son's *American Newspaper Manual*, 1881, 1884, 1886, 1897, 1899, and 1901; A. McKim's *The Canadian Newspaper Directory*, 1892, 1899, and 1901. Occasionally these have been supplemented by the less reliable Central Press Agency, *Directory of Canadian Newspapers for 1900*.

The circulations these publications estimate are for the year preceding the actual date of appearance. Sometimes a directory does not estimate a circulation at all. Sometimes an estimate looks particularly dubious. The authors did take pains to acquire reliable and eventually sworn circulations because the utility of their directories, and hence sale to advertisers, depended upon the accuracy of the estimates. Where other reliable information significantly questions the estimates the figure is adjusted. Where no figure is supplied, material is used from the newspapers, contemporaries, and the like to concoct a 'guestimate.' On the whole, however, the general accuracy of the figures supplied by these directories, has been assumed.

67 Cited in Beaulieu and Hamelin, *La Presse québécoise*, vol. 2, 97.

68 *L'Étendard*, 3 February 1883.

69 The issue of Confederation intervened, and *La Presse* became *L'Union Nationale*, a *nationaliste* organ hoping for a racial union to block the new anglophone conspiracy.

70 For some information on the group see Pierre Godin, *L'Information-opium. Une histoire politique de la presse* (Montreal 1972), 25–33.
71 *Monetary Times* (29 April 1881) 2156.
72 See Mulvany, *Toronto Past and Present*, 236–40.
73 Ibid, 288. That circulation, though, may not have been limited just to country weeklies.
74 Newsboys, especially carriers, of course, had been around at least since the beginning of the century, and probably since the first gazettes.
75 Beaulieu and Hamelin, *La Presse québécoise*, vol. 2, 232–3.
76 *A Souvenir of Canada's Greatest Newspapers*, 15 and 18.
77 *A Story of the Years*, 10 and 51.
78 J.G. Bourinot, 'The Intellectual Development of the Canadian People,' *Canadian Monthly*, 6 (January–June 1881) 119.
79 Cited in [A.E. Millward], 'The Development of the Press in Canada,' *Canada Year Book* 1939, 753; 'The Price of "News", *P&P* (November 1894) 26; A.H.U. Colquhoun, 'The Canadian Press Association,' in *A History of Canadian Journalism*, edited and published by a Committee of the Canadian Press Association (1908), 128.
80 *P&P* (February 1897) 11–13. 'Ems' refers to a unit of measure in printing: the square letter 'm.'
81 E.C.H., 'The Printing of a Great Paper,' *P&P* (September 1900) 6.
82 In addition the *Gazette* and *Herald* of Montreal; the *Mail and Empire*, *News*, and *World* of Toronto; the Ottawa *Journal* and London *Free Press*.
83 *P&P* (April 1894) 1, and Heintzman, 'The Struggle for Life,' 17.
84 Godin, *L'Information-opium*, 41.
85 Heintzman, 'The Struggle for Life,' 5–6.
86 McKenzie Porter, 'The Pulse of French Canada,' *Maclean's Magazine* (15 March 1954) 64.
87 Heintzman, 'The Struggle for Life,' 4–5.
88 Cited in Beaulieu and Hamelin, *La Presse québécoise*, vol. 1, 205.
89 *P&P* (May 1895) 4.
90 For instance, on 3 January 1900, a Wednesday evening, the *Echo* published 'Profit and loss are now receiving due attention.' 'The martial fever is expected to reach its crisis when the second contingent embarks.' ' "Better late than never" may be said of winter, but the other motto should not be forgotten, "better never late." '
91 'The Newspaper Press and the University,' *Journalism and the University: A Collection of Essays*, sponsored by the editors of *Queen's Quarterly* (Toronto 1903), 255.
92 Ibid, 260.

93 Ibid, 261–2.
94 Ibid, 265.
95 David Hall, 'The Political Career of Clifford Sifton, 1896–1905' PhD thesis, University of Toronto, 1973, 430.
96 *P&P* (June 1895) 8 and (December 1896) 2.
97 Charles Bruce, *News and the Southams* (Toronto 1968), 73.
98 *P&P* (March 1899) 2. See also Donnelly, *Dafoe of the Free Press*, 33–4.
99 *P&P* (September 1895) 11.
100 *P&P* (November 1894) 10.
101 Ibid (June 1892) 1; (April 1893) 2; (March 1894) 28; and (May 1898) 10.
102 A. McKim's *The Canadian Newspaper Directory*, 1892, 278.
103 *P&P* (July 1895) 10.
104 Ibid (December 1894) 14.
105 Ibid (November 1894) 7.
106 Ibid (October 1900) 10.
107 Tom Walkom, in an unfinished thesis for the University of Toronto on the Toronto daily press, has used advertising, especially the kind and frequency of classified advertising, to estimate the class composition of a newspaper's readership. His draft chapter IV, 'Readership of the Toronto Daily Press,' notes that by the 1890s newspapers, whether highbrow or lowbrow, attempted with some success to win readers in every class. He has suggested, however, that certain dailies were more closely identified with the business-professional public, others with skilled workingmen, and so on.

CHAPTER THREE / THE NEWSPAPER INDUSTRY

1 Willison, *Reminiscences Political and Personal* (Toronto 1919), 40.
2 The two phrases 'bridging occupation' and 'out relief' come from Philip Elliot, 'Professional Ideology and Organisational Change: the Journalist since 1800,' in George Boyce, James Curran, and Pauline Wingate, editors, *Newspaper History: From the 17th Century to the Present Day* (London 1978), 172.
3 Especially H.J. Morgan, *The Canadian Men and Women of the Time: A Handbook of Canadian Biography* (Toronto 1898), which displayed an unusual liking for the careers of even little-known editors; W.B. Harte's 'Canadian Journalists and Journalism,' *The New England Magazine* (December 1891) 411–41; J.A. Cooper's 'The Editors of the Leading Canadian Dailies,' *Canadian Magazine* (February 1899) 336–52; and occasional biographies in *P&P*. Naturally enough, these biographies concentrate on prominent men and women. Not much can be learned about reporters who never rose any higher.
4 *La Minerve*, 18 January 1895.
5 Willison, *Reminiscences Political and Personal*, 40.

6 St John to Patteson, 7 March 1872, Patteson Papers, Ontario Archives.
7 Charlesworth, *Candid Chronicles* (Toronto 1925), 125.
8 *Le Monde*, 11 March 1896.
9 Cooper, 'The Editors of the Leading Canadian Dailies,' 336.
10 Harte, 'Canadian Journalists and Journalism,' 417.
11 For a discussion of the rise of the reporter in popular journalism, see Schudson, *Discovering the News* (New York 1978), 61–87.
12 'The Daily Newspaper,' 1878, 23.
13 '*The Evening Telegram*,' *A Story of the Years* (1889), 49.
14 *P&P* (December 1892) 4.
15 Ontario, Legislative Assembly, Third Annual Report of the Bureau of Industries, *Sessional Papers* (1885) 17, part 7, no. 84, 44.
16 *P&P* (March 1899) 3.
17 'The Daily Newspaper,' 25. It is only fair to add that the writer thought this time had passed.
18 J.E.B. McCready, 'The Special Correspondent,' *Canadian Magazine* (October 1907) 548–52.
19 See Willison's description of the press gallery in his *Reminiscences*, 113–35.
20 Davin, 'The London and Canadian Press,' *Canadian Monthly and National Review*, 5 (February 1874). 119.
21 *A Story of the Years*, 47.
22 Clark, 'The Daily Newspaper,' *Canadian Magazine*, 7 (June 1896), 102.
23 *P&P* (September 1892) 21.
24 W.C. Nichol, 'The Lot of the Newspaper Man,' *P&P* (April 1897) 12.
25 The mobility of journalists was quite extraordinary. Witness these reports from *P&P* (June 1896) 2: 'Bruno Wilson, formerly city editor of Le Monde, has joined La Presse in the same capacity. Fred Williams, formerly of The Montreal Gazette, has returned from Australia, and joins The Herald staff. Arthur Burns, who lately filled a position on the editorial staff of The Montreal Herald, has left that paper and joined the staff of The Ottawa Citizen in the position of news and telegraph editor. E.N. St. Pierre, one of the leading French-Canadian members of the craft, has resigned his position as city editor of La Presse, and taken the same chair on the new French Liberal evening paper Le Soir.'
26 Ontario, Legislative Assembly, Annual Report of the Bureau of Industries ... 1887, *Sessional Papers*, vol. 20, part 6, 62–6.
27 Laurier LaPierre, 'Politics, Race, and Religion in French Canada: Joseph Israel Tarte,' PhD thesis, University of Toronto, 1962, 368.
28 Ross Harkness, *J.E. Atkinson of the Star* (Toronto 1963), 18.
29 *P&P* believed the treatment meted out to the staffers was criminal. See 'The Empire Staff,' *P&P* (March 1895) 7.

30 Floyd Chalmers, *A Gentleman of the Press* (Toronto 1969), 166–8. That was in 1906, and the negotiations broke down over the price of the property.
31 This kind of arrangement was favoured by *P&P*. See its comments on the new London *News* in May 1896, 1.
32 Bruce, *News and the Southams* (Toronto 1968), 162.
33 Harkness, *J.E. Atkinson of the Star*, 23.
34 J.R. Dougall to J. Dougall, 1 May 1882, Dougall Papers Public Archives of Canada. Dougall's 'both businesses' included the leather shop as well as the newspaper.
35 *P&P* (March 1897) 11.
36 Bourinot, 'The Intellectual Development of the Canadian People,' *Canadian Monthly*, 6 (January – June 1881), 122.
37 E.H. Macklin to J. Mather, 18 September 1900, and A.J. Magurn to Macklin, 19 October 1900, Clifford Sifton Papers (vol. 83), Public Archives of Canada.
38 Director's Report, 6 October 1875, Patteson Papers, Ontario Archives.
39 'Historical Sketch of the Montreal Star,' in Hopkins, *Canadian Annual Review of Public Affairs*, 10 (1910) (Toronto 1911), 85. See also Montreal *Star*, 23 February 1889.
40 Poulton, *The Paper Tyrant* (Toronto 1971), 71.
41 *L'Électeur*, 15 July 1880.
42 Bruce, *News and the Southams*, 148.
43 Poulton, *The Paper Tyrant*, 70–1; Ross, *Retrospects of a Newspaper Person* (Toronto 1931), 34–7; Harkness, *Atkinson*, 36–7.
44 Patteson to Hague, 3 May 1877, Patteson Papers.
45 The financial statistics are taken from a number of sources: Toronto *Mail* in Patteson Papers, Box III, envelope 2; Ottawa *Journal* in I. Norman Smith, *The Journal Men* (Toronto 1974), 21; Ottawa *Citizen* and Hamilton *Spectator* in Southam Archives, Boxes 43 and 44, held by Southam Press Ltd., Toronto; Toronto *Mail and Empire* in the Ontario Archives, the Maclean-Hunter Collection, J.B. Maclean Correspondence, Toronto Mail and Empire file; Montreal *Witness* in the Dougall Papers, vol. 6; and Toronto *News* from the Fifth Annual Report of The News Publishing Company, private possession, courtesy of Michael Bliss.
46 Mulvany, *Toronto Past and Present* (Toronto 1970), 193.
47 'The Globe,' 'A Modern Newspaper Office,' 1896, 1.
48 'The Daily Newspaper,' 11 and 13.
49 Cited in *P&P* (September 1892) 20; (October 1896) 3; and (October 1898) 8.
50 Ibid (October 1898) 3, and (November 1898) 7.
51 Ross, *Retrospects*, 65–9.
52 *P&P* (May 1898) 7.

53 Ibid (August 1900) 1.
54 *A Story of the Years*, 53.
55 *P&P* (December 1898) 6.
56 See Canada, Royal Commission on the Alleged Combination of Paper Manufacturers and Dealers, Report and Evidence, *Sessional Papers* (1902) vol. 13, 31–5, 79, and 171–3.
57 George Carruthers, *Paper in the Making* (Toronto 1947), 487 and 490–7.
58 James Dougall to John Dougall, 8 June 1876, Dougall Papers.
59 Beaulieu and Hamelin, *La Press québécoise*, vol. 2, 99.
60 Special Report, 17 April 1875, Patteson Papers.
61 *Monetary Times*, 2 December 1892, 643; *P&P* (July 1895) 7, and (October 1895) 3.
62 McKim's 1892, 315.
63 H.J. Morgan, editor, *The Dominion Annual Register* (Toronto 1885), 346.
64 *P&P* (May 1893) 10.
65 Ibid (August 1893) 2 and (October 1895) 2.
66 Ontario, Legislative Assembly, Annual Report of Bureau of Industries (1892), *Sessional Papers* (1893) vol. 25, part 6, 42–3.
67 *P&P* (December 1892) 11.
68 Ibid (December 1898) 6.
69 'Delivery of the Small City Daily,' *P&P* (February 1900) 21.
70 Clippingdale, 'J.S. Willison,' 422.
71 *P&P* (April 1900) 4. The Ottawa *Citizen*'s postage bill 1899–1900 was $1,051.
72 For example, *P&P* (June 1896) noted the Halifax *Chronicle* was 'issuing a series of illustrated supplements on the beauties of Nova Scotia as a resort for tourists. They are being supplied by The Toronto Globe.'
73 Facts assembled from the variou Auditor General's reports in *Sessional Papers*, Parliament of Canada.
74 Special Report, 17 April 1875, Patteson Papers.
75 'The Daily Newspaper,' 21.
76 *P&P* (October 1895) 12; (November 1895) 13; (February 1896) 4.
77 J.R. Miller, *Equal Rights. The Jesuits' Estates Act Controversy* (Montreal 1979), 196.
78 See Elzear Lavoie, 'La Clientèle du "Courrier du Canada," ' *Culture*, 31 (March 1970) 45–6.
79 *P&P* (April 1895) 2.
80 'Cheaper Newspapers,' ibid (November 1894) 12.
81 Mail and Empire file, J.B. Maclean Correspondence, Maclean-Hunter Collection.
82 *P&P* (May 1896) 2.

83 Ibid (February 1897) 15.
84 Montreal *Star*, 14 February 1871.
85 Special Report, 17 April 1875, Patteson papers.
86 Poulton, *The Paper Tyrant*, 73.
87 McKim's 1901, 11 (special ad section).
88 *P&P* (April 1895) 4.
89 McKim's 1899, 209.
90 Toronto *Telegram*, 8 January 1886. My thanks to one of my students, Bill Brioux, who turned up this statement in his research.
91 Toronto *Globe*, 23 January 1886.
92 *P&P* (June 1895) 3.
93 McKim's 1892, 254.
94 ? Southam to F.N. Southam, 4 December 1902, Southam Archives.
95 A.J. Magurn to E.H. Macklin, 19 October, 1900, Sifton papers (vol. 83).
96 Glenn A. Welsch et al., *Intermediate Accounting*, second Canadian edition (Toronto 1978), 508.
97 Dun and Bradstreet Collection, vol. 5, 350; vol. 8, 147; vol. 12, 755; vol. 9, 629; vol. 7, 85.
98 Ibid, vol. 5, 109.
99 Ibid, vol. 26, 40 and vol. 27, 144.
100 Ibid, vol. 26, 34, 189, 272, 323, 336; vol. 27, 280.
101 M.O. Hammond, 'Ninety Years of the Globe,' unpublished manuscript, Hammond Papers, Ontario Archives, 132.
102 J.A. Macdonald to T.C. Patteson, 20 February 1872, Patteson Papers.
103 Carruthers, *Paper in the Making*, 502.
104 Mulvany, *Toronto Past and Present*, 199.
105 Charlesworth, *Candid Chronicles*, 129.
106 Beaulieu and Hamelin, *La Presse québécoise*, vol. 1, 57.
107 Ibid, vol. 2, 189.
108 *P&P* (August 1892) 11; (October 1892) 9 and 11.
109 *Monetary Times*, 7 October 1892, 397.
110 Ibid, 7 April 1893, 1189 and 9 June 1893, 1462.
111 Dun and Bradstreet Collection, vol. 5, 160 and vol. 7, 210.
112 Toronto *Mail*, 19 December 1884.
113 Donnelly, *Dafoe of the Free Press*, 30.
114 *P&P* (June 1894) 10.
115 J.S. Brierley to J.R. Dougall, 29 June 1897, Dougall Papers.
116 *P&P* (May 1893) 10.
117 Charlesworth, *Candid Chronicles*, 161.
118 *P&P* (June 1895) 2 and (November 1896) 1.

119 It is, however, only fair to note that the paper's success waned in the next three years, which was why some Conservatives were eager to engage J.B. Maclean in a salvage operation.
120 Information collected from Bruce, *News and the Southams*, 6–79 and financial statements in the Southam Archives.
121 *P&P* (December 1898) 6.
122 Poulton, *The Paper Tyrant*, 97, and Morgan, *Canadian Men and Women*, 1898, 397.
123 *P&P* (February 1897) 22; Hall, 'Clifford Sifton,' PhD thesis, University of Toronto, 1973, 472; Harkness, *Atkinson*, 39; *P&P* (December 1899) 30.
124 *P&P* (June 1892) 5.
125 The information on the CPA comes from Colquhoun, 'The Canadian Press Association,' 1–132.
126 *P&P* (October 1895) 6.
127 Ibid (February 1897) 5.
128 Ibid (February 1894) 2.
129 W.A. Sheppard, 'Objects of the Typothetae,' *P&P* (June 1892) 2. Years later, in November 1900, though, the organ complained that the UTA affiliation had not assisted employers associations very much.
130 P.D. Ross, 'Co-operation Among Local Publishers,' *P&P* (April 1895) 4.
131 The *Journal* and the *Free Press* supposedly 'conspired' to destroy the *Citizen*'s reputation amongst advertisers. See Bruce, *News and the Southams*, 74–5.
132 *P&P* (April 1895) 4.
133 Ibid (July 1895) 18 and (November 1898) 6.
134 Ibid (November 1898) 6.
135 Ibid (November 1898) 6 and (March 1899) 12.
136 Carlton McNaught and H.E. Stephenson, *The Story of Advertising in Canada: A Chronicle of the Years* (Toronto 1940), 31–2.
137 *P&P* (August 1895) 1.
138 Ibid (July 1895) 6.
139 See, especially, A.H.U. Colquhoun, 'A Canadian Cable Service,' *P&P* (May 1897) 6.
140 See Willison's comments at a CPA meeting in *P&P* (February 1896) 12.
141 Colquhoun, 'The Canadian Press Association,' 127–32.

CHAPTER FOUR / THE DAILY FARE

1 Toronto *Star*, 13 December 1895. Sheppard was the new editor of the *Star*.
2 This discussion borrows from the approaches developed by students of semiotics. See Roland Barthes, *Elements of Semiology* (New York 1977). Tom

Walkom's 'The Ideological Structure of the Toronto Daily Press 1870–1910' (a paper delivered to the University of Toronto Economic History Workshop, 7 November 1980) inspired my more modest exploration of the form in which press views were expressed.

3 Magurn to Macklin, 19 October 1900, Sifton Papers.

4 The ad casts some doubt on the old claim that Eaton's was the first Canadian store to pioneer the fixed price.

5 For instance: 'To Professor HOLLOWAY: SIR, – I suffered for a considerable period from a severe attack Erysipelas, which at length settled in my leg, and resisted all medical treatment. My sufferings were very great, and I quite despaired of any permanent amendment, when I was advised to have recourse to your Ointment and Pills. I did so without delay, and am happy to say the result was eminently successful, for they effected a radical cure of my leg and restored me to the enjoyment of health. I shall ever speak with the utmost confidence of your medicines, and have recommended them to others in this neighbourhood similarly afflicted, who derived equal benefit. I am, Sir, your obliged and faithful Servant, [Signed] ELIZABETH YEATES.'

6 S.P. Day, *English America: or Pictures of Canadian Places and People*, vol. 2 (London 1864), 252 and 255. See his chapter 'Sensational Puffing.'

7 'The Daily Newspaper,' 1878, 18.

8 McNaught and Stephenson, *The Story of Advertising in Canada* (Toronto 1940), 44.

9 For instance on 10 June, 1895 the Toronto *Mail and Empire*, *Globe*, and *World* carried a one-column ad for Eaton's which opened: 'They Say/What Say They?/Twenty-five years ago we began to put new notions into trade ways – and people talked. Ten years ago we proved our theories correct – and merchants winced. To-day we hold an imperial position as trade leaders – and the public applauds. But the triumph will not be complete until shoppers learn the difference between fact and fiction – between legitimate business on the one hand, and clap-trap and nonsense on the other. Nobody minds how much some people talk. Nobody cares how much some papers print. There's precious little sentiment in business, and precious little business in sentiment. The world is just about as it was a generation ago – dollars and cents, cents and dollars – with a leaning towards the store that gives best values, and a disposition to trade where prices are the lowest. That's the yardstick to measure by. Success doesn't happen by chance.'

10 See 'Advertising Moulds the Male,' in McNaught and Stephenson, *The Story of Advertising in Canada*, 81–91 and their discussion of John E. Kennedy himself (101–2).

11 Daniel J. Boorstin, *The Americans. The Democratic Experience* (New York 1973), 145.

12 See the biography of May Agnes Fleming (Early) in Marc La Terreur, editor, *Dictionary of Canadian Biography*, 10 (Toronto 1972), 268–9.
13 *The Evening Telegram, A Story of the Years* (1889), 20.
14 *P&P* (June 1898) 1.
15 *Monetary Times*, 23 June 1882, 1570.
16 Bernard Roshco, *Newsmaking* (Chicago 1975), 10.
17 Robert E. Park, 'News as a Form of Knowledge: A Chapter in the Sociology of Knowledge,' in Steinberg, *Mass Media and Communication* (New York 1966), 140.
18 Philip Schlesinger, 'The Sociology of Knowledge,' paper presented at the 1972 meeting of the British Sociological Association, 24 March 1972, 4, as cited in Herbert Gans, *Deciding What's News. A Study of CBS Evening News, NBC Nightly News, Newsweek, and Time* (New York 1979), 81.
19 Sifton to Macklin, 27 July 1900, cited in D.J. Hall, 'Clifford Sifton and the *Manitoba Free Press* 1897–1905,' unpublished paper, 27.
20 Quoted in Smith, *The Journal Men* (Toronto 1974), 22.
21 *A Story of the Years*, 4.
22 'The Daily Newspaper,' 4.
23 Park, 'News as a Form of Knowledge,' 132.
24 Roshco, *Newsmaking*, 11.
25 *A Story of the Years*, 8.
26 *Journal of Commerce*, 11 May 1882, 400.
27 See, for instance, the front page interview with William Van Horne in *La Presse*, 12 March 1896.
28 Palmer, '"Give us the road and we will run it,"' in G.S. Kealey and P. Warrian, editors, *Essays in Working Class History* (Toronto 1976), 116.
29 Park, 'News as a Form of Knowledge,' 136.
30 A reader of the Montreal *Gazette*, 10 March 1896, would have discovered the Queen was en route to Nice and the German emperor intended shortly to cruise the Mediterranean.
31 Often, of course, newspapers did not get the facts right at all. Note this comment by *P&P* (August 1896): 'There was a meeting of Tory politicians in Toronto July 30, and several of the papers had errors in statements of easily ascertained facts. For instance, The Mail said Sir Charles Tupper dined at Government House, while The World gave him to Senator Allan for the same function. The Globe said Dr. Montague arrived in town too late to attend the meeting, while The Mail declared him to have been present. The World said Sir Charles went east to Montreal by Grand Trunk train, while The Globe recorded his departure by the 9.20 train. Both statements were errors, because the ex-Premier left by the 9 o'clock Canadian Pacific train.'

32 Willison, *Reminiscences*, 131.
33 Thus the first three items (13 March 1886): 'Ex-President Arthur is dangerously ill./Bismarck's spirits monopoly Bill has been rejected./There is talk about bridging Bay Quinte at Deseronto.'
34 This analysis has been much influenced by Michael Schudson's comments on 'information' and 'story' journalism in the New York press of the 1890s, though Schudson draws a sharper distinction between the two forms and the newspapers employing them than is true in Canada. Schudson, *Discovering the News* (New York 1978), 88–120.
35 See, for instance, its coverage of the Douglas Morrison case in April 1889.
36 J.S. Willison, 'Journalism,' an address delivered before the Political Science Club of Toronto University, 1899, 16.
37 Cited in Smith, *The Journal Men*, 60.
38 Anonymous, 'Journalism in Canada,' galley proofs, 189?, held by Rare Books Room, Robarts Library, University of Toronto, 2.
39 'The Daily Newspaper,' 22.
40 The *Globe*'s piece (3 August 1874) is self-explanatory; what worried the *Manitoba Free Press* (6 February 1885) were the signs of a social upheaval in the world outside; the *Mail* (6 November 1873) chose to comment on relations between church and state in Europe; and the *Telegram* (2 March 1895) singled out a Liberal hopeful for satire.
41 See this comment by *P&P* (January 1894): 'Of late the Toronto Globe has had a philosophical attitude in its editorial columns that has done much to popularize that paper among the thinking men of the community through which it circulates. The Toronto Mail has a good tone, so has the Montreal Star and the Winnipeg Free Press. The Toronto Empire, Montreal Gazette, St. John Gazette and Halifax Chronicle may be mentioned as journals whose editors have a little to learn yet before they will be as dignified and circumspect as a judge.'
42 See Paul Rutherford, 'The Western Press and Regionalism, 1870–96,' *CHR*, 52 (September 1971) 287–305.
43 For a discussion of the conventions and formulas of popular literature, admittedly focusing on fiction, see Cawelti, *Adventure, Mystery, and Romance* (Chicago 1976).
44 Davin, 'The London and Canadian Press' *Canadian Monthly and National Review*, 5 (February 1874), 119.
45 S.E. Moffett, *The Americanization of Canada* (Toronto 1972), 99. First appeared in 1907.

CHAPTER FIVE / MYTHMAKING

1 Graeme Patterson, 'An Enduring Canadian Myth: Responsible Government and the Family Compact,' *Journal of Canadian Studies* (spring 1977) 13–14.

2 Cited in Jean Hamelin and Yves Roby, *Histoire économique du Québec 1851–1896* (Quebec 1971), 316.
3 *La Patrie*, 7 October 1892, and Toronto *Telegram*, 29 June 1889.
4 Cited in Heintzman, 'The Struggle for Life,' PhD thesis, York University 1977, 81. Heintzman's thesis has an excellent discussion of the idea of progress, or what he calls 'the metaphysics of modernity,' in French Canada.
5 Both nationalisms have been investigated in two unpublished theses: Arthur Silver's 'Quebec and the French Speaking Minorities, 1864–1917' University of Toronto, 1973 and my own 'The New Nationality, 1864–1897,' University of Toronto, 1973.
6 Cited in Gérard Bouchard, 'Apogée et déclin de l'idéologie ultramontane à travers le journal *Le Nouveau Monde* 1867–1900,' *Recherches sociographiques*, 10 (May – December 1969) 267.
7 Heintzman deals at some length with the prevalence of this myth.
8 Toronto *Globe*, 30 September 1889.
9 Note the opinion of the Toronto *Globe*, 9 March 1888: 'The poorer a man is the more in proportion to his means he has to pay. Every man, being taxed, should have a voice in the representation of his country. If after more than a generation of free schools there are some unfit to exercise the franchise, the fault is ours as much as theirs.'
10 The *Mail* was then in its Radical phase. But note this complaint by the very Conservative Montreal *Gazette*, 28 December 1892: 'The cost of legislation in Canada is something tremendous. Lieutenant-Governors, with higher pay than cabinet minister receive; expensive government houses; large cabinets at good salaries; annual sessions of double-chambered law-making bodies, the members of all drawing heavy indemnities; huge staffs of sessional and other employees.'
11 The first five phrases appeared in the Quebec *Chronicle*, 20 October 1864; *Le Nouveau Monde*, 4 February 1880; the Montreal *Gazette*, 22 October 1864; the Saint John *Sun*, 13 February 1886; and *La Patrie*, 18 September 1894. The term 'equal rights' was prominent in the Ontario press in 1889 during the anti-Jesuit agitation, itself employing the rhetoric of democracy.
12 The Canada Firsters, a little gathering of young Toronto types, aspirant intellectuals some of them, pushed passionately for a pan-Canadian nationality which naturally brought their dreams into conflict with French-Canadian views. See David P. Gagan, 'The Relevance of "Canada First," ' in Bruce Hodgins and Robert Page, editors, *Canadian History since Confederation. Essays and Interpretations* (Georgetown, Ontario, 1972), 73–86.
13 20 January 1883.
14 Mercier was Quebec's premier 1887–91; he came to power, and held on to it, by employing the rhetoric of French-Canadian nationalism.

15 Witness the view of a mellowed Toronto *World*, 2 March 1894; 'The English element in Canada is the dominant one, and it will remain such. The disparity in influence and numbers between the two races is becoming more widely marked every year. We can afford to let destiny take its course in a dignified way, without smashing at and trying to kick a weaker antagonist.'

16 This belief, of course, was not confined to Canada. W.L. Burn in *The Age of Equipoise. A Study of the Mid-Victorian Generation* (New York 1964) pointed out the prevalence of such a belief in the England of the 1850s and 1860s.

17 See editorials on 10 January 1880, 31 July 1880, 26 November 1881, 25 March 1882, 1 April 1882, and 7 April 1883 for a sampling of the *Mail*'s range of concerns.

18 *L'Étendard*, 30 March 1883, and the Toronto *News*, 17 May 1888.

19 *Le Monde*, 31 August 1892.

20 *L'Étendard*, 9 January 1893, and Charlottetown *Island Guardian*, 15 February 1894. See also 'Intellectual vs Moral Education,' Montreal *Star*, 12 March 1877, 2; 'La question de l'instruction obligatoire,' by R.P. Paquin, *Le Nouveau Monde*, 18 February 1880, 1; 'Moral Training in the Schools,' Toronto *Globe*, 8 June 1889, 8; 'Les écoles séparées de Manitoba,' *L'Electeur*, 11 August 1892, 1; 'La Morale dans les écoles,' *La Patrie*, 27 February 1897, 2.

21 A copied editorial, from *Le Moniteur du commerce*, in *Le Monde*, 24 July 1893. See also 'Industrial Education,' Montreal *Star*, 15 January 1887, 4; 'Les écoles du soir,' *L'Électeur*, 23 January 1890, 1; 'L'éducation pratique,' *L'Étendard*, 17 March 1893, 1; 'Commercial Education,' Toronto *Mail and Empire*, 3 July 1895, 4; 'The Commercial Course,' Hamilton *Times*, 14 March 1896, 4; 'Les écoles ménagères,' *La Minerve*, 5 January 1897, 2.

22 Thus the comment of the Saint John *Telegraph*, 29 January 1870: 'The best investment, the most profitable that any nation or country can make, is in providing for the education of its youth by means of a system of free schools. No state or country which has ever done so has ever regretted it. All countries who do so stand in the van of progress, and their rivals and enemies fall before them.'

23 Montreal *Witness*, 11 July 1885. See also in the Montreal *Star* 'The Gambling Act,' 5 April 1877, 2, and 'Gambling,' 18 October 1884, 4; 'A Blow at Gambling,' London *Advertiser*, 18 September 1890, 4; 'The Lotteries,' Montreal *Gazette*, 22 April 1892, 4.

24 16 November 1880. My impression is that Anglo-Protestant journals were much harsher in their treatment of poverty. So the Montreal *Star* (21 May 1887) claimed 'the most effective way to conduct an "anti-poverty" crusade is to make war upon the habits, physical, mental and moral, that make for poverty.' See also 'Pauperism in England,' Toronto *Globe*, 4 August 1874, 2; 'The Indigent Poor,' London *Free Press*, 9 February 1889, 4; 'Poverty and Wealth,' Charlottetown *Examiner*, 1 June 1894, 2.

25 *La Minerve*, 7 December 1895. See also 'Pauper Immigration,' London *Free Press*, 14 August 1889, 4, or 'Immigration peu désirable,' *Le Monde*, 7 February 1896, 2.

26 'The criminal classes have it in their own power to cause punishment in every form known to the law to cease. If the murderous class will but lay their bloodthirsty propensities under effectual restraint judicial strangulation will, *ipso facto*, become a thing of the past. And if sensualists will but hold their bestial natures under proper control there will be no further use for the lash. But until this is done the punishment will most likely continue to be inflicted; and though we shall not withhold our sympathy from the unfortunate criminals, our profounder sympathy for their victims, and for endangered society, leads us to hope that it may be administered with exemplary severity' (Toronto *Mail*, 1 August 1882).

27 Cited in Silver, 'Quebec and the French Speaking Minorities,' 380.

28 In the Montreal *Star*, 17 September 1887; Halifax *Chronicle*, 30 April 1892; *L'Étendard*, 21 January 1893; and Ottawa *Journal*, 11 December 1893.

29 Victoria *Colonist*, 22 June 1889.

30 *La Patrie*, 19 February 1903. Cited in Heintzman, 'The Struggle for Life,' 337–8.

31 Cited in LaPierre, 'Joseph Israel Tarte,' 97.

32 For a description of 'moderatism,' which means simply an emphasis on the virtues of moderation in all areas of life, whatever the prevailing values or institutions, see Gans, *Deciding What's News* (New York 1979), 51–2.

33 Commercial Union amounted to complete free trade between Canada and the United States plus a single tariff that would block European competition. Unrestricted Reciprocity did not include the commitment to a single tariff and so avoided the charge of being anti-British but also lacked much chance of acceptance in protectionist Washington.

34 A quotation from Lord Rosebery cited in the Ottawa *Citizen*, 2 December 1892.

35 Hence this splendid promise in the Toronto *Empire*, 7 July 1891: 'No one denies for one moment that preferential duties in the British market upon our produce would give an enormous stimulus to the Dominion; population would pour into our North-West; agriculture in the older provinces would become doubly profitable; we would be closely linked to the richest country in the world; our manufacturers would profit by a great extension of the home market; capital would naturally flow to Canada, because investments would pay in a country where products received favoured treatment in the world's best market.'

CHAPTER SIX / A FOURTH ESTATE?

1 Anonymous, 'Journalism in Canada,' galley proofs, 189?, held by Rare Books Room, Robarts Library, University of Toronto, 1.

2 There is a lengthy description of the whole affair in Charlesworth, *Candid Chronicles* (Toronto 1925), 78–81.
3 Morgan, *The Dominion Annual Register and Review 1883*, 155.
4 *La Patrie*, 14 October 1892.
5 See the accounts in *P&P* (December 1893) 9, and Morgan, *The Canadian Men and Women* (Toronto 1898), 309–10.
6 *P&P* (August 1892) 1.
7 See the reports in ibid (January 1894) 11; (April 1895) 16; and (November 1895) 13.
8 Ibid (November 1894) 19.
9 Ibid (November 1895) 14.
10 Morgan, *Dominion Annual Register 1884*, 362 and 372.
11 Ross, *Retrospects of a Newspaper Person* (Toronto 1931), 26–9.
12 *P&P* (July 1894) 9.
13 Ibid (September 1895) 14 and (October 1895) 13.
14 Ibid (March 1895) 6.
15 Morgan, *Dominion Annual Register 1880–81*, 389–90.
16 Ibid, 241.
17 *P&P* (July 1894) 9.
18 Ross, *Retrospects*, 61–4.
19 *P&P* (January 1894) 16 and (October 1895) 2.
20 J.R. Miller, 'The Jesuit-*Mail* Libel Case: An Example of Nineteenth-Century Anti-Catholicism,' *Studies in Religion*, 7 (summer 1978) 295–303.
21 *La Patrie*, 21 July 1893.
22 Toronto *Mail*, 18 April 1894.
23 Cited in the Toronto *Week*, 18 January 1895, 172.
24 Montreal *Gazette*, 29 October 1864.
25 Bellingham Memoirs, vol. 2, 175–6, Public Archives of Canada.
26 *The Evening Telegram, A Story of the Years* (1889), 45.
27 For a humorous account of the newspaperman's difficulties, see Clark, *Of Toronto the Good* (Toronto 1970) 32–44.
28 F.M. Fairchild, jr, editor, *A Short Account of Ye Quebec Winter Carnival Holden in 1894* (Quebec 1894), i–iii.
29 Day, *English America*, vol. 2 (London 1864), 247–8.
30 White to Macdonald, 28 November 1871, John A. Macdonald Papers, Public Archives of Canada.
31 Cited in the Toronto *Week*, 18 January 1895, 172.
32 Hamilton *Herald*, 23 December 1889.
33 Robert Campbell, 'The Pulpit, the Platform and the Press,' *Queen's Quarterly*, 5 (January 1898) 239.

34 Ibid, 240.
35 Hamilton *Herald*, 23 December 1889.
36 Campbell, 'The Pulpit, the Platform and the Press,' 240.
37 A.T. Drummond, 'Are Our American Newspapers Degenerating?' *Queen's Quarterly*, 3 (January 1896) 193–8.
38 E.H. Dewart, 'The Mission of the Newspaper,' *P&P* (March 1894) 13.
39 Campbell, 'The Pulpit, the Platform and the Press,' 245.
40 Thomas White, 'Newspapers, Their Development in the Province of Quebec,' a lecture delivered to the Young Men's Christian Association, 5 November 1883, 15.
41 Gordon Waldron, 'Newspaper Reliability – Is the Standard Improving?' Canadian Press Association, *Journal of Proceedings*, 42nd annual meeting (1900) 88.
42 J.R. Bone, 'University Teaching of Journalism,' in *Journalism and the University* (Toronto 1903) 286.
43 Clark, 'The Daily Newspaper,' *Canadian Magazine*, 7 (June 1896) 101.
44 This came from the pen of E.E. Sheppard, reincarnated as a moralist at *Saturday Night*. The denunciation of the *Mail* is contained in Clark, *Of Toronto the Good*, 33.
45 J. Brierley, 'The Newspaper and Its Critics,' *P&P* (July 1896) 2.
46 See the comment in *P&P* (July 1894) 17. The writer questioned 'whether a circulation built up with such methods is as stable as one secured upon a service of good healthy news.'
47 Bruce, *News and the Southams* (Toronto 1968), 73.
48 Brierley, 'The Newspaper and Its Critics,' 2.
49 E.J.B. Pense, 'Character and Position of the Canadian Press,' in J. Hopkins, editor, *Canada, An Encyclopaedia of the Country*, vol. 5 (Toronto 1899), 195.
50 London *Advertiser*, 11 March 1872.
51 Ottawa *Citizen*, 31 December 1896. This phrase appeared in an editorial critical of the clerical ban on the reading of *L'Électeur*.
52 Monseigneur Labreque's *mandement* condemning *L'Électeur* in *La Presse*, 11 March 1896.
53 'Un enseignement episcopal concernant les journaux,' *L'Étendard*, 26 February 1883, 1.
54 *La Patrie*, 7 October 1891, 1. Cited in Heintzman, 'The Struggle for Life,' PhD thesis, York University, 1977, 1.
55 *L'Étendard*, 26 February 1883.
56 Ibid.
57 'Lettre pastorale,' *La Patrie*, 28 December 1896, 1. For a lengthy discussion of the Catholic church and press freedom, see Jean de Bonville, 'La liberté de presse

à la fin du XIXe siècle: le cas de "Canada-Revue",' *Revue d'histoire de l'Amerique française*, 31 (March 1978) 501–23.

58 Lavoie, 'La clientèle du "Courrier du Canada",' 57.

59 Laurier LaPierre, 'Joseph Israel Tarte: Relations between the French Canadian Episcopacy and a French Canadian Politician (1874–1896),' Canadian Catholic Historical Association, *Report* (1958) 27.

60 R. Rumilly, *Histoire de la province de Québec*, vol. 3 (Montreal), 147–50.

61 Ibid, vol. 6, 64–5.

62 For instance *La Minerve*, 5 October 1868, 15 February 1871, 13 September 1884, and 1 October 1888.

63 For instance *La Presse*, 20 December 1884 and 3 September 1888.

64 See 'Theorie liberticide,' 4 February 1891, 1, or 'Nos droits de citoyens,' 30 December 1896, 1.

65 *P&P* (June 1899) 3.

66 *La Patrie*, 28 December 1896.

67 Ibid, 6 April 1897.

68 André Siegfried, *The Race Question in Canada* (Toronto 1966), 39–40.

69 Cited in LaPierre, 'Joseph Israel Tarte,' 31.

70 *La Patrie* did not always agree, of course: in 'La décadence d'un peuple' (22 March 1893) a writer claimed 'le clergé catholique ne participe pas à notre vie nationale,' indeed 'ne marche pas avec l'esprit du siècle.'

71 Willison, 'Journalism,' 14–15.

72 See 'L'Indépendance de la presse,' in the prospectus, *L'Étendard*, 23 January 1883, 2.

73 Poulton, *The Paper Tyrant* (Toronto 1971), 52.

74 Young, *Promoters and Politicians* (Toronto 1978), 42–4.

75 The agreement can be found in the Strathcona Papers, vol. 12, Public Archives of Canada.

76 Hall, 'Clifford Sifton,' PhD thesis, University of Toronto, 1973, 418–24.

77 For a description of his grand plans to purchase press support, see Armstrong and Nelles, *The Revenge of the Methodist Bicycle Company* (Toronto 1977), 147–9.

78 Ibid, 154.

79 Porteous to Sheppard, 10 December 1896, and Porteous to Nicholls, 15 March 1898, in Porteous Letterbooks, Public Archives of Canada.

80 D.A. McGregor, 'Adventures of Vancouver Newspapers: 1892–1926,' *British Columbia Historical Quarterly*, 10 (April 1946) 99.

81 Patteson to Hague, 3 May 1877, Patteson Papers, Ontario Archives.

82 Ross, *Retrospects*, 34–7.

83 *P&P* (January 1898) 12.

84 One journalist, J.S. Brierley, was willing to admit 'the trend of circumstance' meant 'in the publisher's eyes, a lessening in the importance of the reader' ('The Newspaper and Its Critics,' 2).
85 In the J.S. Willison Papers, Public Archives of Canada.
86 Cited in Heintzman, 'The Struggle for Life,' 90.
87 Ibid, 88.
88 'Le Droit de propriété,' *La Minerve*, 26 June 1888, 2.
89 See Colin Seymour-Ure's *The Political Impact of Mass Media* (London 1974), especially 156–201, for an excellent discussion of this symbiosis.
90 J.S. Willison, 'Journalism and Public Life in Canada,' *Canadian Magazine* (October 1905) 554.
91 Laurier to M. Jerome, 12 August 1901, cited in H. Blair Neatby, *Laurier and a Liberal Quebec: A Study in Political Management* (Toronto 1973), 158.
92 Charlesworth, *Candid Chronicles* (Toronto 1925), 19.
93 Montreal *Herald*, 23 March 1896.
94 1 September 1898.
95 *L'Électeur*, 10 April 1885.
96 Cited in Beaulieu and Hamelin, *La Presse québécoise*, vol. 2, 189.
97 Ibid, vol. 3, 45.
98 Hammond, 'Ninety Years of the Globe,' Ontario Archives, 214.
99 See R.A. Hill, 'A Note on Newspaper Patronage in Canada during the Late 1850s and Early 1860s,' *CHR*, 49 (March 1968) 44–59.
100 Norman Ward, 'The Press and the Patronage: An Exploratory Operation,' in J.H. Aitchison, editor, *The Political Process in Canada. Essays in Honour of R. McGregor Dawson* (Toronto 1963), 8.
101 I am indebted to Brian Beaven for this example.
102 Undated clipping (from the Montreal *Gazette*) and note, Dougall Papers (vol. 5).
103 Willison to Clifford Sifton, 29 January 1901, cited in A.H.U. Colquhoun, *Press, Politics and People: The Life and Letters of Sir John Willison, Journalist and Correspondent of The Times* (Toronto 1935), 98.
104 Buchanan to Patteson, 19 February 1872, Patteson Papers.
105 Young, *Promoters and Politicians*, 91.
106 McCready, 'The Special Correspondent,' *Canadian Magazine* (October 1907) 548–52.
107 Heintzman, 'The Struggle for Life,' 52.
108 'Memo for Mr. Willison,' included with Hardy to Willison, 8 February 1898, Willison Papers.
109 For instance this comment from *Le Nouveau Monde*, 17 February 1880: 'Chaque élection nouvelle est l'occasion d'un nouveau triomphe pour les conservateurs. Quand les libéraux dégringolent du pouvoir, ils tombent à plat, l'opinion

publique les déserte comme des péstiférés et ils se trouvent bientôt reduits à leur plus simple expression.'

110 For instance this comment from *La Patrie*, 3 December 1881: 'En attendant, libéraux, chacun a son porte. Dans ces jours de crise et d'affollement populaire, restons eximer et attendons avec confiance l'heure de la rétribution.'

111 'Memo for Mr. Willison.'

112 Note this little bit of abuse from *La Minerve*, 25 June 1896: 'Laurier est, par ses études et ses préférences bien connues, anglo-saxon de langue, d'idées, de tendances et d'esthétique; il est canadien-français par un pur et regrettable accident.'

113 LaPierre 'Joseph Israel Tarte' 121–5.

114 Rumilly, *Histoire de la province de Québec*, vol. 6, 214–15.

115 Beaulieu and Hamelin, *La Presse québécoise*, vol. 3, 80.

116 Ibid, 355. *La Bataille* disappeared in March 1896.

117 Macdonald to Alexander Morris, 21 April 1871, reproduced in Joseph Pope, *Correspondence of Sir John A. Macdonald* (Oxford 1921), 145.

118 Macdonald to Bunting, 25 May 1886, reproduced in ibid, 380.

119 Hardy to Willison, 16 August 1898, Willison Papers.

120 11 May 1875, Patteson Papers.

121 Willison to Sifton, 29 January 1901, cited in Colquhoun, *Press, Politics and People* (Toronto 1935), 99.

122 Willison, 'Journalism and Public Life in Canada,' 555.

123 January 1894, 2.

124 January 1897, 1.

125 Bruce, *News and the Southams* (Toronto 1968), 165–6.

126 Toronto *Mail*, 26 July 1880. The *Mail* did admit this ideal was never quite realized in practice.

127 Respectively the Halifax *Citizen*, 14 September 1872, and the Halifax *Chronicle*, 6 December 1894.

CHAPTER SEVEN / CONCLUSION

1 S.D. Scott, 'The Newspaper of 1950,' Canadian Press Association, *Journal of Proceedings*, 43rd annual meeting (1901) 48–54.

2 Morgan, *Canadian Men and Women* (1898), 922–3, and (1912), 1005.

3 See F.S. Siebert, 'The Libertarian Theory of the Press,' in F.S. Siebert, Theodore Peterson, and Wilbur Schramm, *Four Theories of the Press* (Urbana, Ill, 1973), 39–71.

4 'The Press Banquet to Mr. Goldwin Smith, M.A.,' *Rose-Belford's Canadian Monthly*, 7 (July – December 1881) 101–6.

5 In 'On Liberty,' an essay available in many places. My reading was of the edition in *Utilitarianism, Liberty and Representative Government*, Everyman's Library (London 1960). See especially 107.

6 This passion for making judgments, indeed the whole issue of bias in the news, has been investigated by Tom Walkom in 'The Ideological Structure of the Toronto Daily Press 1870–1910, a paper delivered to the University of Toronto Economic History Workshop, 7 November 1980.' Walkom's approach is, perhaps, more interesting than his results, since it grows out of a sound understanding of semiology.

7 R.C. Brown, *Canada's National Policy 1883–1900* (Princeton 1966), 125–211.

8 J.R. Miller, *Equal Rights* (Montreal 1979).

9 Norman Penlington, *Canada and Imperialism 1896–1899* (Toronto 1965), 237–51.

10 The argument about 'need' is drawn from Raymond Williams's *Television. Technology and Cultural Form* (London 1974), 21–2.

11 James Curan, 'The Press as an Agency of Social Control: An Historical Perspective,' in Boyce, Curran, and Wingate, editors, *Newspaper History* (London 1978), 51.

12 A.H.U. Colquhoun, 'Canadian Universities and the Press,' in *Journalism and thc University* (Toronto 1903), 19.

13 Laurier to M. Jerome, 12 August 1901, cited in Neatby, *Laurier and a Liberal Quebec* (Toronto 1973), 158.

14 These changes are explored in W.H. Kesterton, *A History of Journalism in Canada* (Toronto 1967) and Paul Rutherford, *The Making of the Canadian Media* (Toronto 1978).

15 See Lee, *The Origins of the Popular Press* (London 1976), 224–33, for a brief comparison of the experience in those three countries.

16 See Canada, Parliament, *Report of the Special Senate Committee on Mass Media*, 3 vol. (Ottawa 1970).

17 Theodore Peterson, 'The Social Responsibility Theory of the Press,' in Siebert, Peterson, and Schramm, *Four Theories of the Press*, 73–103.

Index